CHILDHOOD BEREAVEMENT
AND ITS AFTERMATH

EMOTIONS AND BEHAVIOR MONOGRAPHS
Monograph No. 8

edited by
George H. Pollock, M.D., Ph.D.

CHILDHOOD BEREAVEMENT AND ITS AFTERMATH

Edited by

Sol Altschul, M.D.

Foreword by

George H. Pollock, M.D., Ph.D.

INTERNATIONAL UNIVERSITIES PRESS, INC.

Madison   Connecticut

LIBRARY OF CONGRESS
Library of Congress Cataloging-in-Publication Data

Childhood bereavement and its aftermath/edited by Sol Altschul; foreword by George H. Pollock.

    p. cm.—(Emotions and behavior monographs; monograph no. 8)
Bibliography: p.
Includes index.
ISBN 0-8236-0772-0:
    1. Children and death—Psychological aspects. 2. Parents—Death—Psychological aspects. 3. Bereavement—Psychological aspects. 4. Parent and child. 5. Psychoanalysis. I. Altschul, Sol. II. Series: Emotions and behavior monographs; no. 8. [DNLM: 1. Attitude to Death—in infancy & childhood. 2. Bereavement—in infancy & childhood. 3. Psychotherapy—in infancy & childhood. W1 EM673 no. 8 / WS 105.5.E5   C535]
BF723.D3C544 1988
155.9'37—dc 19
DNLM/DLC
for Library of Congress   88-2757
                                                      CIP

Manufactured in the United States of America

To Joan Fleming, M.D.

Teacher, Co-researcher, and Colleague

Give sorrow words: the grief that does not speak
whispers to the o'er-fraught heart and bids it break.

Macbeth, Act IV, Scene 3

Contents

Contributors*

Sol Altschul, M.S., M.D. Associate Dean for Graduate
Education, Training and Supervising Analyst, Chairman,
Barr-Harris Center for the Study of Separation and Loss
in Childhood, Institute for Psychoanalysis, Chicago; Associate Professor of Clinical Psychiatry, Northwestern University Medical School, Chicago, Illinois.

Helen R. Beiser, M.D. Faculty, Institute for Psychoanalysis,
Chicago; Psychiatric Consultant, Jewish Children's Bureau,
Chicago; Clinical Professor of Psychiatry, Emeritus, Uni-
versity of Illinois at Chicago Health Sciences Center.

David Dean Brockman, M.D. Training and Supervising
Analyst, Institute for Psychoanalysis, Chicago; Clinical
Professor of Psychiatry, University of Illinois at Chicago
Health Sciences Center.

Joan Fleming, M.D. Formerly Dean of Education, Institute
for Psychoanalysis, Chicago.

Max Forman, M.D. Training and Supervising Analyst, Institute for Psychoanalysis, Chicago; Clinical Associate Pro-

---

*All the contributors to this volume have either been affiliated with the
Barr-Harris Center for the Study of Separation and Loss in Childhood or
they were members of the Parent Loss Workshop of the Institute for
Psychoanalysis, Chicago.

xi

fessor, Pritzker School of Medicine, University of Chicago; Attending Psychiatrist, Michael Reese Hospital, Chicago.

BENJAMIN GARBER, M.D. Training and Supervising Analyst, Institute for Psychoanalysis, Chicago; Clinical Assistant Professor, Pritzker School of Medicine, University of Chicago; Attending Psychiatrist, Michael Reese Hospital, Chicago.

KARITA MIRAGLIA HUMMER, A.C.S.W., C.S.W. Chief Social Worker, Section of Child Psychiatry, Rush Presbyterian–St. Luke's Medical Center, Chicago.

NAN KNIGHT-BIRNBAUM, M.S.S.A. Staff, Barr-Harris Center for the Study of Separation and Loss in Childhood, Institute for Psychoanalysis, Chicago; Institute for Juvenile Research, Chicago.

GEORGE H. POLLOCK, M.D., PH.D. President, Institute for Psychoanalysis, Chicago; Professor of Psychiatry, Northwestern University Medical School, Chicago; President, Center for Psychosocial Studies, Chicago.

ARNOLD SAMUELS, M.D. Director, Barr-Harris Center for the Study of Separation and Loss in Childhood, Institute for Psychoanalysis, Chicago; Assistant Professor of Psychiatry, University of Illinois at Chicago Health Sciences Center; Attending Psychiatrist, Institute for Juvenile Research, Chicago.

HENRY SEIDENBERG, M.D. Dean, Training and Supervising Analyst, Institute for Psychoanalysis, Chicago; Professor of Psychiatry, Pritzker School of Medicine, University of Chicago.

COLIN WEBBER, M.A. Staff, Barr-Harris Center for the Study of Separation and Loss in Childhood, Institute for Psychoanalysis, Chicago.

Foreword

It is with pleasure and pride that we welcome the publication of this monograph from the Barr-Harris Center for the Study of Separation and Loss During Childhood of the Chicago Institute for Psychoanalysis. This center, which provides clinical services to families in need, was founded in 1976 and is the only such facility in the Middle West. Services include diagnostic evaluations of all members of the family (i.e., children and/or surviving parent), recommendations for therapeutic interventions, assistance in implementing these recommendations, and follow-up of how the mourning family members have reacted to the therapeutic interventions in cases where these have occurred. The Center has provided service to over three hundred children and two hundred families. In addition, the Center has undertaken research on such basic issues as the mourning process, the comparison of families disrupted by parental death or divorce, the divorce process, defensive mechanisms used to deny or defend against the mourning process, and of clinical issues such as the therapeutic process as it is unique for adults who had parental losses in childhood or adolescence. The Center has also been involved in educational conferences and presentations to various groups in the community. In addition, the

Center in collaboration with the Teacher Education Program of the Institute and Northeastern Illinois University has undertaken a study of how mourning in childhood can interfere with learning. This research has great promise in opening up a new approach to learning problems in children and adults.

The Center was an outgrowth of clinical research studies undertaken at the Chicago Institute for Psychoanalysis which resulted in various hypotheses that continue to be tested. It was founded on the assumption that adults who "lost" one or both parents through death during childhood or adolescence have personality issues which make them more vulnerable to later life experiences. Some of these individuals either avoid meaningful relationships in order to protect themselves or are high risks for varying levels of decompensation when later life stress-strain events trigger reactions reflecting earlier "unworked" issues.

Early interventions may prevent later adult difficulties, disorders, or even diseases; the outcome can be creative and fulfilled living. We hope that this volume will allow the reader to follow the path from the clinical setting to the research setting and back to the preventive clinical setting. This monograph is the beginning of what we hope will be many more publications from the Barr-Harris Center that will present and elaborate on the exciting discoveries and their application to helping children and adolescents and adults who find themselves in traumatic situations. The Center was established through the great generosity of George Barr, Irving B. Harris, and Neison R. Harris, and we thank them for their support.

George H. Pollock, M.D., Ph.D.

Acknowledgments

During the course of these extended studies of bereavement and object loss at the Institute for Psychoanalysis, a number of colleagues in addition to the contributors participated in discussions where ideas were presented and developed. Participants included Catherine Cullinan, M.D., Linda Cozzarelli, M.A., Renee Gelman, M.D., Mary Jane Jensen, M.D., Joseph Palombo, M.A., Edith Sabshin, M.D., Joy Simon, M.A., and Victor Zielinski, M.D.

In addition, Juanita Dimas, Peej Gordon, and Eva Sandburg provided the necessary assistance for assembling this volume.

David Dean Brockman suggested the very meaningful quotation from *Macbeth* for which I am very appreciative.

Finally, I wish to thank my wife who not only directly helped to bring the volume together but also through the years of my involvement in the study and research on parent loss gave essential support and encouragement, thereby helping to bring the volume to fruition.

Introduction

In the early 1950s, within a short period of time, Dr. Joan Fleming began the supervision of three analytic candidates whose adult patients had experienced the death of a parent during the patients' formative years. Dr. Fleming was familiar with the work of Dr. Josephine Hilgard and her co-workers (Hilgard and Newman, 1959; Hilgard, Newman, and Fisk, 1960) regarding anniversary reactions and preliminary efforts to understand the sources of ego strength following childhood bereavement. This knowledge alerted Dr. Fleming to the possibility that the childhood bereavement of these patients contributed to their current psychological status. However, the specific hypotheses regarding the effects of parental loss by death during childhood did not crystallize until later when difficulties arose in the psychoanalytic treatment and were recognized and worked through (a detailed report of the first patient in the series is presented in chapter 12). As difficulties were encountered in the progress of treatment of these patients, it was decided to establish a research group so that it would be possible to study the complex issues in these patients from a larger pool of individuals who suffered childhood parental death. In this way, experiences could be shared and evaluated in larger numbers than would be available to any of the individual psychoanalysts during his or her professional experience. The development of the Parent Loss Project has been outlined by Dr. Fleming in the book *Counterpoint: Libidinal Object and Subject*, edited by Herbert S. Gaskill (1963).

The difficulties encountered in the psychoanalytic treatment of these adult patients centered around the resistance to the development of the transference. In Gill's view (1979), this could be viewed as a resistance to the awareness of the transference. At any rate, the usual unfolding of the transference and transference neurosis did not occur and a number of mechanisms were utilized by these patients to avoid cathecting or investing in the analyst, and thereby unconsciously preserving the relationship to the dead parent. These mechanisms will be demonstrated in section V, which is devoted to instances of childhood bereavement observed by members of the research group in their adult patients in psychoanalytic treatment. These were patients who had sought treatment primarily for depressive feelings and dissatisfaction with their lives. They usually entered treatment as young adults when they were at a point in their lives where a reorganization or change in their self-image was necessitated by the forward push of life events; for example, graduation, marriage, decisions to have children, and career choices. The fact of a parental death during the years prior to adolescent emancipation was important to these individuals and was often an initial identifying point in the history presented by them. They also conveyed a history of little or no reaction to the loss with very few memories of grief reactions. From our collaborative studies, we postulated that these individuals had adapted to the death of their parent(s) by denying the significance of the loss, although they were quite aware of the fact of the death, and thus avoided the mourning process which in turn led to a state of incomplete and prolonged mourning and an arrest in ego development at the level achieved at the time of the loss (Altschul, 1968). The therapeutic task became the breaking through of the resistance to the transference, or transference as resistance, so that the analyst could be cathected and the mourning process resumed or advanced. Growth and development could then take its long-delayed course.

While this understanding and therapeutic approach was extremely useful for this group of adult patients who had suffered childhood bereavement, many questions were raised and left unanswered. Were we dealing with a group of individuals who were self-selected by virtue of their seeking out psychoanalytic treatment? Must all children who suffer the unfortunate loss of a parent by death suffer developmental difficulties? Since we know how important a function the parent plays in the child's development, how does the absence of the dead parent affect future development? What is the fate of the internalized object representation in the bereaved child? We have previously attempted to answer aspects of these questions in several publications (Fleming, Altschul, Zielinski, and Forman, 1958; Fleming and Altschul, 1963; Altschul, 1968; Fleming, 1975; Altschul and Beiser, 1984) and intend to elaborate on our understanding of these issues in the present volume.

From our previous experience, it became apparent that our knowledge and understanding of this unfortunate event in a child's life would be greatly enhanced by longitudinal studies that would, in contrast to our studies with adults, begin at or near the time of bereavement and continue with periodic observations. In 1976 we were afforded such an opportunity through the encouragement and generosity of Mr. Irving B. Harris, Mr. Neison Harris, and Mr. George Barr, who provided and continue to provide the support needed to carry out the program of the Barr-Harris Center for the Study of Separation and Loss in Childhood of the Institute for Psychoanalysis in Chicago. The Barr-Harris Center was designed to provide service, community education, and research. The community education has been satisfied through numerous consultations, conferences, lectures, courses, and talks directly and through the news media to lay groups, social workers, psychologists, physicians, psychiatrists, psychoanalysts, and other mental health professionals at schools, medical and psychiatric clinics, social agencies, widows' groups, and local and national professional meetings. The specifics of the Barr-Harris service and research will be reported in greater detail in section I. Briefly, children from the ages of two to ten years, who had lost a parent by death within the previous two-year period, were to be seen for evaluation. These age limits were chosen so that we would be dealing with children at the younger age level who were verbal and could participate in the evaluation, while at the upper age level we could avoid the additional complexity due to the turmoil of adolescent development. We hoped to be able to observe children whose development was within the normal range prior to the death of a parent. These guidelines were not absolute, and some younger children and preadolescents and adolescents were seen in the process of evaluations of bereaved families. The service element was provided for in the consultations, evaluations, reevaluations, and a variety of interventions ranging from parental guidance and counseling about caretaking under these difficult circumstances to individual therapy for either child, parent, or both. The investigative aspects of the research were based upon gathering baseline data on the children when first seen through interviews of parent and child or children, plus informational data gained from questionnaires. Subsequent reevaluations were made at yearly intervals. We were interested in observing and determining how children reacted to the loss. Is the loss of a parent by death always a trauma leading to the kind of outcome we observed in our adult patients? What adaptations are children able to make at the time of loss? Is the loss invariably pathogenic? How were the children functioning? Did they show grief and/or depressive affect? Is one of the adaptations children make comparable to or equal to the adult mourning process? Are there differences related to age and sex of the child and deceased parent? Bowlby (1960b, 1961) and the Furmans (1964, 1974) feel that even very young children can mourn, while others, particularly Wolfenstein (1966), believe mourning cannot take place until the adolescent developmental process has been traversed. Another series of questions arose after observing a number of children and surviving parents: Should one intervene in the process; if so, when and in what way? Should interventions be different at different phases of the grieving process? Should one provide group or individual counseling or should one provide brief or intensive individual therapy to the family, the child, or to both parent and child? In other words, what are the best and most efficient pathways to assist a grieving child or family?

It is the intent of this volume to address these questions by approaching the study of childhood bereavement from the combined vantage points of the direct observation of children at the time of parental loss by death and the observations of adult patients with the same childhood losses in whom the long-term consequences of childhood bereavement can be observed and evaluated. In this way we hope to contribute to the knowledge of the adaptations and difficulties encountered in childhood bereavement.

The first section of this volume will present a discussion of the concepts of trauma, mourning, and adaptation from a dynamic point of view. The experience of the Barr-Harris Center will follow. Chapters 2 and 3 are designed to demonstrate an overview of the Barr-Harris experience with children and their surviving parents to highlight the clinical picture observed at the initial and subsequent contacts. Chapter 4 is a commentary on community resources and the importance they can serve for the family in the grieving process. Since the nature of the parent–child dyad is central to the question of intervention, the chapters in section III of necessity overlap to some degree with each other and with the observations set

forth in section II. However, chapter 5, "Diagnostic Intervention with Children at Risk" will focus predominately on the
child while chapter 6 "Therapeutic Work with Bereaved
Parents and Families" will concentrate on the surviving
parent. Special emphasis in section III will be made on
transference and countertransference issues in treating bereaved children while chapters 8 and 9 demonstrate the
mobilization of mourning in a child and problems confronted
in termination. Specific case examples will be presented in
section IV showing what characteristics seem to be necessary
for a child to mourn. These will include a case where the
capacity to mourn is demonstrated, and an instance where a
special creative technique was devised for use with a child
whose loss occurred in the preverbal period.

In section V data from the earlier Parent Loss Project
experience with adult patients will be presented. In the adult
patients we can investigate retrospectively the developmental interference stemming from the childhood bereavement
these individuals suffered. The first presentation, chapter
12, is a reprint of the first case reported from the Parent Loss
Project. The paper is included in this volume, even though it
was originally published over twenty years ago, because it is a
detailed report of the psychoanalytic treatment and still
represents the paradigm for a particular outcome of childhood
bereavement. The paper outlines the problems encountered,
the hypotheses developed, how the resistances were broken
through, mourning activated, and growth resumed. Chapters
13, 14, and 15 all contribute to various aspects of the
resistances, defenses, and mourning process, but in addition
focus on issues of developmental fixation and arrests. The
case of the patient reported by Dr. Seidenberg significantly
highlights the effect of the emotional unavailability of the
surviving parent and contributes to an understanding of the
rapprochement subphase of separation–individuation in the
development of a borderline syndrome. The case presented
by Dr. Brockman allows us to see in an adult the remnants of

preadolescent and adolescent struggles resulting from the arrested development. Dr. Forman's report allows us the opportunity to observe in action the type of defenses against mourning utilized by a six-year-old which persisted into adulthood. The chapter by Dr. Pollock is also a reprint and is included because it presents an example of a creative outcome of the mourning process. This continues a theme of successful outcomes to mourning through creativity that Dr. Pollock has previously elaborated (1975b, 1978a). Finally, there will be a chapter summarizing and giving an overview of the issues encountered in childhood bereavement.

Sol Altschul, M.S., M.D.

Section I

Background

Chapter 1

Trauma, Mourning, and Adaptation: A Dynamic Point of View

Sol Altschul, M.D.

In considering what impact an event such as the death of a parent might have on the psychological growth and development of the as yet immature child, one is immediately confronted with issues of what is trauma or traumatic, what is adaptive, what is pathogenic, and what role the mourning process plays in the adjustment and adaptation to loss.

The concept of trauma is one of the cornerstones of dynamic psychiatry and psychoanalysis. It is a basic premise that early life events and experiences impinge on and contribute to the shaping of the child's psyche. Such experiences can contribute to growth and development, be the stimulus for the organization of psychic structure and character development, and/or through fixations, arrests, distortions, and deviations be the stimulus for or plant the seeds of future psychopathology. The term *trauma* has not always been used consistently. It has been used loosely as a general term for all events that are difficult or painful for the individual to cope with, or it has been used in a very specific

3

way to refer only to those events that overwhelm the ego.* Whether a given event or experience will be traumatic depends solely on how the child or adult processes the event internally. Sidney S. Furst puts it as follows: "It is not so much the experience itself, but the individual's interpretation of the experience and his reaction to it" (1967, p. xiv). For one child, a seemingly insignificant event may prove to be overwhelming, while for another an event that the observer assumes will be traumatic is integrated and mastered without any deleterious effect on development. In fact, such an event has at times been considered a stimulus for development. Beres (1974, p. 69) indicates that whether or not an event is traumatic can only be determined in retrospect; that is, it can only be evaluated by the eventual outcome.

In spite of careful attempts to clarify the definition, there is still some confusion and inconsistency in the use of the term *trauma*. In addition, there is also disagreement as to whether specific events, such as the death of a parent in childhood, are so profound that the results will almost always be pathogenic. Some of the confusion stems from the way Sigmund Freud used the term *trauma*. In his earliest writings, Freud regarded trauma as "Any experience which calls up distressing affects such as those of fright, anxiety, shame or physical pain" (1893, p. 6).

In 1917b, when Freud wrote about trauma, he stated: "We apply it to an experience which within a short period of time presents the mind with an increase of stimulus too powerful to be dealt with or worked off in the normal way, and this must result in permanent disturbances of the manner in which the energy operates" (p. 275). In 1926, Freud saw

---

*It is interesting to note that the concept of stress suffers from a similar problem in definition. "Stress is frequently used interchangeably with stressor to refer to an event or stimulus to which an organism is exposed. At other times, it is utilized to refer to the response of a stressor, and frequently, stress is defined as encompassing the process of a stressor, reaction and consequence" (Stein, Keller, and Schleifer, 1985).

trauma as a state of psychic helplessness, a situation of helplessness that had been actually experienced as differentiated from an expectation of danger. The earlier definitions allow for the term *trauma* to be used when the stimulus causes pain or cannot be worked off in the normal way, while the 1926 definition seems to rule out use of the term *trauma* in instances where there is a defensive reaction to an expectation of danger or a defensive maneuver to avoid helplessness. Such defensive reactions, while they would not be considered traumatic in the 1926 narrow or strict sense, could become the basis for significant future psychopathology. Furst, in his essay in the book *Psychic Trauma* (1967), as I have indicated, emphasizes the important issue that trauma depends primarily on intrapsychic factors and not on the nature of the event. He indicates that when trauma does occur, the acute traumatic state takes one of two forms: "The traumatized child may appear immobilized, frozen, pale, becoming extremely infantile and submissive in behavior or else the trauma may be followed by an emotional storm accompanied by frenzied, undirected, disorganized behavior bordering on panic. Signs of autonomic dysfunction may contribute further emphasis to either picture" (p. 40). Anna Freud, in presenting an overview of various opinions states:

> Whenever I am tempted to call an event in a child's or adult's life "traumatic," I shall ask myself some further questions. Do I mean the event was upsetting, that it was significant for altering the course of further development; that it was pathogenic? Or do I really mean traumatic in the strict sense of the word, i.e., shattering, devastating, causing internal disruption, by putting ego functioning and ego mediation out of action? [1967, p 242].

It is interesting to note that the children of the Chowchilla experience, reported more recently by Terr (1983), did not show such acute symptoms of rupture of the stimulus barrier although they universally developed a variety of symptoms, including fears, perceptual distortions, traumatic dreams, and so on, which were still present at follow-up four years later.

In the book edited by Furst, Waelder (1967) also discusses a variety of situations he considers traumatic, and takes the position that, "Sometimes the stimulus is of a kind that all, or almost all people consider it traumatic. Our two examples are of this class; so are such events as loss of a parent" (p. 229). (Waelder's two examples are those of a boy who watched his father being gored by a stag and a man who was facetiously and playfully teased as a boy with the threat of castration.) Lifton (1982) also supports this point of view when he states: "But predisposition is only a matter of degree: if the threat or trauma is sufficiently great, it can produce a traumatic syndrome in everyone, as was largely the case in the manmade flood disaster at Buffalo Creek" (p. 1014).

Many other authors have struggled with the issue of deleterious or pathological consequences where there is no frank overwhelming of the stimulus barrier. Children who have lost a parent by death usually are presented with a stimulus "too powerful to be dealt with or worked off in the normal way." Yet such children do not necessarily become frozen or overwhelmed, but often seem to carry on as if nothing untoward had occurred or even seem to show a spurt in development. It seems crucial to develop a dynamic understanding of gradations of reactions to important events such as death, divorce, family disruption, and other disasters, and to fit them into a usable, dynamic schema of trauma and its derivatives.

Beres (1974), in summarizing the work on trauma done by the Kris Study Group, also emphasizes the significance of the individual's dealing with the event. He adds a new dimension, however, that of the necessity of long-term effects to determine whether an event can be considered traumatic. He states: "An experience can be considered traumatic in a true sense only in retrospect, i.e., once it has produced a lasting effect on symptom or character formation. The observer's judgment or empathy is not a gauge to measure trauma; only the specific meaning the experience has for the individual can decide that question" (p. 69). This type of outcome elaborated by Beres is not exclusive to an acute, overwhelming experience, but similar lasting effects on symptoms or character formation also follow on such events as the Chowchilla experience, or on defensive maneuvers designed to avoid overwhelming the ego; that is, defenses against experiencing trauma as defined in the narrow sense of 1926. When Freud (1917b) speaks earlier of "an increase in stimulus too powerful to be dealt with or worked off in the normal way" (p. 275), he does not preclude defensive maneuvers which function to avoid a traumatic neurosis, but yet are not the normal or usual mechanisms used by the individual to deal with anxiety. There is no question that the internal experience of an event is crucial to the outcome in any given individual but the internal experience may not be as readily apparent as it may first seem. Defensive or negative maneuvers to avoid the impact of an event also have a deleterious or "traumatic effect" and yet are not processed internally in the same manner as positive reactions to trauma. Freud (1939) in discussing these mechanisms, states:

> The effects of traumas are of two kinds, positive and negative. The former are attempts to bring the trauma into operation once again—that is, to remember the forgotten experience or, better still, to make it real, to experience a repetition of it anew, or, even if it was only an early emotional relationship, to revive it in an analogous relationship with someone else. We summarize these efforts under the name of "fixations" to the trauma and as a "compulsion to repeat . . ."

The negative reactions follow the opposite aim: that nothing of the forgotten traumas shall be remembered and nothing repeated. We can summarize them as "defensive reactions". Their principal expression are what are called "avoidances", which may be intensified into "inhibitions" and "phobias". . . . Fundamentally they are just as much fixations to the trauma as their opposites, except that they are fixations with a contrary purpose [pp. 75–76].

The fixations and arrests in development produced by the mechanisms of disavowal or distortion of the ego which are used in the defensive avoidance of the impact of parental death are examples of such negative reactions.

S. Keiser (1967) adds another dimension to the understanding of these complex issues when he speaks of instances of more discrete cases where there is an overwhelming of specific ego operations: "a particular incident may involve a specific ego function and by overwhelming it may become a traumatic event for that function. The pathological consequences are then likely to be principally within the area of that ego function, even though other functions may also be affected" (p. 793). Other workers have also made efforts to include significant events that are not overwhelming per se, but are pathogenic, and have coined terms to cover such circumstances, including *strain trauma*, and *cumulative trauma* (Khan, 1963; Sandler, 1967).

It seems that to keep to the narrow definition of trauma does not do justice to the complexity of trauma and to the dynamics of living. The significance and outcome of mechanisms that are employed to protect against being overwhelmed are not taken into account and therefore the importance that certain events have in their potential to produce psychopathology is minimized or neglected.

It is the author's contention that we should employ a system of classification that allows for a continuum which includes events ranging from those in which the individual is overwhelmed, to those where the individual is not frozen or overwhelmed but develops symptoms, to those where the defensive mechanisms against being overwhelmed determine the type of outcome (including partial distortions, fixations, and arrests), to those where events ordinarily expected to produce pathology facilitate growth and development instead.

In the past, attempts to find terms to clarify these circumstances have only led to cumbersome classifications. It is suggested instead that we already have sufficient terms in place in our psychoanalytic lexicon to identify, clarify, and simplify the concept of trauma while maintaining the beauty and flexibility of the dynamic point of view. Waelder has suggested that the common use of the term *trauma* is too prevalent to dispense with, and, in agreement with him, it is suggested that we use Freud's original statement of 1893: "any experience which calls up distressing affects such as those of fright, anxiety, shame or physical pain" (p. 6) as our definition of trauma. For the circumstance where an individual is acutely overwhelmed we would use the term *traumatic neurosis;* for the defensive maneuvers, positive or negative, we would use the terms *neurosis* or *development distortions,* depending on whether we were dealing primarily with fixations and conflict or the results of arrested or distorted development. The events leading to growth and development, including even those situations which follow on brief episodes of being overwhelmed, would fit under the category of working through and mastery. Such a scheme keeps us mindful of the many possible pathways for adaptation but does not minimize the potential pathogenic impact of such profound emotional events, such as loss of a parent by death during the developmental years.

We now turn to a discussion of mourning and the types of reaction that children manifest when they have lost a parent by death during the formative years. Confronted with a loss, the child must adapt in some fashion. Children will adapt according to the basic psychic mechanisms they have available to handle conflicts and they must do so within the abilities and capacities they have developed to that point. As one might expect, children's reactions to loss follow the continuum described above, from working through to disavowal and denial, from successful adaptation to maladaptation. Mourning, as observed in the adult, is the model mechanism for working through the loss of a loved object. It is also the prototype for the *working through of all traumatic events*; that is, the piecemeal process of recall and remembering with affective reexperiencing whereby the individual is gradually able to achieve emotional distance from the disturbing event, gradually integrate the event, and reestablish equilibrium in his everyday life. Even normal development, which may in general be proceeding smoothly, has critical periods and phases characterized by episodes of disorganization and reorganization preliminary to growth and development.

A disturbing event that we would now call a traumatic event will initiate some response in the individual. When one's equilibrium is upset, the response which is evoked often proceeds (as it also does in the mourning process) through a sequence of disorganization, working through, and reorganization. The process may get stuck in the original state of disorganization (i.e., traumatic neurosis) or at any other point on the continuum with fixation points, arrested development, symptom formation, or growth and development.

Death of a parent in the formative years seems to be an event of such magnitude that it puts an unusual strain on the child's capacities, and special attention must be paid to the child's ability to cope with such losses. The question of whether or how well a child can process an event such as death has been approached by a number of authors. Some believe mourning is not really possible until the individual has completed the normal adolescent task of separation from the parents. Other authors believe that, given the opportunity, even young children can mourn and work through the loss of a parent. There is, however, a growing consensus that while adapting to the loss of a parent by death can be negotiated successfully, it is a particularly difficult task for the developing child and has an unusual potential for future psychopathology.

Some of the factors that contribute to the difficulty are the child's incomplete development and the continuing reliance and dependency of the child on the parent for support and assistance in continuing development. The death of a parent is the kind of event in which the child would ordinarily turn to a parent for support and assistance in working through the emotional impact of the event. The child in these circumstances will have to lean even more heavily on the support of the surviving parent for help in facing the loss, to grieve, and mourn and so adapt to the best of his capabilities commensurate with his developmental level. The surviving parent, however, is most often deeply grieved and in a process of mourning himself, and may not be available to the degree necessary for the child's needs. The maturity and availability of the surviving parent may be the crucial factor as to whether the outcome for the child is successful or not.

Hilgard, Newman, and Fisk (1960) have outlined some of the factors necessary for relatively successful adaptation to loss. These include the ability of the surviving parent to use the community resources, keeping the family together, the nature of the preloss relationship to both the dead and surviving parent, and so on. E. Furman (1974) has described the importance of using the available resources remaining in the environment, and she, along with Bowlby (1980), has also pointed to the important factor of allowing the child to talk about the loss and express his feelings and clarify his confusion about the experience. Both Furman and Bowlby believe even young children can mourn, but Bowlby in particular has emphasized that if the conditions are not dealt with in an optimal fashion, the child is likely to get stuck in a phase of defensive avoidance, and the parental death is very likely to lead to a psychopathological outcome.

What types of reactions then are we likely to observe? This will, of course, depend on a great many factors, such as the cause of death, whether sudden and violent or the result of a lingering illness; the age, sex, and developmental phase of the child; the developmental progress to the point of the loss; the innate capacities of a particular child; and the type and kind of assistance the child receives from the environment. Given these variables, a given child may be overwhelmed and suffer a traumatic neurosis in the narrow sense. Regression occurs, previous ego gains are lost, so that a child may become enuretic or encopretic, develop nightmares and sleep disturbances; school phobias may become manifest, and the child will be sad and depressed. This is a not uncommon finding in the acute phases of childhood parent loss. Such reactions are, of course, consonant with the opening phase of mourning even in adults, and reflect the fact that the loss of a loved object is, in fact, always initially traumatic. Some adults at times are not capable of proceeding in the process beyond this stage and enter what may be a prolonged period of pathological mourning. Lifton (1982) and others have indicated that symptoms associated with the traumatic syndrome have to do with impaired mourning and the constrictions and strictures of the personality in reaction to the traumatic event.

Another reaction which is quite common is the defensive type where the impact of the loss is defended against. This is the kind of adaptation that is very likely to produce disturbances and pathology later in the adult. It is this type of reaction that produces the psychopathology we have seen in adults in our research on parent loss at the Chicago Institute for Psychoanalysis. This reaction, however, would not qualify for the narrow definition of trauma. These individuals may have a period of brief sadness with some tears or there may be very few outward signs of reaction and they seem to go on with life as usual. This is often compounded by the adults who urge the child to be brave or try to protect the child from the powerful affects. The man described in chapter 10, whose father committed suicide, was told he was now the man of the family, and he found it necessary to control his feelings and to disavow the loss. On the other hand, some of these children are criticized or even punished because they seem to the surviving family to be callous and unfeeling. One woman, who lost her mother at age six due to a lingering illness, recalls being slapped by a relative for playing with the neighbor children on the day of the funeral. For these children who defend against the affect, growth is usually not completely blocked or arrested, but they remain frozen in certain areas of their development and their difficulties in adulthood become apparent to them when they need to move ahead in ways that would force them to develop new images of themselves. It is this group of individuals who are likely to seek treatment when they are faced with anxiety and depression when approaching these new integrations.

In the children described by Terr (1983), we see still another reaction whereby all the children became symptomatic in spite of brief therapy and all demonstrated symptomatology four years later, even though there had been some improvement.

In another group of children, such losses seem to act as a spur to development. Scharl (1961) described two girls who witnessed their father's death in an auto accident. The younger child regressed and lost ground in her development, while the older girl seemed to respond to the loss by an accelerated growth spurt. Children in this category often identify with the goals and interests of the dead parent and use this focus as the departure point for their future life work. A child may become a teacher to follow and finish the parent's career, or he may decide to go into medicine to find a cure for father's fatal illness. Hobbies and activities of the dead parent may be taken up and become a way of continuing the parent within the self of the surviving child. One boy from the Barr-Harris Center began a campaign to honor his father in a very useful and productive way. Such adaptations often lead to creative solutions. Pollock describes how James Barrie began to make up stories to amuse his bereaved mother which, of course, led to an illustrious career as a writer (1978a).

Another group of bereaved children seem to be able to maintain an image of the lost parent and accept another adult as a continuation of or a substitute for the lost parent. This can be thought of as a "piggyback" arrangement (Altschul, 1973), and more nearly approaches the mourning process we see in the usual adult response to the loss of a loved object. We are very aware that the bereaved object is never given up in its entirety—nor would that even be desirable. While one talks about decathexis of the lost object to free energy for investment in new objects, this is a relative matter, and memories of the loved object are retained and even become a source of satisfaction for the surviving child or adult. Anniversary reactions persist and are part of the mourning process that persists over the years. What changes is the intensity and duration of the reactions so that one has energy to reinvest in life processes.

It has been emphasized here that the adaptations to trauma are on a continuum from traumatic neurosis to mastery and growth. The piecemeal working over of the event is necessary for mastery of trauma and is also the sine qua non of the mourning process and aspects of growth and development. Children may adapt to loss of a parent in a variety of ways but they most often need the care of the surviving parent or close caring adults to successfully master the trauma of the death. If such assistance is not available, the child is likely to develop symptoms or use defensive mechanisms to avoid the shock and overwhelming qualities of the event, and development is likely to proceed with pathological consequences associated with arrests, distortions, and strictures of the personality.

Section II

The Barr–Harris Experience

Chapter 2

Parental Death in Childhood

Arnold Samuels, M.D.

The Barr-Harris Center for the Study of Separation and Loss During Childhood has been investigating the effects of parental death in childhood since 1976. It is a part of the Institute for Psychoanalysis in Chicago and is a unique prevention center providing evaluation and treatment services for families disrupted by death, and now by divorce, also. Community and professional education as well as clinical investigation are integral aspects of the Center's operation. Diagnostic and treatment services are provided to families in which children ten years of age and under were orphaned. These families are then followed up with yearly reevaluations. All evaluations involve extensive, in-depth interviews with the surviving spouse and each child, requiring seven to twelve hours of direct clinic time. Questionnaires are completed by the widowed parent regarding the child's experience with the death, his participation in funeral, memorial, or religious rites, his reaction to and the handling of the death. A developmental and behavioral checklist is also completed. Information is obtained pertaining to the circumstances and handling of the death, prior and present functioning of the family, the past history of the family, the marital relationship, and the history of each parent's background, as well as appropriate developmental, school, and medical history of each child. The children are seen and an assessment is made regarding their general psychological status, their level of understanding of the death, and its significance to them, evident reactions to the loss mechanisms utilized in dealing with it, and capacity to do the mourning work. These dimensions are reassessed from the perspective of later evaluations, and change is assessed for each child against his prior interviews.

Some children and parents have required psychotherapy immediately following the initial evaluation; some have required psychotherapy at various later intervals when more significant symptoms developed or when there was sufficient time to observe that the bereavement process was interrupted, deviated, or prolonged without evidence for suitable other adaptation. (Evidence for unabated symptomatology and unchanging, if not identical, associative and fantasy themes was suggestive of continuing psychic trauma, regression, or arrest.) The majority of the families have received crisis intervention and bereavement education, usually with the surviving parent and with the child, less often with the entire family.

The discussion to follow will focus upon the first 128 cases seen at the Center. The families studied have been young families, the parents not usually exceeding the fourth decade of life. All social–economic classes were represented, all regions and races. Two-thirds of the families were Caucasian, one-fourth were Black, and the remainder were Hispanic and Oriental. They were divided equally between the three major religions. In almost 80 percent of the cases in our sample, the father had died leaving the mother. (The Social Security Administration places the death rate among parents where a child in the age group studied loses a parent as occurring in males 70 percent of the time. See the 1980 Census.) There was at least one surviving male child in two-thirds of the cases. The majority of the families considered themselves reasonably well functioning prior to the death. Very few had sought prior psychiatric treatment for themselves or their children. Almost all of the surviving parents saw marriage as a singularly meaningful and fulfilling dimension of their lives. Yet very few had remarried three years later and most had not remarried after five years. [Wallerstein (1984) found that 75 percent of divorced parents remarried "within the first three years of the marital breakup" (p. 446)]. This is highly significant for this age group in contrast to the greater likelihood for remarriage in divorce situations as compared to the widowed (Spanier and Glick, 1980) and suggests that the spouse may not have been able to fully reorganize her life for a very extensive period of time.

These parents and children were not assaulted by the ongoing effects of the disordered and disturbed marital relationship encountered among divorced and divorcing parents (Hetherington, 1980). Rather, the death was an adventitious event unrelated to the preexisting husband–wife and parent–child relationship, except, of course, in those situations of parental suicide and a few in which spousal murder of a parent occurred. Two thirds of our families did experience the sudden or violent loss of life resulting from acute illness, accident, murder, or suicide. Two thirds of these families came to the Center within the first six months after the death. Our sample then was largely made up of families which had suffered traumatic losses with little time for anticipation of the death, for mobilization of personal and social resources, and for buffering, modulating, and integrating the parent's own feelings and emotions, let alone to do so in order to assist the child. The remaining one third of the deaths ran a more chronic course. Here, the families had an opportunity for anticipatory mourning, yet this fact did not in itself guarantee a less traumatic outcome of or smoother bereavement response for the child. Some of these families received "grief work" assistance through the social worker or chaplain services of the hospital where the deceased parent had been treated. Yet these children, too, were traumatized in the aftermath of the death. (This finding in our sample may represent a subgroup of such cases which have inordinate needs for more help or may be less adaptive for reasons intrinsic to their particular family. In other words, it will be necessary to follow families prospectively from the period of diagnosis of the fatal illness to a time far beyond the death in order to properly evaluate their outcome. Alternatively, it may well be that such families are traumatized from the point of diagnosis and continue to be so thereafter.)

The concept of trauma in relation to parental death has been discussed by Dr. Altschul (see chapter 1). When death occurs, the sense of loss is profound and is the most common condition toward which words of consolation are addressed (Garber, 1981). However, we also find the death is almost always traumatic in the disruption it brings to the ongoing life of the family and the flooding of the child's experiencing and integrative capacities. Eighty-five percent of the children were symptomatic with sleep disturbances, nightmares, phobic responses, separation reactions, angry outbursts toward the surviving parent, increased tension states, regressions such as enuresis, soiling, sucking and mouthing objects, attention seeking, confusion, worry, depression, and loss of resiliency.

About twelve to eighteen months after the death, the more regressive behaviors such as enuresis and bed sharing have abated for most of the children, a finding consistent with Hetherington's investigations (Hetherington, 1980), but lessened resiliency, a propensity for separation problems, preoccupation with illness, death-related altered or lowered self-esteem, an uncertainty about the future, and worry about growing up continue as abiding concerns for the children of the Center. At interview, play themes were likely to be the same or similar to those produced during the initial evaluation and have been found not to change in some children over the three to four years following the initial evaluation. Almost all of the children indicate that the death of the parent continues to be an active issue for them many years later.

CASE EXAMPLE 1

Ben was a six-year-old boy at the time of father's sudden death. He had been a buoyant, affective child who took pleasure in his growing abilities and enjoyed sharing his father's interest in sports. At interview, two years after the death, Ben readily experienced the painful feelings of the loss of his father. There was much about his father that he missed. His mother was painfully aware that Ben was no longer the resilient child he had been. He now reacted to minor frustrations with tears and a readiness to anger. His play behavior at interview contained repetitive themes of fighting bouts among the doll figures, the characteristics of which remained unchanged over three evaluations in three years—the smallest figure having to defeat all the others. This "baby" then had to carry the rest on its shoulders only to collapse, and the fighting starting over again. By age ten, the results of these bouts changed so that the largest doll became the super heavyweight champion. Ben now explained that the smaller ones could not really expect to beat the larger, more powerful ones. He was a more serious boy for whom success was very important. He was involved in many activities and did well in school. He was keenly aware of being at a disadvantage and felt that he had to try harder because "other kids have their dads to teach them and practice football with them."

CASE EXAMPLE 2

Alice was nine years old, the oldest of two children and very fond of her father when he had to give up his active professional life and remain home as a result of his brain cancer. He lost sight in one of his eyes and had a scar from previous surgery. Alice was no longer able to enjoy the closeness they had shared earlier and kept her feelings to herself, despite her mother's encouragement to talk. She cried off and on the first few days following her father's death, and has avoided talking about it since that time. Her mother noted a loss of self-confidence since the death, an uncharacteristic lack of assertiveness, and noted that she no longer enjoyed her activities and friends as before.

At interview, Alice was reticent and clearly felt it an imposition to be seen. She avoided any affect-laden issues and responded superficially. She drew two pictures of pleasant scenes such as people swimming in a resort pool. When it was mentioned that there were no men in the pictures, she became momentarily angry and said she had to draw a happy picture of a family on vacation. Alice refused to return for subsequent interviews. She said she just could not talk about it. She became increasingly involved in her father's stamp and coin collection. About a year later, she began talking about father with her mother following a memorial service in which funds were raised commemorating her father's service to the community. Her mother had been seen at regular intervals over that year and helped to understand Alice's pain and the necessity to wait for Alice to be ready. She and her mother then had many poignant conversations in which they could share their grief. Alice expressed her anger at her father's death, her hurt at the disfigurement of his features, and her sense of unfairness at not having him. She was reminded of her admiration for him at the commemoration and was able to reestablish the idealization she had earlier felt for him. There were narcissistic and oedipal issues reflected by this death. The family moved two years after the death to an adjoining state where the bulk of mother's family lived. Alice was looking forward to living near her aunts, uncles, and cousins, according to mother's report.

These reactions hold true for children from reasonably healthy families who have shown a background of higher level developmental concerns, but progressive maturation prior to the death. These children do enter a mourning process, do grieve, are involved in remembering, idealizing, and maintaining a positive image of the deceased parent. They long for and miss the deceased parent. They are likely to identify with aspects of the deceased parent, often mediated and supported through the use of such mnemonic mechanisms as mementos, stories, or actions. So-called "action memories" (E. Furman, 1974) are especially evident in preschool children. The latency aged children of the same sex as the deceased parent, who are principally the boys in our study, identify with concretely perceived and unconsciously experienced qualities and attitudes of the deceased parent. This is often supported by the widowed mother's use of the child as a partial replacement of the dead parent, but is not necessarily nor always related to her encouragement. These children may take on certain qualities of the dead parent such as an "adult" attitude toward work, school, and responsibility, which is reflected in a new, more serious attitude often associated with worry. Childhood is no longer so free of concern for these children (see case example 1). When surviving parents prove to cope effectively, provide for the family, and can empathically assist these children with their fear and pain, longing and missing, the mourning process was supported and the likelihood of eventual acceptance of the death more likely. These children continue to mourn over the years, but not necessarily in an unremittingly intense manner. They have not completed the mourning process and we suspect this was true for those few children whose parents have remarried and who have suitable replacement objects.

The difficulty for us in the situation of remarriage has been that the adaptation of the parent and the desire of the new spouse combine together to push for closure of the mourning process, and the new couple frequently prefers not to continue contact with the Center. As remarriage brings about a kind of closure of the mourning process for the parent, the parent's relative completion or conclusion of her mourning work also tends to bring about premature termination of treatment for the child. The Center takes on the quality of cemetery visitation and represents a holding on to the past, interfering with the parent's wish to go on with life, to begin again. At least prior to the remarriage to a suitable, potential replacement for the child's lost parent, these children have a need to hold on to their memories and do not decathect nor resolve the loss as yet. They try to keep the parent's function alive, but cannot quite succeed. With the remarriage, there may be reinvestment in the new object with or without decathexis of the old and the possibility for growing identifications and experience within a two-parent family more supportive of the child's total development.

The picture of latency age boys who have experienced the loss of a father by death frequently depicts a sad and suffering child who manifests depressed ideation, mood, and fantasy at interview, despite otherwise functioning well. A significant number of these children, however, have shown various difficulties in learning, but on the whole, these difficulties were not generally sufficient to impede their overall school progress. In addition, phobic symptoms, intense longings, and wishes for reunion with the deceased parent, pseudomaturity, vulnerability or uncertainty about their personal adequacy in situations of separation are the more prominent symptomatic features of this group of otherwise healthier children. Many were fearful of growing up; others showed conflicts with aggressive feelings. It is of particular importance to note that at interview most were in great pain over the death. A few of these latency boys more completely denied their feelings or disavowed the impact of the death upon their lives.

For the preschool group, temporary regressions have been more commonly encountered. These children were seen as sad from time to time, but their intolerance for sadness and pain did not allow this feeling state to predominate. So, rather than overt depression, we encountered regressive behavior, phobic or fearful reactions (especially to the initial interview situation), and a facade of playful or happy feelings. Some of these younger children were striking, nonetheless, in the expression of plaintive, sad, mournful feelings. Others developed a somewhat controlling, manipulative, and demanding attitude. This was especially true of oedipal aged girls. These girls were aggressive toward their interests in trying to attract the interest of a father by at times intruding upon the relationships of young friends with their fathers. For this group of younger children, the vulnerability to trauma was such that painful feelings more often had to be fended off. In addition, their more immature level of development created further difficulties in being able to sustain a mourning process. Sad feelings were not only painful, but frightening and potentially disorganizing.

When the child was overwhelmed by the death so that he could not maintain his emotional equilibrium nor internally organize the experience, when the surviving parent was lost to the child in her own bereavement, when the death was unexpected, sudden, violent, or related to serious pathology in the parent and within the family, such as in the circumstance of parental suicide, the child was more likely to be traumatized and unlikely to establish and maintain a mourning process. In fact, when the death was the result of murder or suicide, no child was judged able to mourn this type of death without intervention. Such children were more likely to have preexisting psychopathology and were not doing well since the death. They remained traumatized. The children of suicidal parents tended to have preexisting deficits; the families were more likely to be enmeshed (Adams, Bouckoms, and Steiner, 1982) and not well differentiated. They had difficulty with aggression, had deficits in object relations and self-esteem, were disorganized, were unable to buffer stimuli, or manage their own tension states or frustrations, and either became withdrawn or aggressive. Their parents tended to be unempathic and unable to support and accept their children's feelings about the loss and tended to misinterpret alterations in behavior rather than to appreciate the behavioral expression of fears, frustration, and anger resulting from the loss. The parent's capacity to work and economically provide for the family was by itself not sufficient to prevent significant impairment in the child.

In circumstances of murder, compensatory grandiosity, wishes for revenge, fear vulnerability, conflict with, acting out of and reaction formation against aggressive impulses resulted. In one family, the son of a murdered father identified with the aggressor and became delinquent; his younger sister expressed the wish to become a policewoman who would put murderers in prison. In another family in which the father committed suicide after threatening to kill the mother if she did not help him hold the gun, one child became identified with the victim and engaged in and allowed himself to be led to self-destructive activity. The older child turned his rage against the mother and attempted to go after her with knives taken from the kitchen and was hospitalized.

CASE EXAMPLE 3

Allen was seven-and-a-half years old when his father was robbed and murdered while working as a taxi driver. The men who were responsible for the death had been apprehended and were given long prison sentences. His mother was narcissistically self-absorbed, hypochondriacal, and depleted. She would often go out "to get away from her loneliness." She was not able to assist her son in his grief. Allen idealized his father and could not understand why anyone would want to kill him or how this could happen. He became very compliant at home following the death, but was in difficulty in school because of poor attention, inability to sit still, clowning, and initially, fighting, which had stopped by the time of the evaluation. He had repeated nightmares.

At interview, he spoke without affect about the facts of his father's death. He said of the two men, "I don't hate them. I don't hate anyone." He said his father appeared to be asleep when he saw him at the funeral. He added that he knew he was dead when he touched his hand which felt like paper. He did not cry at the funeral and thought that his father was an angel in heaven.

He began having dreams of a man chasing him with a big stick. He would bite the man's finger, which would turn soft and the man would change into a witch, then a giant, and he would awaken.

He drew pictures of houses which became haunted, car races in which his car was impervious to the shots of the other contestants, the bullets bouncing back and causing them to crash—"No, to have flat tires."

This child was seen weekly in therapy, and his mother was seen weekly and then every other week. Issues of danger, annihilistic fears, rage, omnipotence, and phallic narcissism thus were replete.

Sudden, violent, unexpected death was more highly

traumatogenic than death by illness, ending fatally over time. When the type of death resulted from an illness or accident, the facts of which could be more readily assimilated by the child, a mourning process was much more likely to be in evidence. Overall about one-third of these cases demonstrated an effective bereavement process within the limits of development of which the child was capable. We expected that the opportunity for "anticipatory mourning" would involve a lessening of the traumatic impact of the death; this was not true to the extent expected. When the child could have increasing familiarity with the fact that the parent was ill, that he was dying, that the consequent alterations in function and within the family could support the ongoing needs of the child and maintain his routine, that everything possible had been done, and that confused feelings could be understood and the grief shared, he would be more likely to adjust well over time. For the families in our study it proved to be the ideal. For most, various facets of traumatization were observed. For example, the predeath or dying period of gradual but not incipient deterioration was for some younger children a period of pleasant and greater availability of the parent—a gratification, not a privation. Such a child became a sort of "lap" or "sick bed" child and was gratifying to the dying and surviving parent as well. The child did not actually understand that the parent would no longer exist as a result of the progression of the very situation that felt so good. In other situations, the child was actually further traumatized during the terminal illness, which brought about changes in the ambience of the home, the daily routines, sensitization to physical changes, and alterations of mood and emotional and psychological state of the dying and healthy parent. There was also sensitization to hospitals, nurses, and equipment, failing and failed vital function, greater absence and unavailability of the surviving parent who often had to provide for the family, and a household organized around active mastery, which often ran counter to dealing piecemeal with the questions and feelings aroused in the child from day to day. Such households were on a kind of emergency status during the terminal illness and the surviving parent was not necessarily more emotionally available after the death, as there was often an unconscious element to the relief which was directed toward reorganization and normalization. The traumatization of the child was not perceived by the parent and not understood as a result.

The availability of an adult to support and facilitate the bereavement of the child is of great consequence to the child's adaptive potential. When the parent was involved in active mastery of the loss experience, she was found to cope reasonably effectively for herself in about 50 percent of the cases. However, this was often done at the expense of the child's need for continuity of parenting functions, the availability and capacity for which was considered appropriate in only slightly less than one third of the cases.

When the widowed parent was the father, active mastery, continuing providership, and early remarriage, often within the first or second year after the death, was more likely. There was also a tendency to move from the family home. Not infrequently, the move was out of state. It was more difficult as a rule to be able to follow up the surviving father and his children. There were a few families in which the father was extraordinarily sensitive and empathic to his children, others in which a daughter became unintentionally exploited as a substitute for the wife, or was effectively abandoned in the father's efforts to find a new companion for himself and to avoid the painful reminders extant in the home.

In our cases, the parent's period of bereavement may represent half the life of a young child and parental functions of stimulus buffering, mediation of tension states, modulation of mood and affect states, accurate and empathic perceptions of when and what the child needs to integrate about the death, may become inconsistent and unreliable (see chapter 3).

Whether the widowed parent is more or less depressed, still has difficulty accepting that the spouse is dead, or is preoccupied at times with thoughts and memories of the deceased can have important effects upon parental function. For example, those widowed parents who have had to use their child as a partial replacement of the lost spouse, interfere greatly with the child's reality perception and stimulate denial and omnipotent fantasies in the child. Others may have such a great need to preserve the memory of the deceased spouse "for the child," that they may unwittingly flood him with evidence of the existence of the parent when the child is either attempting to apprehend his absence or gain temporary distance from the traumatic awareness of his disappearance. All widowed parents have the wish to spare their child unnecessary pain; few in our study have the capacity in their burdened state to effectively provide for the ordinary needs of the child and the now extraordinary needs plus facilitation of the child's mourning process (see chapter 3). It would be best for such a parent to do so, but the parents of the Center are not likely to be able to do so for a considerable time period. Only about 25 percent of the surviving parents were able to actively support the child's bereavement.

In conclusion, the complexity of what is lost with the death of a parent can be understood as involving multiple kinds of losses which effect disruptions in the ongoing life of the family and within the internal representational world of each individual, involve potentially regressive revivals of earlier psychological states or concerns, and stimulate certain defensive operations serving mastery and adaptation, or pathological outcomes.

The death is a traumatogenic agent and affects the child in that the impact of the death shatters the child's comprehension, his reasonable sense of security, and the belief in his parent's omnipotence. It is on the one hand an overwhelming stimulus sorely taxing the child's ego capacities, and on the other, may interfere with his sense of self, self-esteem, and the differentiation of certain aspects of fantasy from reality. This traumatic state may be long lasting under a variety of circumstances usually relating to the capacity for adaptation which the child brings to the death, and the opportunities internally and externally available to him or her at the time of and in the aftermath of the death. The interplay between this nucleus of trauma within the child, the alteration of his actual life subsequently, and the deprivations to the developing self resulting from the lack of modifying influences inherent in progressive processes of identification and internalization in relation to interactions with a living parent adds to the complexity of the loss paradigm (Tolpin, 1971, 1978).

There exists an ongoing need for the object to support the development of internal mental structures, stabilization of mood and mediation, and modulation of need and tension states. The adequacy of the child's sexual identity and its attributes of masculinity and femininity are dependent upon progressive identification with a like-sexed parent and recip-rocally with the opposite-sexed parent. Pathological possibil-ities or opportunities for integration may unfold at different times depending upon the significance of the parental object and his or her attributes for the child at the time of the death or after, when the child's later development requires specific interaction between the object and the self attendant to its new(er) aspirations. To illustrate, a girl lost her father when she was two years of age. At that time, she manifested separation anxiety. Three years later, the separation anxiety was still present and associated with dependency problems, but concerns about bodily damage or missing parts were added. She felt deprived of father's response and interest in her and blamed her mother for this privation.

When the experience of the loss threatens the child's

narcissistic integrity and interferes with the establishment or reestablishment of his emotional well-being, when the impact of the pain is too great, the individual too vulnerable, or, when the adaptive means are otherwise unavailable, then the child uses defenses to prevent, avoid, or otherwise deal with the pain (Joffe and Sandler, 1965). The array of defensive mechanisms varies with the developmental level of the child, sufficient experiences with the deceased parent, the capacity to maintain a bank of positive memories of their common history, and the possibilities provided by the current life circumstances of the child. They include identifications, idealizations, yearning, and remembering which serve reunion wishes as well as denial and disavowal of the significance of the death and/or its attendant affects, among others. If the loss is neither perceived nor understood, if its significance to the child is defensively avoided, the full measure and meaning of the loss will lose its reality for the child (E. Furman, 1974). His sense of reality with respect to the death will be distorted and mourning, with its potential for reinvestment in others, in life, and in his own creative capacity, will be less likely to occur.

The work of mourning is fundamentally an attempt to integrate the traumatic effects of the death within the psychic structure of the bereaved. Reality dictates that the loss has occurred and the child struggles to maintain his emotional equilibrium in the face of the loss. This situation is precarious for the child as a result of the immature status of his cognitive and emotional mental structures and functions. He is more likely to attempt to ward off the painful affects of grief (H. Deutsch, 1937; Wolfenstein, 1966). Such intense feelings are difficult to bear and tend to be overwhelming. For adaptation to be served, the child must negotiate between denial and repression and sensitization (Lazarus, Averill, and Opton, 1974) by way of remembering and reexperiencing. This process may continue throughout the developmental period of childhood and adolescence. The active mourning may be reactivated and reworked at significant developmental junctures across the life cycle (Pollock, 1978b). So long as overall development is progressing, despite periods of intense preoccupation with the loss, the child may not be arrested in his development (E. Furman, 1974). The same may be true for periods of repression.

Further defenses which seem to manage various aspects of the loss could be enumerated. However, no defensive organization in itself was predictive of good or poor outcome, with the exception perhaps of idealization of the deceased parent by the more adaptive child. It was far more significant if the defenses remained fixed over time and overall development was not proceeding well. In some individuals the resultant outcome then may have to await the relative completion of development, at least through adolescence.

Overall, the children who functioned the best had an immediate grief reaction with sustained, not necessarily continuous mourning. They maintained good relationships with peers and adults, achieved in school, had positive relationships with the deceased and surviving parent, and maintained a positive, if not idealized image of the lost parent, so that they could consider subsequent positive relationships. They did not totally deny or disavow the significance of the death. The conclusion was reached and supported that progressive maturation of the child with evidence of capacity to invest in life, in his own functions, and in others was the most significant indicator of adequate adaptation. In addition, it was clear that bereavement would proceed over the course of the developmental period, be reactivated at certain significant times, and was suggestive of adaptation when it would seem that the work of mourning was proceeding.

The ultimate outcomes then are likely to include one of the following: (1) an arrest in development, the concept posed by Fleming and Altschul (1963) and Altschul (1968) in their early work and consequent risk to later breakdown; (2) an encapsulation, perhaps similar to arrested development, but more circumscribed, associated with apparent mastery and adjustment; (3) as a symptomatic organizer, a concept in which the impact of the death organizes and fixes preexisting difficulties, now given new meaning by the death; and (4) a nonsymptomatic organizer of character based upon adaptive identifications with the image of the deceased parent, often idealized, but not necessarily excessively rigid, which would then allow for progressive development with relative stability.

Chapter 3

The Influence of the Recent Death of a Spouse on the Parenting Function of the Surviving Parent

Karita Miraglia Hummer, A.C.S.W.
Arnold Samuels, M.D.

INTRODUCTION

The meaning of the effects of death upon children of differing developmental stages has been studied, but the effects of loss of a spouse upon parenthood and the discrete parental functions of the surviving parent have not been systematically investigated. When distinctions are drawn, these are about widow or widowerhood, not often about widowed parenthood.

From the point of view of the life cycle, the people in our sample were widowed parents with younger children, and they were involved in the early parenthood phases of the life cycle (Benedek, 1959). These families were disrupted by death at a point in the life of the parents when psychological intensity could be expected and husbands and wives, fathers and mothers could look forward to the benefits of interdependent and creative living, confident nurturing, and adequate providership. Mutually based family functions of sharing of work, determining of goals, establishment of roles, and decision making, evolving psychological and sexual intimacy, mutual warmth, respect, empathy, and shared and differentiated caretaking of the children (Zilbach, 1979) are radically changed by the death of a spouse. The qualities of motherliness or fatherliness (Benedek, 1970) previously supported by the spouse are sorely taxed for a variable period of time, and may affect the parent–child interaction for a number of years beyond the death. The emotional tasks which challenge the adaptive capacity of a bereaved parent are of great consequence to the surviving parent and child. The widowed parent must accommodate to the loss, mourn, reorganize his or her life, secure themselves in the real world, and provide for the orphaned children while maintaining affectionate bonding and emotional intimacy. The surviving parent and child require protection from a sense of emotional emptiness, isolation, and traumatic disillusionment emanating from the internal and external disruptions brought on by the loss.

Widowhood has been properly appreciated as a study of coping and adjustment to trauma. It has been studied from the point of view of age differences (Clayton, Desmarais, and Winokur, 1968; Marris 1974); personality factors or status as a psychiatric patient (Parkes, 1965); type of death (Clayton, Halikas, Maurice, and Robins, 1973); and psychosomatic considerations (Madison and Walker, 1968; Parkes and Brown, 1972). It has been shown that widows in the fourth and fifth decades of life tend to do less well than those over sixty-five years of age. Such widows are less likely to remarry, especially if no attempt has been made in that direction by the end of the first year. In fact, very few of the still younger widows (less than forty years of age) in our sample had remarried three years later, and many of them remained unmarried five years and more later. The realignment in living that is required at this time is very difficult for many widowed parents and practical opportunities are often limited. When remarriage does occur, special problems may result in the context of the parent's "readiness" for a new relationship, compared to the "readiness" of the surviving child.

There have been studies which deal with the duration of bereavement to the point of lifting of the depression and psychic reorganization. In his classic paper Lindemann (1944) reported the resolution of acute grief within six to ten weeks. Clayton et al. (1968) reported improvement for 81 percent of their sample within six to ten weeks. However, Parkes and Brown (1972) reported that more than 50 percent of the young widows in their study were still mourning beyond the first year after the death. In fact, Parkes found that when young widows were compared to nonbereaved controls, depression remained high for up to three years following the death of the spouse. Our sample is representative of this longer bereavement period. Therefore, a significant and prolonged period of adjustment is more likely for a child as a result of the parent's prolonged bereavement and the potential for an adequate adaptation for the child may be decreased. There is an increase in the demand for empathic and effective parenting. Under such circumstances, the requirements for mastery polarize the widow's attempt to reduce the affective strain of her bereavement while encouraging and facilitating the mourning work of her child, which requires even greater empathy and effective parenting. Whether the widowed parent is more or less depressed, still has difficulty accepting that the spouse is dead, is preoccupied with thoughts and memories of the deceased (Bowlby, 1963), or has prematurely removed herself from the work of mourning, will have important effects upon parental function.

THE BEREAVEMENT SITUATION

Mourning may be defined as a human reaction to loss. The loss may be real or imagined, an object or attribute, a function, ideal, or aspiration. It has been used both in this sense, or more restrictively, to denote the adaptation to the loss of a meaningful love object through death. Pollock (1978b) prefers the term *bereavement* for the adaptational process inherent in the death of a person. He considers the mourning process "a universal adaptational and transformational process having sequential phases in stages . . . present as a reaction to loss . . ." (p. 258). Mourning is a process and requires emotional work. The adaptation is brought about by the separation of the individual from an important love object. It brings with it a psychic disequilibrium and requirement for a new equilibrium based upon the reality of the absence of that important figure and an alteration of emotional investment in the lost object and its significance for the bereaved. It requires a reinvestment in the self and in other objects and in the continuation of life without that person. It is based upon the perception of reality and the capacity to alter previous adaptations.

It is a process well described since Freud and includes delineated stages and attendant affects of grief. The grief gives expression to the feelings of loss; the mourning process includes the grief reaction and proceeds to relative (decathexis and) detachment from the lost object.

The cardinal features of bereavement include psychic pain, anxiety, sadness, longing, anger, guilt, disappointment, and shame. It is associated with symptoms of depressed mood, sleep disturbances, and crying. Loss of interest in the outside world, anorexia, or weight loss also occur frequently, as do increases in somatic complaints and increased use of drugs (usually tranquilizers, alcohol, and tobacco) (Clayton et al., 1968).

The capacity for the work of mourning is dependent upon the capacity for emotional object constancy, the capacity to know and test reality, the age and stage of life of the mourner, and the opportunity and ability to invest in new relationships. A factor which should not be underemphasized is the degree of ego strength at that period of life in which the death occurs, and the resources and limitations brought to bear upon the adaptation by the overall personality of the bereaved.

The process of mourning has been divided into component phases which provide a fairly clear-cut, overall pattern, despite individual and phasic variations. It includes a series of stages from shock or numbness at the loss, to hypercathexis of the lost object, often by means of memories, identifications, and yearning in association with the affects of grief, and gradual, bit-by-bit detachment of emotional interest in the lost object and reinvestment in living; that is, in life itself. The detachment (decathexis) is probably never complete, but successful completion of mourning probably is best assessed by the overall adaptation that prevails. Erna Furman (1974) makes the point that the degree of decathexis and identification is less important than the capacity of the surviving parent to invest in the living family, work, and possible future relationships. The last factor is also variable in that a widow or widower may choose not to marry and still be capable of successfully resolving the loss and maintaining effective parenting.

The duration of the phase of shock or numbness may vary from a few hours to one to two weeks (Parkes, 1965, 1970). It represents a state of psychic immobilization as a result of the traumatic impact of the death upon the survivor. It will vary according to the opportunity for anticipation of the death and the catastrophic, violent, or chronic circumstances of the death. It may include a sense of disbelief or give way to panic. In that the ego may be temporarily paralyzed by the advent of the death, a parent may not be able to respond in an organized manner to the numerous demands which the death brings. Decision making may therefore require assistance from supporting figures and the parental response to the surviving children may be limited. Some individuals may be capable of effecting decisions, despite the shock, but may not be able to experience much by way of feeling.

The second phase of mourning is associated with intense psychic pain—crying, fatigue, and anorexia are expressions of acute grief. Longing and yearning become manifest as time goes on. The yearning is accompanied by the repeated realization that the object is gone, the ego depleted, and the grief waxes and wanes as the reality of the death sinks in. Regression, depression, irritability, and anger begin to evolve as the individual experiences the narcissistic depletion of life without the deceased. Day-to-day activities and functions are often difficult. Certain periods of the day are very hard; those which involve memories of the deceased, the dinner hours, bedtime, and so on. Sleep disturbances are common. Many widows find themselves struggling with the separation, loneliness, and despair with the result that they are either unable to sleep in the marital bed or cannot discourage the children's wishes to share the bed with them.

Affective expression becomes gradually less intense, but smooth modulation of emotional states remains difficult. Parents experience frustration and either may not have the necessary buoyancy or patience for their children, or regressively may respond to certain sectors with the child and not to others, or withdraw, with disruption in their capacity to empathize with their children. Mediation of the children's tension states and facilitation of their bereavement is often difficult. During this phase, there are differences in the widow's and widower's adaptation.

In traditional families, bereaved mothers are more likely to be depressed, and fathers more likely to channel their grief into work, providership, and activity in an attempt at mastery over the pain of loss; that is, a defended avoidance of it.

The third phase of mourning is a reparative one which brings with it an integration of the fact that the loved object is irrevocably dead, a decline in the emotional investment in the object, an internal reparation of self and object representations, which requires a realignment of the internal mental representations, and a gradual reorganization of and reinvestment in life without the deceased.

The final point to be noted before we turn to the effects of bereavement upon focal parenting function involves the factor of time or the duration of bereavement to the point of lifting of the depression and psychic reorganization. As stated above, the widowed parents in our sample actively mourn at varying intensities for years after the death. While mourning among widowed parents in this age group tends to be long or chronic, this fact alone does not indicate "chronic mourning" in the sense of pathological mourning. The effectiveness of the overall parenting as well as the capacity to cope well and provide for and support the family (Hilgard, Newman, and Fisk, 1960) in conjunction with a bereavement process are the best indicators of a healthy adjustment to the loss of a spouse.

PARENTAL FUNCTIONS

The bereavement process of the parent and actual alterations in the living conditions of the family affect certain essential parental functions. These functions pertain to general needs for the growth and development of the surviving child, and specific needs occasioned by the loss.

Meeting reality needs, such as warmth, food, clothing, shelter, and education, are obviously basic, and providing assurance that these will be met promotes a sense of security. Protection is another function closely related to reality needs, which involves attention to the preservation of a child's physical safety. Psychological protection is also required, against more stimulation than the child's ego can absorb, and in this sense, the parent serves as a buffer against potentially traumatic agents. Similarly, soothing and tension regulation are requirements for children where these functions are not yet internalized. Empathy is essential for a child to feel confirmed and validated and to preserve the psychological relatedness to the surviving parent. Support of ego functions such as integration and synthesis are essential when these capacities have not developed or when regressions have occurred, as frequently happens when the child sustains a parental loss. Optimal frustration and guidance are self-evident. All of these functions are then related to meeting children's basic and general needs for growth and development. Moreover, the functions of empathy, assurance that reality needs will be met, stimulus buffering, soothing and tension regulation, and assistance with integration and synthesis are parental compliments to the child's internal capacities and are prerequisites for the child's mastering grief and undertaking mourning.

Pertaining to the loss itself, children, in addition, need information and verification of perceptions; that is, assistance with reality testing, assistance with verbalization of affects, the provision of a constant, familiar environment, and the permission and opportunity to share grief, which requires the parent's attention to and judgment about proper dosing. Proper dosing implies achieving a balance so that a child is assisted to move beyond denial and yet is protected from traumatic flooding by his own grief and that of others. The empathic parent must also accept the child's different experience and the different meaning the loss has to him, and the different timetable for adaptation to the loss.

What then is the impact of the parent's own grief, mourning, and accommodation to the loss on her capacity to meet the general needs of the child and the needs specific to the loss?

From Freud's classical description of mourning, it would

appear that there is considerable potential for disruption in the parental exercise of the functions described above. Freud refers to "painful dejection, cessation of interest in the outside world, loss of the capacity to love, [and] inhibition of all activity" as the attendant characteristics of mourning. He says: "It is easy to see that this inhibition and circumscription of the ego is the expression of an exclusive devotion to mourning which leaves nothing over for other purposes or other interests" (Freud, 1917a, p. 244). However, from our experience, the "devotion to mourning" in the surviving parent rarely is so complete that there is nothing left over for their children. Rather, we see a relative diminution of parental functioning. The continued investment in a child and the functioning pursuant to that investment is relatively preserved for several reasons.

Insofar as a parent experiences a bond with the child in the loss, that the ego ideal of good parenting is preserved, and the child is connected to thoughts of the loved object, the spouse, the child remains an integral part of the parent's world and investment in the child is preserved. However, while such factors are safeguards, they do not provide total immunity against the effects of ego absorption attendant to mourning; that is, the internal burden of accommodating to a loss. It is a burdened parent, then, who is faced with the ongoing and new, death-related needs of the child. Both parent and child are burdened by their psychological tasks, so that by virtue of the parent's weakened state and the child's greater need, it is expected that there is some impoverishment in parental functioning, however partial, minimal, or temporary this may be. Despite their absorption, however, some parents are capable of profound empathy for their children.

Ego absorption, inappropriate defenses with respect to the loss, parental regression, and the work of accommodating to the reality of life changes present potentially deleterious interferences to optimal parental functioning. There exists a wide variety of defenses encountered during bereavement. To the extent that the parent remains in a traumatic state or erects defenses which are maladaptive and abiding, the quality and adequacy of parenting will suffer. Suppression, repression, activity defenses, such as work and doing, and circumscribed avoidance mechanisms are employed in an attempt at active mastery. The active mastery here involves the more immediate solution of some external problem. For example, while the parent's capacity to assume a dual parental role is positively associated with good outcome for the bereaved child (Hilgard, 1963), this activity may, where used too much, and for too long a time, serve the purpose of repression and denial of the internal meaning of the loss and result in a greater potential for an aborted mourning reaction. What results is a certain ego constriction or precocious, pseudomaturation in the child based upon this model of inadequate coping with the internal and interpersonal dimensions of the loss while giving the appearance of successful adaptation. The very same mechanism may serve effective adaptation when utilized temporarily or in emergency circumstances to avoid traumatic flooding of the ego, followed by mechanisms serving neutralization, synthesis, integration, and internal adaptation leading to effective coping and mastery externally.

The defenses stirred by grief and mourning that may directly interfere with a parent's functioning are many. We see a range which includes denial of the significance of the loss, displacement, magical thinking, activity defenses, avoidance, repression, identification as a way of preserving the object, isolation and intellectualization, among others. The parent's defenses, insofar as they are maladaptive, serve as inadequate models for their children.

Parental defenses serving to rationalize, intellectualize, isolate, disavow, or deny in one way or another the emotional significance of the loss and the painful affects of grief interfere with the surviving spouse's ability to perceive and/or mediate the surviving child's reactions to the death. When the widowed parent is involved in such distancing mechanisms, the child's bereavement likely will go unattended. Other attempts at avoiding pain may be partially motivated by realistic capacities for nurturance, concern, and protection that result from the almost universal wish among parents to spare their children such pain. Memorialization and idealization may also have healthful as well as harmful effects. Such effects will depend upon the extent to which the reality of the loss and what was lost can be accepted, and how efficiently such mechanisms may serve to modulate the intense dysphoric states rather than deny the loss by way of a type of substitution. Remembering, in itself, may serve as a kind of substitution or state of reunion with the deceased.

The process of identification is a complex, inherent, explicit, and culminating attribute of bereavement. All losses result in identification. The identifications are evident in child and surviving parent and occur primarily during the second and third stages of bereavement. The more global, concrete, and lasting the identification, the more likely it is to be pathological. It may serve to deny the attributes of what is lost by the creation of a phantasy of replacement through identification. However, it may serve to preserve a more ideal state associated with the deceased and support and strengthen the ego ideal. The parent may encourage appropriate identifications with the deceased parent in the child which foster adaptation. The parent may also encourage identifications with effective coping and mastery evinced by appropriate parental behavior in the present loss situation and beyond, thus supporting the progressive maturation of the growing child.

The tendency toward sympathetic identification by the

parent is a frequent problem during the bereavement process, which often causes the parent to misperceive the child's need to establish some momentary distance from the loss experiences from the child's need to talk and express feelings about the loss. The widowed parent may either excessively attend to nuances of the child's expression of feelings of pain, sadness, or missing, or the parent may wish to share his own pain and loneliness when the child is trying to maintain a certain equilibrium without such tension. The parent also may limit the child's comprehension by distorting information, using ambiguous euphemisms, and/or excluding the child from sufficient concrete experiences with the death and involvement in the mourning rituals "for the sake of the child."

Another interference in the parent is regression, particularly ego regression, resulting in serious impairment in judgment and organizational skills. When loss is experienced as a trauma, by definition the ego is in a regressed state and is overwhelmed, overburdened, and disorganized. The burden of parenthood becomes a major overload. By virtue of the trauma, the longing for the object, the deprivation, and the lack of support resulting from the absence of the object, and external demands, there can be other regressions with a revival of needs and conflicts from an earlier period. Narcissistic vulnerability is exaggerated and depressions are more likely. Under these circumstances, the child's own regression and attendant behaviors may be perceived as an assault or injury. This is particularly true if the child's regression is to the ambivalent and conflictual object relations sector; for example, with such behaviors as tantrums, power struggles, sleep disturbances, and separation protests. What the child brings to the equation may compound the stress of the parent and further reduce overall effectiveness. Here the child is experienced as an added stress.

Reality life changes, such as moving from the family

home and community, entering the job market, beginning educational programs, and dating, further deplete the parent of energy and time available for the children. This frequently creates a conflict between the needs of the parent for reorganization and the child's needs for continuity. It is a conflict that is external between the parent and the child and one that is internal for the parent between ego-ideal aspirations for themselves as individuals, now single, and ego-ideal demands of being a success at parenting tasks. When parents do not match their ego-ideal of themselves as parents because of this conflict (or because of other interference noted above), lowered self-esteem may result in depression, further undermining capacities. There may be a guilt-induced reaction formation and other inappropriate attempts to compensate their children for the loss. On the other hand, there are many parents who reject their new representation as a single parent and have difficulty carrying on with the more demanding burdens of single parenthood. They have difficulty making reality life changes because these represent a confrontation with the reality of the loss. For many of these parents, receiving support and narcissistic supplies from their spouse had enabled them to provide needed supplies to their children. Without this resource for themselves, then, they find it harder to give to their children and to assume new burdens.

Aside from important practical issues inherent in managing the family as a single parent, the widowed parent is more likely to be subject to regressions and identifications (not necessarily regressive) which might set a boundary to the adaptational outcome for that parent. It is also likely that having young children may support positive adaptational modes, necessitated by the need to care for the child as well as the parent's inherent individual assets. However, for those parents with unresolved issues emanating from their own developmental experience, now reactivated by the traumatic loss of their spouse, there exists a higher risk for interferences and distortions in the parent–child relationship. For example, Mrs. Lev, a young woman, lost her husband when her child was two years old. Her own childhood was characterized by multiple losses. She and the child presented a picture of depression and symbiotic clinging when the child was seen at age four. In another case, Mr. Brown died during the early latency of the couple's only child, a boy. Mrs. Brown sought to become a pal, which had the quality of an identification with her deceased husband and the nature of the relationship enjoyed by the son and his father at the time of the death. Yet, the character of their interaction was like that of peers. Identification as an attempt to maintain the relationship with the deceased is not unusual in the bereavement situation. What was of further interest here was the fact that the mother had a "pal" relationship with her father during her own childhood and that this reactivated position did not support the taking on of a more effective dual parental role.

That these reactions are overdetermined is no doubt true. However, the effect of these parental identifications should be considered in terms of whether the emotional functioning of the family and the work of mourning are supported or to what extent these identifications interrupt or distort the mourning process of the parent and the child.

The lack of synchrony in the timetable for mourning between the parent and the child can constitute yet another interference in a parent's ability to assist a child through stages of mourning. If the parent is ready to move on, there may be a wish to hurry the child, and, if the parent is not ready, he or she may attempt to force a child to continue to mourn too long. An additional consequence of the experience of the death of a spouse is that parents sometimes become fearful about the well-being of their children, identifying the child with the deceased parent. This may account for one of the reasons why so many mothers bring their children, particularly boys, to the Barr-Harris Center for evaluation. Such fears can lead to fretful and overprotective parenting.

It should be understood that the parent's preexisting personality traits may exaggerate these many stresses and, of course, influence the parent's management of the children. Social and cultural mores and customs may also interfere with adaptive handling of the child's grief and needs as well as support it.

These interferences in a parent's functioning have greater or lesser consequences for the child, depending on age and developmental achievements, such as level of ego maturity and level of object relationship, and regressions brought on by the death with respect to these achievements. The child more or less suffers a double loss, though the psychological loss of the surviving parent may be very brief, and there may be other factors that reduce this loss. One such factor might be the availability of a grandparent, other relative, or friend to meet ongoing reality needs and general needs as well as provide direct assistance with mourning; for example, providing information, verifying perceptions, permitting, containing, and showing grief, and helping the child with reality testing.

The relative loss in the parent's functioning, then, with respect to the child's needs, has numerous implications. With respect to needs in general, obviously, where the child's reality needs are not met, or where reassurance about these is not forthcoming, there is tremendous anxiety. The child is in physical danger where protection is not available. Breaches in empathy around all issues result in disappointments, sadness, and diminished self-esteem. Inadequate soothing and stimulus buffering by the parent results in greater tension, regressed ego functioning, and potential disorganization. Inadequate support for ego integration and syntheses of a child's everyday experiences and crises tax the young child, so that a full understanding of various experiences is not achieved and the child may be confused and anxiety ridden; for example, a preschool child may appear quite frenetic. Where these parental deficiencies persist, especially when the child is vulnerable because of age, developmental interference may occur with inadequate structure formation and inadequate internalization of functions as a result.

With respect to the child's grief and loss, when parenting functions are diminished the child's capacity to mourn to the extent that the capacity was developed, becomes undermined. Erna Furman (1974) states: "At all stages of development, a child's ability to mourn is greatly facilitated when his surviving love objects also mourn, accept and support the child's reactions, and allow him to mourn with them" (p. 115). Robert Furman (1964) understood a parent's use of denial and the inability to model mourning behavior as interferences in a child's capacity to mourn. Without empathy, such children are engulfed in their sadness and they may feel that their emotions are inappropriate. With insufficient attention to their coping mechanisms, children are more likely to institute inappropriate defenses to deal with the loss.

The failure in empathy may also result in the child being given too much information or exposure to parental grief, the problem of dosing, which again may lead to flooding and being overwhelmed. Without information and assistance with reality testing, there is inadequate assimilation and integration of the experience of the death.

DIMINISHED PARENTAL FUNCTIONS IN NORMAL MOURNING

In considering case examples of the impact of diminished parental functioning on the child, it is difficult to completely differentiate this component in the etiology of a child's reactions from other factors, such as those that derive from his own mourning, reaction to trauma, and adjustment to the absence of a most needed figure. When considering case material one must, therefore, keep in mind the principle of multidetermination. Nevertheless, for the sake of discussion, material will be presented that, at least in part, reflects the shifts in parenting resulting from a parent's bereavement. Consequences for the child in general and with respect to his needs around the death will be considered.

Case Example 1

Mrs. Smith was a thirty-five-year-old mother of three children, two boys and a girl, ages two-and-a-half, six, and eight years. She called the Barr-Harris Center for an evaluation because she was having great difficulty coping with her children. She sounded overwhelmed and frantic. She complained that the children were constantly bickering, occasionally defiant, and frequently uncooperative with chores. It had been ten months since the sudden death of her husband. The relationship with her husband had been a very good one. She reported that her trouble with the children was uneven. She observed that sometimes she had an easier time than at others. The most difficult times were when she was preparing to go to work at a part-time job in a professional field, newly undertaken since the death. (This highlights the impact of change of routines on the surviving parent.) Since the death, she had been receiving a great deal of support from her family. She was not sure if the "problem" behavior was a result of her children's own reactions to the death of their father or to her inability to cope. She often felt overwhelmed by painful feelings which she could not always anticipate. When moods had been most severe, she had retreated into her bedroom and called a friend or her mother for comfort. The moods used to last two days. At the outset of the evaluation, these moods were less frequent and less intense. Discipline had not been a problem for her before the death, and the children generally had been cooperative. Following the death, she felt less patient. What irritated her most were all the children's teasing and tattling, her middle child's tantrums when thwarted, and her youngest child's developmental struggles. In her first interview, she seemed very weighed down and profoundly sad, though it was quite controlled. She seemed hurt and wounded, greatly burdened, and very unsure of herself. As she attempted to describe her concerns or complaints, she became vague. By the second evaluation interview (a month later), she began to look on the children's behavior as more normal sibling rivalry. It appeared that her view of their behavior and her capacity to handle it fluctuated with her own internal reactions to the continuing experiences of bereavement and the burden of carrying on with the responsibilities alone.

In contrast to some diminished ability to handle their general needs, this mother generally handled her children's reactions to the death quite well, so that, in this area, it was difficult to discern much interference deriving from her own mourning, although her own grief and sense of loss had been profound and did temporarily affect her ability to cope with and deal with the children.

Case Example 2

The Lee family, composed of a mother, age twenty-eight, daughter Harriet, age two-and-a-half years, and older adolescent half-siblings, were evaluated four-and-a-half months following the death of father. He had had several hospitalizations preceding the death and Harriet was witness to his growing illness. Harriet had begun to have a very special relationship with her father, quite distinct from the relationship with mother. With mother, she had been less mature and less cooperative. Though this child had essentially continued the thrust of her development it became clear after several evaluations that a crystallization of issues around separation and anger was beginning to occur in the child with impact on her general functioning. Though the Barr-Harris Center staff speculated that these effects were in part multideter- mined, they could be attributed to mother's input, derived partially from her own grief and mourning, and from ongoing personality dimensions, exaggerated by the death. Instances of inappropriate parental handling corresponded frequently to the phase in which mother was in the bereavement process. For example, before father's death, mother antici- pated her daughter's grief and loss, and seemed prepared to attempt to undo some of the experience of pain and loss. Shortly before father's final seizure and collapse, but sub- stantially after the beginning of his serious decline, Harriet had lost a piece of her family life puzzle, the father piece. Mother quickly went to the company for a replacement. As the time of father's death became imminent, she made repeated requests to the company. She restricted the use of the puzzle until the missing piece arrived. The missing piece arrived a month after father's death. Harriet's immediate response was to be happy, but then she stared at the father puzzle piece, said, "Daddy died," and had little use for the puzzle after that. Her mother became perplexed about how to handle Harriet's confusion and avoidance. As Mrs. Lee reacted to the immediate trauma, in her absorption and lack of energy, she altered some routines. For example, she altered the meals, essentially changing the type of food she had been giving Harriet. Harriet developed a transient eating disturbance. During the phase in which the memory of her husband was hypercathected, she drew the child's constant attention to the subject of father. It was our general impres- sion that this mother pressured her child to deal with it too much, with the effect that her daughter would sometimes parrot her mother's explanation, "Daddy died," with mother and daughter both caught up in this repetitious attempt at mastery. In fact, whenever mother sounded the least bit serious in calling her, Harriet would repeat this phrase, "Daddy died." In Harriet's first interview, which was conducted with Harriet and mother, mother repeatedly introduced the subject of father, presumably to aid the evaluation, but in a similar fashion to the pressured way she was having Harriet deal with the death.

As mother began to reconstruct her life, breaches in empathy became more pronounced, though these were of a somewhat different nature. Approximately three months following the death, mother had become very active. She engaged in numerous pursuits, taking up sports and dancing, and beginning to date. There appeared to be some attempt to distance herself from the affects of the loss and the work of mourning, on the one hand, and some beginning, genuine readiness to move on, on the other hand. In any event, there was a feeling of urgency to get on with these pursuits and to make up for lost time. Though she was thoughtful about the impact of these activities on Harriet, she became quite impatient with her daughter's tantrums and protests in these situations. Though she could generally anticipate the child's anxiety in many situations that did not interfere with her new plans, she sometimes used quite insensitive techniques to avoid dealing with Harriet's anxiety at times of separation. For example, she altered familiar arrangements for the dinner hour and left the sitter to handle some of the arrangements. One sitter would sometimes put Harriet to sleep before mother would leave in order to avoid the protesting tantrums, a technique mother condoned. It was convenient; it was a temporary solution to the conflict between their needs. This behavior was uneven and, at times, she could better prepare Harriet that she was leaving. Such unevenness appeared to be partially an artifact of the reorganization phase of mother's bereavement. Thus, the interferences can vary substantially according to phases in the process of bereavement.

PATHOLOGICAL MOURNING AND
PARENTAL FUNCTIONING

When the bereaved parent engages in various mental mechanisms, which serve in one form or another to persistently deny or disavow the emotional significance of the loss, or to regain the lost object with its relevant associated experiences significant for the individual's emotional well-being, mourning will be interfered with, deviated, more or less completely aborted (Pollock, 1978b), delayed (Raphael, 1983), or prolonged. Such pathological reactions may be associated with the type of death (with unexpected death, especially suicide and murder); the external circumstances of the bereaved family in the aftermath of the death (serious financial hardship, much change, and the lack of a supportive familial or social network); and the preexisting personality of the surviving parent (especially those characterized by dependency and ambivalence) (Bowlby, 1980). Internalizing needs of incorporation and introjection of the lost object and global identification with the lost object may be characteristic of such personalities. Bowlby (1963) categorized four major variants of pathological mourning. These include: (1) pathological yearning with the aim of reunion (often in the absence of outward grief; (2) angry reproaches (displacements) directed at the self or others; (3) overconcern for the suffering of others; and (4) denial of the permanency of the loss usually through the use of ego splitting mechanisms. A greater incidence of symptom formation generally results and includes protracted grief and prolonged, intense yearning, agitated depression and frank melancholia, hypochondriacal reactions, euphoric states, anniversary reactions, and suicide.

In 1980, Bowlby described three personality patterns typical of pathological mourners (pp. 202–213). These included individuals (1) who form anxious and ambivalent attachments to others as a result of unresolved problems emanating from childhood and are likely to be clinging, demanding, anxious, depressed, guiltful, angry, and disorganized. They have not infrequently experienced significant disruptions and losses in childhood as well. It would not be difficult to appreciate that such individuals, as parents, would be likely to induce confusion, insecurity, and ambivalence in their children. In fact, Mary Main (Personal Communication, 1985) reported finding a higher incidence of disorganized, insecure children raised by mothers who suffered an early loss. Bowlby characterized the second type of pathological mourner, as having a "disposition toward compulsive care giving" (p. 206). These individuals had abiding character defensive organizations of this type, were likely to have selected spouses who were needful or disadvantaged in some respect, and were likely to be overprotective and possessive as parents.

The third type was described as giving a picture of "emotional self-sufficiency" and "independence of affectional ties" (p. 211). Both stable and vulnerable character organizations were described. Childhood circumstances which were not sufficiently nurturing or actively discouraged the desire for empathic caretaking, as well as the same defensive attitudes to prior loss would be more typical of these individuals. As parents, it might be expected that self-sufficiency rather than empathy will be encouraged. Such a parent would less likely be available to a surviving child as an effective mediator and facilitator of mourning and might have to encourage the child to be too much "the good soldier."

Each of these paradigms of pathological mourners, then, emphasize preexisting pathological determinants in the parent, already influencing the parent–child relationship, but now made worse by the death. Many but not all of these parents have had significant, unresolved losses in their childhoods. The death, as a unique determinant, combines with previous pathology to produce a significantly disturbed reaction in the parent.

The ability to parent is seriously diminished. The interferences are many. Many of them are the same as previously described, but they are either more exaggerated, or more exaggerated in a particular sector of parental function. For example, an anxiously attached parent in Bowlby's sense is more likely to affectively flood the child. In such instances, the parent not only insufficiently protects the child against breaches in the stimulus barrier, they are themselves the breach. This is particularly the case where a parent experiences a heightened traumatic reaction with disorganization because of a combination of extreme circumstances surrounding the death (e.g., suicide), prior pathology, and inadequate support system in the crises. In this, in compulsive caregiver situations, and others not so typified, the separation anxiety triggered in these parents can lead to exaggerated concerns for the child's health. They may use the child as a replacement, need-meeting object. Guilt reactions and loss of self-esteem due to diminished capacity to parent further break down the capacity for empathy and frequently result instead in primitive projections.

Unrelenting anger, sometimes at the deceased and sometimes about the situation, is a mark of pathological mourning. It may take various forms: identification with the aggressor, defenses such as threatening abandonment, displacement of the anger toward the child who becomes identified with the lost or depriving spouse, or generalized resentment toward all the children and significant others. In pathological mourning, the death becomes an organizer of the parent's character and defensive structure, providing the child with a maladaptive model of mourning. Such interferences in parenting are greatly prolonged, they contribute to major developmental interferences for the child, skewing development, and diminishing the overall quality of the child's life. The consequences for these children are qualitatively different from those bereaved children whose parents mourn more normally their shared loss, in that arrests and deviations in development are more likely to occur.

Case Example 1

Mrs. Dempster, a mother of five children, called for an evaluation for her son Sam, who was then age seven years. Father, an attorney, had died after a long illness, about one-and-a-half years prior to consultation with the Center. Sam was said to be unruly, demanding, insolent, and selfish. In addition, mother described impulsive behaviors, hostility, abusiveness toward her, reluctance to attend school, lack of energy and interest in activities, and fantastic claims about and wishes to do dangerous things.

Mrs. Dempster presented as an intensely anxious, self-doubting, and depressed woman. She felt she could not manage her children and she was an easy target for them. Alternatively, she seemed highly demanding toward them. She had been unable to resume her career and had isolated herself from former activities. She occasionally contemplated suicide. She felt so overwhelmed by her pain and was so depressed that she felt her children would do better without her. She contemplated placing several of her children, including Sam, in a boarding school. Six months after the death of her husband, Mrs. Dempster developed a serious depression with hypochondriacal symptoms, requiring extensive medication and treatment.

When Sam was evaluated, he still greatly idealized father, and the need for him was all the greater as a result of the ambivalent care in the relationship with his mother and her essential deterioration. The continual psychological and physical absence of his mother left this seriously troubled, vulnerable child alone. Therefore, it was essential for him to preserve his father. He had neither the external support nor internal structures to withstand the onslaught of the trauma. The result was ego weakness and a serious regression in object relations.

This child's inadequate structure prior to the death was itself related to previous parental functioning that was not optimal. The death had the effect, then, of traumatizing the child by magnifying the pathology within each and between Sam and his mother. Mrs. Dempster, a woman who was psychologically vulnerable to depression, became incapacitated by the death. A major narcissistic regression ensued. Her functioning as a parent was seriously compromised and Sam's future development would have been seriously disturbed without intervention.

Case Example 2

The Dawson family, mother, age thirty and son Matthew, age four-and-a-half was seen two years following the death of father due to a train crash. Father had been a salesman. At two-and-a-half years of age, Matthew had a highly idealized relationship with father. They had gone many places together and Matthew would eagerly await his father's return home from work. At the time of the evaluation, the child day care program reported that he was not responding well to limits and, when reprimanded there, he would stare into space and act as if he had heard nothing. He was said to be an extremely restless child who could never remain quiet. He was always creating a commotion and needed a great deal of individualized attention and structure.

Mrs. Dawson was immediately sedated following the death and left the care of the child in the hands of relatives for several days, though in close proximity to her. The facts of father's death were not disclosed to him during that time, though he was exposed to the family turmoil surrounding the death. What ensued from that time was a series of experiences that resulted in a cumulative trauma for the child. Many of these experiences derived from external changes that mother initiated in an effort to avoid her pain and to deal with the reality of being the only provider. She immediately changed apartments and returned to her former work that involved long hours and night work. A relative, whom Sam had not previously known, moved into the home with her own child and assumed major responsibilities for Matthew's care. He was placed in a day care center from 7:00 A.M. to 5:00 P.M. Mrs. Dawson increasingly began to defend against the loss with still more activity, returning to school in addition to working. She also began to date and was then out additional evenings. Matthew complained to his mother that she was always working. At home, she had an expectation that he be mature, and she realized that she also frequently expected him to be a companion to her. She claimed that she did not observe any of the reactions at home that were noted elsewhere.

In his interview, during the course of the evaluation, then two years after the death, Matthew appeared to be still quite traumatized. He was flooded by violent images, impulses, and fantasies. His fantasies included themes of great danger, destruction, reparation, disillusionment, alternations between grandiose regressions, and searches for protective, magical, empowering figures; for example, a dragon snorted smoke, devoured cars, went on rampages, collapsed, died, and needed to be "fixed" with blood. Then he would declare that he was very strong. Trains crashed, but cars and pedestrians were protected. He fantasized about straw people who could not get hurt.

The trauma was made greater by too little information and mother's limited awareness of his psychological needs, especially in light of her efforts to disavow the loss. Mother's empathy was interfered with initially by the sedation and then by her self-absorption and defensive accommodation to the mourning task, and finally, by external factors which brought some necessary burdens that greatly distracted her.

SUMMARY

In conclusion, the tasks of the bereavement situation for widowed parents with young children has been outlined. The tragedy of the early death of a husband or wife places enormous demands upon the capacity of the surviving parent to integrate the experiences for her or himself, to manage the family, and to support the mourning process of the child. It is an overburdened parent who must continue to mediate not only the ordinary needs of the surviving child, but the needs intensified by the loss. Interpretation of reality, modulation of tension and mood states, empathic caretaking and support of the child, encouragement of the capacity to experience the effects of grief, as well as encouragement of progressive development, and the capacity to cope and provide for the family are among the critical functions requiring preservation in the face of this trauma. The fact that the bereavement period can and often does extend from months to years and involves a significant period in the life of the young child is an important component of the bereaved parent–child relationship. The potential for multiple losses attributed to the death is inherent for both the surviving spouse and child. Some parents are able to respond adaptively, others develop pathological reactions, which encumber their parenting ability. Early intervention for high-risk parents should attempt to assess the status and evolution of the parenting function.

Chapter 4

Support Systems

Helen R. Beiser, M.D.

The loss of a parent does not take place in a vacuum. It happens not only in the context of a family, but also in a complex community. This poses a problem in studying the effects of death because the number of family and community variations seems endless. Although we have been most interested in the effect of parent loss on the internal world of the child, we have been aware that such effects may be modified for better or for worse by the support or lack of it available from others.

The surviving parent is of primary significance for the child, and the individual reactions and personality factors in this parent have been explored elsewhere (see chapter 3). This parent, however, is also the bridge for the child to other support systems, especially important for only children. The direct support the surviving parent is able to give the child may be dependent on how much of a social network the parent has readily available, or how much professional or nonprofessional help he or she is able to find. A parent who lives in the same locality as the family of origin, or else has been in the same place for a sufficient period of time to have a circle of friends, is in a very different position from one who has just recently moved to the location in which the spouse died.

The surviving parent's choice for support is an individual matter, and some offers from well-meaning others may be rejected. Hardest on the child is the situation where the child himself is the first choice for providing the parent with comfort and support. However, the older the child the more support he or she can give to the parent as well as to any younger children. For example, in a family with eighteen-year-old and ten-year-old sons, after the father's death from cancer the older boy took on the father's role, supporting the mother, and acting as a role model for the younger child (see chapter 10). A seven-year-old boy, the oldest in a family seen at the Barr-Harris Center, started to take over his dead father's mail as his prerogative. His mother encouraged this, as well as using him as her confidant. Girls whose mothers die may take on household responsibilities beyond their years, and act out their mother's role. The father may look to the daughter for sympathy and encourage the attention she gives to him. A grieving parent may be only too willing to lean on these frail staffs, and others may have to intervene to protect the child from excessive burdens. Although children may seem to enjoy this seemingly real oedipal victory, it is also necessary to protect them from the accompanying guilt.

In families with large numbers of children, a loss may be easier to bear if the children are able to support each other. Social agencies have always tried to place siblings together for that reason. If they remain with the surviving parent, however, there may be an extra physical and emotional load arising from the need to care for many children. There is great individual variation, however, depending on the ages of the children, and the quality of family relationships which existed before the loss.

Although supports can be roughly divided into practical and emotional, it may be hard to make a clear differentiation. A lot of emotional support may accompany what looks like practical help. First, depending on the length and type of illness and cause of death, arrangements need to be made relating to medical care, payment of bills, funeral and burial plans, and for the future living place and sources of financial support for the survivors. Emphasis may be different for surviving fathers than for surviving mothers. Fathers may feel more comfortable with the multiplicity of financial arrangements that need to be made, but need more help in arranging for the care of children, especially if there are any of preschool age. In fact, child care issues may be of major importance in planning for the future of the motherless family. Some surviving fathers may think that early remarriage is the easiest solution to these problems, but incomplete mourning on the part of the father, and resentment from the children may produce complicated familial problems.

Working mothers may face the same problems of child care as fathers, but usually have the additional problem of reduced income. The nonworking mother does not have the same need for child care, but her financial problems may be great. Insurance may be of assistance, but even without actual financial need, she may have to be much more active in planning and handling money than before the loss. Although most women are quite capable of dealing with these responsibilities, the pain of the loss may be accentuated when they take over tasks previously performed by the dead partner. Reduced income brings into question whether the family can afford to continue to live in the same place or in the same style. There may be value in moving closer to helpful family members. If a move is necessary, it should be carefully planned. For children, it is best to retain the familiar neighborhood, friends, school, and teachers, at least for awhile. If at all possible, a move should be coordinated with the end of a school term, so that a new school can be entered at the beginning of a term. Such natural endings and beginnings can make the loss of old ties and the start of new ones less painful. Teenagers feel the loss of friends and school with special sharpness. Those who have already achieved considerable emotional separation from family might choose to stay in the original location, perhaps in order to graduate from their familiar school with their friends.

Parents may also differ in what help they will take to handle their internal feelings of loss and destitution. In the experience of the Barr-Harris Center, surviving fathers are more likely to deny feelings of loss, need to show themselves as self-sufficient, and find it difficult to enter a supportive therapy situation. We do not feel it is just because there is a statistically higher frequency of father loss as compared to mother loss that the Barr-Harris Center has served far more surviving mothers than fathers. Some mothers actually underestimate their material as well as emotional resources.

Most often, surviving parents will turn to their families of origin at a time of loss. Their own parents can be of great practical as well as emotional support, both to the surviving parent and to the children. They may give at least temporary shelter or child care, financial assistance, and/or advice about future planning. Much of this depends on their available resources, geographic proximity, and emotional closeness. We have seen surviving parents who have lost one of their own parents fairly recently, which produces a repetition of the feelings of loss. If the surviving parent has siblings, they may be as helpful as the grandparents, especially if family relationships had been positive. Relatives of the same sex as the dead parent may be especially important to the child or children of that same sex as role models, and as at least temporary substitute parents. When mothers die, sometimes grandmothers become the permanent mother substitute. We have seen some tragic situations where the death of that grandmother subjected the child to a second loss.

The family of the dead parent is a far more variable source of support. Of course, they might be of as much help as the family of the surviving parent, but their own sense of loss may make them unavailable, a burden, or even a detriment to the surviving parent and children. For example, in the case of the death of a five-year-old boy's mother, the maternal grandmother repeatedly called the father and accused him and the doctors of causing her daughter's death. For years the father suffered from headaches and nightmares, eventually requiring psychotherapy. In the boy's analysis, five years after his mother's death, he demonstrated unconscious fears that all adult males might well be killers. The grandmother had told the boy that his mother was going to the hospital to have a baby, rather than that she was seriously ill, and his analysis also showed that he felt childbirth was destructive to mothers. He had behavior disturbances when his stepmother had her first child, but when she had her second, the support and understanding he obtained in analysis helped to correct this distortion (see chapter 10 for details of this case).

Sometimes the dead parent's family may try to woo the child for its own needs. One paternal grandfather spent his visits with the children of his dead son in the cemetery, actively involving the children in his wishes to reunite all family members with those lost in the Holocaust. This was interfering with the mother's more optimistic plans for the future. The suspicion that the surviving parent at least was not an adequate spouse seems to be very hard for some parents who lose young adult offspring to overcome. The dead parent's siblings may be less bitter, and can be important supports to the surviving parent and to the children, especially those siblings who are the same sex as the dead parent. In some circumstances, various extended family members may also offer much practical and emotional support.

Beyond the family, there are many possibilities for aid

during periods of tragedy. If the family has lived in its present location for a long time, friends and neighbors usually respond. In fact, when a young parent dies leaving small children, there might be almost too much initial sympathy, which may be difficult if it is then followed by withdrawal. Aside from emotional support for the surviving parent, immediate child care can be of great value while the parent makes the necessary arrangements following a death. The child can be with familiar people, who are probably the parents of his friends. Some neighbors may have actually witnessed the death, and are better able to interpret the facts to the child than the distraught parent. It is to be hoped that they can also allow the child to grieve, rather than offering distractions or otherwise encouraging suppression of feelings. After the initial period of shock and grieving has passed, and the family is continuing in the same home, they can be of even greater assistance to the child. The parents of neighborhood friends can see that a bereaved child is included in group activities that require the presence of a parent, and offer to be the substitute. "Parent's Night" can be particularly stressful for the child without the designated parent.

If the family had been active members of a religious group, the same kind of support as from friends and neighbors may be available. Funeral arrangements are often centered around the church or temple, and there may even be some sort of counseling available for parent and children. In Jewish families, the author has found that the ceremonies marking the first anniversary of the death allow for a reworking of the feelings, or else allow them to be expressed for the first time. A religious group may supply a philosophical framework for the understanding and eventual acceptance of death. Of course, in the process of depth psychotherapy it becomes clear how such ideas can be perverted, even to making the dead parent into a ghostly companion, but this does not mean that the idea of a constant supernatural father may not be a source of comfort to adult and child alike. Some religious communities are like families, supplying much practical and emotional support for their members. If a move is necessary, a related religious group can be very helpful in making the transition easier.

Except for the very young child, the school is a most important institution, occupying a large part of the child's day. Although not ordinarily seen as a support system, it can be of great use to the bereaved child. Adults in the school can be quite sympathetic when they learn of such a tragedy, and are usually understanding of the child's temporary lack of interest in schoolwork. They can also inform the child's classmates in a way to arouse their support. If available, a school counselor may give the child a chance to ventilate feelings away from the classroom. Younger children may cling to the teacher for awhile, but older children are more likely to withdraw from the teacher and classroom activities. As time goes on, the school may be in the best position to pick up symptoms that can be helped by therapy so that they do not become chronic. One symptom which schools may unwittingly support is an excessive interest in studies or other activities. This may be adaptive if it is not a technique to avoid dealing with the feelings of loss. The Barr-Harris Center saw a boy who felt that his loss should not keep him from moving ahead, and he devoted himself excessively to athletics, to the detriment of his interpersonal relationships.

Sometimes events in school trigger reactions related to past losses. Schools can be sensitive to such sudden changes in behavior or mood. For example, the boy whose grandmother had told him his dying mother was having a baby reacted to the pregnancy and subsequent leaving of his teacher by failing to learn (see chapter 10). The boy whose father died of cancer when he was ten returned to his therapist at fifteen when his school noted his depression. Not knowing his history, they were unaware that the trigger was the illness which had forced his physics teacher to leave his job. As these examples indicate, teachers may be seen as parent substitutes, and, if they remain healthy, can become important persons to bereaved children, especially in the later years.

Children may belong to formally organized peer groups, such as scouts, outside of school or church. Some may be introduced to such groups for the first time as part of the attempt to establish meaningful relationships to adults other than the surviving parent, as well as to peers. The adult leader of such a group can act toward the child like the schoolteacher, offering sympathy and support, and interpreting the child's loss to the other children. Although intense involvement in such groups may be adaptive, like excessive preoccupation with studies, it may be symptomatic of avoidance of mourning. The value of such a group to the depressed child may be limited, as a voluntary group has no control over dropouts. As the number of single parent families from all causes increases, groups must seriously consider how to plan those activities in which the participation of one or both parents is encouraged or required. Embarrassment over not having the appropriate family member to participate may cause dropping out by some children who need the group experience very much.

Besides these more usual or generally expectable support systems or institutions, specialized professional or semiprofessional services can be found in some communities. The Barr-Harris Center is one such professional service which not only gives direct help to bereaved families, but offers help and advice to other resources. Social agencies are sensitive to the impact of loss on both adults and children. They may offer supportive psychotherapy, as well as child care services, if such are necessary for the working parent. On the nonprofessional side are self-help groups specifically for the bereaved—one of the major sources of referral to the

Barr-Harris Center has been widows' groups. They help the new widow to express her feelings in a group of women who have suffered a similar loss. As time goes on, they help each other to enter and use a wider social network, or seek treatment if this is needed. Such groups, or even professional services, may be of particular value to those women who do not have family in the immediate geographic area.

A variety of other types of support may be available for certain situations. In some dangerous occupations like police, firemen, and the armed services, there are special provisions for survivors of members who die in action. Family physicians, pediatricians, psychiatrists, or other psychotherapists with a long-term relationship to a survivor may give special support after a loss. Unexpected support may come from insurance adjustors or funeral directors who have become aware of the emotional impact of loss. Similarly, a lawyer may be of more help than in merely settling estates or selling property.

In summary, it is important to deal with each case in an individual manner. Death has a powerful impact which can lead to disruption of the personality in the survivors, but with appropriate supports to previously healthy individuals, can be expected to have time-limited results, if grieving is allowed and mourning facilitated. For those who, either as professionals or nonprofessionals, find themselves trying to help families who have suffered bereavement, it is important to discover what would be most helpful. In general, it is best to make changes slowly. Separation of family members or change of location may be necessary but should be done one step at a time. A surviving father's primary need might be child care, while a widow might more likely need legal help, and for each, the family and community support systems need to be explored. If money is an issue, expensive modes of support are of no value. The ages of the surviving children are a consideration in planning. Older children may be so hostile that they will accept no help, at least not directly. It must also be remembered that different methods of support are suitable at different time periods after the death. Even the most sensitive funeral director cannot continue counseling past the time of the burial. Often there is an excess of help immediately after the death, and a dearth later on. If symptoms are prominent, especially after the period of obvious grieving is over, professional help may be required. In the initial stages grief should not be mistaken for depression, nor evidences of regression for serious pathology. On the other hand, we have found that the death of a parent may bring to professional attention problems in the children *or* the surviving parent that long preceded the death. It may be extraordinarily difficult to separate those symptoms due to the loss from those due to long standing problems, because a need to idealize the dead parent may obscure previous family dynamics. The failure of ordinary support systems to bring the bereaved family members back to a reasonably functioning state in a reasonable time can be one indication for considering professional treatment. In conclusion, it takes a lot of imagination, tact, and skill to help a bereaved family find and use supports that are available and specific for their needs, as well as refer them to professional help for symptoms which do not respond to support alone.

Section III

The Barr–Harris
Experience—Intervention

Chapter 5

Diagnostic Interventions with Children at Risk

Colin Webber, M.A.

As psychotherapists, we are interested in providing an understanding of the impact that the death of a parent has on a child. At the same time we are concerned about what can be done to lessen the pain and to prevent psychopathology. The diagnostic consultation provides us with the necessary data to develop an idea of the mosaic of the family, which in turn forms the basis for our diagnosis and possible interventions. When one observes the pain and confusion that these bereaved families experience, it is difficult to restrict oneself to conducting the diagnostic assessment of the family, and one naturally wants to intervene. However, intervening in the usual sense would be premature and would take us beyond the specific tasks and goals of the diagnostic consultation. A question does arise as to whether, in this early phase, one can fruitfully conduct both the diagnostic assessment and simultaneously begin to provide some therapeutic assistance to the family.

In the experience of the Barr-Harris Center, the diagnostic consultation does indeed provide multiple functions in the therapeutic process. While the purpose of the diagnostic consultation is to develop an understanding of the impact that the death of a parent has on the child and his family, it is through understanding the meaning of the loss that we then begin to form our interventions. These interventions can range from education and support to psychotherapy for the surviving parent and/or child.

A survey of the literature gives the impression that there is a paucity of psychoanalytic articles dealing with the diagnostic phase of treatment, and more so in regard to the topic of parent loss. Work by A. Freud (1965), Kohrman, Fineberg, Gelman, and Weiss (1968), E. Furman (1974), Sours (1978), Palombo (1981), and Mishne (1983) are a few examples of articles which begin to touch upon this topic. Although there is a lack of data on this early phase, it should not be interpreted to indicate that the diagnostic phase is unimportant. However, the lack of material leaves the diagnostician with limited guidelines for approaching the bereaved child. Although the diagnostic process with bereaved children is similar to that of nonbereaved children, there are some unique factors which need to be considered and will be approached later.

The diagnostic consultation is a time of primary importance in establishing rapport and a working relationship with the family. This relationship is assisted in its formation through creating an environment of trust, which can then facilitate the surviving parent's and the child's sharing of their thoughts, feelings, and worries.

During the diagnostic consultation at the Center the surviving parent, all of the children in the family, and other significant adults are interviewed. Although we have found it most effective to meet with the parent first, it is also possible to begin by seeing the child and subsequently interviewing the parent as necessary through the diagnostic process. The interviews with the parent are for the purpose of collecting the necessary information that will provide a base for approaching the interviews with the children, as well as assisting us in understanding the parent's process of mourning. In addition, the interviews with the parent are extremely important in establishing a working relationship with the parent so that they may facilitate the child's coming to the Center. We have found that as parents feel more confident and trusting of the clinician, they will be better able to support the child being seen and to share their feelings. Many times children resist coming to the Center or are unable to separate from the parent for an interview. Such resistance can be due to the surviving parent's ambivalence about the child being evaluated, as well as the child's own resistance to confronting their feelings, especially as they related to the parental death.

Allowing the child to be evaluated may also mean to the parent that more of the parent's self will be revealed. Freud (1917a) discussed how the bereaved often feel a lowered self-esteem. It is this lowered self-esteem that we often see as contributing to the parent's feeling that their children will reveal negative aspects of the parent's personality and parenting skills. For some parents the child carries the parent's infantile self. To let the child be evaluated may mean that their own fears and dependencies will be exposed.

In addition, the resistance to bringing the child to the Center often stems from the parent's desire to protect the child from further hurt and pain. When families are seen at the Center we anticipate their initial contacts to be difficult. The Center may come to represent many different images to different families. To some, we are perceived as supportive and a link to life. To other families the Center can come to represent death and a prolongation of their grief. It is with these latter families that we find the parents having the greatest difficulties in supporting their children coming for an evaluation. Most often, family members will feel frightened, ambivalent, and confused when first seen following the death. It is because of these feelings that it is essential to engage the parent in a supportive, buffering manner that can assist them in managing their flooded ego so that they can do the same for their child.

One must be careful not to ignore the intense feelings of humiliation and shame which a parent may feel in bringing their child for consultation. It is difficult under usual circumstances for parents to bring their children in for treatment, but when it occurs at the time of a death, parents are more open to narcissistic injuries and vulnerabilities, often feeling that their role as a parent is being questioned. It not only exposes the parent to what has been lost, but also becomes a reflection of who they are.

During the initial contacts with the parent, we are looking in several directions simultaneously. First, we are examining the parent's current functioning and their various roles as a parent, at home, work, and in the community. In their role as a parent, we are observing their ability to remain physically and psychologically available to their children. If they are able to accomplish this, they will then be available to provide the support necessary for the children to begin their mourning. It is when children are left emotionally alone that they encounter the greatest difficulty in mourning and adaptation to a parental loss.

While we are assessing the parent's availability to the child, we are also examining the parent's ability to engage in a mourning process themselves. This is influenced by their own psychological development. The parents who demonstrate the greatest ego capacity and development and have achieved a significant degree of structuralization are those who have the greatest capacity for mourning. On the other hand, the parents who have limited ego resources and lack the necessary structural differentiation are most likely to experience difficulties in their own mourning process. It is these parents who will not only have difficulty in their own adaptation, but will also be unable to provide an appropriate holding environment for the child (Winnicott, 1960).

An additional area of exploration with the parent involves the family's genetic and historical background. We will be looking for strengths and assets, as well as early ruptures and disruptions in both the child's and the parent's development. This would include evidence of any specific constitutional deficits or assets which a child may possess. Any early life experiences relating especially to issues surrounding loss and separation or any specific traumatic event in the child's life is important to discover. These events are significant since they point to areas of strength or vulnerability. Through this material we listen for events which have shifted the developmental history of the child. We are also examining how the child and the parent interact, the specific functions that the child and the parent provide for each other, and how capable the parent is of engaging in relationships with their external support systems. A final area to be explored with the parent is the child's current developmental phase. This is useful since it will provide an indication of the specific developmental landmarks which have been reached, the developmental task which the child was struggling with at the time of the death, and the child's current developmental tasks.

The gathering of this material with the parent is useful in many ways. First, we are able to learn who the parent is, how they understand the child, and their view of the meaning of the event in the child's life. An additional benefit of the diagnostic material with the family is that it begins to give a form and structure to their current state of anxiety and can help remove the feeling of isolation the family may be experiencing. It is also through the gathering of this information that we begin to develop what one could refer to as a family's myth. The information we receive from the family is the parent's version of how the family developed, and is colored and modeled according to the parent's past history. What we need to remember is that this material is much more useful when we begin to understand it as a version of history and not as objective, concrete data. It is with this information that we begin to appreciate and understand the child's and the parent's milieu.

Each child, even though growing up in the same family, will experience the death of a parent in a different manner. Understanding the death and the meaning that it has for each child will vary according to the experiences of that child. These will include other losses the child has experienced, their position in the family system, the role that they fill in the family, and the specific relationship with the surviving parent and with the deceased parent. The developmental stage of the child also affects the meaning and understanding the child has of the death. Because of the multiple relationships and individual meanings of the loss for each family member, the meaning and adaptation to the loss will vary considerably. Our work is to develop our empathic understanding of what the child has lost and the specific feelings the child has at the time of the death. This is important because each loss means something unique to each member of the family and the family as a whole. It is these varied meanings of the death that makes the task of diagnosing in this area difficult. As seen in work with the families at the Center, and the work of others, death is a tragic, overwhelming event in the life of the family. It is important, however, not to assume that we understand what and how it is tragic for each individual family member.

We cannot assume that an individual will respond to the death of a parent in any specific manner or that a specific type of death such as an illness or an accident will produce a specific reaction. In our work, we are discovering some common reactions that a child may have to the death of a parent, but to respond to these general ideas without focusing specifically on each individual child would be incomplete and a disservice to the child.

Following the diagnostic interviews with the parent and the establishment of a working relationship, the parent and clinician establish an appointment for the child. The diagnostic consultation with the child begins before the child is actually seen. This is done through the work with the parent. The parent is asked to speak to the child about coming to the Center. The discussion should include the reason for coming in, presented in concrete terms. For example, "Since your Dad has died you seem very angry, fighting with your friends and with me." Or, "I am concerned that we have not talked enough about your Dad and every time we try, you stop talking."

Being concrete and simple assists the child in understanding that the parent is concerned and understands that the child's behavior has meaning and that the consultation has a specific meaning and purpose. We ask that the child be told who they will see, the length of the appointment, and what will occur. This is explained by informing them that they will be speaking to someone who understands children and is interested in knowing about their worries and concerns and to talk about their parent's death. It will also be explained that the clinician will help them to talk through drawing and playing. The parent is also encouraged to convey her support and interest in the consultation.

This process of preparation is beneficial to the child as it again helps him to speak with the surviving parent about the deceased parent; it also buttresses their defenses by partially preparing them for the meeting. It is our belief that children adapt best when they are provided with appropriate information.

The children who are seen at the Center come at varying

points on the scale of adaptation. Like their parent, they are often frightened and overwhelmed. Each child manages the consultation using whatever ego resources are available. They are notably resistant, cautious, and concerned about being flooded further by their fears of death, annihilation, abandonment, and the pain from the emotional disruption of their object attachments. Emptiness and confusion stemming from not understanding the drastic changes in their lives adds further difficulty to the evaluation process. As the child's defenses work to protect them from these intense emotions they can also operate to distance the child from the clinician and the diagnostic process. This initial contact with the clinician is important in helping the child appreciate that the clinician is aware of and is interested in understanding the pain and vulnerability of the child.

When our approach to the child is in an empathic, introspective frame of reference, and we focus our attention on the child's experience at that moment and use this material as the pivotal point for the interviews, the structure of our questions in the interview will take form from our empathic understanding of the child. For example, if we ask a child to tell us about the deceased parent and he becomes emotionally frozen, we then have a clue to the child's experience and a beginning understanding of his psychological state. An example of this is a four-year-old boy who was seen three months after his father's death by suicide. He was not told the truth about the death, even though A. was present at the time they discovered his deceased father. In our first interview, he was extremely anxious and managed his feelings through his hyperactivity. During the interview, when he was asked why he thought we were meeting, he burst out with the statement that his father had died. When asked to tell about this, his mouth moved forming words but no sounds were produced. A. was in essence telling us several things: first, that he was overwhelmed and frightened; second, that he could not find words to express the experience; and third, that it was an unspeakable topic in his home. He was not pressed more at that time, but instead the session was allowed to take its course, knowing that over time he would be more able to answer the necessary questions. In addition, the material that A. conveyed was used to begin our intervention both with him and his mother.

This vignette demonstrates the primary source of material used in diagnosis and in forming the beginning of our interventions. The interchange between the clinician and the child from the very first encounter forms the basis of our understanding of how the child manages his internal and external world. The content of the session becomes a second source of information which is obtained through the child's verbalizations, play, drawings, and nonverbal behavior, as well as what he omits.

While we are observing the child, we are simultaneously processing the material in many ways. First, we are listening for how the child has experienced the death. What is the child's understanding of death in general, and then specifically, the death of the parent? Second, we are asking how the child is experiencing and managing this death. Is the death viewed as a natural consequence or is it experienced as an abandonment and rejection, with the child left in a lost and confused emotional state? What psychological mechanisms are being utilized by the child for adaption? For example, is there evidence of grief and mourning, or is the child using denial, avoidance, acting out, or withdrawal? How capable is the child of experiencing, managing, and integrating the painful affects and feelings? Finally, what does the material tell us about how the child thinks (his or her cognitive style). In addition, we are, of course, developing a picture of how the child's development has progressed and whether regressions have occurred.

During our initial interview with the children there are

several tasks which will occupy the clinician. First, is to engage the child in a manner that will facilitate his relaxing and developing a working rapport. We can assume that the child will be anxious and apprehensive at encountering a new person and an unknown situation. Considering that he has had recent encounters with many new and unknown situations filled with sadness, pain, and confusion, we would expect the diagnostic situation to be viewed with caution.

As the goal is to engage the child so that we may learn about his struggles with adaptation to the death, we must initially suspend our agenda and allow the child to set the pace of the consultation.

An ongoing struggle in our work has evolved around whether the interviews at our Center should be structured or unstructured. Our dilemma surfaced as we worked to maintain a nonintrusive psychoanalytically oriented approach, while at the same time gathering the necessary data for our research and to help the child. Our decision has been to develop a semistructured interview. The structure of the diagnostic consultation evolves from the child and the clinician. The clinician brings his specific individual style, a set of questions which need to be answered directly or indirectly, and a nondirective mode of listening. The child brings his specific personality structure and style of relating to others. Through a nondirective orientation the child and clinician set the pace of the work together. Due to our research and the fact that this is for diagnostic purposes only and we do not necessarily want to enter into treatment, we attempt to obtain specific information in a limited time. In order for this to be accomplished, we have developed a set of questions which are introduced by the clinician.

This approach to the diagnostic phase has benefits for the child as well as serving to obtain the needed data, but it demands a great deal from the clinician. It requires him to adjust his style and to accommodate himself to the pace and style of the child. The clinician's task is to empathize introspectively with the child to determine the degree of structure and direction that must be provided. The degree of intervention is determined by the quantity and quality of the structure needed to facilitate the child in sharing his worries and concerns. Ideally, intervention is kept to a minimum.

Each child will vary in the degree of structure that is needed. In fact, the type and quantity of structure will vary within the same child as he continues to adapt to the death. There are many children who can benefit from an active, directed, and structured approach. These tend to be the children with the greatest degree of ego strain. The more immobilized and overwhelmed the child is, the more structure he needs. Without this structure the experience of the diagnostic consultation only adds to the already existing trauma. The purpose of the structured consultation is to lend strength to the child's ego so he is able to communicate his psychological experience of the parental death.

During the diagnostic consultation, which generally lasts for three forty-five-minute interviews, the therapist is continually monitoring through listening, thinking, and observing the meaning of the child's communications. The material from the child is obtained from a variety of sources which are common to child therapy, such as play, dreams, drawings, and the interaction with the clinician.

The type of play used by children is, of course, based on their developmental age. The youngest children's play is simple and repetitive (i.e., the two-year-olds). With this age we are looking for regression in their ability to play, fixations in play, or specific repetitive actions or sounds. Some examples are: B., age two, who was seen following the murder of his father by his mother. (This case is discussed in greater detail at a later point.) His play consisted of pushing two toy cars around the room, crashing them together. Another child, a precocious four-year-old, enacted a dinner scene during which the parent was murdered, using a chair and a paper tissue for props. P., age four, played with blocks, constructing a fence to cage a stray dog the family had taken in, as this family had also taken him in following his mother's death. S., age seven, during his second interview brought in his He-man figures with which he constructed battles between his figures who struggled for power and victory to demonstrate both his wish for power and the battles he was encountering. Children will use whatever toys or material are available to tell their stories, but for the purposes of research we have tended to standardize the toys so all clinicians have similar ones available.

The use of drawing is also extremely valuable in assisting us in understanding the children we see. Generally, we ask the child to draw a self-portrait, a family portrait, a house–tree–person, and a drawing of whatever they choose. The material we gather is rich in meaning. For example, M., age nine was seen following the murder of her mother. Her self-portrait was a pair of eyes, a nose, and a mouth on an otherwise blank piece of paper. M. was demonstrating her lack of structure, her feelings of nothingness, her loss of identity, and her sense of fragmentation. Another child, age nine, drew a picture of a rainbow over a dark patch on the ground. In the sky flew a bird separated from a larger group of birds. In this drawing the child illustrated not only her concern over the grave and the separated, deceased parent, but also her defensive stance of pretty colors covering her sad depressed feelings. This is a child whose mother felt she was happy and unaffected by the father's death. Many more examples exist of how the drawings add to our knowledge of the child's primary fears and longings, their defenses and their attempts at mastery and adaptation.

Dreams are less frequently heard and are generally given only when asked for. They, like the drawings reveal the child's longings, wishes, and fears. The children that spontaneously share their dreams are those that appear to be in a traumatized state. It is when the child's defenses are erected that dream material becomes less available. An example of a dream during the diagnostic is from M., who was mentioned earlier. Her dream was of a large monster breaking into her house and killing everyone. This was an attempt to work through the overwhelming memory of her mother's murder.

The final tool from which we obtain our material is the interaction between the child and clinician, including the clinician's countertransference to the child. The interaction between the child and clinician demonstrates to us the child's object differentiation, the degree of object permanence, his capacity for object attachment, and the quality of his attachments.

Many times the children who are seen are hungry for an attachment and attach extremely quickly to the clinician. Other children appear more cautious, attaching slowly and in a limited manner. There are still other children who are phobic and unable to even enter the consultation room, let alone form a relationship with the clinician. One contributing factor to this extreme reaction is that being involved with the clinician evokes the child's longings for attachment and consequent rage at the wished for but unavailable object.

While we are examining the child's reaction to the clinician we must also examine the response of the clinician to the child. The degree to which the clinician can be available to the diagnostic process will significantly influence the child's ability to engage with the clinician. The intensity of the children's longings for a relationship, or their rage and the tragedy they express often make it difficult for the clinician to immerse themselves in this process. It is often the result of the clinician's own unresolved mourning that makes it difficult to be fully involved with the diagnostic work. When this occurs, the child will also avoid intimacy. Another potential interference in the diagnostic process is the clinician's inability to discuss death, and their discomfort with their own rage, sadness, and dependency. It is difficult at times to ask the necessary questions when they involve suicide, murder, or sudden illness and death. This may be based on our wish to protect children from pain, but it seems that it is especially true when we also wish to protect ourselves from the pain.

As we approach the child with questions, we must constantly remind ourselves of the pain, disorganization, and vulnerability these children may be feeling. When we keep this in mind, we remain much more sensitive to the child's struggle. If the clinician remains empathically tuned to the child, the evaluation will not be harmful. It is when the clinician loses touch with the child that the evaluation can be disruptive.

At the initial interview, the clinician is observing the child's reaction from the moment they meet. It is helpful to be cognizant of the interaction between the parent and child and how they negotiate the situation. As the child enters the consultation room the stage is being set for the unfolding of his story. Already, we are able to learn about the child's mood. Is he or she coy, curious, passive, compliant, or hostile and aggressive?

After the child has entered the room and a sufficient period of time has elapsed for him to spontaneously begin, and a rapport is established, the clinician can slowly begin to discuss the purpose of the interview. This will include asking what the child knows about the appointment and what they feel may happen. It is at this point that the clinician can clarify any confusion and explain the frequency and length of the appointment. We have also found it useful to explain our interest in understanding the child's worries and concerns and their reactions and feelings about any specific problem the child may be experiencing. If the child does not mention the parental death, it is brought up at this point by the clinician. First, it is essential to determine whether the child is aware that the parent has died. This may appear to be an obvious question, but there are instances where the surviving family has either not told the child about the death, or the death has been described in such a way that the child does not know if the parent is actually dead or away on a trip. This occurs a great deal when the child is under four years of age. The purpose of explaining the death in such a fashion is not malicious, rather it is the family's attempt to protect themselves and the child from the pain of the death.

These explanations are not only confusing because of the incorrectness of the information, but also due to the children's limited cognitive development. This is particularly true in children under eleven who have limited abstract abilities. The vagueness of the explanations are additionally problematic since they support the child's defenses of disavowal, denial, and avoidance. Even when given all of the correct information the child may continue to struggle with the reality of death.

A boy, age five, had explained to him in appropriate detail the circumstances of his father's death, and attended the funeral. His ability to verbalize his knowledge of the illness, the death, and the funeral gave the impression that he had a clear understanding of the meaning of his father's death. This impression was further supported by his affective response of rage and sadness. It was only later that one could hear him say to the clinician and to others that his "dad was hibernating just like the bears." This appeared due to both his defensive fantasy and his cognitive limitations. It is essential to understand what the child has been told by the family in order for us to understand how the child is processing these ideas, but it is not sufficient for a comprehensive understanding of the child's reaction to the loss.

At this point, questions focus directly on the circumstances surrounding the death and how the child is adapting to the loss. The process by which a positive adaptation occurs is referred to as the mourning process. Mourning, as it has been defined by various writers (Freud, 1917a; Fleming and Altschul, 1963; A. Freud, 1967; E. Furman, 1974; Bowlby, 1980; Nagera, 1981; Palombo, 1981) has as its goal the gradual decathexis of the internal representation of the deceased parent so that the child would later be available to invest in new relationships. Pollock (1961) has identified three stages in bereavement which overlap. They are (1) shock; (2) grief reaction where despair and sorrow are experienced; and (3) separation reaction which involves a reorientation of self and object.

It is a difficult task for the clinician to obtain from the child the specific information which can assist us in determining the degree to which the child has mourned or entered the mourning process. Questions begin with the very basic yet difficult question of the child's understanding of the meaning of death and what the child feels or knows about what happens to someone when they die. As we explore further the child's understanding of the death we will focus on whether the child has been told and understands the cause of the death, and if anyone is felt to be responsible for the death. Was the child present when the parent died and if so, what was observed or heard? For example, M., age nine, and D., age six, were in their rooms preparing for bed when their father returned home and began to beat their mother. Both children could hear mother's cries for him to stop and her gasping for air as she died. These memories of the sounds were still being experienced by the children when they remembered their mother.

We will also ask the child what he believes happens when a parent dies. Some children give a biological explanation for death, but most talk of the parent going to heaven. The child's fantasies regarding heaven help us to understand his acceptance of death and his wish to keep the parent alive. As we are asking these questions we are also listening to the child's affect as he discusses the death and his association to the death; that is, distractions, disaster, frustration, anger, guilt, and sadness.

The next step in the diagnostic process with the child is to explore family relationships. This includes memories of the deceased parent. The children are asked to describe and to share their memories of each parent. They are also asked to describe their relationships, what they remember, and the positive and negative qualities of both parents and what they miss most about the deceased parent. Similar questions are asked about the siblings, with a special focus on how they support each other.

During the second interview the focus shifts to discussing the children themselves. They are asked to describe themselves now, as well as before the death, and how they have changed. The children are asked about their play, their night and daydreams. We also ask the children about their expression of affects such as anger, sadness, and happiness, and what contributes to those feelings. It is during this phase of the interview that we will ask the child to draw and to discuss with us their relationship with peers, teachers, and other significant adults.

At the end of the second diagnostic interview we explore the child's thoughts about his future, which include his hopes and fears about an occupation and marriage. This important information can be useful for our understanding areas of identification with the deceased parent and an important indicator of the child's prognosis for mourning. Our final question relates to any changes that the child would like in his life and any other thoughts or feelings he would like to share. The end of each session is generally summarized for the child, and plans for future evaluations are briefly discussed.

After we have completed the interviews with the child, an appointment is scheduled to meet with the surviving parent to share our impressions and recommendations. When the family is being seen during a crisis, ongoing interventions are often conducted with the parent.

The specific information from the diagnostic interview with the child that is essential for us to obtain in order to determine the course of the child's beginning adaptation evolves from the following areas: (1) the child's capacity to manage his anxieties alone or with somebody; (2) the child's degree of object differentiation and capacity for object constancy; (3) the child's cognitive understanding of such concepts as the permanence of death, the irreversibility of death, and the time framework—past, present, future. It is with this information, along with the data from the parent interviews that the clinician is able to form his beginning understanding of the child's overall ego capacities.

It is our experience that the child who has developed the strongest ego is the child who is the least likely to experience a disrupted mourning process. The task of determining the child who is at greatest risk is difficult as we anticipate that all children and adults who are under extreme stress will be momentarily stunned and traumatized. In the immediate crises, the child's ego is flooded and overwhelmed, more so when the loss is sudden and violent (Pollock, 1961; DeLeon-Jones, 1979). The symptoms of the trauma, however, are not necessarily indicators of potential pathology or the necessity to intervene (see chapter 1).

In order to determine whether the loss is being adapted to pathologically, one needs to follow the child over time. As we know with adults, the process of mourning can go on for years. Unfortunately, we do not have unlimited time to wait for the process to unfold during the diagnostic period. Instead, in order to determine the child's status we need to examine his developmental progression at that point to determine the degree of traumatization. If, in any area of the child's life, his forward developmental movement is derailed, we then assume that the child is adapting negatively to the death. With a negative adaptation, the child can appear to have adjusted to the death through his external behavior, while his internal adaptation has not proceeded in a forward direction. It is in these cases, as seen in adults, that we see the developmental arrest as described by earlier writers (Fleming and Altschul, 1963; Altschul, 1968). This configuration brings us to an important area of diagnostic differentiation; that is, between the child who is at risk and adapting negatively and the child who is temporarily traumatized. Both the at-risk and the nonrisk child may be traumatized, and both may demonstrate similar behavior, in that both may be frozen and overwhelmed, with the normal ego functions disrupted. It is at this point that the material obtained from the parents can be beneficial. Prior to the death, the child whose development was already disrupted will be at the greatest risk. It is difficult enough for a child to adapt to the death of a parent, but when the psychological tools they possess do not function well or when they are not able to use what they have available to them, the task becomes even more difficult, if not impossible.

The child who is not at risk prior to the death may be less vulnerable to the effects of the death. The response to the trauma will fluctuate and only momentarily will the child be in a traumatized state. They will be capable of instituting defenses and engaging others to buffer and filter the stress.

This becomes an important area for diagnostic distinction significant for children whose parents have died. It is beneficial to determine the child's capacity to tolerate stress, the degree of traumatization, and his capacity to bounce back from the moments of trauma. (Trauma is being defined here in the narrow sense [Furst, 1967] as a state of being overwhelmed; for example, when the child's ego is immobilized by a flood of affects.) By determining the child's developmental history and current functioning, as seen in the direct interviews, we will have a clearer idea as to his capacity to tolerate the flood of affects associated with the mourning process.

The clinical vignettes which follow demonstrate our task of differentiating diagnostically between the child's capacity or incapacity to tolerate the death of a parent, and to focus on examining the child's developmental level of progression, his or her propensity to vulnerability, and the ways in which this information can be used for early interventions.

EXAMPLES OF CHILDREN AT RISK

Case Example 1

B., age two, was referred for assessment following the violent murder of his father by his mother. The initial concern of the court was whether this child would be affected by the death of the parent and whether the child should be placed in foster care during his mother's incarceration.

B. was his mother's only child. She was not married to B.'s father. His father had minimal contact with the family during the first year-and-a-half of B.'s life, but at that point, he moved into an apartment with B. and B.'s mother. Initially, it was felt to be a good decision, beneficial for all of them financially and emotionally. However, the family situation deteriorated quickly. Although Mr. R. worked, he provided little for the family, spending his money on drinking and gambling. Mrs. B. continued for some time to provide him with money for his activities, but gradually she became resentful and began to complain. The couple would fight and often he would beat her. Mr. R.'s contact with his son seemed distant and inconsistent. He was often neglectful of B. in a manner which was physically dangerous to the little boy. Mr. R. would frequently leave B. wandering around the apartment when Mr. R. had passed out in a drunken stupor. Other times, he would fall asleep while the infant, at that time a year-and-a-half, would lock himself out of the apartment.

Mrs. B., a large, talkative woman, professed much love for her son. However, she appeared to be a dependent woman who also placed B. in a dangerous position by leaving him with his father, whom she knew was incapable of caring for him. Her ability to care for B. was limited, as evidenced in her poor decision-making ability and poor ability to regulate her own impulses. B. had grown up in a violent home with parents who demonstrated poor capacities for self-regulation and need gratification.

Through this brief history, we can begin to see a child who is at high risk for psychopathology. B. is a child who has been neglected and not protected from potential harm, a child who has been with parents who have difficulties meeting their own needs and regulating their behavior.

During the interview, B. was totally nonverbal, even though his mother claimed that he had a vocabulary of approximately twenty words. He demonstrated no separation anxiety, and in fact, initially gave no evidence of being aware of his mother leaving. This was not the first time that we had met. B. had been present for parts of two earlier sessions with his mother. B. immediately went to the drawer in the office where the toys were kept and took out two vehicles he had played with previously, one a tow truck and the other a van. He proceeded as before to crash them together head on, this time in total silence. Over and over the cars crashed while he made no effort to include the clinician in the play. After a short time the clinician began to talk with him about our visit, saying that he knew B.'s father had died and that just before that, he had seen his mom and dad have a big fight. At that point, he closed his eyes and then crashed the cars. Then he again covered his eyes and held his head. The clinician said that seeing all that must have been upsetting for him. He then repeated closing his eyes and holding his head with an intensely worried expression on his face. B. then proceeded to lie motionless on the floor against the wall. After a short while he got up, rolled the cars across the room, and lay curled in a corner of the room alone.

B. demonstrates a traumatized child who is at great risk developmentally. He was overwhelmed by the event he witnessed and wished to not see it, although it was always with him. His ability to engage and use others was limited, so his adaptation to the loss was more problematic. He appeared depressed, empty, and alone in his overwhelmed state. His propensity to retreat in the face of aggression is evidence of an already existing difficulty in his ability to manage and express his aggression. Of course the death of father was not the only factor contributing to B.'s difficulties; his young age, the witnessing of the violent death of his father by his mother, and the loss of both of his parents through his father's death and his mother's incarceration added to an already preexisting neglected family life. His parents' inability to regulate and meet their own needs as parents further contributed to B.'s difficult if not impossible task of mourning his father's death. At this point, mourning is not the primary concern. A more basic issue will be to facilitate the family's management of the traumatized state.

Case Example 2

The second vignette is of a four-year-old boy who demonstrated a greater capacity to engage with the therapist, yet remained a very vulnerable child. C. presented a distorted speech pattern with facial and digital tics which were of an autoerotic nature. The initial concern with C. was that he was a very disorganized child with poor ego functions. He demonstrated a poor differentiation of self and appeared to be an extremely traumatized child who was evidencing a severe regression with a mild thought disturbance. C.'s father had died two months previously from a chronic illness that had spanned approximately a period of eighteen months. During this time the family had moved twice, and mother had returned to professional school. His mother, a very concerned woman, had found the task of mourning her loss extremely difficult. She had directed her attention to school and avoided discussion of her husband's death.

Although C. was extremely verbal during initial contacts, he perseverated frequently and his thoughts were disjointed and inappropriate. Gradually, C. became more involved with the clincian including him actively in his play. For example, in the third diagnostic session, C. played that a fire was raging in the closet. He held a rope in his hands, which was to be the fire hose, and then connected it to the clinician, as he was to be a fire hydrant. As they played, he spoke of his father dying and repeated the factual realities of his father's death, countering these thoughts with magical wishes of his father returning to life again. Through this play C. was demonstrating his need to have an object available to assist him in regulating the feelings that were raging inside of him.

C.'s capacity to understand the meaning of death was limited and under the influence of magical thought. His mother's lack of psychological availability had left him on his own to manage his feelings of confusion and anger regarding his father's death. The flooding of affect and feelings of confusion influence his tenuous ego and led to his disorganized thoughts, his withdrawing, his tics, and perseveration. C. demonstrated a child with developing though precarious ego skills which had not yet consolidated in an ability to self-regulate. He was very much in need of his mother to be available to assist him in mourning. This had been extremely difficult for his mother due to her own disrupted mourning process. C. was a child who, with help, could make an adequate adaptation. Without interventions he would continue to move in the direction of a negative adaptation.

Case Example 3

A third child, a four-year-old girl, revealed herself as in possession of strong ego development, a high intellectual ability, and a precocious understanding of her mother's death. The death of the mother, who was murdered by robbers while shopping, came as a sudden shock. Her father, who was also with the mother at the time of the murder, was injured and recovered quickly. D. was seen initially as a bright, verbal, precocious child. She was dishevelled and appeared to be a child who missed her "mother's touch." During her first session, she reenacted the trauma of her mother's death as she understood it. She repeated numerous times her thoughts and image of how her mother died. As we began to talk of her mother, D. would curl up in a big chair, suck her thumb, and rub her hair. No tears appeared; instead, there was an empty, depleted expression.

After a brief period with comments about how much she missed her mother, D. would engage again with the clinician in play which was reparative to her momentary feelings of being flooded and regressed. D. appeared to be a child who was able to engage with people in an active process of talking about the death and was capable of experiencing the affects of grief momentarily, returning to her normal developmental tasks with little interference to her current level of ego development. She was able to maintain a fairly cohesive sense of her self and was not severely disorganized over a prolonged period of time in the face of her mother's death.

These three children, all close in age, experienced a tragic death of a parent. Each child responded to the death as a trauma and in each we found a very different ability to adjust. The capacity of each child varied based on their early life experiences and the significance of the early bonding to the primary psychological parent. B. was the less structured, more fragile child, who experienced a less significant relationship with the deceased and the surviving parent. B.'s mother had not been able to engage in a mourning process and was actively involved in warding off what she experienced as her "going crazy." B.'s tendency to withdraw and to self-destructive behavior indicated an inability to soothe himself or to rely on his mother to soothe him, leaving him in a very risky position for future pathology.

C., who appeared extremely disorganized and evidenced a language and thought disturbance, was able in a short period of time to become involved with the clinician and to use this experience to assist him in psychologically organizing. This points to a greater capacity to use people in his life and is evidence of greater structural capacity. Although his mother is now unavailable, due to her difficulties in mourning, the potential for growth is much stronger than the first child. D., because of her strong constitutional endowment and what appeared to be a strong, solid attachment to a primary mother, was quite able to experience the loss, to regress, and then to recoup.

One point which differentiates these children in their ability to manage the trauma of loss is the degree of resiliency that each child possessed when faced with a traumatic event. The fact that D. was able to experience the loss of her mother, yet continued to progress, put her in a stronger position to mourn her mother's death. The other two children, because of their limited ego resources and less adequate holding environment, appeared to be at greater risk, and needed significant interventions for themselves and all of their family members if they were to manage and mourn the death of their parent.

By examining the children's early history, observing their ability to engage with objects in their lives, and the resiliency to regressions in the face of the trauma, we become more capable of appropriately focusing our interventions. This brings us then to a further questions of how the diagnostic phase can be seen as a form of intervention. What occurs in the diagnostic period that appears most therapeutic can be seen in three ways. First, as a cathartic experience of being able to talk and to reexperience the events of the death. This follows the theories that have been pointed out in the crisis intervention theory. It is explained that this offers an opportunity to review, reexperience, and then begin to master the events. This idea has also been recently discussed in an article written by Lenore Terr (1983), in her work with the traumatized children of Chowchilla. Each of the children described previously did just this during the diagnostic phase. D. pretended that she was at a store and fell on the floor over and over again, reexperiencing how she had heard her mother had died, attempting in her manner to understand and gain control of this event. B. crashed cars together in a violent manner, repeating this action continuously through the session, then lying on the floor immobilized. The crash of the cars was understood to represent the repeated fighting of his parents.

Second, the diagnostic phase offers an opportunity for education. This can provide the child and the parent with important information that can facilitate the parent's ability to parent the child and increase the child's understanding of what has occurred. For example, with the case of A., who was mentioned earlier, by encouraging mother to speak to A. about his father's death and explaining the actual cause of the father's death in an honest, direct manner, mother allowed herself to become more physically and psychologically available and reaffirmed the child's knowledge of what had happened.

A third function of the diagnostic phase is to offer a structure for the family to begin to experience their mourning. Through establishing contact with the clinician and beginning to discuss the loss, the family's early history, and the family's structure, the family is reviewing the past, reexperiencing the joys, the sadness, and a full range of appreciations of what they had, what they can have, and the direction in which they are moving. The family also experiences the regrets and disappointment for what never was and now can never be. What occurs is the beginning formation of what can be viewed as an early phase of mourning. In this framework, a family can use the sessions to regulate the erecting or razing of their defenses.

Our diagnostic work is complicated in many ways. One complication is the reaction of the clinician to engaging with the family. In order for a family to engage in a diagnostic process, the therapist must be able to create an environment conducive to the unfolding of the family's history. Such an environment will consist of trust, knowledge, and a feeling that the clinician is capable of tolerating their extreme pain, anger, and loneliness. In order for this to be experienced, the clinician must be comfortable with his own range of feelings and be willing to immerse himself in the grieving process of the patients. The continual immersion in these feelings can be extremely taxing on the clinician's ego. The outcome of such a situation, though, can be extremely positive.

Difficulties arise, however, as the clinician is exposed to his own unresolved struggles with separation and loss, leaving him vulnerable to his own worries and fears of these losses and separations. The cicatrix of previous losses often cause the clinician to be vulnerable to the pains they still hold. It is just this pain that we hope to avoid. We are constantly in search of a pleasurable, homeostatic position and attempt to avoid unpleasurable situations.

In discussing the roles of parenting, Thérèse Benedek (1959) pointed out how those points in the parent's development which were conflicted and have not yet been resolved, will reemerge when their children reach similar phases of development and ask parents to do with them what the parent has never had done for himself. This often ends in a repetition of previous disruptions. The same holds true for the therapist. When faced with bereaved families with their intense grief, we are again faced with our own pain in the areas which may not have been substantially resolved, making it extremely difficult for the therapist to be emotionally available to the patient.

SUMMARY

The task of assessing a child's adaptation to the death of a parent is complex. The child's ability to mourn is dependent on his developmental level, his previous life experiences, the type and form of death, and the degree of availability of the surviving parent. The child, if he is to mourn, will need a secure and consistent environment.

During the diagnostic phase one examines the areas of strength to build upon and deficits that are in need of reparation. Through the diagnostic phase, the process of mourning can be facilitated and supported so it can buttress the child's forward development.

We need also to be alert to the ways in which the diagnostic process can impede the mourning process. As in the case of any behavior, the diagnostic phase can be used for defensive purposes, supporting resistance. This can be seen if the child uses the therapist or the diagnostic phase as a substitute for the lost parent. In this case, through the attachment and involvement in the diagnostic process, the child attempts to fill the loss and thus avoid the experience of the death. If this occurs, the child may appear to be adapting appropriately, but actually is defending against the loss, so psychologically it is never experienced. One way we have found to manage this is to structure the interviewing process early on, especially in regard to the frequency of the interviews.

It is important that our diagnostic work not interfere with

the child's and the family's normal mourning process. Freud (1917a) pointed out that we would never think of interfering or diagnosing grief or the normal grieving process as pathological, and the same is true today. It is not reason enough to recommend treatment just because a child experiences symptoms following the death of a parent. Our efforts are directed toward understanding the meaning of the loss to the child and discovering his capacity to perform his own psychological work with the assistance of his parent. The therapist's transference and countertransference can be used as a means of observation to gain an understanding and to modulate the therapist's own interventions. How we intervene should be for the benefit of the family and provide an appropriate catalyst for the child and the family to continue on in their mourning process.

Chapter 6

Therapeutic Work with Bereaved Parents

Nan Knight-Birnbaum, M.S.S.A.

Work with bereaved families at the Barr-Harris Center for the Study of Separation and Loss in Childhood has shown that the care provided by the surviving parent forms the foundation for the child's subsequent adaptation to the loss. Consequently, clinical assistance to the parent is the initial intervention offered.

There are several additional reasons for assisting parents at the first intervention. First, the average good parent is not ordinarily faced with the task of helping a child mourn the loss of the other parent, but if provided with support and a schema for understanding the child's developmental capacities for mourning, the surviving parent is in a unique position to help because of their empathic closeness to the child. Second, the normal process of recovery for the surviving parent extends over several years. This is well beyond the acute phase of grief usually described for adults (Parks and Weiss, 1983). The parent's bereavement and the family's recovery process can therefore potentially affect the child over the course of several developmental periods. Early assistance to the parent can support the parent–child relationship and the parent's role in facilitating the child's adaptations to the loss. It has the potential for preventing a developmental interference stemming from changed family circumstances which complicate the nature of the loss.

Third, work with the parent assists all the children in the family, when individual help for several children would be or might be inappropriate and impractical. We are conservative in our approach, working with the parent first and recommending more inclusive treatment for the child, such as psychoanalytic psychotherapy, only when it is clear that the loss has contributed to a fixed interference in development.

Our emphasis on work with parents is supported by the literature on the importance of adaptive handling by the parent (Ottenstein, Wiley, and Rosenblum, 1962; Kliman, G., Feinberg, Buchsbaum, Kliman, A., Lubin, Ronald, and Stein, 1969; E. Furman, 1974, 1984; Pruett, 1979; Garber, 1981; Palombo, 1981; Raphael, 1983; E. Benedek, 1985). Providing permission to mourn and giving assistance in doing so are aspects of the parent's task emphasized by Pollock (1978b) and Garber (1981). They postulate a developmental line for the capacities for mourning. Garber comments:

> If the child is to undergo a developmental progression, then he also needs to experience a milieu which will permit, support and enhance such a change. Although the child may possess the necessary skills for some type of mourning activity, it is equally important that the surviving parent be able to mourn as well as be able to empathize with the child. If the parent himself is unable to mourn and is also unable to facilitate the child's task, then the child's mourning activity may move in one of the following directions: the whole experience may be repressed or denied; the child may mourn silently, or he may continue

the unfinished mourning work during some later developmental phase [p. 17].

The Furman group recommends work with the parent early in the bereavement because of the complications and limitations of direct assistance to bereaved children.

> The extent to which a bereaved patient can be helped and the preferred form of treatment depend on the psychology of his personality before the loss and on the nature of his life circumstances at the time of and after his bereavement. This may interfere with the patient's ability to cope with the death and to continue his development, and this may also augment earlier pathology. Among these circumstances are the forms of death, the availability of realistic information, the consistency of physical-need fulfillment and emotional support for mourning, coincident stresses, and opportunity to form a relationship with a new parent figure at the appropriate time. The previous pathology and the effects of attendant and subsequent circumstances both determine the nature of the patient's difficulties and their accessability to therapeutic intervention. . . . In this connection it is pertinent to mention another of our findings, that is, that assistance is most effective when it occurs at the time of bereavement or shortly thereafter. One does not think here of individual therapy as an initial form of help but of assistance to the surviving parent in the form of counseling. Through such work the attendant and subsequent circumstances of the death may be ameliorated so that the child has an optimum chance of utilizing his capacities for mourning. This does not prevent all difficulties but forestalls some [E. Furman, 1974; pp. 294–295].

THE DIAGNOSTIC CONSULTATION

In the diagnostic evaluation we are oriented to the issue of loss. We try to understand the specific anxieties and concerns that motivate the parent to seek service at this time. A minority of families are seen within the first few weeks of the loss, with the greater portion coming within six to eighteen months after the death.

Generally, parents who contact the Center within two months of the loss are traumatized, anxious, and dealing with the immediate, overwhelming circumstances of the death. They act out of a strong sense of parental responsibility and protectiveness. They seek advice about the child's inclusion in funeral rites and rituals. They are concerned about responding in the best possible way to the child's early reactions. Families that come after the first six months have similar concerns and are dealing with later consequences and reactions to the loss. They come for a variety of reasons. One or all the children may be symptomatic; there may be management problems. In some families, the child is not symptomatic but the parent wants to take preventive steps to protect the child's adaptation, to mitigate the impact of the loss on development. Some reasons may be related to difficulties the parent is experiencing in the mourning process. The format of the consultation includes an individual interview with the parent and with each child in the family. The focus of this discussion will be primarily on the diagnostic process with the parent, as the work with the child has been discussed elsewhere (see chapter 5). Our goal in the completion interview is to describe each child's current dynamics and how these relate to attempts to deal with the loss. We convey our understanding of whether the child is stuck in the process of adaptation or is struggling with the issues, and what those issues may be. We indicate the ways in which the parent can help in their care and management of the child at home. We anticipate the child's psychological tasks in the mourning process. We highlight the strengths and capacities evident in the child and in the parent's care.

The recommendations need to be thoughtful and empathically geared to the parent's needs and capacities. Suggestions need to be offered with acknowledgment of the parent's previous attempts to help their child. The discussion is an opportunity for the parent to question, digest, and do further psychological work on the issues that have been addressed. One hopes that the recommendations and feedback will not be surprising to the parent after a productive diagnostic interaction.

The Center adopts a conservative approach in recommending only the degree of intervention necessary to assist the parent and child to mobilize their self-righting capacities by supporting the normal bereavement process. Many families demonstrate remarkable sensitivity and capacity for dealing with the loss. Told that their children were coping successfully, reassured and supported by the orientation of the evaluation, these parents did not need or desire more intensive contact at that time. The recommended format was for reevaluation after a specified period of time, usually six months to one year later. We attempt to match the frequency and intensity of continuing consultation with the needs of parents.

The recommendation for another large group of families was for ego supportive parent guidance. These parents were interested in child management assistance with goals of helping to stabilize the family situation. This was the most common type of therapeutic intervention for those families who sought further assistance. For the child showing severe difficulties it was often difficult to determine which factors are contributing to his disturbance and its permanence. The child might be reacting to the parent's bereavement and depression, which temporarily decreased the amount of support the parent could offer. The child's difficulty could be related to a preexisting parent–child conflict, or to the intensification of a prior developmental difficulty. In these situations or where it is too early to determine if the bereavement was problematic, it was also useful to offer parent guidance. This allowed time for the family situation to calm, and for the child's self-righting capacities to be mobilized. We then reevaluated the child after an interval of several months.

For a proportion of families, the consultation or a later reevaluation indicated significant and unchanging interference in the child's development. Some parents returned for individual psychotherapy for the child based on the alliance formed in the original diagnostic consultation.

A much smaller group of parents sought the service of the Center as an opportunity to enter their own psychoanalytic psychotherapy with a focus on their own bereavement. They were aware that problematic issues were being reactivated by the loss, or found themselves immobilized at some stage of the mourning process. Particularly traumatic circumstances of the death led some parents to seek therapeutic services for themselves.

The therapeutic value of the consultation lies in the opportunity for the surviving parent to experience, express, and begin to integrate the meaning of the loss. The parent begins to understand the meaning of the child's behavior. Reactions may have been experienced up to this point as fragmented, overwhelming, and disconnected from the loss. The family begins to find cognitive and emotional meaning in the distress. The parent may also have had an opportunity to reorganize their efforts on behalf of the children. Engagement in this effort supports self-esteem, contributes to mastery, and leads to a sense of control in the situation.

We discovered that the consultation format has value for a group of families who most likely would not have sought psychotherapeutic services for their children under any other circumstances. Psychological services were not an accepted part of their cultural milieu or congruent with personal values. These parents expected to handle the bereavement in private and to help their children independently. They accepted help only because the job had become more than they could manage. Under these circumstances they were able to use a time-limited, initial service which had preventive goals.

One unique characteristic of the diagnostic process in parent loss is that the family is coming for a preventive service because of an overwhelming life experience, rather than because of psychopathology within the child or a disrupted parent–child relationship. The preloss situation of the family contributes enormously to the meaning of the loss, to the course of mourning, and to potential adaptations. Ordinarily, however, our clinical orientation is to see a normative bereavement process in which regressions, especially among younger children, are triggered by the trauma of the loss.

There are also unique characteristics in dealing with parents in the throes of grief. The sense of injury and loss of self-esteem which accompany grief, intensify the parent's narcissistic vulnerability. The child's pain magnifies their own. They may be aware that the mourning has led to a regression in their usual ability to care for the child, as they find themselves impatient, irritable, and exhausted. Explicitly or implicitly, they ask for bolstering in the relationship with the child. Additionally, the parent is often preoccupied with painful memories of the death. Decision making is difficult. Extreme anxiety about injury to themselves or to the child is common. Brief normal separations from the child can provoke intense anxiety. The parent may temporarily be more dependent or highly defended against their dependency. Under these crisislike circumstances, the therapeutic alliance tends to form rapidly and intensely. Collaboration early in the bereavement concerning the child's funeral attendance, and initial reactions to the death also contributes to the rapid alliance. The alliance is also shaped by our willingness to be available rapidly, to consult over the telephone, and to arrange session times immediately.

Another unique aspect of the consultation with the bereaved parent is that the trauma of losing a spouse will often reactivate unresolved conflicts and developmental anxieties. Defensive efforts to deal with the stress are also prominent. It is useful to understand characterological issues in the context of the parent's regression during the bereavement. In this way, the mourning issues are not overlooked and the diagnostic process does not become a quasi-therapeutic exploration of these issues for which there is as yet no shared understanding or contract. Instead, these communications about characterological issues can be understood in terms of how the parent's mourning may affect the child, and eventually, whether the parent can support the child's mourning.

PARENT GUIDANCE

Ego-supportive parent guidance is a didactic, teaching model that includes advice giving, reassurance, and managerial suggestions. It is an educational approach which explains the complexity of childhood reactions to loss and then assists the parent to examine the child's attitudes and behavior against the schema. Weekly or bimonthly sessions have the goal of supporting the parent in efforts to stabilize family life and facilitate the child's adaptation to the loss. We understood that the parent's bereavement made both tasks more difficult. Parent guidance is offered to most families initially as the next phase of therapeutic intervention beyond the phase of the diagnostic consultation. It is indicated for those parents who can integrate educational and management information, rather than for those whose failure to adapt stems from personality deficits.

We find parent guidance to be useful in situations where the diagnostic assessment indicates that the parent–child relationship has been progressing well and parental functioning has also been adequate prior to the loss. In such cases, disruptions in parent's capacity to care for the children, if they existed, seemed related to the normal vicissitudes of their own grief. These basically well-functioning families might be highly traumatized, with family members showing severe symptomatology. However, the clamor and intensity of the suffering was not an indication of failure to adapt and the family could often respond rapidly to guidance which dealt with the trauma. Parent guidance is often recommended before treatment for the child when interferences in bereavement are evident but do not seem static or fully internalized. The supportive approach with the parent on behalf of the child seems a useful way of helping during family reorganization by giving the child time and support for self-righting efforts.

Parent guidance is also recommended when the priority is to assist the parent to stabilize family life. Life may have been organized around a parent's serious and debilitating illness, affecting parent–child interactions and the child's developmental course over many years. Cumulative trauma from many stressful experiences may have affected interactional patterns within the family in both obvious and subtle ways, and such families are exhausted and numb. The first phase of intervention was often recognition of the experience they had lived through. As a result of our providing a holding experience, these parents gradually began to reorganize family life and to feel some of the affects suppressed in the course of living in emergency circumstances. When the death was the result of murder, suicide, or violent accident, guidance aimed at stabilization was offered as the first intervention. When both parents died, and relatives assumed guardianship of the surviving children, we provided support to the bereaved relatives in their efforts to create psychological stability and security. The opportunity to form ties to these relatives as new psychological parents depended upon security and sensitive handling of the loss. Work with guardians took into account the developmental needs of each child, the nature of the prior relationships to the deceased parents, and the specific circumstances of the double loss. We also need to take the mourning of the related care givers into account.

Effective parent guidance depends upon the creation of a relationship which provides a holding environment for the parent. The therapeutic task of the guidance involves acknowledgement of and sympathy with the parent's feelings of loss, and interest in their attempts to care for their children alone. The guidance alliance is often a carryover of the alliance formed during the diagnostic consultation. As clinicians, we are often seen as highly idealized teachers, or at times as a "second parent." The therapist functions as an auxiliary ego. Temporary substitution of the function of the therapist for that of the deceased spouse is not uncommon early in the bereavement when the parent is most burdened by grief. Mourning can take place in the presence of the therapist because the therapist provides crucial psychological functions which were previously supplied by the spouse. When the parent is less overwhelmed and better able to deal with the loss, the various meanings of the relationship to the therapist can be clarified, interpreted, and worked through.

Ego-supportive guidance has as its primary educational function helping the parent to understand the child's developmental capacity for mourning. They are prepared for the reality that the mourning process will take place over a long period of time with many resurgences. The parent learns to recognize signs that an internal process of adaptation is under way when the child seems affectively as well as cognitively engaged with the loss. The parent becomes aware of the child's shorter tolerance for the pain of grieving, and the child's pattern of engaging the mourning feelings and then disengaging for periods of time. Parents can see the disengaged phase as an effort on the part of the child to stave off traumatic flooding of their coping capacities. They are then able to assess the dosage and timing of their comments to the child. The parent's early comments might address the confusion and fear engendered in the child by the loss. Later comments might be more specifically addressed to the child's yearning and longing for the deceased parent. Preparing the parent with an overview of the child's adaptational course can allay inordinate anxiety. It helps them to recognize and support a new step in the child's mourning. Guidance information is more meaningful and better assimilated when it is related to the child's current functioning and areas of strength and to the parent's initial questions and anxieties. The recognition of a process which will unfold over time can also convey to the parent that the child will be able to bring newly acquired cognitive and maturational capacities to the task. Helping confirm the significance of the loss can interrupt certain defensive operations. The seriousness and degree of the loss are conveyed by acknowledging that the loss is not a one time event, but a series of experiences that require different integrative tasks on the part of the child over the course of years.

Guidance work early in the bereavement often assists the surviving parent to provide the children with clear, simple, and age-appropriate information about the circumstances and nature of the parent's death. Particularly difficult, but important, is dealing with traumatic, violent deaths such as murder or suicide. The surviving parent's willingness to answer questions as well as to discuss the child's perception of the events surrounding the death was most helpful in the process of integrating the event. Children need assistance with their reality testing. They may have witnessed the event, been part of the accident, or observed the parent's gradual illness and deterioration. Their perceptions of the death and its meaning will be colored by their age and developmental stage. Their perceptions can be significantly different from the adult's view of the experience. The surviving parent can help by correcting distortions held by the child and also by verifying the child's accurate perceptions. Sharing information works well when it is provided in small doses which the child could integrate slowly with respect for his need to ward off such discussion. The process involves repeated discussions over time as the child raises new questions. The capacity to talk to the child about the circumstances of the death requires that the surviving parent has sufficiently allayed her own anxieties about the death. This is also a gradual process for the parent which follows phases corresponding to their bereavement.

Case Example 1

The importance of providing truthful information to assist a child to begin to integrate a highly traumatic loss is illustrated by the guidance work with a maternal grandmother, Mrs. A. She was raising her seven-year-old granddaughter M. after the girl's father murdered her mother and then committed suicide. The apparent precipitant had been divorce proceedings and the husband's worsening depression. The child may have heard threats over a period of time and had been symptomatic at school. She was visiting relatives when the deaths occurred and was simply told that her parents were dead and that grandmother would raise her. The grandmother sought help both in telling M. what had happened, and because M. was troubled by intense separation anxiety, sleep difficulties, and fears of intruders shooting grandmother and herself. She either clung to grandmother anxiously or had explosive tantrums in which she was physically aggressive. Guidance work addressed grandmother's traumatized feelings, and only gradually was she able to express the grief, pain, and guilt she had suppressed for fear of having to discuss the deaths with her granddaughter. As the work proceeded she was able to tell the child the basic facts of the deaths and respond to subsequent questions and perceptions about events leading up to the tragedy. Guidance continued and the child eventually entered individual psychotherapy.

The case illustrates another aspect of the parent's role in supporting the child. The younger the child, the more help is needed in developing an understanding of the concrete aspects of the death and in mastering anxiety. This understanding requires the parent's assistance to enable the child to differentiate his own fate from that of the deceased parent. If the child is very frightened of dying as the parent had died, then to think about the parent and experience the grief as a first step in the mourning process is impossible. The surviving parent plays a crucial role in helping the child by addressing his fears in order to permit this differentiation.

Similarly, it is helpful when the parent appreciates and can help the child test reality around expectable, related fears that the surviving parent or siblings will die, or that the surviving parent will abandon them. Dealing with intensified separation anxiety is a common issue in the guidance work. We also deal with the child's fears and guilty feelings related to particularly intense and unacceptable affects or impulses experienced around the time of the parent's death. Guidance work with Mr. Berger, for example, initially focused on his discussions with his seven-year-old son, Sam, about the boy's perception that a week-long separation from his mother during her terminal illness had been caused by his misbehavior and underlying anger at mother for her emotional withdrawal. The visit to relatives had in fact been arranged with the motivation of lessening Sam's exposure to mother's pain and to medical procedures which were part of the hospice care at home. The boy returned home for the last several weeks of his mother's life. Sam's perceptions arose out of his effort to understand what was happening to mother, to feel in control of events when he felt quite helpless and frightened. His reaction to the brief separation was one factor contributing to intense guilt after her death. Father's explanations about the illness, the visit, and discussions of Sam's feelings were guided by our understanding that Sam was also interpreting events in terms of the particular cast of his oedipal relationship with both parents. Father dealt with the fact that mother had become depressed as she faced her death and separation from this beloved son. She had always been disturbed by his assertiveness and aggression. Sam's anxiety during this last phase of mother's illness had in fact been expressed in ceaseless motoric activity. Mr. Berger's work with Sam about these issues was the first phase in understanding the boy's excessive guilt feelings and in assessing his need for psychotherapy.

Parents often seek consultation as to whether to include the child, particularly a young one, in funeral rituals. Guidance at this stage takes the form of assisting the parent with such decisions. We offer information about the bereavement process in young children and assess with the parent, the child's anticipated reactions and ways in which the parent can help. The opportunity to share grief by participating in the funeral and other family and religious rituals is generally seen as an important first step in supporting a child's mourning. If the parent or other close relatives can go through the experience with the child, even the youngest children seem able to participate to some degree.

At all stages of development, the child's ability to mourn is greatly facilitated by the surviving parent's acceptance of the child's reactions and including the child in the mourning rituals. The child's participation can be paced by the parent according to the child's capacity to comprehend and manage the particular experience. The concrete experience of participating in the rituals assists in the task of integrating the reality of the event. The child's first-hand experience of the physical reality of the inanimate state of the parent, of knowing about the disposal of the body, all contribute to his beginning understanding of death. At the time of the funeral, when adults in the family are able to express their feelings of sadness and grief they provide permission for the child to express such feelings.

Discussions with the parent anticipate the child's reactions to funeral rituals and signs of anxiety so that the parent can adjust how much the child is involved. The child may appear low-keyed in affect or may be shocked in the presence of the deceased parent's body. The child may be so overwhelmed as to seem nonreactive when, in fact, the experience is being actively denied.

We often address the issue of the stability of the care provided by the surviving parent and other relatives. Such stability and continuity is important for supporting the child's sense of security. When caregivers and routines remain relatively consistent, the child's psychological energies can be used to address the issues of loss and not be burdened with additional tasks of adapting to other changes. The continuity of the ongoing relationship with the surviving parent permits the child to continue to feel some pleasure.

Case Example 2

This predictability of care as a prerequisite for mourning was clear in the situation of the Miller family who were seen at the Center eight months after Mrs. Miller died of cancer, following a two-year illness. Mr. Miller was raising their eight-year-old daughter, and four- and two-year-old sons. He was concerned that Emily, the eight-year-old, was becoming increasingly withdrawn, provoking punishments, and blaming herself for mother's death. Despite being overwhelmed and grieving deeply, Mr. Miller was able to maintain family routines and continuity in the care from the baby-sitter who had known the children for years. Father and the sitter had assumed the major portion of the care for the children during the last year of mother's illness. Mother had chosen the sitter, who came to know the children's preferences and routines. Mrs. Miller had remained emotionally available to the children and the transition had been gradual. While Mr. Miller had been severely depressed in the first six months after his wife's death, one of his means of coping was to throw himself into organizing family life and continuing to care for his children.

The stability of the care and Mr. Miller's active presence and emotional availability to his young children made it possible for them to express their anger, grief, and frustration at the loss of mother to an unusual degree. They did so in words, play, and behavior. It was precisely because of the good care and relative absence of other changes in their daily lives that these children could tolerate the many feelings engendered by their mother's illness and death. Mr. Miller was able to listen empathically to the children's complaints without becoming defensive, angry, or overwhelmed by his own sadness. Such abreaction was a first stage in their adaptation to the loss.

The significance of good substitute care in providing the foundation for mourning has been emphasized by Furman (E. Furman, 1974). She notes that the child's attachment to the surviving parent and to good substitutes remains distinct from what is felt toward the deceased parent. The original attachment is not automatically transferred to a substitute care giver. In the case of the Miller family, the children maintained distinct memories of mother and her care, and did not have to defensively deny the attachment to these memories. The baby-sitter's care provided assurance of adequate need fulfillment and permitted energies to be available for the task of mourning.

Remaining in a familiar environment also provides stability for the family. Relocations may be necessary for economic well-being and the security provided by extended family. However, such change at the time of bereavement can be an added stress because adaptation to the move compounds the psychological tasks. In general, immediate relocations seemed also to be related to the emotional balance within the surviving parent. Their sense of emotional impoverishment and depletion was often tied to the striving for economic improvement; the sense of abandonment led directly to the wish to be closer to extended family. When the home presented painful memories and intolerable reminders of the lost spouse, motivation for relocation was driven and impulsive. Remaining in a familiar environment for a period of time can be very valuable, particularly for the younger child, because it provides reassurance that not everything has changed. Home surroundings are suffused with memories of the parent and of interactions with them in the daily routines of life. Memories are also supported by the presence of the parent's possessions.

We recognize the fact that the children are generally in a regressed state. Parents are often concerned about the child's inordinate greediness, irritability, demandingness, and lack of resilience. Parents tend to feel all the more responsible for the disruptions in family life and for their children's psychological vulnerability following the death. To some extent this sense of responsibility was a part of the parent's attempt to ward off a sense of helplessness in the face of the loss. Not only were parents distressed by seeing their relatively well-functioning children revert to immature and troublesome behavior, but they tended to experience this as the result of a failure on their part and were narcissistically injured. Interpreting such behavior of the child as symptomatic of regression tended to allay the parent's anxiety.

We addressed the general difficulties most parents had in providing soothing and pacification for children during the bereavement. We helped parents appreciate the internal and external sources of overstimulation. The internal overload for the child consists of the meaning he or she attaches to age-appropriate libidinal and aggressive impulses in the light of the parent's death as well as the intensity of affects in relation to the loss. The external overload consists of the family atmosphere of grief and depression. Early in the bereavement, too many visitors and too many changes in the family's routines are sources of external overstimulation.

The surviving parent's capacity to insulate and protect almost universally diminishes during the early stages of their grief. When the parent remains traumatized and mourning is protracted, the disruption extends beyond the early stages. The soothing and tension regulation which a parent normally provides are also disrupted during the bereavement. The surviving parent is coping with a stimulus overload. The loss of spouse and partner in caring for the children upsets the normal means of regulating tension. Early in the bereavement close relatives and friends may have been available to care for the children when the parent was preoccupied or were able to take over other responsibilities so that the parent was free to involve herself with the children. Later, as the routine of daily life resumes, the parent is faced with having more responsibility as the adult in charge of the family.

As we discuss regressions in the children, interpretive comments about the children's distress and inability to calm or regulate themselves, often elicit intense responses in the parents. Parents see their experience mirrored in that of the children in terms of feeling deprived, exhausted, and irritable. They make the link between their own anger at the deprivation and that of the children. Discussions of weekly life lead to expressions of frustration over the situation in which they find themselves and their profound sense of unhappiness. Many express the feeling that life will never be the same again in terms of experiencing peace of mind and contentment in family life. Anger toward the deceased spouse, as opposed to anger at their situation is generally less available. Anger at the spouse is frightening and is usually displaced onto other aspects of the frustrating experience.

As the parent verbalizes the anger and sense of deprivation related to this phase of their own bereavement, they begin to have a framework for understanding the regressions.

While unique to each child in form and content, the regressions are seen as a resonse to trauma. They are also an indication of the child's frustration at being deprived of the ongoing relationship with the lost parent. Some children are unable to maintain psychological accomplishments, particularly those newly gained, in the face of the loss. Some of the regression is also linked to the children's characteristic way of dealing with anxiety. This understanding gradually permits parents to tolerate children's regression and provide support during such episodes.

The therapist's posture is of listening empathically and trying to understand the parent's intense distress. This stance is one which essentially conveys "these feelings and this phase are survivable." We suggest approaches to the care of the children which can buffer them from further stress. We discuss practical ideas about moderating external demands on the parent's time and energies. Often parents have to adjust internal expectations for their own performance. In acknowledging that everyone is under strain and can no longer maintain the same schedule or pace of activities, the parent is acknowledging the loss and coming face to face with the reality of how life has changed. This step in the mourning process is often difficult, particularly for families who have lived in a mobilized emergency state during a parent's protracted illness, or for parents whose mode of coping with the initial grief is exclusively one of active mastery. We address the parent's fear of being overwhelmed by affect if they slow the pace of their activities. Many parents describe feeling empty, detached, or incapable of experiencing any feelings. This dilemma is often a continuation of the traumatized state of suppressed affect during the illness. With the emergence of affect parents can recognize that the family is in a recuperative period. The parent then has greater freedom to set a manageable pace for family life. These issues were apparent in the work with the Conrad family.

Case Example 3

Mrs. Conrad came to the Center two months after her husband's sudden heart attack and death. She was concerned that her ten-year-old son, Darrell, had cried very little after his father's death and seemed unable to talk about father or the incident to any extent. The traumatization of the family had been intense and circumstance contributed to a complicated bereavement. The children had no opportunity to see father before his death which had occurred late at night. When mother told them the next morning, the cause of the death was still unclear, and mother and children seemed frozen in their responses. Mrs. Conrad's sense of disbelief and unreality about her husband's sudden death continued for most of the first year. Mrs. Conrad had a persistent sense that her husband was emotionally present and that his return was imminent. She maintained dialogues with him in her mind, and interpreted odd occurrences in the house as communications of his advice. Her grief seemed delayed; she showed little feeling in front of the children. She occasionally cried when alone at night when her feelings of desperate unhappiness and loneliness overcame her. Darrell and his eight-year-old sister rarely mentioned father.

Mrs. Conrad carried on the family business. Her efforts made her feel less helpless and also contained a degree of denial of her husband's death. While she was emotionally available to the children to some degree, it was also clear that she was preoccupied. Her intense level of activity seemed a means of slowing down the process of integrating the reality of her husband's death. They all had difficulty sleeping and banded together during the difficult evening hours when her sense of loss was most intense.

The children fought incessantly and daily routines became hectic and disorganized. They seemed to be displacing frustration over the loss of father, and the loss of emotional contact with mother, into battles with one another. Mrs.

Conrad coped with her grief by working hard to do everything her husband would have done. Mrs. Conrad described her frustration over the wildness of the children. We saw a corollary between their state of overstimulation and what she described as her difficulty in maintaining control of the situation and her feelings. She reviewed the circumstances of her husband's death, including signals of his ill-health over the previous year, which he had ignored, despite her efforts to have him consult a second physician. She gradually described her anger at his resistance, and her dependence upon his knowledgeable self-assurance in other matters. We supported the gradual emergence of the feelings of rage and betrayal at what she experienced as an abandonment. In sessions the focus was the children's behavior and its meaning and on Mrs. Conrad's warded-off feelings. She gradually understood that maintaining a sense of her husband's presence was a means of continuing their relationship, and a defense against feeling helpless and abandoned. During sessions, Mrs. Conrad slowly experienced and expressed the sadness, loneliness, and sexual deprivation she felt in the late evenings. A careful modulation of the affects as they emerged was helpful. She then was able to change the pace of her family's activities. As a result of being affectively more available to her children, she reduced the external sources for their tension states, and helped them deal better with their own feelings.

An additional educational issue dealt with in the parent guidance work is that of the parent's role in granting permission for the child's expression of feelings. The parent's stance can convey either that these matters are safe to talk about and that the affects involved can be mastered or that discussion is prohibited. The crucial role of verbalization in the child's mourning adaptation has been emphasized by a number of authors (E. Furman, 1974; R. Furman, 1978). The parent can begin this process by discussing his own feelings in a comprehensive way that does not overwhelm the child. It is particularly useful for the younger child when the parent helps to define and connect the child's dysphoric or anxious moods to possible feelings about the deceased parent or other aspects of the loss.

A growing tolerance for experiencing painful affects develops throughout childhood. Parents have a role in modeling this tolerance. The surviving parent's capacity to tolerate the child's expression of ambivalent, rageful, and frustrated feelings contributes to the child's growing mastery. Modeling varies with the parental personality, phase of mourning, and with the nature of the prior parent–child relationship. It also depends on the parent's current degree of denial or disavowal and acknowledgement of the child's pain. Verbalization of mourning indicates that some degree of integration and mastery has occurred.

Some families have taught their children about verbalization of feelings prior to the loss. For these families, discussions of the loss are a continuation of their child-rearing practices, but these discussions are nonetheless highly charged and difficult for the surviving parent. Guidance often supports the parent's efforts to continue communicating with the child and promoting the child's expression of feelings as a crucial step in coping with the death (E. Furman, 1981).

Case Example 4

Work with the Rollins family illustrates the guidance process with a mother who helped her three-year-old daughter deal with witnessing father's cardiac arrest and death at home. We focused on supporting her efforts with her daughter and addressing her exceptionally high expectation of herself as a parent. The child's precocious verbal capacities served to ensure emotional contact with mother when mother's preoccupation and depression were most intense.

By the time she came to the Center, Mrs. Rollins had

entered her own short-term psychotherapy for her sense of abandonment and guilt. She sought a checkup for Luisa. Luisa had witnessed her father's collapse and some of the subsequent medical procedures. The sudden and traumatic nature of Mr. Rollins' death, the rapidity of the autopsy and cremation contributed to mother's sense of disbelief and shock and was reflected by a delay in choosing a burial site. Mrs. Rollins' grief was profound and intensely painful. The Rollinses had been an intimate and supportive couple; Mr. Rollins had been an involved father. Luisa was a precocious, bright, and highly verbal child. Mrs. Rollins thought Luisa was coping reasonably well overall. She sought confirmation for how she had been handling things with Luisa and had questions about how to help Luisa enter nursery school.

Parent guidance work was agreed upon after a diagnostic evaluation. Mrs. Rollins was frightened by the prospect of raising Luisa alone. She was anxious about Luisa's sudden quietness about father after weeks of constant talk and questions. Luisa seemed more distant, and bedtimes and sleeping were becoming difficult for her. She was afraid that she might not be dealing enough with the loss and that problems would go underground. She felt intense sadness for Luisa who had been deeply attached to father. Mrs. Rollins also worried about Luisa's ongoing development without father's presence. She questioned whether Luisa could understand the permanence of the loss and whether she should be told about the cremation. The close mother–child relationship, mother's support and directness, and Luisa's excellent verbal capacity had been apparent in the initial handling of the events. Mother gave Luisa a simple explanation of the subsequent events. Mother also followed Luisa's lead in responding simply to her series of questions. Luisa's initial grasp of the reality was indicated by her immediate and intense response of crying with mother and wanting to read a favorite story that dealt with loss.

Luisa struggled to understand father's physical disappearance, what had happened to him, and with fears of calamity befalling mother and herself. She asked why people had been shoving on daddy's chest and had been "kissing" him. Mother explained the efforts to resuscitate father. Luisa told the story to friends, played "falling dead" with them, and repeatedly enacted the scene with her dolls. She brought new questions to mother almost daily. She asked why father had been lying on the floor looking dead. Mother, in simple words, explained why this was so and what had happened to cause father's death. Mother explained the "special sickness" in daddy's heart that made it stop working and that neither she nor Luisa had this kind of sickness. Luisa wondered why she had been sent out of the room, why mother's voice had been very sharp when she told her to leave, and why she could not stay to watch. Luisa was sorry she did not have a chance to say good-bye to father. "You got to say good-bye to him, I didn't. He was my daddy, too." Mother responded to Luisa's obvious confusion and frustration at being deprived of the relationship with father. In the guidance work, we considered some of the worries, anger, and age-appropriate fantasies behind Luisa's questions. Luisa struggled with the concept of death and fearful identification with father's illness. She went around the house labeling those objects which were alive and those which were dead, and those which had hearts.

Luisa's frustration grew at not having father's daily presence. She occasionally had intense screaming and kicking tantrums with mother. She insisted that she wanted her father back and that mother should get father for her. She said that mother was playing a mean joke on her. Mother gently confirmed the fact of father's death, reviewed what it meant for father to be dead, and that Luisa felt sad and angry that dad was gone and that mother could not bring him back. Luisa told her that that was a terrible thing to say, that mother should say she was sorry. Luisa would collapse in tears and mother would hold and rock her. Mrs. Rollins had to cope with similar feelings about the loss and her helplessness to restore father, in order to help Luisa in such a sensitive way. Luisa's lament was draining to hear, a lament not so different from mother's own feelings.

One day, six months after father's death, Luisa spent some time with a carpenter who was doing repairs on the family's apartment, watching his work and asking him questions. The workman, clearly delighted with his audience, had been friendly and playful. Luisa commented to mother on what a nice man he was. When the carpenter left, Luisa sat down, and suddenly, like a cloud burst, began sobbing. She had not cried as openly and intensely in many months. Mother held and rocked her and they talked quietly for some time about how the carpenter had reminded Luisa of father. They talked about all the times Luisa had done things with father around the apartment. The contact with a kind man and the enactment of "memories in action" had clearly stirred Luisa's yearning for father. Mrs. Rollins was able to hold Luisa through this experience and to help give words to the feelings.

We attempt to teach the difference in timetables of children's and adult's mourning. Parents have often noted that, in particular, their young latency aged children had great difficulty talking about their feelings or the experience of their parent's death and have even shown a kind of phobic response to the parent's gentle attempts to discuss it. Children of latency age often had greater difficulty and fearfulness when they observed their parent's grief. Instead of expressing overt grief, such children were moody, vulnerable, cried easily, and seemed to experience diminished self-esteem and resilience. Children sometimes provocatively misbehaved. The passage of time and greater stability in the emotional balance of their surviving parent seemed to be factors that made it possible for this group of children to ask questions and express feelings about the loss. An important aspect of our guidance intervention was to help the parent remain patient when the children were unable to talk about their distress directly. We helped the parent follow the child's signals of readiness to actively mourn.

Case Example 5

The difference in timetables for mourning is illustrated by work with the Russell family. Maternal aunt and uncle were raising their six-year-old niece and ten-year-old nephew after the children's parents were killed in an automobile accident. The children reacted to the loss with intensely regressive behavior. We worked with the couple for over a year helping them to deal with the children's traumatic reactions and gradually to form closer attachments in the new family. The families had been close, and Mr. and Mrs. Russell grieved deeply for their sister and brother-in-law. They were worried and surprised by the children's infantile behavior. The ten-year-old boy never spontaneously discussed his parents' death. He seemed frozen and frightened. Immersing himself in school activities and athletics, he avoided being at home. He distanced himself from his aunt and uncle. His six-year-old sister was visibly depressed. We supported the Russels in their efforts to help each child cope with the issues. As Mrs. Russell discussed memories of her sister and differences in the family life between the two households with the children, her nephew gradually started talking to her about his feelings. It became apparent that the boy needed additional help with the mourning process and they were able to help him enter psychotherapy two years after the loss, when attachments within the new family were stable and supportive.

GUIDANCE IN THE SECOND YEAR OF BEREAVEMENT

A detailed description of the impact of the bereavement process on surviving parents is provided in chapter 3 of this monograph. Here, we will outline some of the vicissitudes of the mourning we have seen in our parent guidance work.

The bereavement process is punctuated by anniversary phenomena, not necessarily related to calendar time, but to configurations of feelings or interactions significant to the lost relationship. Some anniversary reactions emanate from new developmental acquisitions on the part of the child which cannot be shared with the deceased spouse and thus heighten the awareness of the loss and intensify the pain of caring for the children alone. Birthdays, graduations, holiday gatherings, or changes in seasonal routines can elicit renewed preoccupation with memories and painful comparisons to the time when husband or wife was alive and well.

The second half of the first year tends to be a very painful time. In the early period of bereavement some numbing and the greater availability of consoling friends and family tend to moderate the level of pain. In the second period, supports are generally reduced. The surviving spouse is faced with the fact that life is different, and there is no control over the loss. One must cope independently without one's spouse. The surviving parent enters a phase in which grief seems unendurable and relentless. The parent feels deprived and lonely. They are exhausted, irritable, and at times frightened about not being able to manage the children. Making decisions about the children is difficult and lonely as this was usually shared with their spouse. The loss contributes to feeling narcissistically depleted and shakes their confidence as parents.

As noted above, the child may be more symptomatic in the last half of the first year and into the second year. The child's response is often delayed because of developmental limitations in the capacity for mourning in the absence of active facilitation from the parent. Trauma also contributes to a delay because the child is too frightened to mourn. Fear may stem from identification with the parent's fate, from anticipation of further injury and separation, or from the environment's collapse. It is important to differentiate those symptoms which signify affective engagement with the loss from those which seem maladaptive to the situation. In families where the parent's functioning is restored and the supportive relationship is assured, the child is more able to undertake mourning, perhaps because parents are able to perceive and recognize distress more accurately. The child's reaction of guilt, lowered self-esteem, and anxiety are particularly painful for the parent and often instigate an effort to seek professional help.

In the second year of bereavement, individuals can feel disillusioned when the passage of the first anniversary of the loss does not lead immediately to a respite from the grief or an improved feeling of well-being. They may feel disillusioned despite feeling more independent and proud of having coped with the events of the past year. The pain of missing the spouse and the reality of going on alone are often experienced more sharply in the second year. The middle phase of bereavement may bring an even greater sense of desolation and may mobilize a variety of defenses. The disruption to the ongoing life of some families is still so great that life remains pressured and disorganized.

Widowed parents often date or consider the possibility of new relationships after the first or second year. Dating as a transitional phase is usually disorienting for young widows and widowers. Their life course had been set. They had defined themselves to some degree as an integral part of a couple and were carrying out the family life they had planned together. Having made choices and commitments, they are suddenly in the position of defining themselves as separate individuals and making new relationships.

The transitional phase is usually marked by episodic but intense grief. New relationships can buffer against the feeling of loss and desolation. Elements of the relationship may preserve the feeling of the old object tie. As new persons and interactions are contrasted to the old relationship, the loss is brought into perspective and can be felt very intensely. There is anxiety and guilt over "abandoning" the old relationship. The person wishes to remain connected to the image of the spouse at the same time that he is investing in a new attachment. Movement toward greater acceptance and resolution of the loss are likely under healthy conditions. Being involved in a relationship, per se, is not the measure of successful mourning and can indicate an aborted or pathologically organized bereavement. At the same time, a widowed parent's wish not to remarry may not be indicative of an arrested mourning process.

The focus of guidance is determined by the phase of the parent's bereavement as well as the parent's changing concerns about the children. The clinician must be sensitive to the progressive shifts in the parent's recovery which signal the gradual restoration of energy and investment in the children, or help in understanding the nature of ongoing interference. When the child is seen for reevaluation, the clinician must be alert to new environmental factors and shifts in the parent–child relationship which affect the child (Pruett, 1984).

PSYCHOTHERAPY RELATED TO THE BEREAVEMENT

Parents who are aware of difficulty coping and of something having gone awry in the process of their bereavement may seek psychotherapy. They may also have difficulty managing the children and functioning without a spouse. Most have not considered seeking psychotherapy prior to the loss; others may have considered it, but do so now because of regressions brought about by their bereaved state. Deaths which were the result of murder, violent death, suicide, or a particularly devastating illness, often lead to a more complicated or potentially pathological bereavement.

The recommendation for individual treatment for the

parent may evolve out of an initial contract for parent guidance work. Parents often identify problem areas in their own mourning when they are exploring their children's difficulties (Chethik, 1976; Hoffman, 1984).

Individual psychotherapy was recommended when the initial diagnostic evaluation indicated that the parent had a severe characterological disturbance which had actively contributed to a disturbed child–parent relationship prior to the death of the spouse, and/or appeared to block the child's adaptation to the loss. We have found that such character disturbances lead to difficulties in the adult's capacity to mourn and integrate the loss, deficits in parental capacity, and developmental problems in the child. Those parents with severe character pathology represented a small minority among the parents seen for diagnostic consultation at the Center, but it was a group that needed therapeutic assistance. We saw individual treatment for the parent as a necessary contribution toward a better outcome for both parent and child. Many parents in this group were not amenable to the recommendation for psychotherapy when it was first discussed. In view of their reluctance, psychotherapy may not have been recommended to the parent as a first level of intervention. In these instances, parent guidance was recommended with its focus on dealing with the traumatic aspects of the death and stabilizing family life. Parents often felt that this recommendation was more in keeping with their needs and wishes. The development of a therapeutic alliance with such parents was often a gradual and difficult process and in certain circumstances, guidance provided an opportunity to see what progress could be made toward initiating psychotherapy. When successful, a therapeutic alliance was formed with the parent around work with their own issues. As family circumstances changed, some parents then were able to enter psychotherapy. We tried to establish a distinct contract and a separate format from the previous parent guidance.

Those parents who had a history of prior object loss, particularly childhood parent loss, often benefited from individual treatment. For some individuals, unresolved mourning of that original relationship presented an interference in the current bereavement. The loss of the spouse represented a retraumatization. The old vulnerability stimulated defensive measures against the current pain and anxiety.

Prior loss may strengthen certain capacities and provide a kind of immunization to the experience if the individual had support from family and was able to mourn the earlier loss. However, the individuals seen at the Center tended not to have had such experiences. They were exquisitely vulnerable to the loss of their spouse, mourning was difficult and seemed more likely to be pathological. Psychotherapy did appear to make a difference in assisting them to allow a mourning process and to begin and continue to some resolution.

A small minority of such parents sought or accepted the recommendation for their own psychotherapy, often their first experience with psychological counseling. The majority, however, chose to use the format of periodic reevaluations for the children. The Center came to be seen as a special and safe place, less threatening and distinct from the larger world of psychiatric services. There was often a strong institutional transference as well as an alliance with the diagnostician. The inherent task of considering the past through the meaning of the present was often experienced as a threat. The threat entailed a reexposure to potentially overwhelming feelings. They had achieved an equilibrium and adaptation which they did not want to disrupt any further. Throughout the children's diagnostic evaluation they often voiced the feeling that they had designed family life to protect the children from ever experiencing the loss that they themselves had suffered. In identification with their own bereaved children, they were overwhelmed, frightened, and angry. The loss of the spouse was met with disbelief as well as a secret conviction that, in fact, they had been doomed to lose the "spouse–parent."

The psychotherapy with surviving spouses was complex and difficult as the defenses and resistances were extraordinarily strong and imbricated within their character. Nevertheless, certain characterological issues were more addressable as a result of a shift in defenses brought about by the current bereavement.

Psychotherapy with widowed parents who had functioned reasonably well within a stable marriage and family prior to the loss brought the mourning process into focus and aided their understanding of the multiple meanings of the loss. Concomitantly, therapy might assist the parent to manage the child's difficulties in the light of the bereavement. Individuals who used the therapist as a replacement object for the lost spouse, mourned more fully because emotional equilibrium was maintained during the bereavement process.

The following case is an example of psychoanalytic psychotherapy with a focus on bereavement. The mourning process was affected by two factors. First, death was sudden and unexpected. Second, mourning was more difficult because the loss reexposed the individual to earlier experiences of abandonment, traumatic overstimulation, and massive deidealization of his spouse.

Case Example 6

Mr. Adams sought psychotherapy for himself several months after his wife's death from a heart attack. The couple had three children ranging in age from six to thirteen. Mrs. Adams had experienced transitory symptoms in the year before her death but had dismissed them and refused to consult a doctor. There was a history of heart disease in her family and she reacted to the symptoms with denial and a fatalistic attitude. Mr. Adams remained in shock for months after her death. He initially withdrew from the children, finding their sadness and battling intolerable. His eleven-year-old son became restless and impulsive in school, as well as aggressive with his brother and sister. Mr. Adams absorbed himself in work. The children were intensely needy and demanding, and grew more frantic as father maintained his isolation from them. The children rejected a succession of housekeepers as family life grew chaotic. Mr. Adams began to drink heavily and became suicidal. Relatives finally urged him to get help for the children and himself.

Mr. Adams initially discussed how life seemed empty and meaningless without his wife. He was frightened of living without her. They had worked hard together; he felt insecure about functioning professionally without her support. He could not imagine finding anyone like her again. At the same time, he felt ashamed and humiliated by his failure to function in his usual controlled, organized manner. His detachment from the children puzzled and frightened him, but they were such constant reminders of his wife that he could not stand to deal with their neediness.

Mr. Adams reviewed the last year of their life together, particularly the few months before his wife's death, trying to understand how they both dismissed mild symptoms she had had. He was preoccupied with memories, dreams, and flashback experiences of the heart attack. For a long period, Mr. Adams talked about his guilt over not recognizing subtle signs of his wife's fatigue. He felt that had he been more emotionally available her heart attack could have been prevented. The psychotherapy gradually dealt with the multiple determinants of his guilt and rage at his wife emerged. He surmised that his wife suspected that she was ill but minimized it in order to protect both of them. She had perhaps been so frightened that she denied the importance of the symptoms and refused to see a doctor. The death of many relatives during her adolescence predisposed her to a kind of fatalism about her own health. Mr. Adams realized that he acquiesced in her denial, and in fact became emotionally detached from her. His response entailed an extreme suppression of affect. Only gradually did feelings become available to him again in the months after her death. Despite his admiration for her courage and capacity to live in the present, he felt abandoned. Her fatalism about her possible illness felt like a devaluation of their life together. Her refusal to seek help was a negation of her attachment to him. He had failed to protect her. Her death opened up his vulnerability to abandonment and depreciation. He was enraged with her. Mrs. Adams' denial and fatalism was a traumatic disappointment to his highly idealized opinion of his wife. In part, it was massive deidealization which made the early phase of mourning intolerable and brought him into treatment. He was flooded with feelings about past disappointments in significant relationships, particularly those with each of his parents.

Mr. Adams experienced more direct grief as these issues were explored. He entered a phase in which he considered how past experiences with each parent and with siblings had motivated his choice of a spouse. The marital relationship had been exhilarating and intense. The dynamic issues which predisposed Mr. Adams to react to his wife's death in this suicidal manner were an intolerance for experiencing his own feelings in identification with his mother, who denied, minimized, and depreciated her son's feelings. His mother flooded him as a child with frightening and overstimulating stories of her immigration to this country as well as mistreatment at the father's hands. As a child he felt that his small childhood woes were insignificant and unworthy of consideration. There was a direct failure of support, nurturance, and protection within the relationship with his mother. Mr. Adams' father was an alcoholic who deserted the family when Mr. Adams was eleven years old. Before the desertion, Mr.

Adams was also exposed to father's frequent physical abuse of his mother, to his parent's mutual hatred and depreciation. His mother acted in a martyred manner, denying the meaning of the abuse. Throughout childhood, Mr. Adams had to "close his ears" to their fighting and to dissimulate his feelings in order to defend against his fears, and the anger toward both parents. Mother's sister cared for him throughout early childhood when his mother worked and after father's desertion. However, the aunt abruptly disappeared from his life when a conflict arose between the sisters. Family ties were marked by intense rivalries and feuds ending in severed relationships. Mr. Adams met his wife when they were in high school. He left home to live on his own when he was still an adolescent.

Gradually, the meaning of Mr. Adams' relationship to his wife took shape against the background of these childhood experiences and the defensive adaptations he had made. Mrs. Adams was deeply devoted to him and built her life around supporting him and caring for their children. She was playful, loved life, and was a charismatic person who made every experience intense. Her humor, capacity to keep difficulties in perspective, and hopeful optimism counteracted his tendency toward depression. They were intensely wrapped up in one another. He felt acknowledged and valued for the first time. He contributed a complementary seriousness and basic stability to the marriage. His wife's warm acceptance and easygoing nature stood in contrast to his mother's bitterness. There was reflected glory in his wife's charismatic liveliness and popularity. She made him feel alive, and when she died, he felt deadened.

He was able to put into words what was lost to him when she died, how vital her qualities and activities were to his sense of well-being. He came to understand the nature of earlier experiences with his parents which threatened repetition within the bereavement. During the first year of treatment, Mr. Adams feared that the therapist would be like mother, that she would expose or subject him to painful feelings, rather than bringing wished for relief. He feared that he would be submerged in inescapable, painful feelings. At the same time he anticipated that the therapist would leave him alone to cope with the pain after flooding him with feelings he had warded off. A related transference theme was his wish and fear that the therapeutic relationship would replicate an aspect of the relationship with his wife by supplying essential and legitimate experiences. He wanted to feel enlivened and connected again in an empathic relationship. The psychotherapeutic relationship helped him understand his need for these qualities in a relationship. He also understood the difficulties he had had in grieving because his wife could no longer play those roles for him. There were other aspects of the transference which emerged in the course of the treatment but they will not be dealt with here because of the primary focus on the bereavement work.

Mr. Adams reacted to the separation of the therapist's first vacation which came several months before the first anniversary of his wife's death. The vacation experience coincided with a resurgence of grief related to memories of that season the year before when his wife had some suspicious symptoms. As the first anniversary approached, Mr. Adams feared it would be overwhelming. He grieved intensely within the context of the support provided by the therapeutic relationship.

In the second year of treatment we examined Mr. Adams' relationship with his wife. He could also turn toward investigating his own personality structure. Periodically, Mr. Adams focused on issues with the children and their complex adjustment to the loss and to a housekeeper. Discussions of the children also seemed to be a way of discussing aspects of his internal states. He experienced periods of quiet sadness and yearning for his wife alongside periods of well-being. As he considered meeting new people and eventually did so, new episodes of mourning were ushered in by the contrast between the women he dated and his wife's personality. The psychotherapy also gradually dealt with the issue of managing his work life to be as available as possible to the children. The psychotherapy provided a framework for mourning work, which probably could not have proceeded as thoroughly without engagement in the psychotherapeutic relationship.

SUMMARY

This chapter has considered the three types of intervention with parents provided in the context of a bereavement treatment service. The author would like to briefly consider commonalities and distinctions between these interventions. The therapeutic work in each is guided by an understanding of the vicissitudes of the surviving parent's bereavement. The diagnostic consultation and the ego supportive parent guidance work are considerably more focused on the bereavement orientation than is the psychotherapy. These interventions specifically have a goal of facilitating the parent's and the child's adaptive bereavement. Each has a clear educational and guidance component, while the psychoanalytic psychotherapy has an open-ended agenda, whose content and process is determined by the emergence and management of transference themes. The therapist's interpretations are based on knowledge of the mourning process, yet avoid a single-minded focus on bereavement issues. The scope is broader and characterological issues can be dealt with in the context of the emerging alliance and transference. References to the children and refocusing on them can be heard as communications about the parent's self objects and internal states. Work with surviving parents in all three contexts is challenging and calls for sensitivity and an empathic effort to encounter the multiple meanings of loss.

Chapter 7

Some Common Transference–Countertransference Issues in the Treatment of Parent Loss

Benjamin Garber, M.D.

INTRODUCTION

The patient's transference reactions to the therapist as they occur in every therapeutic encounter and the therapist's countertransferences have been described as the drive that constitutes the essence of the therapeutic process. Whatever other interactions may occur, whatever the therapeutic strategies may be, it is the transference–countertransference interplay that gives the therapy its dynamic direction and its energetic component. The variety and range of transference and countertransference reactions set each therapy apart from all the others. The style and substance of these interactions will, in large part, be determined by the personality and psychopathology of the patient as well as by the personality, and we may hope to a lesser extent, the psychopathology of the therapist. Such variables are beyond the scope and discussion of this chapter for they can be addressed and examined only on a case by case basis. However, in certain psychopathologic configurations or as the result of a particular set of traumas, there occur transference and countertransference interactions that seem to be ubiquitous in their presence and repetitiveness. It would seem that aside from the other variables involved, a particular form of psychopathology tends to manifest itself in a particular transference gestalt and also seems to elicit a rather specific countertransference response. Freud (1905a), in his early cases, especially the case of Dora, set the precedent for these types of interactions, and since then psychoanalysts have expanded and contributed to the fund of knowledge and understanding of these various configurations.

Most clinicians are generally aware that the seductiveness of the hysterical personality will typically elicit a mixture of sexual excitement and anger from a male therapist. Or for that matter the sterile speculations and intellectualizations of the high-level obsessional will invariably draw the therapist into discussions about somebody's hostility, while the mood swings of the narcissistic patient will stimulate feelings of excitement, boredom, hopelessness, and ultimately a sense of confusion.

A similarly repetitive clinical interplay occurs between the child who has lost a parent by death and the therapist who treats him. When viewed from a purely theoretical perspective, the role of the therapist with the child whose parent has died is relatively clear-cut. The task of the therapist is mainly to facilitate the child's mourning activity in keeping with what is developmentally appropriate (Garber, 1981). However, as is so often the case in our work, the theory generally outdistances the clinical possibilities.

The ambiguity prevalent in the clinical approach toward the grieving child is such that sweeping assumptions are often made about treatment and treatability. At one extreme it has been stated that the loss of a parent by death is such a uniquely traumatic event that every child is in dire need of professional intervention. At the other extreme, it has been proclaimed that death is the natural culmination of life's events so that every individual, whether child or adult, needs to come to terms with the loss in his own natural, adaptive style. Extraneous theoretical models and/or expectations need not be imposed on the child's manner of dealing with the loss, so that his reaction may take its predestined course without interference.

When a child whose parent has died is referred for an evaluation, the diagnostician will usually recommend treatment whose major focus is the mourning for the lost object. Yet, how often is the question posed as to whether a particular child is capable of engaging in a mourning experience. Clinicians, working mainly with children, will reflexively prescribe therapy to include mourning, without considering whether the child has the necessary cognitive skills and/or emotional equipment so essential for mourning to occur. In part, the expectations have to do with the application of an adultomorphic model of mourning to the child and an associated idealization of the latency child's status and capabilities. The other aspect of such expectations is related to the overpowering sympathy for the parent loss child, so that we automatically opt for therapy without considering whether the child is indeed capable of complying with such a demand. Consequently, the child's need and longing for a caretaker and the therapist's need to take care, become intertwined in the initial diagnostic contacts.

How the surviving parent deals with the loss vis-à-vis the bereaved child may have a profound impact on how the child is able to deal subsequently with his own feelings about the loss. Bowlby (1973) was impressed by the enormous influence on the child's response to the loss of what and how he is told by the surviving parent. It has been found that the younger the child, the more likely the parent is to delay in telling about the loss. In a series of patients studied by Bowlby, the child was told what happened to the other parent one week after the loss in almost one third of the cases, while information about the disposal of the body was postponed for as long as a year after the death.

Why then is such significant information withheld from the child, especially since he will often suspect the truth anyway? If he does not suspect the truth then there is a good possibility that his phantasies and distortions are far more frightening and bizarre than the reality.

Most well-intentioned adults will tell you that they do it to protect the child from the pain and the trauma of the death. But how does a delay in telling, or a distortion of the facts, protect the child? Does it indeed make sense that a one-week postponement will in some way immunize the child with regard to the pain? Or does telling the child that the dead parent was buried instead of cremated diminish the trauma?

Yet such practices are not unusual in spite of their lack of logic or common sense even among people who know what to say and how to say it. Consequently, such withholding is only partly to shield and protect the child from the pain of death and mourning. The withholding may also have something to do with protecting the adult. It would seem that the adult may need some protection from the directness and the pointedness of the child's questions and statements which tend to underline the reality of the loss.

Adults have the ability to philosophize incessantly about the meaning of death, to intellectualize about the continuity of life and death, and to rhapsodize about life after death. The child, on the other hand, not being shackled by such constraints, is able to ask some rather direct and specific questions which no adult is able to answer knowledgeably, simply, and honestly. Even the most learned of priests, ministers, or rabbis would find it difficult to answer the child's simple questions in a manner that is plausible, understandable, and sensible. The best that the child can hope for is a benign catchphrase or a sterile intellectualized response to which he will shake his head in mute compliance; while both he and the adult will be relieved by their mutual silent pact.

Consequently, in delaying or avoiding telling the child, the adult is in essence avoiding his own confrontation with the reality and the finality of the loss. The child in his direct, simple, and straightforward manner has the capacity to confront and bring home the reality of the loss more strikingly and starkly than the adult. So that the adult by avoiding the questioning of the child is in essence avoiding the child within themselves, who is always clamoring for the truth.

The problems involved in dealing with children who lost a parent by death have their origins in how we explain death to our own children which in turn depends on how death was presented and explained to us. I can remember very distinctly a time when my six-year-old daughter, for reasons only known to her, began to question me about death. I felt rather proud of myself as I fielded her questions as to which of my belongings would be hers and which ones would be inherited by her sisters. However, when she plaintively said that she would not like for anyone that she loved to be stuck forever in the cold, hard, and wet ground, I sensed a shiver go up and down my spine. It makes scant difference as to how much we know or how much we think we know and understand about death and dying, the child's statements and questions will invariably elicit responses compounded by pain and discomfort. This is done not out of anger, hostility, or malice, although these may be components of the interchange. Rather, the mind of the curious and inquiring child has the uncanny ability to focus on the essence of the most complex and painful issues with a directness and simplicity that eludes the most sophisticated of adults.

With adult patients one can always take refuge in the delicate niceties of a philosophical and/or existential discourse. We do this as adults because we also sidestep the pain that may be prevalent in such direct encounters. The child, on the other hand, whose thinking has not yet been contaminated by such profound speculations, will make us uncomfortable and evasive when dealing with the twin mysteries of human existence—sexuality and death.

In the treatment setting such avoidances in dealing with the parent's death are not uncommon, in fact they are the rule rather than the exception. One of the more striking experiences that was noticed at the Barr-Harris Center was that for the first two years of the center's existence, children were not asked directly about their loss unless they brought it up spontaneously. In many instances, the diagnostic evaluation was completed, yet the death of the parent was not mentioned nor discussed in the process. This occurred in spite of the fact that the diagnostician was constantly poised for material related to the loss, while the child knew that he was being evaluated because of his reaction to the death. The rationale for such an avoidance was that ultimately the material would emerge, so that there was no need to traumatize the child by asking questions as to why he was here.

A similar situation was encountered in reviewing the interviews of normal adolescents in Offer and Peterson's (1982) Longitudinal Study of 315 upper-middle class teenagers.

In this group of normals there were seven youngsters who had lost a parent by death in latency. In almost every instance the interviewers avoided any references or questions about the parent that died. It was almost as if each child was the product of one and only one parent.

Within the treatment similar avoidances may occur. Children whose parent died will seldom be asked questions about the death, the events that led up to it, or even more general questions about just what happens to people after they die. If the death was sudden and violent, then it's almost assured that it will never come up nor will it ever be mentioned or asked about. In fact, should the child happen to bring it up spontaneously or in play, the chances are that the therapist will not notice it nor make any comment about it. Such is the unwritten pact in any treatment contract— some things are just not to be mentioned.

Due to the intensity of feelings that are elicited in the therapist by the child as well as the constant deflection of longings, no therapist should burden himself with too many parent loss patients. The therapist who finds himself over-burdened by too many grieving children who insists on seeing them consecutively during the working day will more than likely find himself drained. There is a very subtle quality to the demands exerted by such patients. While not obvious to the clinician initially, the debilitating effects of the demands will be manifested with the passage of time. More than any other psychopathology, the depression of loss will cast a pall on the therapist that may spill over beyond the working day.

There is the initial interest and a marked empathic response by the therapist who starts working with a child whose parent has died. The child is sad, unhappy, withdrawn, and lonely; sometimes he may appear to be in the throes of a chronic traumatic state. In the latter instance any seemingly appropriate intervention will elicit a painful response and a flood of tears. The therapist, for his part, has very little difficulty in being responsive and empathic to the child's grief and sadness. There is probably no reaction known to mankind that elicits empathy and sympathy more consistently than the lonely, unhappy, and sad orphan. Exalted by writers and filmmakers, the lonely waif in search of a parent has remained a heartrending figure throughout the history of mankind. Seeing a small child who is lost and looking for its parent will cause almost any adult to stop what they are doing and concentrate their efforts on searching out the missing caretaker.

This initial phase of the treatment in the parent loss case could be appropriately labeled as the honeymoon period. For eventually the time comes when the child reaches a leveling in his sad affects and then he or she may begin to wonder as to what the return will be for such painful and gut-wrenching encounters. The child may question the value of such inter-actions even more if the depressing moods persist beyond the sessions and spill over into daily functioning with peers and family. The price for such painful meetings may be extremely high for other children are not eager to interact with a child who is depressed.

At the same time, the therapist may begin to wonder about the next stage, or just how long this sadness will continue as the primary currency of the therapeutic exchange. Often the initial sympathy and empathy becomes replaced by a sense of boredom followed by withdrawal and irritation. The initial good feelings that one experiences from being in tune with another human being, who is suffering, are replaced by other feelings and thoughts which may make the therapist question his empathic stance and therapeutic effectiveness.

This mutual dissonance may manifest itself by the child being silent and complaining of boredom while the therapist either withdraws or becomes overly interpretive and active in his interventions. These interpretations are often related to the death of the parent and they are brought forth from sources other than the patient. At this point in the treatment coming late and missing appointments is a common occurrence. The child and surviving parent have a host of valid excuses subsumed under the philosophical stance that life must go on. The therapist may enter into collusion with this approach by rationalizing the positive aspects of the child's involve-ment in all these activities as a reasonable compensation for the loss.

A variation of the above treatment situation which occurs rather commonly is one where the child will discuss all varieties of issues and problems, but will not deal with his feelings about the loss. While the patient comes to his appointments dutifully, he disclaims any feelings related to the death. Although the child maintains an absence of feelings, the therapist will find himself insisting that he is just denying, disavowing, or avoiding the overpowering affects. In most cases, it is almost impossible to win an argument with a patient, and even if the argument is won the treatment may be lost.

In spite of claims to the contrary, parents do find ways of interfering with the child's expression of powerful affects. There are a number of ways in which the parent may do this, whether it be by example, directly, or by more subtle maneuvers. There is, for example, the overly intellectualized parent who may talk with, at, under, and all over the child each time there are feelings to be dealt with. The more driven parent will distract with scheduling and myriads of activities every time affects rear their ugly head. Then there is always the possibility that younger children have not been taught anything about affects so that a therapist may have to begin the treatment by teaching the child about that mysterious something called feelings. It is equally plausible, that while the child does have feelings about the loss, it may well be that he is not ready to talk about them at this particular time and place, but may do so at a later period in his treatment or development. Since the child has not yet developed the finely honed skill of intellectualizing about feelings, then his choice of interaction in therapy is narrowed either to recounting daily events, or silence.

The basic affects of the mourning process have been variously considered as grief, sadness, longings (or yearning), anxiety, and anger. Clinical practice would seem to indicate that therapists experience the greatest difficulty in tolerating the expression of anger toward the person that died. Among researchers on the process of mourning, Bowlby (1960b) and Pollock (1961) regard the anger and frustration in mourning as inevitable and relate it to the initially primitive and insatiable nature of the yearning for the lost object. They have attributed a special constructive role to the presence and discharge of the anger in the mourning process. Yet, there is something about allowing oneself to sense anger, especially to feel it and then say it toward the one that died, that borders on trespassing into forbidden territory.

Children, far more easily than adults, acknowledge anger at the dead, both for having died and for their shortcomings, real and imaginary, when still alive. Children are far more likely to direct their hostilities not only at death itself, but at the love object's shortcomings prior to the death. Children often have an overriding need to recount and remember the flaws and the disappointments they experienced with the person that died. Such an expression may have a driven, self-propelled quality, an urgent need for discharge as a viable part of mourning.

The child's anger toward and about the loss is expressed in a number of differing styles. The chronic grumbling and sulking of the indirect passive–aggressive manner is probably the more comfortable for most adults. On the other hand, anger that is expressed by the child in sudden, direct, intense, and brief outbursts may be potentially startling and unsettling to the most well intentioned of healers.

One of the more memorable therapeutic encounters that I experienced was with an eight-year-old boy whose father had died two years previously. While it was apparent that he was attempting to contain his hostility and anger by grumbling and sulking, he steadfastly denied the slightest amount of irritation. About halfway through the treatment, after some energetic prodding, he suddenly jumped up with clenched fists and screamed at the top of his lungs: "Okay, okay— so I hate his guts for having died on me— so what do you want me to do, go to the cemetery and stamp on his grave?" It is reasonable to assume that in addition to being startled by his outburst, I also sensed a fair dose of anxiety; not only about the sudden explosiveness, but also about what this sweet, pleasant, likable little boy could possibly do to me.

The therapist may have an extremely difficult time in allowing the child to express the anger because of its intensity, its lack of disguise, and its directness. Instead, the therapist may be more sensitive to and more comfortable with the child's longings and feelings of sadness and loss. The child's indirect expressions of anger via complaints of boredom and sullenness may be ignored and discounted with maneuvers to pacify and to indulge. Aside from the expression of anger for anger's sake, the child may even need some acknowledgment and validation of the objective reality that stimulated the rage.

The child's expression of anger toward the lost object is probably overlooked, deflected, or not recognized by the therapist far more than any other affective state.

Such a countertransference response may be doubly motivated. In part it has to do with a basic tension or anxiety that one experiences when expressing anger toward the dead. Such tension is probably closely linked with a powerful element of guilt. The other component of the response is based on an awareness of the primitiveness and directness of the child's rage. For there is the tendency to interpret this rage as something that may actually hurt us, just the way it must have hurt and perhaps even destroyed the lost object.

The recognition of the anger and the rage toward the lost object needs to be considered as an essential component of the treatment in every parent loss situation. It may well be that in those cases which stalemated or in which the treatment was not completed, the neglect of the anger toward the lost object was the primary component responsible for the result.

One of the more common countertransference problems

that emerges in the treatment of parent loss cases is the making of special allowances which foster a moving away from and a distortion of the treatment contract. The basic interaction in any therapeutic process vacillates around the to and fro of the therapeutic contract which is usually spelled out in the beginning of treatment. The verbal agreement about the mutual responsibilities of the patient and the therapist constitutes the essence of the practical framework around which any therapy is constructed. The therapist spells out the nature of the contract and the patient usually hears it cognitively, but not emotionally. In fact, it may be assumed that the patient spends the rest of his time in treatment learning the meaning of the original contract; once the contract has been mastered then the therapy is at its termination point.

When working with a parent loss case, there is more of a tendency to overlook the elements of the original contract. Such issues as the missing of appointments, charging for missed appointments, or not adhering to the agreed upon frequency, are just a few of the practical day-to-day transactions that tend to be overlooked. Such oversights can be usually rationalized in a variety of ways for they all come under the general category of "a realistic appreciation of the hardships encountered by the child whose life has been disrupted by the loss of a parent." They may also be looked upon as expressions of sympathy for the child and/or parent who has experienced an overwhelming trauma. If not sympathy then these oversights may be described as attempts to strengthen the relationship or valid compensations for the child's deprivation. Lesser variants of the above may be the giving of food or presents, once again to fill a deprivational void, albeit symbolically.

Such occurrences are usually part and parcel of any therapeutic situation, except that in the case of parent loss they are accentuated by the therapist's collusion with the acting out. For it seems that the therapist's acting out is much easier to rationalize in a situation where the child's parent has died.

However, what eventually occurs is that the therapist has a difficult time following the continuity of the process, since the only process available is one of disruption, missed appointments, cancellations, lateness, and avoidances. The surviving parent, who is aware of this, as well as their own guilt about sidestepping the treatment, will eventually demand a progress report. When the therapist has nothing to report except his own sense of frustration and lack of understanding there is a reasonable chance that the treatment will gradually phase out with a mutual sense of disappointment and relief.

With the child whose parent has died there is very little that the therapist can do in a realistic sense to make the child's life easier. The therapist cannot bring back the dead parent, and if the therapist is of the same sex as the lost parent it may only heighten the child's hopefulness and ultimate frustration and disappointment. The younger child does not wish to dwell upon his grief but longs for an immediate replacement, for nothing short of that will alleviate the pain and the sense of loss. Consequently, a recurring external issue and internal problem is that a child whose parent has died will often harbor the phantasy that the therapist will become a substitute for the lost parent. This is more likely to occur with younger latency age children. Frequently this type of restitutive phantasy is shared implicitly by the surviving parent and the child. When some time in the course of treatment the child begins to realize that his phantasy will not materialize there may ensue a profound disappointment, anger, and a feeling of having been betrayed. This in turn may interfere with the treatment temporarily and sometimes permanently. For once the child senses that the therapist will frustrate his longings a major component of the initial motivation for treatment falls away.

One of the most difficult transference–countertransference issues that emerges in the treatment of a parent loss case is the nature of the child's attachment to the therapist. The child will automatically attempt to put the therapist in the place of the lost parent.

Such an expectation by the child is not necessarily indicative of severe psychopathology, but is rather a developmental imperative that goes beyond one's ability to test reality. The resulting problems gain in complexity, for the child will not express this need overtly, but will rather do so in subtle, covert, and indirect ways.

The initial manifestations of this longing may appear in the diagnostic process, wherein the mother will make a joking offhand comment as to how her son expected her to marry the therapist or at least invite him to dinner. Such comments are usually *not* interpreted in the diagnostic as they tend to make the parent and therapist equally uncomfortable.

Within the sessions, the transference elements of such an involvement will tend to emerge in their silent, subtle manifestations. Initially, there may be occasional comments or questions by the child about the therapist's interests and/or leisuretime activities. Such questions will often elicit a realistic response as the therapist may not wish to deprive and frustrate the child by withholding. Such responses may be rationalized as vehicles for strengthening the real relationship or the therapeutic alliance. They may also be labeled as appropriate responses to the child's realistic needs and affect hunger for a relationship with an appropriate role model that is not currently available in his milieu.

Often the gradual shift in the therapist from a neutral therapeutic stance to a more "real person response" may be indicative of the child's demands and expectations that the therapist become the real parent. Such a shift in the therapist may be gradual and almost imperceptible. Yet, there is an unconscious response to the child's longing for the missing parent. So that when the eventual mutual frustration and disappointment comes about neither the child nor the therapist are exactly aware as to why this happened. The need of one played into the need of the other without either one being quite aware of what may have transpired.

An increase in frequency of the therapist's meetings with the surviving parent may also nurture the aforementioned phantasy. Such problems may be compounded if the meetings with the parent are not alluded to in the child's treatment.

The variety and frequency of real person interventions by the therapist neither tend to further the therapeutic process nor do they strengthen the working alliance. The child's requests and demands, once realistically responded to, will show a temporary respite. However, the next time they return just as insistently for that one more bit of seemingly useless information which has mushroomed into a life and death issue. The therapist may then recoil from the child's greediness, demandingness, and seeming sense of deprivation. The therapist's guilt may shift to anger when there is the realization that the twin causes of insight and the therapeutic process have not been served by such maneuvers.

This period of the treatment is probably the stormiest of times, for the mutual frustration, disappointment, and anger between patient and therapist is such that the therapeutic process may derail temporarily and sometimes permanently. With the passage of time it becomes apparent to the therapist that the child has become preoccupied and withdrawn. What makes the behavior seem even more puzzling is that there does not seem to be a discernible precipitant. The child on the other hand, is equally puzzled as to why the therapist will not come forth with his true intentions. He may interpret the therapist's seeming coyness as an act of withholding, aggression, betrayal, and a promise that was never kept.

When one works with a case of parent loss there is an implicit expectation as to how long the child needs to mourn for the parent that died. Whether this expectation is internally motivated by the therapist's experience as well as theoretical understanding, the fact remains that we do have some kind of timetable composed of various stages. Although one may forgive the child for not having read the proper books and thus complying with our expectations, we are not as likely to forgive the surviving parent.

Based on our sense of right and wrong as well as our identifications with being a parent, we have a definitive notion as to how long and in what manner the bereaved adult needs to mourn his loss. Although we favor a reinvestment in normal routine as well as compensatory activities by the survivor, we maintain a definite sense of when it is appropriate to date or remarry after the death of a spouse. Such idiosyncratic expectations are more a function of our own history and often have little to do with what is reasonable and appropriate for a particular patient.

Should the surviving parent start dating, take trips, and plan remarriage without having experienced an "appropriate mourning process" with or without treatment, it is not uncommon for the child's therapist to experience a sense of resentment. The reaction is compounded with a sense of betrayal if the parent has made all these plans without consulting our expertise. The ultimate feeling of resentment, betrayal, and outrage emerges if the parent then proceeds to remove the child from treatment. This is not an uncommon occurrence as the parent may actively stop, short-circuit, or even complete a mourning process; while the child, due to the immaturity of his psychic apparatus, is still in the midst of dealing with his grief. One of our most intense countertransference reactions becomes manifest when the surviving parent flees the mourning process and takes the child with them. For while the child remains anchored in mourning work stimulated by the treatment, he becomes the conscience of the parent and tends to elicit feelings of guilt and resentment.

One of the easier solutions to this dilemma is for parent and child to unite against the therapist and terminate treatment for the sake of restoring some equilibrium within the family.

There are a number of situations in which a child who has been in treatment for a lengthy period of time, will slowly, but persistently and tenaciously insist that he wishes to stop. He is quite consistent in this demand which he proceeds to present to the therapist as well as at home. It becomes apparent that this wish has been initiated by the child and gradually it may even receive some lukewarm support from the parent. The therapist, having considered all possibilities of resistance, may resort to the gamut of interpretations, but to no avail. The child cannot be persuaded from, nor distracted from this all-consuming passion of ending the treatment immediately. More than likely, he will continue to come, but the litany of complaints is such that eventually the therapist has no choice but to agree to a termination time, otherwise the parent will withdraw the child from treatment. A retrospective examination of the therapeutic work does not reveal any major errors in theoretical understanding nor in technique. These are the situations in which a child who has experienced passively the sudden loss of a parent is driven by an overpowering need to master the trauma by actively leaving a significant adult. The predisposing elements may be a youngster of a passive–dependent or passive–aggressive nature who has always been vulnerable to an overwhelming sense of helplessness in the face of significant traumatic events. An attempt to master actively what one has experienced passively may sometimes become the first step in the direction of coming to terms with the loss.

CONCLUSION

From Freud's earliest exposition of the genetic point of view (1905b) until the present, psychoanalysts have prided themselves on their ability to consider developmental issues. An assessment of the impact of genetic influences on personality formation as well as psychopathology has remained an essential component of diagnosis and treatment. Although such has been the stated view it is reasonable to wonder whether developmental issues are given their due in one's daily work with adults and even with children. To what extent do we take note of the necessary leisurely back and forth or ebb and flow of progressive and regressive trends in trying to master a developmental conflict? We may fluctuate from expecting an overnight shift in developmental concerns at the one extreme to a lack of recognition that such shifts have indeed occurred. We may also fail to recognize that just because the child has been stymied in resolving a particular issue now, does not necessarily mean that he will not go back and attempt to reresolve that very issue at a different developmental stage. With the current recognition that there may be continuities as well as discontinuities in developmental competencies (Kagan, 1980) such assumptions about the future have more meaning and a greater significance. In our paper on mourning in children (Garber, 1981) we argued that most children will mourn according to what their unique developmental capabilities may be at a particular time. We also addressed ourselves notion that there are certain cognitive skills and emotional capabilities which are essential for the work of mourning to proceed. It is not too far-fetched to assume then that although the child may not be able to continue his mourning process at the current level of development, he may be able to pursue such work at a different developmental plane; given the confidence that some or perhaps most of the necessary competencies will come into being.

Such an appreciation as well as faith in the developmental imperative is essential for any therapist who may expect the child to mourn according to an adultomorphic model of mourning. Otherwise, the child, the surviving parent, and the therapist will part in a manner that may not facilitate the child's awareness of the possibility that he has a choice. That choice implies that if you cannot, or perhaps do not wish to complete it now, then you can do it later in keeping with your own needs and developmental timetable. Such a message to the child is perhaps one of the most important things that any therapy could possibly offer.

Chapter 8

Johnny: Mobilizing a Child's Capacity to Mourn by Means of Psychotherapy

Karita Miraglia Hummer, A.C.S.W., C.S.W.

INTRODUCTION

The purpose of this paper is to demonstrate the significance of psychotherapy for a latency child who possesses the structural prerequisites for mourning. We selected an individual who could demonstrate the ability to engage in a mental process that reflected an internal adaptation to loss, an awareness of the significance of the loss, with a relative ability to withstand the concomitant pain, and who could articulate and observe the vicissitudes of his experience. The experience included shock, grief reactions, some measure of decathexis, and changes in identificatory processes, all of

The author is indebted to Dr. Sol Altschul and his helpful comments in reviewing this chapter and to Dr. Benjamin Garber for his very thoughtful discussion of this case in an earlier presentation on January 19, 1978.

which are among the steps of mourning, a "complex internal reorganization of cathexes" (Altschul, 1968). In treatment, the child's material reflects the ebb and flow of the mourning process, its forward momentum, and the defenses and resistances in opposition to that momentum.

CRITERIA FOR MOURNING

The criteria for mourning include ego maturity and strength, the achievement of object constancy, and the sufficient internalization of narcissistic supplies. Ego maturity includes good reality testing, basic acceptance of the reality principle and impulse controls, ability for verbalization and identification of affects, the presence of stable and differentiated self and object relationships, adequate memory, perception, and understanding of time concepts, capacity for integration of the experience, the ability to distinguish between living and nonliving, and the achievement of causal thinking (A. Freud, 1960; R. Furman, 1964). The term *object constancy* includes perceptual object constancy, the capacity to maintain drive investment in an absent or frustrating object, the capacity to recognize and tolerate loving and hostile feelings toward the same object, to keep feeling centered on a specific object, and the capacity to value an object beyond its need-meeting qualities (Burgner and Edgecombe, 1972).

INTERFERENCES IN MOURNING FOR A CHILD

Though a child may have all the prerequisites for mourning, the impact of the loss of a parent by death sorely tests these capacities. The more recently acquired the structural capacity, the more vulnerable it is to the impact of trauma. Regression, even though temporary, is likely to occur in most children. Ego vulnerabilities or weaknesses, regressions in object relationships, and narcissistic imbalance may require periods of strengthening through supportive psychotherapeutic efforts before a child may truly be able to undertake a mourning process. The work of mourning is difficult and even the strongest of children perceive it to be fraught with danger, so that even though a child may have a very advanced psychological structure, the process may not be activated without external mobilizing efforts.

Once underway, interferences in a child's mourning process do occur. Premorbid personality structure and conflicts can be at work. The need for the missing parent in order that development may unfold makes decathexis particularly difficult. This developmental need for the object may result in a variety of defenses against the loss such as displacement, substitution, denial of the significance of the loss, or incorporative and pathological identificatory modes. The affective grief components of sadness, longing, frustration, psychic pain, and anger frequently overwhelm the ego integrity of the child, become traumatically frightening experiences in themselves, and require modulating and/or defensive mechanisms for containment, further compromising the work of mourning. The temporary or prolonged loss of, or changes in the surviving parent's functioning can be an overload that further interferes with the mobilization or continuation of mourning in a child.

THE VALUE OF PSYCHOTHERAPY

Child psychotherapy enables and helps a child sustain mourning in a variety of ways. Through supportive measures, consistency, reliability, soothing, and assurance, it can strengthen ego capabilities, stabilize the level of object relationship, and assist in internalization of soothing and tension regulation necessary for narcissistic equilibrium. Where there is some externalization of the latter (i.e., a regression in self-regulation and equilibrium), a therapist may provide restorative functions, though ideally not as a replacement for the lost parental object, and, we may hope, only to the extent necessitated by the temporary diminution in the surviving parent's functioning. Needless to say, the proper attention to a child's feeling of comfort and reassurance must always be maintained in child psychotherapy as a general context for psychotherapeutic interventions.

In addition to supportive elements, insight oriented psychotherapy assists the momentum of mourning. It gives focus and encourages the initiation and unfolding of the mourning process through interpretive interventions that interfere with the resistances and pathological defenses, and ideally prevent the formation of new maladaptive mechanisms. The child's experience, observation, and understanding of the mourning process is especially heightened by interpretations of transference manifestations. Through such handling of transference manifestations, ego mastery of future experiences related to the loss (such as anniversaries) become more likely. The transference affords an access to the child that would be unlikely to be achieved in any other manner, thus establishing a level of ego integration that probably would not occur under most other circumstances.

CASE EXAMPLE

The case selected for illustration is of a child who had the basic ego maturity, level of object relationships, and internalization of self-regulating mechanisms that provided him with the structural capacity for mourning. However, because of some regressions in these sectors, which even preceded the death, due to the strain of the parental illness, the actual experience of the loss, and the traumatizing effects of his own ongoing affects, treatment was undertaken to strengthen and mobilize his capacities to mourn, with the hope that a permanent developmental interference could be prevented.

The material presented is of a case, then, in support of the hypothesis that certain latency age children, with given maturities, are able to undertake, at least partially, the complex work of mourning. The material will cover a latency age child's reaction to the loss of his father, at the age of seven, and will follow the vicissitudes of these reactions as observed during the course of his psychotherapy. The material on the treatment course is also offered as typical of the way the Barr-Harris Center approaches the evaluation and treatment of those children who fit the criteria for insight oriented psychotherapy. The treatment process is discussed from the standpoint of the child's use of defenses as reflected in treatment, the nature of the transference as it emerged, and something of the resistances which occurred.

Johnny was seven years old when his father died. He was evaluated two months later. He was the oldest of three siblings, having two sisters, five and three years of age. The family was Catholic with deep working-class roots in an ethnic community. He was referred by the family's physician. During the evaluation, mother was in tremendous distress and was having a difficult time coping with her own grief as well as her children's. She expressed concern about Johnny's nightmares, his difficulty in getting to sleep, his fear that father would return to take him to heaven and his encopresis. A large extended family's support was experienced as engulfing.

Father died at the age of thirty-three after a prolonged illness due to a chronic kidney disease. The children were witness to much of his pain during the illness. When father was nearing death, Johnny had remarked that his father was "very young to die; he's only thirty-three years old." Thereafter, despite the imminence of father's death, he tried to ignore it and to go routinely about his business. However, after the death, he had a very difficult reaction, which persisted for many weeks following the death. He would cry and scream, "It's all a bad dream!" He would pound his pillow and be unable to sleep. Alternating with this, there would be no mention of the death at all. At the time of the evaluation, he was experiencing almost daily tantrums, crying, screaming, kicking, flailing about, saying that he wished to be in heaven with his father and crying out, "This has to be over with!" He began to lash out at mother, who had become afraid to openly share her own grief because of a fear of triggering an agitated reaction in him. He avoided family photographs of father, but did consent to listen to a tape of his father's voice which resulted in uncontrollable sobbing. A symptom of encopresis became exacerbated.

Johnny had begun to open his father's mail since father's death. Mother told him it was not his to open. He stated that everything of his father's in the house was now his; mother told him otherwise. While his siblings would tell their mother to get a new daddy, he would tell her, "We're not getting another daddy and I've decided you shouldn't marry." He said, "I am the dad of the house now, right?" Mother said, "No." "But I am the only man of the house now," he said, "right?" Mother would tell him, "You're the only little boy."

Father had managed to remain close to his children until the time of the actual death. He pushed himself to be active with the children and spent a great deal of time with all of them. For example, he extended himself to help Johnny learn and participate in various active sports and he would try to be everything for his son that he felt his own father had not been for him. He was firm with Johnny, expected very high performance, and was quite demanding of him about these expectations. During his illness, he made tapes for his son to be played at a later time.

In the diagnostic interviews, Johnny presented himself as very much in command of the situation and initiated discussion energetically and actively. Initially, he was unable to talk about his father and made no reference to him. However, when he inadvertently brought the subject up himself, he went on to talk increasingly about father, despite some occasional hesitance. As he continued, he spoke of an incident before father's death when he had gone home and discovered that the car was not in front of the house as usual, indicating the kind of ongoing trauma he experienced through his father's illness. He told of taking on some of father's functions; for example, opening the mail still being addressed to father by individuals who were unaware of dad's death. With some pride, he said he not only got his own mail, but he got father's too. As he talked about his father in these interviews, he became increasingly tired. He spoke of how the loss intruded on his thoughts. In reaction, he tried to say prayers at night to rid himself of thoughts of father's death.

His material shifted from present to near past to far past and back again. He told of the day of father's heart attack. He had gone to his sister's kindergarten room to go home with her, had discovered that she had not come at all, and then had run all the way home anticipating once again a new assault on father's health. His young sister greeted him with news of father's collapse. As he pondered what it meant to him not to have father with him, he gave some poignant examples. He described how he had been very good in some sports such as ice skating the year before and how he had done pretty well while his father watched. Now he did not do so well. He also conveyed how helpful his father had been in other ways, with directions, for example, indicating his need for his father's assistance. He shared a number of hypercathected memories of his father, such as the Fourth of July when the family had had a picnic the year before and the "Christmas of '79." These all had a kind of idealized ring to them. In the initial interview, Johnny gave the impression of a child who was very anxious, controlled, bright, perceptive, resourceful, with considerable depth, richness, and maturity, and very likable.

In the second diagnostic interview, he again seemed

somewhat anxious, fidgeted, and had certain nervous mannerisms. He also seemed very serious and came to look even more tired and sad. Getting sadder, he told more details about the episode surrounding his father's heart attack which were moving and saddening to hear. He went on to tell of inheriting his father's treasures, his watch and after-shave lotion. He said all of his father's possessions were now his and he reiterated his claim to father's mail. He also told of assuming father's former chores.

Johnny was in great pain over the loss of his father and was engulfed by grief and memories of him. Father's illness had resulted in a developmental interference for Johnny several years preceding the death. The episodic encopresis of the last two years was a manifestation of that interference. This appeared to be a critical time for Johnny and it was felt that we needed to determine whether he had the resources to overcome the experience, even though he seemed well endowed. He was a child with considerable psychic structure with evidence of superego development, ego ideal formation, and high-level defenses of intellectualization, isolation, and avoidance. A tendency toward regression seemed to be the most serious problem, despite the seeming attempt to be so grown-up.

When the case was reviewed by the Case Review Committee at Barr-Harris, it was felt that Johnny was demonstrating a clear entry into a mourning process in which he had moved from an initial stage of denial to identification, albeit a very massive one. It was doubtful that the boy would continue to traverse the steps of mourning without help. It was pointed out that the boy saw himself as the incarnation of father, an incorporating mode which appeared to be in danger of becoming predominant. He had taken over in fantasy father's functions and roles, which loomed as a tremendous internal burden for him at his young age of seven years. It was from this vantage point that the recommendation for psychotherapy was made. It was determined that the treatment goals of working with him were: (1) to prevent further developmental interference and to overcome the regression which had already occurred as a result of cumulative trauma, the last being the death itself; (2) to facilitate the mourning process and to work with the massive identification, so that it would not be so global, freeing him of some of the burden of having to be so grown-up; and (3) to help him develop and internalize more adaptive processes.

The process of the treatment will demonstrate this child's reaction to the death of his father, the nature of the transference relationship that evolved, and the usefulness of the psychotherapy, including the handling of transference in mobilizing the mourning process and helping him sustain it.

Treatment was initiated approximately two-and-a-half months after the completion of the evaluation, four months following the death, and continued for ten months in twice-a-week sessions. In his first treatment session, he appeared very depressed, very tired, with a slightly angry and still more anxious edge to him. His face was contorted and he appeared on the edge of tears much of the time. With the introduction of the contract for treatment, he was most uncomfortable but denied his discomfort. He reflected that there had been a lot of changes around his house. He followed with contradictory statements to the effect that there had been no changes around the house, that nothing had changed in the house since father left, and, indeed, he did not miss him. In response to the therapist's comment about his looking sad and after having told him that kids sometimes push sad feelings away because they are so painful, he talked of knowing a boy like that in his school. He could tell that his friend was sad, even though his friend would deny it. However, he pointedly remarked that he himself refrains from telling his friend that he thinks he is sad, giving the therapist a cue that she should follow that course.

Soon after treatment had begun, he talked about a "projector" in his head that in some ways would replace his mind. This projector would go off whenever there was a bad film showing and he had to replace it with a new projector altogether, signifying his attempt at denial or disavowal of the experience of the loss. He spoke metaphorically, too, of a fantasied tape recorder whereby he could control when to listen to old memories. When he talked of rejecting any bad material from the "reel" in his mind, the interpretation of the wish to avoid bad memories was easily made and acknowledged by him. Through the use of such metaphors, he attempted to control the therapist's interventions. He would go about ejecting the therapist's comments from his projector–tape–recorder–mind by mechanically answering, "Right, wrong," to various of the therapist's comments without further thought. These comments had the multiple purpose of resistance, dismissal, and avoidance of therapeutic interventions, while gaining control by an attempt to measure and test me through a mechanism of devaluation. Devaluation of the therapist quickly gave way in the next session to an improved rating, going from 3,000 wrong and only 30 right to 3,000 right to 200 wrong comments.

At one point, he spoke metaphorically again of an audiotape that had broken; he became quite concrete in the metaphor and spoke of the broken tape as a broken bone in the heel of his foot. He felt the tape needed to be replaced by a new tape now, and seemed to convey the confident expectation that a replacement would occur in treatment. It appeared that in the transference the therapist was being experienced as the need-satisfying object who would provide certain functions, who could heal his broken self and make him whole again, replacing the missing part-object pieces of himself. He appeared also to be describing the work that lay ahead in therapy with the expectation that the changes would be mental ones; that is, a new tape was necessary. However, he did not seem completely aware that the old tape in the form of mental representations would have to undergo some change first.

After approximately a month into treatment, he began initiating more material about father and for a while there was a tremendous focus of attention on father. He shared memories of father and longingly recalled particular events. Anniversaries such as an upcoming holiday like the Fourth of July would trigger these memories. He would comment that, while there would still be a picnic on that day, it would not be the same. That picnic had been a major occasion in which father had played a very special role as an announcer and Johnny was sure that no one could do the job like dad had. Eventually, he talked about memories of the funeral itself, commenting that the funeral had been close to his birthday; he was sure on his next birthday he would be thinking of the funeral. Using an isolation defense again, he talked again metaphorically about having a mental tape recording of the day of the funeral, which he had placed on the shelf. On the day of the funeral, he had recalled dad's promises to him. He expected that his mother would not keep father's former promises to him. For example, should he get all A's upon turning fifteen, he would get the choice of any new car he wished. If he got B's, he would get a used car; with C's, he was still to get a car, which was to have been father's selection, but presumably now would be mother's selection. Thus father was to be kept alive through the remaining parent.

A real sense of a therapeutic alliance emerged early in the treatment. He began to refer to the office as a story room where each session had a hundred pages. He developed a sense of the rhythm of the sessions; he could usually tell when it was close to the end of the time. He also shared that he had had a startled feeling one day when he had the sensation that he had missed one of the therapy sessions, reflecting both the growing attachment and the fear of loss of the relationship.

Though he would anticipate feelings of sadness about

future events of a kind that he had shared with father in the past, when these events actually occurred, he would try to deny their significance for him. For example, on Father's Day, he referred to it as having been "the greatest day of my life." He made a lot of references to that day without talking of any sadness and instead talked about all the great things he had done that day with other relatives. When the therapist suggested that maybe it had been somewhat of a hard day, too, he denied it with great exaggerated casualness. He claimed it had only been difficult for his mother, casually adding that he had liked carrying out some of father's responsibilities that day, such as carrying chairs to the patio. Still further he said, "Speaking of Dad, I saw these T-shirts with the words printed on them 'Superdad' and 'Superkid'." He said that had father been living, he would have given father this shirt and he would have had a Superkid shirt, thus permitting some of the sadness he was feeling to emerge. Following the Fourth of July, as with Father's Day, he came in saying it had been "the greatest day of my life," clearly a reversal of affect.

Increasingly, he began to show his feelings of attachment in the sessions. He would show concern about any separations in the course of the treatment relationship. For example, after missing a session, he came in and referred to how long the interval had seemed to be from his last session. Though it had not been the reason for the missed appointment, he spoke emphatically and in great detail of a minor physical injury that occurred in that interval. He had felt as if he might almost have required hospitalization, though this certainly was an exaggeration. It appeared that the brief loss in the transference resulted in feelings of abandonment, depletion, and hurt that stirred reunion needs. As the therapist's vacation neared, he made more references to it. He associated not only to her going away, but to others going away and his having had a year of bad luck. He thought this bad luck had been caused by opening an umbrella, denying that he thought it had any connection to father's death. This was typical of his disavowal. He expressed some concern about whether he would be able to find his way down to the office after the therapist's vacation and acknowledged her reflection of his concern about being able to find her. At the same time, he expressed some ambivalence, saying he was glad he would miss some parts of it, such as the traffic jam, and so on. In the session just preceding the vacation, he wished he had brought a camera so that he might take a picture of the room and the therapist. He was then able to acknowledge that he would miss coming, recalling a poem he had read once in school with the words *I love you* in it. Upon the therapist's return, he talked of having seen a raft in a swimming pool and that it had made him think of her while she was away, an obvious transference depiction of her functional role in keeping him afloat.

As the treatment continued, there was focus on a number of issues, one of which was his uneven maturity and the conflict he felt about wanting to be grown-up. For example, in the sessions he would not deign to play and was highly intellectualized, but for a period would routinely wet his pants. The therapist introduced that in the therapy he and she could help him build a middle part which was what he actually was, a seven-and-a-half-year-old boy. Nevertheless, he found his pseudomature defenses difficult to relinquish. He referred to the whole last year as a disaster in which his mailbox only brought "bills, bills, bills" and no fun mail. The demand upon himself to be more grown-up thus continued, while the underlying regression persisted.

As new anniversary events came up in which he had participated with father, he would become very active, very excited, and very anxious. With respect to a block party, he kept speculating on what could go wrong at the block party and seemed to expect to be disappointed. At the same time in his obsessional attempt to control, he was trying to avoid the disappointment. After that party, he did not use the typical reversal of affect and did say that he had had a double-deep disappointment; there had been no popcorn machine that he had hoped he could work on and no disc jockey had come to the block party. He could then associate directly to sad feelings he was having about father, became increasingly aware of how much he was missing him, and was increasingly in touch with his grief in general. He asked, "When does the sad feeling go away?"

Whenever an announcement was made about the therapist being away, he became increasingly persistent that she should not go away and once demanded, "You are *not* going away!" As he looked back on the year as the anniversary of father's death approached, he commented on what a "great drag" the year had been for him and how he was looking forward to becoming eight years old, so he could get this "seven" off his back. He could also talk about looking forward to being eight as a new time. Adaptive movement and magical defenses appeared to be at play simultaneously. He was given confirmation and understanding for the heavy load that he had been carrying, but he and the therapist also reflected on his hope. He initially tried to give superstitious explanations for why the year had been so bad; in response to the therapist's comments that they did have some explanations, he acknowledged, albeit casually, "Oh, you mean Dad died this past year, right?" He himself went on then with associations about having a bumper sticker on the car that read, "Help Cure Kidney Disease," and how he tried to protect this when he was washing the car.

As treatment went on, his anxiety about separations persisted. He associated on one occasion to some "nervousness" that he had felt when mother had not shown up at the expected time at school to pick up his sister. He had become alarmed that perhaps she was sick or perhaps had had an accident driving. This ridicule of mother's driving was multidetermined, relating to his exaggerated and idiosyncratic identification with an adult male role in which it is typical to devalue female competences, and in some measure was an accurate perception of his mother's difficulty/inadequacies as a reliable, protective figure. To control his anxiety, he demonstrated his ridicule with mock driving.

Later, he told a story in therapy about a boy climbing a mountain. He had said that his therapy was like a mountain. In his story, he told of a little boy who might be climbing up a mountain, who has a rock in his pocket and the rock is like the therapy. If the boy should drop the rock, which would be a very bad thing, he would need some other means to secure himself. He would need a lasso. He talked of some danger of the boy slipping down the hill. He further talked of his father and the therapist as like the rock, but was not sure mother was like the rock. He was able to acknowledge some doubts about mother's ability to look after them. The therapist thought there were some transference implications as she connected it to Johnny's worries about her reliability and her coming back, too. He spoke of how the boy should take the rock and place it high on a mountain so no one could steal it. The therapist reflected how precious all this was to him. Once, in a session, he referred metaphorically to his therapy as a train and said, "Eventually there will be a caboose." He looked very sad at that time. He referred to marking his calendars with the days that he "sees Mrs. Hummer," and marked the days that he did not come for sessions with an E, standing for empty. He referred to the days he missed as like a malfunction in a car. He likened starting again after a break to the difficulty of starting up a car that had broken down. He assured the therapist, however, that his tapes of all his sessions, along the line of the metaphor discussed above, were all preserved. This was both a sign of an isolation defense, whereby he kept the therapy quite separate from his everyday experience, and the need still to attempt magically to preserve missing objects, which was similar to the defenses he used with his real and metaphorical tapes of father. His increasing metaphorical depictions of the importance of his therapy reflected the intense transference relationship he had developed.

When the family planned to move, Johnny was quite enthusiastic following a very brief show of reluctance and anger. He turned to an anticipation of good things to come and negated any unpleasantness about it. It remained a question through this time as to whether or not, in his enthusiasm for moving to a new home, he was attempting to avoid the old, thereby denying current feelings. Much of this time, both elements, movement forward and avoidance, appeared to be occurring simultaneously or alternately. Using his metaphor of ejecting tapes he did not like, an interpretation was made that he might be attempting to "eject" the old for the new instead of possibly having both memories and new experiences.

As the time for the anniversary of father's death neared, he began to dread the day and said it was like "being afraid of a ghost." He associated to his upcoming birthday so close to the day of the anniversary. Around that time, too, he advised the therapist if she ever had a relative who died, that she should allow herself to cry. He was very close to tears himself. Nevertheless, as the time drew still closer to the anniversary, he avoided the topic altogether and could only focus on the happy anticipation of his birthday just preceding it; but he also shared many happy memories of father around that time. Ultimately, on the day of the anniversary of father's death, the therapist did mention it and he replied, "I did know it and didn't know it." He said that he tried to pretend that dad was alive and put someone else in dad's place. Further, he spoke about leaving his metaphorical tape about father on the shelf, but that he might play it again when the time was right, meaning the right session. Again, he was using this symbolic device to distance himself from the mourning.

Shortly after the family actually moved into their new home, it became necessary for mother to give their dog away because the dog was so destructive in the new environment. Johnny had been very attached to this dog, but attempted to be very casual about it. With attempted casualness, he said, "Oh, she's gone. That happened a couple of days ago," as if it were all finished. When the therapist called his attention to "ejecting" the experience or "erasing" it, he professed confusion, but then acknowledged it. When it had been suggested that feelings did not just evaporate, he said he knew this and he knew that feelings had a beginning, a middle, and an end. When the therapist agreed and said that she thought they had not come to that point with respect to his dog, he wondered very poignantly if she thought they had arrived at that point with dad yet. Later, Johnny was able to wisely suggest some help for himself in another metaphor. He told of a song from school that he liked, a song about valleys and mountains, of wise men who had to cross these valleys and mountains, of good times and bad times, in quest of a star, concluding himself that there was time for the wise men to find the star. These comments reflected a remarkable capacity for observing and comprehending the unfolding of a mourning process: the flow between the psychic pain of loss and yearning and the hope for renewed ventures and new relationships.

While Johnny was seen in treatment, his mother was also seen for supportive counseling and parental guidance as well. She made less use of the treatment than did her son and had less capacity to mourn than he did. She seemed to have less tolerance for pain and was more impatient than he. As she began to distance herself from the work of her own mourning and, indeed, interrupted it so that it began to be a pathological process for her, she began to be less tolerant of Johnny's continued feelings of loss and to be unreliable in supporting Johnny's treatment. Ultimately she interrupted his treatment without allowing time for a termination.

Under the best of circumstances, a parent's capacity for optimal parenting around a child's general needs, and needs regarding the loss, is often undermined by their own mourning process due to absorption in the task of their own mourning, their own defenses around the mourning, their demanding reality life changes and burdens, the potential regressive impact of the trauma, the need for a partner to assist in carrying out parental functions, and the different timetables with respect to mourning. These factors frequently can interfere with a parent's consistent and effective handling of their children's needs in general, for empathy, soothing, stimulus buffering, integrative, and synthetic functions, and specifically for assistance with and reassurance around the grief, for reality testing, and for parental mediation of the trauma.

Further, should a parent become engaged in a prolonged or pathological mourning of his own and/or is unable to tolerate his own mourning and distance himself from it, the capacities of a parent are still further undermined and the needs of the child are less tended to. Such parent's depression, refusal to accept the reality of the death, inadequate defenses, increased irritability, heightened traumatic state, make them still less available to their children for dealing with ongoing needs and their children's feelings of loss and grief. The child is alone in having to integrate and synthesize the experience and, in addition, is confronted by a pathological model for mourning. With respect to general needs, the child feels uncertain and anxious about being adequately cared for; and with respect to the loss, their inappropriate defenses are supported, condoned, or ignored. Such was the situation with Johnny.

In returning to Johnny's treatment, as it drew close to the time when mother would abruptly interrupt it, increased material about trust began to emerge. He began to say that he felt certain he could not trust anyone and that the therapist would have to prove to him that he could trust her. In retrospect, it appeared that he had begun to predict the interruption. Increasingly he used stuffed animals for comfort. He said he could trust his stuffed animals, "They don't drink, they don't drive, and they don't smoke" (as his mother did), and apparently were in no danger. Ultimately, he said about himself that the only one he really could trust was "Me, myself, and I."

While this last material suggested a narcissistic retreat, a defense against the quite possibly anticipated loss of the transference object, the potential for self-replenishment was there. His material always reflected a child of depth and richness with many inner resources. There were, indeed, then, resources that he could trust to overcome another dreaded loss such as that of his therapist. The treatment offered him an experience and a model for using his resources toward the reestablishment of the momentum for development. This is a positive note regarding his treatment and premature termination. Admittedly, this is a hopeful conjecture, because the possibility of the untimely termination contributing further to the cumulative effects of trauma with potential for developmental interference must also be considered. Nevertheless, this child afforded the therapist the opportunity to observe closely the unfolding of a clear mourning process in the content of psychotherapy, despite this process not continuing to completion.

SUMMARY

Johnny is an illustration of a case which had the basic prerequisites for mourning. However, regression, under the impact of multiple traumas, parental deficiencies in the surviving parent, defensive measures of ego splitting and isolation, occasional denial of the significance of the loss, and nearly pathological identification with father, required considerable ego strengthening for him to feel safe enough to approach the work of mourning. This was accomplished through supportive, narcissistically enhancing, and preparatory therapeutic interventions. Systematic and timely interpretations of defense and resistances moved the treatment to a level in which it became possible to work with transference manifestations. At this point, he was capable of considerable toleration of pain and was able to make direct expressions of loss, need, and longing for his father and for the therapist. An ongoing internal process of working through specifically highly cathected memories was occurring. Though he would resort to his isolation defense, he became increasingly aware of his own potential for the defense, observed it, and described it.

He came to perceive that he was engaged in a process, both in his treatment and in his mourning, that there was a beginning, middle, and end. A genuine caboose would come along. The need would not be so great. He could see that a process, the mourning and the treatment, would end. Though he was not yet ready to end either, he could envision such a day with some equanimity and even hope. Such reference to certain endings to come clearly showed movement from the extreme phase of hypercathexis to at least a contemplation of a time of decathexis, with a measure of some reorganization taking place. Affectively, he was clearly less depressed, with considerable demonstration of new, restored levels of energy. He became more childlike, less omnipotent, and perhaps less wholly identified with adult roles. His own observations of the dual process of mourning and its reexperience in the transference demonstrated a considerable level of ego integration of the traumatic experience of the loss.

It was most unfortunate that this case was not followed through to completion. The premature termination prevented further ego integration and mastery of the loss for the child. It is hoped that the direction was set strongly enough so that he could undertake the remainder of the mourning work himself. However, we have no final answer as to the outcome of the process.

We are, however, enormously enriched by this case. It demonstrates the value of psychotherapy in mobilizing a mourning process for a child who had achieved prerequisite maturities, but who was also experiencing a pathological regression (see chapter 9).

This case raises an important question about childhood parent loss and psychotherapy. Do most children who have high levels of structural development still experience regressions and defenses that almost universally require interventions such as psychotherapy to mobilize their mourning potential? Would they achieve restoration sufficiently on their own to eventually undertake mourning themselves perhaps with the assistance of an empathic parent? Even if this were to happen, would the results be as complete, or would as full an understanding be reached as it is in the more systematic work of psychotherapy? In any event, what are the differences and the long-term results? Should therapy be generally offered on a preventive basis? These will be questions for the Barr-Harris Center to explore further through continued research.

Chapter 9

Termination and Endings

Karita Miraglia Hummer, A.C.S.W., C.S.W.

INTRODUCTION

The termination phase in psychotherapy has almost always been seen as a time for reworking the significant issues and conflicts pursued during the course of a treatment whereby greater mastery and resolution are achieved. It is a time for consolidating gains and strengthening the internalization of therapeutic functions of the psychotherapist. Interpretations are reworked, resistances can be reduced, and self-observing skills gain ascendancy. In psychotherapy with bereaved individuals, termination especially affords the patient an opportunity to further master the experience of loss and mourning. Termination should assist in effecting a resolution and acceptance of the loss in reality.

From the author's experience with cases of children with parent loss due to death, this ideal of a genuine termination has been difficult to obtain with any degree of regularity or uniformity. This difficulty may be a measure of the large task confronting a child in undertaking the work of mourning, or

187

may be a measure of the frequently adverse external circumstances in which the child undertakes such a process, including the weakened capacity of the surviving bereaved parent. Resistances and interferences, well beyond the ordinary resistances encountered in child psychotherapy, and abrupt endings, were more frequent, despite long and significant therapeutic experiences.

THE RANGE OF TREATMENT TECHNIQUES, USEFUL MODELS

The treatments undertaken at Barr-Harris have always had a link to the experience of death. Therefore, it has not been a completely open-ended treatment; objectives related to the promotion of healthy adaptations to parental loss, such as promoting healthy identifications, acceptance of reality, cathexes of new objects, and ego integration and synthesis. In a sense, the type of treatment was a type of sector analysis, though to be sure, the effects of loss had profound potential for influencing a number of personality dimensions. Treatment techniques were guided by the principle of doing only as much as is necessary to promote and restore a forward thrust in development with respect to phases or general modes of functioning (Gedo and Goldberg, 1973). Such an approach is guided by the kind of principle of limitation suggested by Winnicott, "in [psychoanalysis] one tries to get the chance to do as much as possible . . . in [child psychotherapy] one asks, how little need one do?" (Winnicott, 1965, p. 213).

Nevertheless, however limited the objectives and scope of treatment might have been, an attempt was made to utilize techniques that were specific to the patients' capacity to use them, in line with their stage of development.

Using Gedo's and Goldberg's terminology, techniques may range from pacification, unification, optimal disillusion, to interpretation. Shifts in the use of such techniques were in accord with modal and phasic regressions and progressions (Gedo and Goldberg, 1973).

The therapeutic repertoire of Gedo and Goldberg corresponds will with treatment techniques as recommended in *Normality and Pathology in Childhood* by Anna Freud (1965) for a variety of childhood pathologies which can be applied to pathological conditions in bereavement as well. Miss Freud discussed the "widening of consciousness," interpretation of transference and resistance, verbalization, clarifications, "auxiliary ego" techniques, suggestion, corrective emotional experience, and reassurances, as the variety of techniques available to a therapist, each of which may be used as the primary technique or in combination with others, according to diagnosis (A. Freud, 1965, pp. 227–235).

More recently, the Blancks, in *Ego Psychology II* have proposed that all therapeutic techniques be subsumed under the general conceptualization that the primary and basic functional role of the therapist is that of a catalyst for reorganization; as such, the therapist employs techniques which are dictated by a patient's developmental organization and which will promote growth. Some of their suggestions of ego building techniques such as affect differentiation, assisting the patient to develop self-soothing mechanisms, and attention to patient "replications of experience in the dyad . . . for purposes of retention of the object" are among their useful techniques that have application to the psychotherapy of children experiencing parent loss (Blanck and Blanck, 1979, pp. 210–255).

TERMINATION READINESS

The achievement of treatment objectives should provide a readiness signal for undertaking the termination phase.

In his seminal book on *Latency* (1976), Sarnoff suggests

some very practical guidelines, or requirements, as he calls them, for establishing readiness for termination. His requirements include the resolution of the presenting problem; success in social and academic developmental tasks and activities, generally commensurate with levels achieved by peers; the establishment of age-appropriate defenses (such as reduced "access of fantasy to motor activity"), to the extent possible; the greater development of the child's understanding and awareness of causes for his reactions, and use of such understanding to aid in problem solving; the selection of friends that reflect his emotional growth; the attainment of a developmental momentum that can be maintained by the child through natural processes of growth (Sarnoff, 1976, pp. 250–251).

In addition, in childhood bereavement cases, we would look for the achievement of such objectives as the following:

1. The restoration of equilibrium and management of stimuli;
2. A diminution of pain, and perhaps enhanced capacity to tolerate some increments of pain;
3. A restoration of ego functions lost through regression;
4. Interference in the compulsion to repeat traumatic experiences;
5. Ascendancy of reality principle functioning (i.e., some ability to accept the death); and
6. Reduced feelings of vulnerability to the self.

Objectives then must not be so idealized or so fixed as to be out of tune with the principle of epigenesis, which allows for maturation of functions and structures, while carrying the seed of earlier modes of functioning, which, while modified, persist in some fashion. Samuel Weiss referred to the model of the helix, whereby earlier issues get reworked at increasingly higher levels of progressive development, but worked over, and reworked they are (Weiss, 1979). With such considerations, there can be no such thing as fixed endpoints at the conclusion of a treatment.

In the practice of psychoanalytically oriented child psychotherapy, one seeks to have termination, determined by the discernible shifts in the intrapsychic life of the child. As Sarnoff indicates, the progress and shifts within the child's inner world constitute the reality by which the therapist, parents, and child should recognize readiness for termination. Ideally, such evaluation and planning should coincide with the child's recognition and acknowledgment of the dictates of this reality; that is, the progress or lack thereof. For example, Sarnoff recommends for a period preceding a termination date, that a child become actively engaged in a process of self-evaluation and examination with the therapist, to determine readiness for termination. The therapeutic alliance should enable such planning, but resistances may complicate smooth acceptance of establishment of a proper timing for termination. Sarnoff's guidelines offer the child psychotherapist an ideal for therapeutic endeavor. His suggestions are the more noteworthy because of the dearth of technical literature on termination, and, most particularly, in the area of child psychotherapy.

Beyond the confinements on the side of the patient with respect to the achievement of ideal objectives for establishing termination readiness, timing of termination is further modified by the multiple external variables, such as parental support or lack thereof, and other environmental considerations, including those introduced by the therapist.

What requires greater understanding, explanation, and possible suggestions for remedy, are the factors that impede the movement of therapy to a point of termination readiness and to an ideal termination as described above for child psychotherapy patients of parent loss due to death. There will be an attempt to discuss and explain some of the factors of premature, interrupted, and incomplete psychotherapies.

As suggested above, the termination phase affords any child patient a very intense period by which therapeutic gains can be reworked, maximized, and solidified. For the child of parent loss, by virtue of the intrinsic separation issues, as repeated in the transference, termination provides the additional value of an unparalleled opportunity for resolving and completing the work of mourning. It is important, then, to examine child psychotherapy, parent loss cases to understand dynamics and to compare those which approached the ideal of complete psychotherapy and those that did not. Through such examination, it is hoped that issues of termination with such children will be better clarified, and will assist other clinicians in the following ways: to be better able to consider ways of potentiating therapeutic gains for such children when it is necessary to plan for premature interruptions; to know better when termination is genuinely indicated and to suggest some possible techniques for conducting termination. This aim is admittedly ambitious and such goals will only be partially achieved in this discussion. It is further hoped that the clinical examination of some of the Barr-Harris cases as pertain to issues of termination, will in some small measure suggest some answers to the theoretical questions raised by our group: can children mourn? Are there incremental levels to such mourning capacities? When children do not or cannot mourn, what are some of the adaptations they do make? Can therapy with children mobilize mourning capacities, reduce trauma, and restore equilibrium, and how is this effected (see chapters 8, 10, 11)?

SUGGESTED TERMINATION CLASSIFICATIONS

Fifty-eight children were seen for evaluation by the author at the Barr-Harris Center. Of these cases, sixteen children were seen in treatment; eight children were seen in extended individual psychotherapy; and one child, a two-year-old, was seen in psychotherapy in the context of his family; namely, in the presence of mother and younger sister. Seven were seen for limited, brief interventions in family therapy. (A number of the remaining forty-two children also established therapeuticlike relationships as their longitudinal periodic evaluations unfolded, providing further insights into the capacity for utilization of a therapeutic figure.) A suggested classification for treatment is as follows:

1. Those cases that could be viewed as approaching the ideal for terminated cases: where therapeutic objectives were met in the context of a psychotherapy that included a genuine termination phase, set in motion by a genuine recognition on the part of parents, child-patient, and therapist that objectives had been met and that changes were persistent. Only one case met these criteria to any measurable degree.

2. Those cases where termination was initiated by patient or therapist due to external factors, but where, nonetheless, significant therapeutic gains had been achieved: these were at least partially recognized by all participants, a termination phase was initiated and completed, with adequate time for preparation and mastery, and, where in good measure, the imposed termination affords an opportunity for corrective emotional experience. Three child psychotherapy patients met these criteria. Seven other children from two families in brief and/or more limited family therapy interventions met these criteria in some measure.

3. Situations of premature termination, initiated by the patient, where there was insufficient readiness for termination: significant changes were minimal, and there was inadequate preparation for termination, despite some announcement on the part of patient and/or family to end treatment; where there was some, if brief, measure of work about it, but where the

overall quality was one of departure, rather than completion, and/or resolution. Two children met these criteria. In addition, one parent seen for her own treatment ended therapy in such a manner.

4. A cases where there were unanticipated and unannounced endings, where there was no preparation for the patient, not even a completion interview, where the endings were abrupt and untimely, despite the presence of significant therapeutic gains and rather strong transference relationships of some duration. The only feelings left to process were those of countertransference feelings of shock for the therapist. There were three such cases, all of which were very involved, with treatment ranging from eight months to just short of nineteen months.

APPROACHING THE IDEAL, WHERE OBJECTIVES HAVE BEEN MET AND THERE HAS BEEN A TERMINATION PHASE

Case Example 1

The single case that approached the ideal was that of Matthew, the youngest of five boys, who was seen at the age of eleven-and-a-half years following the sudden death of his stepfather of some years. Several years earlier, when the child was in his early latency years, he had sustained the loss of his natural father after a long terminal illness. Matthew, who attended a private parochial school was referred by the pastor of the family's church. The child had become quite invested in his stepfather and spoke of him as the primary paternal object in his life, referring to stepfather as his own father with little qualification. There was, nonetheless, some forced quality about the relationship, even some superficiality, and there was some sense that stepfather had satisfied narcissistic needs for Matthew not to be different, to have a father and an intact family.

Matthew was reported as being quite uneven; mature in the use of language and ability to reason, and concerned (or overconcerned) with family finances, but quite immature in other respects such as in his food indulgence, school, and work habits. To mother, his initial displays of grief appeared as precocious imitations of adult behavior, as compliances with what he considered to be expected responses, but did not reflect his own genuine feelings. Mother was also annoyed by his attempts to become her caretaker.

From the first diagnostic interview, he engaged fully in the treatment. He appeared to have come with an expectation of continuing, which, despite some element of compliance, seemed quite genuine. He obtained a measure of relief and restored comfort after an initial outpouring of grief.

From the diagnostic assessment, he was seen as a child in deep psychic pain, who appeared very vulnerable, but who was defending mightily with pseudomature defenses, such as intellectualizations, rationalization, isolation, and obsessional controlling mechanisms. He talked a blue streak. Identificatory processes were global, and he felt endangered and victimized. The experience around the earlier death appeared repressed, but it seemed likely that some of his grief response in the current situation was a displacement from the earlier loss. Tension regulation was inadequate. From his oversolicitousness toward mother, attempts to control her schedule away from home, and the dread he felt about a sibling's departure for college, separation anxiety, and regression were apparent in an otherwise neurotic personality organization. Neurotic personality organization was suggested by obsessional thought, a range of neurotic defenses, most particularly isolation and intellectualization and a triadic level of object relationships, which, while established, had not moved beyond familial triadic investment. Within the construct suggested by Gedo and Goldberg (1973), he was at a phase that included superego formation and a repression barrier (Phase IV), but under the trauma would regress to modes more reflective of separation anxiety, infantile narcissism, and a defense of disavowal.

The Barr-Harris Committee in reviewing this child's material agreed that the earlier death, in contrast to the latest death, was of greater consequence in the presenting symptomatology and pathology. The Committee viewed therapy as preparatory to psychoanalysis and this information was communicated to mother. The psychotherapy would continue at the discretion of the patient, but be allowed and even enabled to end if he desired. Immediate treatment goals were to help him restore equilibrium, to integrate the most recent trauma, and to help him restore the level of functioning he had achieved prior to the second loss. There was a general goal to foster more acknowledgment of and access to genuine feeling.

Early in his treatment, he was so obsessional that he came to worry about worrying; it was around the discomfort his obsessional worry caused him that he genuinely entered into a treatment contract. Nevertheless, he felt some shame about requiring treatment and, while he became reconciled to treatment, he did so with feelings of martyrdom and narcissistic injury about being an exceptional child who had problems. Once initiated, he engaged actively in the treatment, capable both of observing the process and fully experiencing it. As some narcissistic discomfort about treatment persisted, he defended through idealization of the therapist, reaction formations, and active maintenance of positive feelings in the transference. It was throughout an essentially genuine positive transference, however.

Using Gedo's and Goldberg's framework, techniques included: (1) some pacification; (2) unification through the silent establishment of an increasingly significant therapeutic relationship; (3) some measure of optimal disillusion; and (4) interpretation of defense (most notably around anger). The first two techniques were consistently successful, while the latter two techniques had more variable success. All of these were primarily directed to achieving greater integration with respect to loss and issues of vulnerability. The neurotic structure was essentially unexplored.

The notable achievement was his greater integration of the significance of the two deaths, its multiple impact, with his regaining and permitting memory of earlier experiences with his first father. His recall of the actual traumatic events of the first death, with genuine expression of sad affect was further evidence of some of the integration that was achieved. His guilt in replacing his first father was not interpreted.

Another achievement which suggested some restored momentum for growth and development, particularly along the lines of separation–individuation, was his ability to overcome his anxiety and take public transportation to his therapy sessions on his own. Altogether, he showed a deepened awareness of himself, while he became less serious and more capable of enjoying himself. His affective expression was more genuine and there was less use of isolation techniques. Tension and anguish were reduced, as he was no longer flooded by painful and uncomfortable affects, and instead had more appropriate expression. He appeared less worried, less adultlike, and more capable of differentiation from others, notably from his mother. These gains appeared to be internalized in some measure.

In one interview that, indeed, was a signal for termination, he delivered the following material in a most genuine manner. He said that he had his own moods now and was no longer unhappy when mother was unhappy. He said that, though he could appreciate someone else's feelings, the more so because of his experiences, he no longer had to share such feelings directly. He said that he no longer got overly concerned about his family. He thought that his past experiences were interfering less now with his being able to have a good time. He was not forcing himself not to worry; he just wasn't doing so. He thought all this was subconscious, that it was going on even when he wasn't in therapy, and it was happening with his hardly being aware of it. (One is reminded of Dr. Pollock's comment on termination: "The observing ego of the patient becomes sufficiently expanded and integrated for observation, interpretation and experiencing to occur autonomously and non-volitionally" [Pollock, 1961, p. 354]).

Matthew credited his gains as having come from his therapy and reflected on the therapist's comments about his having had the potential within himself for such gains. When he wondered if he would have gotten to this point anyway without therapy, he concluded, in an amazing release from his obsessional grip: "What difference does it make? What really matters is that I am doing better than before."

The subject of termination came up on two occasions. After having started a new school year and finding leaving school early for sessions to be somewhat embarrassing, his conclusions and even pretentions that he was ready for termination appeared to be rationalization, resistance, and a flight into health. Nonetheless, in accord with the initial qualifications in undertaking the treatment of this bereaved, but essentially neurotic child, his request was weighed over several weeks. In this context, when a young maternal uncle required sudden major surgery, Matthew was very glib and light about this and mother questioned terminating under such circumstances. His defenses were interpreted and he concurred with the recommendation then that he was not ready for termination under such internal and external circumstances. The setback was brief, and in the following two-and-a-half months he became increasingly genuine and produced the kind of material described above. Progressive shifts and changes became solidified and genuine. The therapeutic alliance became increasingly strong. The nature of his therapeutic bond was discussed, and he made a statement that he was glad that he had "waited it out."

Following such growth reflecting sessions, he announced again that he thought he was ready to end his therapy. He saved this discussion for a therapeutic session and made no prior mention to mother, as he had done in the first instance. The evaluation for termination, then, was altogether a therapeutic endeavor. He indicated that, while he wished to terminate, he preferred to consider it a break from therapy which could be reevaluated after several months to determine if his gains remained subconscious, as he put it; that is, remaining available as internalized gains. Clearly, his request was multidetermined, having some resistance, defensive, counterphobic, and ambivalent components to it, in part as a reaction to the intensity of the recent therapeutic sessions. Because the request was in accord with the treatment plan and followed significant gains, and because the therapist wished to confirm and recognize these gains and to support his strengths and positive components, his plan was accepted, pending discussion with mother. This request did induce anxiety in him and was accompanied by some regression and renewed use of pseudomature defenses. A termination date was set, and the nature of his therapeutic gains was discussed further. His own emphasis on these gains was, in part, a defensive reassurance to cope with separation anxiety. His thrust for autonomy, however, continued to be supported therapeutically, despite the expectable renewed anxiety. His plan to return for an evaluation was also quite multidetermined. Among possible reasons for his plan/wish were compliance with distorted expectations (e.g., possible fantasied expectations that mother and/or therapist did not wish him to be autonomous), his own ambivalence about letting go, and genuine therapeutic cooperation on a more conscious level, toward the therapeutic objective of staying well.

In his last full treatment interview, he was again more

genuine and comfortable. He spoke of a number of current painful realities in the family, big events that had hit that week: a family friend's cancer, an accident involving his mother's car, though she had not been in the car, and a proposed change for his stepfather's grave site. He was not traumatized by these events, nor defensive about them in his discussion. Indeed, he associated further to reconstructive memories of the first paternal loss. He recalled how shocked he had become when his natural father died. In the context of the therapist's suggesting he had grown through all his difficult experiences, there ensued some discussion about the definition of genuine maturity versus pretense. He used terms himself such as *maturity* and *illusion* to make such differentiation. Though such responses were somewhat compliant and intellectualized, there was self-observation and insight in this material as well. When his comments about the week's traumatic life events were dealt with as displacements of the transference experience of renewed loss due to termination, he quickly avoided the subject. When his defense was interpreted, he acknowledged his avoidance and shared that saying good-bye on this day was, indeed, "a very big thing." With genuinely sad affect, he said that he thought he and the therapist had come to know each other very well, that, indeed, the therapist had come to know him better than some of his relatives knew him. It seemed that he had come to acknowledge the significance of the relationship for himself, with less use of denial and ego splitting mechanisms. This appeared to be somewhat similar to the adult case described by Fleming and Altschul (1963) who, after initial resistance, had come to acknowledge the significance of transference relationships in psychoanalysis (see chapter 12).

Evidence of his having sustained a developmental thrust appeared in the follow-up evaluation several months after termination, though the overall neurotic character organization remained essentially intact. He had become definitely more actively engaged in autonomy struggles with mother, in the manner of an early adolescent. Some new defiance and testing of limits was exhausting for mother, but she was helped to see this as movement away from regressive modes and as typical, appropriate adolescent strivings for separation–individuation. What seemed clear in the follow-up evaluation was an overall attachment to excitement. He described his life as having been more exciting than that of his peers, as packed full. He thought he would always prefer a seventy-second minute in contrast to the fifty-second minute for which many of his friends settled. This boy experienced cumulative trauma with respect to repeated deaths of paternal figures (a grandfather and two fathers) and major illnesses of close individuals. He retained an attachment to trauma and stimulation that left him characterologically alert, excitable, and somewhat tense. However, anxiety and feelings of helplessness were reduced.

THERAPIST OR PATIENT INITIATED TERMINATION DUE TO EXTERNAL CONDITIONS THAT WERE NONETHELESS SUCCESSFUL, WHERE SIGNIFICANT GAINS HAD BEEN MADE, AN ADEQUATE TERMINATION PHASE WAS INITIATED AND COMPLETED, AND THERE WAS READINESS FOR TERMINATION OR TRANSFER

Case Example 2

Such a case was Katie. She was the only child of a couple of Quaker background who had met and married in the Peace Corps. Katie was seven-and-a-half years old when father died suddenly by choking during a light meal late at night. The child, who had been asleep, was awakened by the commotion of the ambulance and accompanied mother to the hospital. In the initial interview, a month following father's death, she would freeze whenever the topic of father's death and surrounding circumstances arose, or, initially, whenever any questions were addressed to her at all. She then would push herself to proceed. While for a very long time she could not speak of her father's death, she could speak in loving detail about him and of her experiences with him. Though she required some assistance, she could talk of her sadness and her wish that this "whole thing were nothing but a dream." She was in acute pain and her material was painful to hear. In addition to expressing grief about father, she also lamented all the changes in family plans that followed; for example, changes in Christmas plans, her bedroom would not be painted, and so on. This highlights the significance for children of not only the loss of a parent, but loss of continuity in the home environment.

This child was very verbal and never used play material. In all ways she appeared to have achieved a high level of psychic organization prior to the loss, appropriate to her age level. In Gedo and Goldberg's model, this was a child at a phase of high ego differentiation, superego development, with high level defenses, who was guided by reality principle considerations and ideals. At the time of her evaluation, she engaged quickly in and seemed needful of a therapeutic relationship. Because of her suffering and apparent wish to continue to receive such help, it was agreed to see her weekly on a preventive basis. She had an exceptional ability to tolerate and sustain the affects of grief and to maintain momentum and continuity in her psychotherapy. She developed a very positive transference and utilized the support of the therapeutic relationship to continue to face and work through the significance of the loss. Though she shared some feelings of loss with mother and showed sensitivity to mother, she had seemed to sense that, because of mother's defenses around the loss, she could not burden her mother with the depth of her own feelings of loss. She also seemed to wish to preserve a sense of privacy regarding her feelings about father in relationship to mother. This preserved her appropriately mature levels of separation–individuation and may have been related to oedipal rivalries with mother as well. Clearly, she had had a very special relationship with father, very distinct from her relationship with mother, in the context of an overall triadic level of object relationship.

Psychotherapy, then, was utilized by her in two ways: (1) to work through feelings of bereavement, and, therefore, not to excessively burden a deeply grieving mother who was perceived as not capable of managing the full onslaught of the child's feelings, and (2) to maintain the appropriate boundaries achieved with mother.

She was in psychotherapy for approximately a year. For at least a full half of that year, material focused on memories of father, sometimes appearing to be the bit by bit hyper-cathexis and decathexis of memories involved in the work of mourning, and sometimes appearing primarily to be a hypercathexis aimed at preserving father. Over and over again, she would report the fond memories of activities and experiences such as going to his law office in the Loop, meeting the partners in his firm, the special treats father would buy her, fantasies of where a gift may have been purchased, the games they played together, some mutual teasing and the flattery she had felt when he had asked her how she liked his newly grown mustache. At times, she clearly had felt quite stimulated by father. She vividly recalled a puppet stage father had planned to construct for her and the puppet characters they had planned to make for it. It was to have been a rainy day project, as she and father had called it, but it had never been completed. Despite her idealization of father, she came close to acknowledging that father had postponed their project and spoke of that unfulfilled promise.

Nevertheless, she mostly continued to see her father as nearly perfect and said so. The loss and grief were thus related to what had been, and of the promise of things to come. She shared a dream of going on a roller-coaster with father, then going to a restaurant with both Mom and Dad, being served a lobster that came alive, which was ultimately announced by the waiter in the dream as an April Fool's joke. Clearly, there was the wish to undo the loss and to make the dream a reality, a bad April Fool's Day joke.

Much of her early material related to happy memories, and the unfolding of this material was permitted. Eventually, her experience and pain of loss was more directly handled and confronted by the therapist, in an "optimal disillusion technique" manner. After really getting in touch with her sadness, she was able to recall with assistance the events of the traumatic circumstances of father's death. After this recall, though she had many continued associations to father, they diminished, and increasing interest in other reality concerns became clear. She made many more references to school, her enjoyable activity there, going on vacations, and so on. Her material was more directly affective, both happy and sad. The quantitative recount of preloss memories of father diminished, while the experience of loss and pain had greater direct affective expression.

Her first words on learning that the therapist was leaving the Clinic, were, "Oh, my God!" She looked stunned and initially lost for words. However, in contrast to her early frozen states around such affect, she utilized therapeutic assistance to express feelings of sadness.

Altogether, she was given six weeks for termination, in contrast to Sarnoff's recommendation of two, which the author believes minimizes and reduces the potential therapeutic use of termination, particularly in regard to instances of parent loss. The length of termination was in marked contrast to the suddenness of her father's loss, and it gave her time for preparation and the opportunity to master feelings of abandonment and sadness. In contrast to Sydney Smith's discussion on the negative impact of "forced terminations invoked by the therapist," the opportunity appeared to offer her a corrective emotional experience, in which the ego work in assimilating the experience was a form of active mastery. Her strengthened ego was reflected in her increased capacity for self-observation and understanding. It must be noted that some of her material appeared to reflect some strengthened ego capacities, as well as reaction formation and counterphobic defenses which may have been adequate defenses for her stage of development.

Despite its obviously deep significance for her, the termination phase really never appeared to stun her into her earlier mechanisms of affect avoidance, isolation of affects, or into a preoccupation with memories that served the purpose of preservation, rather than the new "mourninglike" acceptance processes demonstrated in this final treatment phase. In her very last session, some dwelling on memories occurred, but did not dominate her session. These memories, as commonly seen in relatively abbreviated fashion, represent the adaptation of mourning.

Her increased self-observation, mastery, as well as defenses were reflected in the following material: she likened ending therapy to how it had felt when she had gone from a tricycle to a two-wheel bike. She recalled her parents' encouragement to move on to the two-wheel bike from her tricycle, but described her own initial reluctance to the idea and wish for compromise. Her renewed fear of moving on, growing up, and letting go, especially in the absence of her admiring and admired father, were therapeutically clarified. A discussion ensued about evaluating readiness for ending versus the need for treatment, the legitimacy of having treatment when it is required, and how to secure an evaluation of the need for therapy for herself in the future. In contemplating the possibility that psychotherapy might again be required, she expressed reluctance in that it would be necessary to have a different therapist. Nonetheless, she confirmed again her own conviction that she was ready then to terminate. She shared her self-awareness of her renewed interest in life, when she very genuinely described having learned that "life can go on" in an interesting way, even without father.

In her last session, she brought in a cartoon clipping of a farewell scene, depicting cartoon characters with a variety of feelings associated with separation. She stated clearly how much she would miss coming. Interestingly, because of a conviction about her readiness to terminate therapy, her termination never stirred any countertransference feelings of having abandoned this patient, as might happen in untimely terminations imposed by the therapist. (In this case, it is likely that the subject of termination would have been soon introduced in any event.)

It should be noted further that this mother could not have withstood the additional burden of arranging for treatment interviews much longer. The weight of her continuing grief, its cumulative effect of fatigue for her, and her greater, somewhat defensive involvement in her work would probably have made her daughter's continuation in treatment quite difficult.

PREMATURE TERMINATION INITIATED BY PATIENT AND/OR FAMILY

Case Example 3

Carl, the second of three children, was nearly seven years old when his father, a poorly controlled diabetic, died following insulin shock. Carl was given to outbursts of temper and some poor impulse control even before the death, but most especially following the death. In general, he was described by mother as an aggressive child, who liked his independence.

Mother was a somewhat even tempered person who was forever jolly, saw the "bright side of things," and had little tolerance for prolonged experiences of sadness. She was vulnerable to narcissistic injury and defended herself through action defenses. She was hurt by the lack of support from in-laws following the death of her husband.

From his clinical diagnostic interviews, a month following father's death, Carl appeared depressed, without zest and helpless. He actually would fall on the floor in a heap in an angry but utterly thwarted display of helpless frustration. In the diagnostic interview, he was evasive and it was initially difficult to make any real therapeutic contact with him. Though he nuzzled his stuffed animal next to the therapist, he would alternate this by teasingly using it to hit the therapist. Altogether he was preoccupied with thoughts of horror and danger, and would make wild challenges against the therapist. He was seen as defending against feelings of powerlessness and helplessness, with grandiose defenses and other manifestations of regression, use of devaluation defenses and denial. He was seen as a child with good autonomous ego skills, but with weak secondary ego skills in capacities for delay, frustration tolerance, attention span, and tension regulation (or with such skills weakened by regression). Tolerance for self-observation was limited. In Gedo and Goldberg's framework, he would be seen as a child capable of superego functioning operating in a regressed mode of functional organization, with separation anxiety, omnipotent illusions, projection, and magical defenses.

The Barr-Harris Center Committee perceived the loss of father, an ego ideal figure, as devastating for Carl. In the committee case review, the possibility of a developmental interference occurring with chronic feelings of helplessness was predicted. It appeared that the death could become the traumatogenic agent preventing the natural resolution of fixations. The goal was to reduce the traumatic effects of the loss, to restore equilibrium, and to promote ego strengthening.

An evaluative period of several months to determine if natural healing processes could take hold preceded the initiation of treatment. At a point when his struggle with mother became very intense, it was decided to start treatment. He was started in weekly sessions which were increased to twice weekly sessions, with treatment spanning six months.

During the treatment course, he established very strong negative and positive transference reactions. Throughout, he was caught up in strong approach–avoidance behavior and struggles reflecting early fixations exacerbated by the death of his idealized father. These struggles were all absorbing and exhausting to him. His ambivalent struggle was reflected in one of his nicknames for the therapist, "Mrs. Bummer."

In his first treatment interview, he expressed alarm that he might forget the image of father, and resolved to prevent any such loss. While he would react to direct reflections or interpretations with boredom or other resistances, he would accept metaphorical interpretations. Such metaphorical interventions were stories that had been taped for him, for soothing and restoration, essentially utilizing clinical techniques of pacification and unification. These stories also encouraged some assimilation, but the patient used them too passively and repetitiously to be truly ego integrative. For example, he repeatedly asked to hear one of the therapist's stories about the "Beetle Bug," a metaphorical interpretation of his feelings of and defenses against powerlessness and helplessness. The therapist had created a character for him, Beetle Bug, that felt small and powerless, angry about not being grown-up, always being told what to do, and not being permitted to make decisions for himself. Similarly, he would request another favorite story, metaphorical tapes of a prehistoric animal who would rely on his friend, a cave dweller, to calm him down. This was a metaphorical depiction of the therapist's understanding of the role father had played for him. It was as if the reactivation of the memory of father's calming influence helped him restore such feelings in the present.

In contrast, in his own play themes, his fantasy animals would frequently run amok with anger. One of his puppet characters provided Carl with considerable satisfaction, a dog called Laddie that felt justified in his rampages because his family had deprived him of the right food (e.g., feeding him a concoction of orange juice and milk). Such food had not only been wrong for a dog, but had tasted bad. In his story, Laddie repeatedly had not cared when his family ultimately died because of feelings stirred by such poor, inappropriate care. Indeed, in this metaphorical play vignette, Laddie tried to "double kill" his family. Such vignettes depicted Carl's inconsolable state of irritability, narcissistic rage, and revenge fantasies. These vignettes also reflected the lack of genuine complementarity in his environment to his needs, historically and currently.

Four-and-a-half months after the initiation of treatment, mother, who received periodic parental guidance counseling, called and left the following message with the secretary: "Mrs. Hummer is not going to like this, but we're moving to Houston to join relatives."

In Carl's next session, aware as he was about plans for moving and the need to terminate, he requested the story tapes. Thus, he obtained soothing, while possibly devising a way to assure and fix remembrance of the therapeutic experiences since splitting mechanisms greatly interfered with a sense of object constancy. He brought a stuffed animal as he had on much earlier occasions. This one had been a birthday gift he had intended for his father, but had never been able to present. He once again became very tired and listless. Over the next six weeks, at various points he became still more resistant, hyperactive, distractable, and devaluing. At the same time, he became more direct about wishing to preserve the relationship with the therapist and tried mightily to prevent missing any sessions, even when external circumstances made it necessary to do so. Despite steadfast resistances, he began to show psychological clinging behaviors toward the therapist.

His play was more active during this phase. Some of his playful activities afforded the opportunity for therapeutic interpretations. For example, through the use of his pretend phone calls to the therapist in which he would portray refusing to speak, metaphorical interpretations could be made about his ambivalence and renewed feelings of approach–avoidance in the premature termination phase. Such techniques would restore some measure of greater organization, encourage greater willingness to engage in therapeutic endeavor, and provide him with an avenue for some expression of his feelings. It was always in such playful therapeutic exchange that the therapeutic working relationship and positive transference were at their highest level.

In some of his play he took delight in having an avenue for expression of some of the anger he felt about needing to leave. The play served as the vehicle for displacement of anger toward mother about her decision to move and further about the death itself. In his telephone game, he would call the therapist's secretary and gleefully dictate notes to her such as, "Dear Mrs. Hummer . . . you rat . . . I won't be coming to see you next week." He would make dictations, hang up, and hide. While approach–avoidance behaviors were at a high point, the overall transference tone eventually became slightly more positive, and the suffering, when expressed, a little more direct. Turning passive into active and identification with the aggressor defenses were clearly at work during such play periods, and at these times, depression was lifted notably. The play, too, was a more adaptive mastery of his feelings of helplessness, reducing the possibilities that a developmental interference would solidify, the initial concern of the Barr-Harris Committee. On the other hand, he refused to acknowledge affective connections between his play and the forced termination. Instead, distancing from the significance of the therapeutic breach implied in termination, he insisted that the hardest part of leaving would be the packing.

When mother was late on one occasion, he was nearly swinging on the proverbial rafters (in this case, clinic doors), making quite a commotion in doing so. When mother returned, he announced that he thought she had died, which had the tone of extreme ambivalence, anxiety, and fear of loss due to both loving and hostile feelings.

At times during this phase, it took considerable effort to help him contain his anxiety and restore calm. On one occasion when he shot paper planes at the therapist, he ignored her comments about the overdetermined significance of such play; his declaring war in this active manner and that, after all, it would be a plane that would take him away from Chicago and therapy. After a metaphorical suggestion to land the plane, he did so. While further plane attacks on the therapist ceased, his extreme agitated motion could not be contained. Eventually he required a pacification technique, reading a story which calmed him. It became necessary to use pacification techniques quite frequently early in the termination phase to help him regulate the excessive stimulation due to severe ego regression, precipitated by the anticipated premature termination.

Fortunately, pacification techniques finally mobilized and strengthened more adaptive capacities, and severe regression occurred in only one other instance during the final course of this forced termination. It appeared that a repetition of genuine trauma was averted. While this child was in no way ready for termination and in no way were objectives fully met, perhaps the termination itself did lead to some very small but fragile gains. The following material reflects some restoration of function and even some signs of budding new functions.

Again, metaphorical interventions were successful in reducing resistances. After trying to "eat the therapist up" with his puppet and ignoring the attempted interpretations of implied ambivalence, he finally agreed to permit the therapist to play the part of a dragon puppet provided that it were lots of fun—the caricature of the dragon should be very angry, just as he would have played the role. In this role, through projective play techniques with the puppet, the therapist could demonstrate and clarify Carl's angry feelings and much of his transference manifestations. For example, through the portrait of the dragon, the therapist conducted a dialogue with Mrs. Hummer, telling "her" about mixed and complex feelings and how angry the dragon could feel when his feelings were confronted. Carl initially attempted to use the therapist's intervention as permission for impulsive discharge as demonstrated when his own puppets acted out the dragon's feelings rather wildly. To promote the alliance, the therapist ultimately was able to elicit Carl's agreement to work on a puppet team with the therapist. His puppets suggested that Mrs. Hummer had tried to kill them, revealing defenses of projection, displacement, and renewed feelings of devastation and victimization and even annihilation anxiety. The therapist encouraged the whole team or gang of puppets to work it out and understand it. In the role of the dragon, the therapist could go between the two positions, "theirs" (the gang) and the therapist's, and allow or suggest that the gang of puppets continue to be open to some truth as his puppet had been in the instance around the expressed feeling of being killed. Thus, the working relationship was reestablished during this difficult period.

He became newly able to alternate between symbolic

play and direct expression. In his last two sessions, he was directly able to acknowledge and show self-awareness both of some feelings and of some of his defensive processes. For example, with definite awareness, he demonstrated that his drawings of happy faces that depicted "mad" feelings, and happy faces that depicted "sad" feelings, and so on, were attempts at reversal of feeling and denial. He unabashedly asked to keep the tapes of therapeutic stories that had provided soothing in his past sessions, a request which was granted. He directly acknowledged his ambivalence about leaving Chicago and his therapy, expressing in part a wish to go to Houston and in part a wish not to go. As in one of the steps of mourning, he did some remembering of earlier times in therapy: he leafed through the appointment calendar, enjoyed comments about earlier sessions, and, having brought out one of the old tapes, listened to it in a seemingly hypercathected review of old memories. Ultimately, he angrily tore out his birthdate page from the calendar, several others from that month, and the page with the date of father's death, writing on it, "MY DAD DIED," after a request for aid with the spelling. The activity with the calendar appeared to condense the feelings of rage and grief regarding the loss of father and the loss of the transference relationship. The author's interpretive comments about his loving feelings for father and his many memories of father were received with a measure of equanimity and some ability to listen.

At the actual point of departure he was very low-keyed in leaving. After joining his mother and siblings, he looked past the door when he passed in marked contrast to his siblings who waved good-bye profusely. He was still an angry child who had discomfort with both angry and positive feelings. Nevertheless, in his termination, he had been able to show a deep poignancy, which evoked some mutual feeling of loss.

To paraphrase Sydney Smith (1982–1983), for anyone who has established significant transference manifestations, any termination would likely have been difficult and intense. An intense child like Carl would have experienced an intense termination regardless of the timing. However, by its untimeliness, because of his intensity and pathology, the termination experience could well have been an added trauma which, by virtue of our mutual efforts, appeared to have been averted.

It seemed more likely the child would require treatment again soon for two reasons: his own pathology and his mother's deficient repertoire of parenting skills. Maternal skills appeared insufficient to provide this particularly vulnerable and needy boy with the soothing and ego restoration measures that he had yet to internalize for himself.

UNANTICIPATED AND UNANNOUNCED ENDINGS WITH NO PREPARATION FOR COMPLETION INTERVIEW

Case Example 4

In chapter 8, Johnny was described extensively in relation to the mobilization of mourning in a young child, and the case will be reviewed here only briefly insofar as it was paradigmatic for the issues of abrupt ending of child psychotherapy in a child with parent loss.

Johnny appeared to be a child with considerable psychic structure, with evidence of superego development, ego ideal, and high-level defenses of intellectualization and isolation, with a tendency, nonetheless, toward considerable regression. In terms suggested by Gedo and Goldberg, he was a child with a well-differentiated psychic structure appropriate to his age in a regressed mode of functioning, where narcissism, castration issues, and defensive disavowal and isolation were heightened. At times, the regression was quite extreme with rather severe anxiety. In reviewing his material, the Barr-Harris Committee noted some genuine mourning capacity in

Johnny. The Committee hypothesized a massive whole identification with father in contrast to more partialized identifications. This was seen as becoming very burdensome for him. The diagnosis for Johnny was a developmental interference and treatment was recommended. Treatment goals were to prevent further developmental interference, to facilitate mourning capabilities, and to assist him in internalizing more adaptive processes. Mother was seen for purposes of parent guidance and supportive service for herself.

Though in his initial treatment interviews, his face was contorted and he was on the verge of tears, he made the wild claim that he didn't miss his father. As treatment proceeded, he talked metaphorically about a "projector" in his head that in some ways replaced his mind. He said the projector clicked off whenever there was a bad film showing, saying that occasionally he replaced it with a new projector altogether, demonstrating his use of isolation, ego splitting mechanisms, and disavowal of the experience of the loss. Though he would return to such defenses at times, he sustained the ability to share feelings and have a discussion about his father for prolonged periods. His pain was acute. Techniques of optimal disillusion and direct and metaphorical interpretation were the principle techniques utilized.

The transference relationship became very intense. He began to mark his calendar days with a big E for empty on those days he would not be coming for therapy and gave numerous metaphorical descriptions of the therapist's significance to him. With sadness, he would refer to his certainty and awareness that one day his therapy, like a train, would have a caboose. Sometimes he would attempt nonchalance around separations in therapy or at home. However, when once he acknowledged genuine feelings about the loss of his dog, he also remarked on his awareness that strong feelings such as these have a beginning, a middle, and an end. He wondered then if the therapist thought he had approached the end of his painful feelings about losing dad, but agreed with her reflection at that point that he had not done so yet.

As his treatment drew close to the premature and yet unannounced interruption, material about whether he could trust anyone began to emerge. When such material was interpreted as distortion, which, in retrospect, was an error, he expressed the view that the therapist would need to prove to him that people could be trusted. He increasingly began to use his stuffed animals again, saying, "They don't drink, they don't drive, and they don't smoke." His stuffed animals were, therefore, in no danger while mother, on the other hand, did all these things. In a narcissistic retreat, he thought the only one he could really trust was "me, myself, and I."

Not long after the emergence of such material, at a point one year into a very intense treatment, his treatment abruptly stopped. He never returned following a planned interruption due to a vacation that his mother had taken. In her own supportive counseling sessions which had become more sporadic, mother had shared her exhaustion with all her continued burdens and her rageful feelings of never having any fun, and the need for relief and respite in planning and taking a vacation. She had become increasingly angry with her son, intolerant of his regressed behaviors, and cynical about her world. She primarily wanted the therapist to make her child more manageable in the home. She was weary of her own grief and increasingly resorted to alcohol and avoidance behaviors; she was irritated by her son's ongoing expressions of grief.

Calls to the home produced no results. They were not answered. A letter describing the importance and necessity for at least some closure and the deleterious possible consequences of not having a completion interview for the child suffering from the prior traumatic loss met with no response.

Johnny had obvious strengths. There was some hope that

the self synthesis and integration that he had begun to accomplish in therapy would further develop his own resources. However, his lonely work would need to be conducted under the handicapping circumstances of what appeared to be a parental model of pathological mourning. Johnny, therefore, was potentially in danger of increased, unrelenting rage and strengthened maladaptive defenses with greater developmental interferences.

Case Example 5

Thaddeus was another case whose psychotherapy ended without warning, after a treatment that lasted one-and-a-half years from age seven to eight-and-a-half. Thaddeus, an only child, with two stepsisters many years his senior, lost his father suddenly at age three due to a fatal cerebral embolism. In his evaluation at age five, he was seen as mature with good psychological structure, but extremely lethargic and depressed with actual symptoms of sleep loss. Mother had been reluctant to initiate a psychotherapy for him, though she showed awareness of friends who utilized therapeutic services for their children from a child therapist, whom she herself idealized. Mother became more accepting of the recommendation for psychotherapy after Thaddeus had awakened one night with hysterical symptoms of feeling unable to walk. His entry into therapy was marked then by mother's approach–avoidance about the subject. From the diagnostic material he appeared to be a child with precocious superego structure, but who was quite repressed. He appeared to be highly defended against all affect, good or bad, with frequent experiences of separation anxiety as well as anxiety about loss of love.

His treatment was a very slow, tedious process wherein he resisted therapeutic commitment, and denied the significance of the therapist to him. He was like the patients that

Altschul has described with a negative traumatic reaction, with defenses against repeated experience of the trauma (see chapter 1). He remained adrift in a defensive fog. In fact, this metaphor of a fog was eventually used with some benefit to his therapy. A variety of therapeutic techniques were utilized, including unification, optimal disillusion, and metaphorical and direct interpretations, with varying degrees of success. In his early treatment, his reluctance to express anger and his fear of punishment became quite focused. His general defensiveness and resistance to treatment were focused in the latter part of his treatment. Metaphors, such as his seemingly sailing out to sea in a fog, were utilized to reflect his distancing mechanism. He came eventually to find such distancing defenses as discordant.

Just prior to the abrupt ending, he engaged in play with puppets that depicted his feelings of deprivation, guilt for these feelings, and a wish to "get to the bottom of the meaning of this." When his puppets spoke about "having no friends," he corrected his puppets' "distortions." Reflected in his corrections and advice to his puppets were reaction formations against feelings of neediness, some newly realistic appraisal and awareness of the availability of objects for himself, including his therapist, and identification with the therapeutic function of the therapist.

At the moment of such breakthrough, mother entered the hospital; upon her return, claiming that he had done very well in his separation from her, she insisted that therapy should be terminated and that, to prevent any feelings of reengagement, he should not even return for a final session. She had just terminated her own therapy with a private psychiatrist at the time he changed his office. Thaddeus's continuation in treatment was recommended strongly and an even stronger recommendation was given for enabling him to have a termination phase. Mother adhered to neither recommendation and refused any request for interviews for herself to discuss her decision.

Thus it was that Thaddeus's treatment ended, just as the significance of the transference and usefulness of the therapist were beginning to be acknowledged, and just as there was some lifting of depression as seen in enthusiasm for his therapeutic play activities and themes. While there had been brief, episodic breakthroughs in his defenses before, this breakthrough just prior to the untimely interruption of treatment seemed much more sustained and persistent and of much greater promise. It appeared that mother was projecting and replicating ambivalent feelings about her own termination of treatment. There is a good possibility further that she could not sustain support for her son's treatment as long as she was not in psychotherapy herself, possibly because of feelings of envy and the inability to postpone action without the aid of a therapeutic figure. It is likely that this child showed no resistance to ending in this manner. His powerful characterological defenses of negating loss and avoiding the significance of transference, as well as new relationships, likely became reestablished with renewed strength. This was the only child among the author's cases at Barr-Harris where the loss had occurred at such a long interval prior to treatment. This child's adaptations to loss appeared to have become more solidified in an all-pervasive, characterological defensive structure that depleted him of energy, created ego constriction, and left him nearly inaccessible to comfort or much assistance from outside objects. Such results greatly strengthen the case for early intervention.

DISCUSSION

From such case material, it is clear that some children who have lost a parent due to death have the ability, or can be enabled to reach a satisfactory conclusion in their psychotherapy, while others, because of a variety of circumstances, internal and otherwise, cannot reach such completion. (It is all the more noteworthy that achieving such closure appears even more remote for those cases where treatment has been of longstanding duration.) The importance of termination has been underscored throughout the chapter. The dangers, or at the very least, risks of premature termination or abrupt endings also include the following:

1. The abrupt ending may join forces with the traumatic experience of parent loss and strengthen the compulsion to repeat traumatic experiences of loss or may strengthen defenses against loss which are also under the sway of the repetition.

2. Arrestations at the development point at which the loss was sustained may become solidified, with increased rigidity of structure occurring (Altschul, 1968).

3. Regressions in ego, drive, and narcissistic sectors induced or exacerbated by the trauma of parent loss or the traumatic circumstances of the parent loss may become further solidified by the new loss of the therapist.

4. Some children may develop precocious defenses. In fact, they may move forward quite precociously along intellectual or sexual lines, with the certainty that their only hope is to parent themselves. Such precocity would attempt to overcome helplessness and lack of control, experienced through repeated precipitous loss with the abrupt termination being another event for which they were unprepared. Such short-circuiting in the developmental process may lead to unevenness, lack of integration, a sense of deprivation, and shallowness of some structures.

5. The child, though his own resistances may have played into such a termination, may not feel inclined to return to therapy having once been disappointed. The child may have felt betrayed, as if he could not again trust a psychotherapist.

It is hypothesized that such premature terminations or ruptures of therapeutic relationships are traumatogenic or, to a lesser degree, become experienced as an unfulfilled therapeutic promise of resolving parental loss.

It is imperative, then, to obtain as great as possible an understanding of the dynamics interfering with therapeutic closure, so that we will be better able to prevent such unwanted results. Following a lead set by Freud long ago in his article on "Analysis Terminable and Interminable," "the question should be asked of what are the obstacles that stand in the way of such a cure" (Freud, 1937, p. 221).

The factors that complicate closure are quite extensive, multidetermined, and multifaceted. They can be classified from three standpoints: those emanating from the patient, those from the surviving parent, and those from the therapist.

INTERFERENCES IN CLOSURES OF CHILD PSYCHOTHERAPY IN PARENT LOSS CASES ON THE SIDE OF THE PATIENT

In Freud's article on termination, his statement that the "ego treats recovery itself as a new danger," has particular relevance to all child psychotherapists. Resistance to change appears in the characterological defense mechanisms that have been utilized to deal with earlier dangers. For the child of parent loss by death, the same defenses that have been employed to avoid the experience of loss are frequently the same defenses that serve resistance to changes in psychotherapy. Changes are perceived as dangers that finalize the experience of the parent loss making the death all too real and finally challenging the child to find new objects. Cure can be perceived as dangerous and may at times be avoided by flight. In addition to characterological defenses, Freud postulated that certain predilections of an almost constitutional or inherited nature are found in some of the resistances that interfere with psychotherapeutic goals. Such resistances include (1) difficulty in forming new cathexes; (2) the oversuggestibility of some, so that changes do not endure; (3) the lack of plasticity, an intransigence; and (4) the tendency to masochism or suffering. The latter has great bearing on the subject of parent loss, because of the peculiar potential for suffering and guilt that can follow in the wake of the loss of a parent. The defensive resistances and even those of a more constitutional nature are powerful counterforces to the maintenance of treatment for a child despite a strong attachment to the therapist.

The opportunity afforded child psychotherapy patients by parental interferences and parental collusions may, indeed, be exploited unconsciously or consciously by the child in the service of such resistances. While it is impossible to know the exact extent of the reactions or contributions of the two child patients whose treatments were discontinued in the abrupt fashion described above, there was no protest on the part of either patient that sufficiently countered the parental interference.

Children have a whole host of resistances to psychotherapy, and these have been described quite well in the literature. Anna Freud cited a great number of these, including the child's limited capacity for insight, the limited wish or motivation to get well, the lack of an exclusive relationship with the psychotherapist, and the reliance on a parent for the decision to enter and maintain them in psychotherapy. In a further consideration of obstacles in the treatment of children, Anna Freud points out other difficulties peculiar to them. Included are the child's short-term tolerance for psychic discomfort and low tolerance for heightened pressures from the negative transference and unconscious material, the child's predilection for acting out or discharge, the greater rigidity of defenses, the greater access to primitive defenses alongside the more mature defenses, a tendency to amnesia of some developmental experiences, the child's potential for externalization, and more primitive superego processes.

Many, if not all of these resistances were manifest in the treatment of all the children described above for each of the classifications. Those general childhood resistances that appeared to have the most deleterious effects on the above children's capacity to maintain a treatment relationship were:

1. Characterological defenses against painful affect: flight, avoidance patterns, denial, externalization, and devaluation.
2. The child's greater ego allegiance to resistance as a whole.
3. The psychological rigidity of defenses.
4. The lack of plasticity of some children, possibly due to genetic forces.
5. Externalization and projection; that is, the unwillingness to accept difficult behavior and feelings as their own.
6. Negation of interpretation.
7. Negative transference resistance.

In addition, there are a number of resistances to treatment that derive directly from the experience of parent loss by death. For example, the yearning for the parent, the hypercathexis, continued need for "a" parent as well as for "the" parent, makes reality adaptation an unpleasant, unwelcome experience, with the child finding it difficult to perceive the need or the gain in making such an adaptation. The child has the potential to become arrested in an early phase of bereavement which threatens to undermine the resolution of the parent loss and interfere with the maintenance of a therapeutic alliance sufficient to preserve the psychotherapy.

Garber (see chapter 7) has suggested that the child's realization that a fantasied restitution has not occurred, indeed, cannot occur in the psychotherapy, is often a deep disappointment for a child. The transference object is ultimately frustrating and cannot provide the full replacement they would like or need. Garber also cites the therapist's countertransference fantasy of providing restitution as a collusion with the child that heightens the impediment to therapeutic movement.

Despite all the possible resistances, it must be stressed that the children described in this chapter never actively sought to leave psychotherapy themselves. Instead, their resistances appeared to fuel passive compliance to parental decisions to terminate treatment prematurely. Thaddeus, who, in his low-keyed way, had occasionally protested coming, protected as he was by his characterological, defensive lack of zest and enthusiasm, probably made it the easiest for his parent to remove him from his psychotherapy.

It can be speculated that all of the children who experienced precipitous endings did experience disappointment and letdown. However, it is encouraging to recall that none of the children, with the exception of Carl, were so vulnerable as to lack a sufficient repertoire of defenses to protect themselves against too deep or prolonged regression or narcissistic insult.

ON THE SIDE OF THE PARENT

A child's resistance may cause difficulty for the course of psychotherapy and predispose the child toward flight solutions, but most therapists have an adequate repertoire of techniques to counter these resistances in order to preserve and strengthen a minimal working relationship with most children. This proved to be almost universally true for child treatment cases of any duration at the Barr-Harris Center.

However, obstacles to therapy introduced by parental inter-ferences and resistances ultimately proved to be of the greatest consequence and were the most difficult to overcome.

Some suggestions regarding the reasons for parental interference have already been considered at points in the elucidation of case material in the body of this chapter. When one considers the depth and range of parental resistances or interferences, one is impressed with the great number and range of parental resistances or interferences to supporting a child's continued treatment in situations of parent loss by death.

First are the interferences in overall parental functioning in the specific handling of the death with the child that derive from the surviving parent's experience of mourning the loss of a spouse. Such interferences and their consequences have been reviewed in another chapter and will not be discussed to any great extent here (see chapter 3). Here it is sufficient to underscore the significance of normal and pathological mourning processes as potential interferences in a parent's capacity to sustain a commitment to their child's psycho-therapy. Such attendant problems as energy depletion as a result of internal adjustment and the experience of feeling overburdened and fatigued by external adjustments tax a parent's capacity to act uniformly in the best interest of their child. Such a psychological overload for the parent can make the physical trip once or twice weekly to a child's therapist a further source of energy depletion.

Under the weight of feeling burdened or, in fact, being burdened, the child's regression can become an intolerable overload to the parent and the therapist can be blamed for the child's regressions. This is exaggerated by the parent's magical expectations for quick cures and increased manage-ability in the home. Such parental reactions may follow a very positive, initial attitude toward their child's treatment. This may happen to a greater extent when a parent sought treatment for a child at the outset due to a temporary introjection of the ego ideal system of the lost spouse. In such a situation, the surviving parent temporarily carries on with the values with which they have imbued the deceased. For example, it seemed possible that Johnny's mother, in addition to being under the deleterious impact of prolonged patholog- ical mourning reactions, was also returning to her more general mode of functioning when she abruptly withdrew him from treatment. Without the aid of the initial identifications with the ego ideal functions of father, who had greater capacities to understand and meet the needs of his children, she could not sustain the empathy necessary to maintain the requirements of Johnny's treatment. Mother appeared to have always been less empathic toward her children and to have had less patience with them than father had. It must be noted further that a child and surviving parent at a point of greater detachment or decathexis themselves in their own mourning process may become impatient by their child's prolonged grief, which now threatens the parent's freedom.

Defenses in the parent, pathological or adaptive in the aftermath of the loss of a spouse, can constitute additional parental resistance to the support of their child's participation in treatment to the point of an appropriate conclusion. Rationalization, denial, disavowal, action defenses, avoidance, displacement, projection, and isolation are among the type of characterological defenses that can contribute to parental resistance in any child's psychotherapy. When such charac- terological defenses in a parent are combined with defenses selected specifically to deal with their experience of losing a spouse, the result can become all too destructive for a bereaved child's psychotherapy. The projection of parental pain onto the child, the occasional blurred boundaries in doing so, and the projective identification mechanisms further complicate the parent's ability to perceive the extent of their child's pain, and the exact nature and significance of it in contrast to their own. There is sometimes a very fine line between pathological projections on the one hand and empathy on the other based on the bond of shared experience and mutual identifications resulting in genuine understanding and even the legitimate wish to spare and protect the child from pain. When the parental experience is primarily one of projection or projective identification, there is far more chance of parental collusion with the child's resistance. Under such circumstances, the parent may actively mastermind the flight or avoidance for the child in a misguided effort to protect him from pain, but which serves to protect the parent from pain as well.

An opposite defense, perceived in some parents, was the displacement of rage toward the missing spouse onto the child with a concomitant identification of the child with the lost spouse. This was particularly true when the child was the same sex as the lost spouse. Under such circumstances, the child is treated as if he were the frustrating lost object and retaliative mechanisms may be employed against the child. Punishments, including removing the child from gratifying experiences such as a positive therapeutic relationship, may be enacted. Even under the influence of more benign reasons, such as an attempt at restitution or identifying the child with the lost spouse, there is bound to be frustration and disappointment, despite attempts by the child to measure up and please the surviving parent.

Parental pathology that existed prior to the loss of a spouse is another predisposing condition on the part of a parent that could interfere with a child's treatment. These can range from mild interference in the capacity for empathy, where perceptions are uneven or inaccurate, to severe narcissistic pathology where the child is not perceived as having an independent center of initiative. Such pathology may include a parent's inability to tolerate the child's development of an extrasystemic relationship. In addition, a parent's extreme ambivalence conflicts, obsessional doubting, and transference reactions based on primary object relationships, rebelliousness toward authority figures, and a tendency to regression have deleterious results for most child psychotherapies. Parental reactions in the wake of their own loss and their own preexisting pathology constitute powerful potential interferences in the course of a child's psychotherapy.

ON THE SIDE OF THE THERAPIST

In addition to the factors contributed by the patient and the parent, one must also look to factors within the therapist. The therapist's emotional responses, attitudes, and reactions, the therapeutic actions and counteractions that are a mixture of technique and countertransference, must be examined as well.

In child psychotherapy with parent loss cases, the potential for countertransference reactions are great and can interfere with appropriate technical interventions when the "going gets rough." During periods of high resistance from either parent or child, countertransference or counteridentifications can lead to a distorted understanding of data. Kohrman, Fineberg, Gelman, and Weiss (1971) provide a classification of countertransference in child psychotherapy which includes universal countertransference, countertransference proper, and the therapist's transference reaction to a patient. Their classification can assist the clinician more specifically in examining personal reactions.*

---

*The definitions of countertransference as reviewed in Kohrman et al (1971), are as follows: Universal countertransference is the "total response of the child analyst to the patient, the parents, and the therapeutic situation." It includes a clinician's characterological givens, including style, personality, and culturally determined attitudes as well as the clinician's own views toward children. Countertransference proper is the specific reaction in the analyst that occurs spontaneously in response to a given patient's transference material, which may include the patient's unconscious attempts to induce reactions in the therapist. Third, genuine

The universal countertransference response for most child psychotherapists is a sense that the child has been unfairly treated by life circumstances and a wish to spare him further pain. Such attitudes can lead to confused messages, uneven technique, and collusion with a patient to avoid pain. In situations of parent loss, universal countertransference reactions may lead to an avoidance of endings to prevent pain, either by becoming too passive in the face of evidence about impending ruptures (i.e., not initiating preventive measures in timely enough fashion), or by prolonging termination beyond a point of readiness to avoid the inevitable pain renewed in the separation from the therapist. On the other hand, a therapist may initiate premature terminations based on too fixed a notion of what constitutes cure or the nature of mourning or adaptation to loss for a child, thus limiting therapeutic goals and ignoring a given child's capacities for adaptation and/or mourning based on the child's level of object relations, ego strength, and developmental achievements. Such preexisting attitudes may dispose a therapist to attempt to work toward matching the child to preconceived notions so that the child may be short-changed from experiencing the adaptation of which he is actually capable. The child may attempt to comply with the therapist and achieve the suggested "results," whereby little is accomplished except for an imitation of a fantasied cure.

The fantasy of rescuing a child may derive from all three types of countertransference reactions, for example: (1) on the universal side, the characteristic reaction to and views about the semiorphaned, especially in the face of parental deficits, may lead a therapist to have rescue fantasies; (2) in countertransference proper, there may be a positive response

---

transference reaction on the part of the clinician, in the context of a treatment relationship, is the "spontaneous, unconscious, conflictual and immaturely determined reaction" to a given patient, the therapist's projections, despite minimal cues in the patient.

to a given child's reaching out for such rescue, because of the child's intense feelings of helplessness and powerlessness about the loss; and (3) in genuine transference; for example, when a therapist may have had similar personal experiences of early parent loss causing him to distort the data and project a need for rescue with minimal cues from the patient. In all these circumstances, the management of termination can produce the same difficulties, not recognizing a patient's readiness for termination or defensively terminating too early. When the countertransference attitude colluded with a child's wish for restitution, the therapist and patient may be operating on an unconscious assumption and expectation of permanence. When the therapist's rescue fantasy provokes further countertransference reactions of guilt because of inabilities to rescue the patient, appropriate consideration of termination can be further undermined. When the surviving parent has genuine deficits, the fantasy of rescuing the child and providing actual restitution can become particularly intensified. In such situations, the parent may feel excluded and react by the premature removal of the child from therapy.

After hurried and abrupt departures, the therapist's reaction can include a range of feelings from frustration and disappointment to shock, sadness, and even anger. At times, even relief will be felt if a patient and/or family have been severely resistant. This range of feelings is the same as those experienced in a bereavement experience. To the extent that such reactions in the therapist are externalizations of the patient's or parent's continued feelings of grief and mourning or are responses to provocations, the therapist's reactions fall into the category of countertransference proper. In such an instance the therapist's insight at that point is of little or no therapeutic value for the former patient and constitutes the ultimate frustration of therapeutic ambition for the therapist.

Because of the circumstances of a relative absence of information and frequent lack of warning in abrupt departures, it would appear that the potential for true transference reactions in the therapist, as Kohrman et al. have defined these, is great (1971). Although these are feelings that are evoked in the context of a premature termination, they belong more strictly to the therapist and leave him or her with an integrative task to master. Such mastery is most important for the therapist to achieve so that whatever therapeutic possibilities still exist can be affected: a proper letter or phone call, an avenue back for the patient now or in the future, should such a suggestion be considered appropriate.

REMEDIAL SUGGESTIONS

The task for the therapist of parent loss cases is a most complex, demanding, and challenging one. To carry such treatments to proper points of conclusion challenges the therapist to strike just the right balance: to evaluate what capacities a given child might have for mourning or adaptations to loss; to determine what kind of help should be used in assisting a child in reaching his or her potential, and, when therapy is indicated, to evaluate at the outset both the child's ability to engage in the treatment process and the presence or absence of proper parental and external support for the child's psychotherapy. Remedies to premature terminations can be viewed from the same vantage points as were the obstacles.

On the side of the patient, while the therapist has every responsibility to know proper techniques for managing resistance and assisting the momentum of psychotherapy, it is ultimately the patient in therapy who must overcome resistances, make the internal adaptations, and achieve a reorganization of cathexes that results in the resolution of parent loss. (It is understood that some children may well be able to achieve such results through inherent self-healing processes, without the aid of psychotherapy; others require psychotherapeutic assistance.)

From the standpoint of the parent, for psychotherapy to be effective for a child, the surviving parent must support and give sanction to the endeavor. Otherwise, the child feels undermined in his undertaking and may feel greater conflict and even disloyalty as he approaches the therapeutic work. As important as it is to attempt to predict such an ability and to assist the parent in meeting his or her end of the responsibility, it is impossible to foresee all the pitfalls that might ensue in the course of a parent's support for their child's treatment. Diagnostic prediction of parental support is made still more difficult when stages of a parent's bereavement camouflage the parent's characterological potential for support or disruption for the child's treatment. For example, in the acute stages of shock and grief, Johnny's mother was all for the treatment; in her later stages of bereavement, support ground to a halt.

It is impossible to predict all parental resistances, yet the therapist is obligated to engage in appropriate assessment and diagnosis in an attempt to predict and influence the outcome. Enlisting the patient and parent in a therapeutic contract, the therapist must match goals to the possibilities and probabilities of a given child within a given family context and refrain from inappropriate countertransference positions of overzealousness and excessive therapeutic ambition.

The goals and rationale of treatment should make sense to the patient and parent. To avoid obscurity and to heighten awareness, treatment objectives should be presented in understandable and sometimes quite concrete terms. The therapist must be vigilant in retaining focus and in maintaining the treatment alliance. At the onset, the therapist must educate and prepare parents for typical resistances, reactions, and feelings that can occur in the course of a child's psychotherapy. The parent should be made aware of: (1) general bereavement processes in children and what appears to be specific bereavement reactions in their child; (2) the typical conflicts around such experiences within a child and between a child and parent— such as the different pace at which a child and parent might move through the bereavement process. Such educational measures may still have significant limitations, but they should be attempted. They are ideals and may be only partially achieved.

Throughout the treatment, the therapist must remain alert to opportunities to anticipate and avoid inappropriate endings. The therapist must be alert to both the signals of increased resistance in the patient and must recognize the different levels of countertransference as therapeutic interferences and as a source for understanding the road blocks that occur in the patient.

From the standpoint of direct therapeutic intervention with the bereaved child, the therapist must become adept at utilizing a full range of psychotherapy techniques such as pacification, unification, optimal disavowal, and interpretation and must match them to the progressions, regressions, and resistances of the patient.

In the face of the pain and narcissistic vulnerability experienced by the child during bereavement experiences, the therapist must exercise caution, using appropriate delicacy and sensitivity when assisting the child to acknowledge the disavowed affects of sadness and anger, and must move cautiously from outer layers of here and now experience to those that pertain to memories of the lost parent. Inappropriate technique can lead to wishes for flight or greater defensiveness and resistance. Inevitable disruption in the therapeutic relationship due to vacations, failures in empathy, inexact interpretation, or technique applied inappropriately for the level of pathology or defense, requires the use of techniques and patient understanding which repairs the therapeutic alliance and gets the treatment "back on the track."

Despite such challenges, perhaps the most technically demanding task for the therapist is to anticipate and handle the parental resistances to permitting the conclusion of a child's psychotherapy. In addition to the preventive education measures already suggested, other technical remedies with parents can be utilized throughout the course of the child's treatment.

The therapist should maintain an attitude of appropriate inclusion of the parents in the overall work, whereby they are viewed as a member of the treatment team. While the therapist must protect the privacy of the patient, useful insights about the child can be shared with the parent to be utilized in their own child management. Such inclusion and assistance helps preserve the necessary parental alliance, counters regression of parental functions, and leads to the maintenance or restoration of parental functions. In this way, a parent may be engaged in the kind of active mastery or adaptation in the service of their child that might help undercut the type of defenses that could otherwise lead to their actualizing resistance by removing their child from treatment. Including the parent in ongoing evaluation of their child's progress as it is demonstrated in the home, and assisting the parent with new concerns that emerge, further affords them a sense of genuine active mastery and restored self esteem in the aftermath of their own bereavement.

It must be noted that there may be additional issues to be worked out in the child's treatment as a result of such parental contact, though these may remain silent in the child for a long time while confusions and resentment might build. The therapist, however, confronted with the realities of the child's familial context, must attempt to deal with the conflicting demands and requirements of the total treatment process, be alert to manifestations of the patient's feelings about them, attempt to anticipate them, and deal with them as they emerge.

The description of parental inclusion is once again an ideal, which may or may not be achieved fully. Some parents, already overwhelmed by the intrapsychic burden of mourning and the everyday burdens of survival, view such contact with their child's therapist as yet another burden and are only open to the most minimal involvement. Nevertheless, the therapist must be empathically alert to and in tune with the vicissitudes and shifts in parental readiness or demands and/or needs for involvement so that the surviving parent might become fruitfully engaged in the process. In this manner, premature terminations may be averted, the goals for the child's treatment appropriately supported, and parenting functions enhanced.

In the end, therapists are challenged to expect no less of themselves than they do of their patients. The therapist must accept the reality, should patients or parents choose to leave in what appear to be untimely ways: to do what one can and to recognize what one cannot do, to do the self-analytic work of countertransference, and to mobilize the energy to attempt new techniques; to stay the course but to know when to be ready and able to let a patient go; to recognize termination readiness when gains are sufficient; to avoid attempts at control and/or manipulation, and to avoid placing the child in conflict with parents. Lastly, the therapist must accept difficult endings with grace, good humor, and openness.

CONCLUSION

The ultimate goals in psychotherapy with a child of parent loss are to provide him with an opportunity to make adaptations to loss that will lead to mastery and integration and to free the child of the encumbrances of repetition compulsions that would otherwise restrict him to a limited repertoire of behavioral and emotional experiences and choices. Precipitous endings were viewed as a manifestation of the deleterious impact of the phenomenon of repetition compulsion following trauma. Abrupt endings were seen as being potentially traumatogenic agents with the further potential of organizing pathology around loss and separation. It is hoped that this chapter provides the therapist in such circumstances with a proper sense of caution and alertness to the seemingly greater potential for traumatogenic, pathologically repetitious endings in child treatment cases of parent loss. It is hoped that signals will be more rapidly perceived and recognized and that timely remedial efforts can be attempted with greater precision and increasingly greater success.

Section IV

Developmental Issues

Chapter 10

Early and Late Effects of Bereavement: Requirements for Mourning

Sol Altschul, M.D. and Helen R. Beiser, M.D.

The effect of parent loss can be studied either prospectively or retrospectively. The Institute for Psychoanalysis started with studies of adults in psychoanalysis (Fleming and Altschul, 1963), showing that such persons had a deficiency in mourning, and many had an arrest of development at the stage at which the loss was sustained. Those who were parents showed difficulties in their parental role due to their own lack of such experiences from the dead parent (Altschul and Beiser, 1984). Pollock (1978) has also studied mourning and grief, demonstrating how adults often react to previous traumas with anniversary reactions. When one looks at the literature relating to children, there are many case studies describing the reactions to death at different ages, but much difference of opinion as to whether children are capable of mourning in the sense that adults mourn. Garber reviewed the pertinent literature in 1981. Bowlby (1960b) represents one extreme view, believing that mourning can occur in infancy, while Wolfenstein (1966) presents the view that mourning is not possible until adolescence. Most authors seem to be moving toward the position that there is considerable variation, depending on the differing circumstances as well as the developmental stage at which the loss occurred (Nagera, 1970). One very important variable is the support available in the environment (Bowlby, 1980; see chapter 4). E. Furman (1974) describes in a very moving way the reactions of children in a nursery school to the death of a parent, with many excellent suggestions as to how important adults may help.

The Furmans (R. Furman, 1964; E. Furman, 1974) and Kliman (1973) believe that the process of psychoanalysis is the best way to facilitate mourning in children. Although a number of children at the Barr-Harris Center have received once- or twice-weekly therapy, none so far has gone into psychoanalysis. However, one of the authors recalls two cases of child analysis from the 1950s involving two boys who had sustained parent loss. These cases not only present interesting material regarding the ways in which children deal with loss, but can be compared as to the effect of loss at two different stages, and as to the loss of parents of different sexes. It would be interesting to compare the examples of John and Bob presented here who were treated in childhood with similar cases treated in adulthood. Unfortunately, only a case of father loss at the same age as Bob was available. Of course, the examples of John and Bob do present the differences seen between early and late treatment with Mr. A.

A CASE OF MOTHER LOSS AT AGE FIVE

John (a fictitious name) was a much wanted child born to a couple who had spent the first five years of their marriage in the armed services. Father, who was gradually becoming deaf from otosclerosis like his mother, had been an honor student in college, but felt he had never lived up to his potential, and ran a small business. Mother was very close to her own mother, and very much wanted children. She suffered from toxemia during the pregnancy with John necessitating early induction of labor. The baby weighed about five pounds, but seemed healthy. He was adored by both sets of grandparents. When he was three-and-a-half years old, his mother developed a mysterious illness of the blood which caused her to be extremely susceptible to infection. She became depressed after repeated bouts of infection without obvious cause and with slow recovery. In retrospect, she probably suffered from a disease of the immune system. When John was five years old, his mother was taken to the hospital rather abruptly and died. His grandmother told him she had gone to have a baby, and he was not told of her death for two weeks. For a long time the maternal grandmother called and hysterically accused father and the doctors of killing her daughter.

John and his father lived with the paternal grandparents until father remarried two years later, a widow whose first husband had died of leukemia. During his stepmother's first pregnancy John became very upset, fighting and crying, and was taken to a family social agency for evaluation and brief treatment. The parents took him back to the agency just before he was ten with concerns that he was doing poorly in school (he had never done well), stuttered (he had done so since age three), and had to be pushed to do anything. Psychological tests showed him to be of average intelligence, but he was in a school of very high achievers. His stuttering was mild, and on the positive side, he did well in sports and had friends. The agency now saw this configuration of school difficulties and stuttering to be the consequence of long-standing personality problems, and recommended psychoanalysis. The stepmother made the arrangements and took the responsibility for bringing him. She was a warm, caring person who had received some supportive treatment at the social agency when her first husband died. She was sensitive to the fact that John's father's symptoms of insomnia and headaches were related to the death of his first wife, and supported him in seeking treatment for himself toward the end of John's analysis. Father could not discipline John, and had broken down and cried and apologized the one time he punished him. Although not as motivated as stepmother, father supported the analysis out of his concern for John's poor schoolwork. John would provoke stepmother by being passively resistant, and she bore the main burden of disciplining him as well as for the care of her son, now eighteen months old. John expressed considerable fondness for his half-brother.

The analysis was short, covering a period of one-and-a-half years. In the first phase, John was friendly but passive, waiting to be told what to do. He drew a peaceful scene of birds in a nest and a man cultivating a garden. When asked what he remembered about his mother's death, he said he cried at first, and then crawled under a sofa and watched television. He accepted the prospect of help by participating in rescuing toy soldiers with parachutes made of tissues. Gradually he enlarged his play activities, sometimes bringing toys and games from home. The first of these was a large plastic airplane. With a burning tool he made an opening in the underside to insert the toy soldiers. He became anxious when he realized he had ruined the plane. Another time he brought a tampon with him, expressing the fantasy that it was a piece of dynamite, although consciously thinking it was something his stepmother used to take care of his half-brother. The meaning of this play seemed to indicate that babies, or males, could harm mothers. In the transference, he played this out by having great difficulty winning games. In checkers he found it impossible to penetrate the king row, even when given specific suggestions that this was necessary to win a game. Although overtly fond of his half-brother, even bringing him into the office at one time, he indicated his sibling rivalry by locking the reception room door on his way out so no one else could enter. He also took more than the designated number of dominoes at the start of a game, even though this would lessen his chances of winning.

Other themes related to his mother's illness. His play with cowboys and Indians indicated mysterious happenings or attacks. His ideas about cause and effect were replete with magic, also related to the mystery of mother's death. When he had upper respiratory infections, usually correlated with brief separations, it was learned that the family worried that he might have inherited his mother's illness, just as father had inherited his own mother's deafness. Once he painted his fingers red to teasingly worry his stepmother that he had been hurt. At the end of the school year, although he had shown some improvement, it was decided that he should repeat the fifth grade. Unfortunately, vacations arranged before the analysis started produced a very long summer break. In the short time available he was more resistant to finding meanings in his play, and was unable to talk about his feelings about not passing, or about the long interruption.

When analysis was resumed in the fall, it was learned that John's stepmother was pregnant. This ushered in the second phase, which lasted until the birth of the baby. The frequency of treatment hours was gradually diminished as stepmother felt considerable fatigue and illness. In retrospect, it seems likely that stepmother was at least unconsciously planning another pregnancy when she first wanted treatment for him, hoping to avoid the behavior in John that had been so upsetting during her first pregnancy. His teacher was also pregnant and left in a couple of months. John refused to maintain the analytic frequency by coming alone on public transportation, fearing he might go past his stop. During this phase he was much less friendly and more overtly aggressive.

He ran cars and a toy stagecoach along the top of the desk, and almost deliberately let them fall off, breaking the tail off of one of the horses. He was now taking more direct blame for harming mother, and included symbolic castration of the male. He was much more resistant to help, perhaps a transference reaction to father's pushing. More material related to father, both as attacker and nurturer, and he identified with both aspects. He continued the attack and rescue play with cowboys and Indians, but also spent time feeding birds on the office windowsill. Although much more knowledgeable, he still avoided winning games, except by accident. His anxiety about the coming delivery, and its relationship to his mother's death, was expressed in a series of dramatic happenings as the time of delivery approached. He brought in two facsimile front pages of old Chicago newspapers, one describing the assassination of Lincoln, and the other reporting the great Chicago fire. He also brought in a current news report of a major air crash. He blew up balloons in the office and became anxious when he overexpanded one and it burst noisily. On the more constructive side, he accepted a boat model for his eleventh birthday in January instead of a pushbutton toy which he wanted, and worked hard and carefully, almost as if he were creating a baby. When the baby was born, a little prematurely, in February, he wanted to name her Helen. The parents compromised on Ellen, which memorialized a great-grandmother.

In the third phase, after the baby's birth, the stepmother was too busy to bring him, but he was sufficiently mature to come by himself. However, he only agreed to come once a week. In spite of his previous fear, he only passed his stop once, but managed to find his way, and was only a few minutes late. He continued with aggressive play, but with a more joking tone. There was oedipal material expressed by a sequence of carefully killing off all cowboys and Indians, leaving himself alone with the stagecoach, the symbolic mother. In contrast to his previous handling of interpretations by politely listening and then proceeding with his play without response, he was able to connect the stagecoach play with his old habit of locking the analyst's office door to prevent anyone else from entering. As the summer break approached, he talked with some annoyance of the long interruption of the previous summer. When it came time to resume in the fall, mother called and said he did not want to come anymore. He did come once more, and showed a combination of friendliness and defiance, but held fast to his decision to terminate. This could be seen as retaliation for what he saw as desertion the previous summer. Without greater motivation from the parents at this time, it was not possible to continue, although, in spite of improvements in the third phase, his continued inability to win at games was evidence that he still was inhibited in his aggression. Six months later the stepmother called complaining about his oppositional behavior, but she seemed to want a quick solution rather than continued analysis.

Five years later the parents made contact again, this time with father having more appreciation of the meaning and possible seriousness of John's behavior than stepmother. Father had gotten rid of the family dog for biting, and had not told the boy that he had had him killed. John had been having outbursts of angry crying, quite different from his usual behavior. Since the analysis he had been fine as far as his relationships with people were concerned, and even now was pleasant to people outside of the family. Recently he had acquired a girlfriend. The only problem was that he still was only barely passing in school. The recommendation was made that father tell him what happened to the dog, and tie this up with his old confusion as to what happened to his mother. John refused an offer for an interview. In a recent attempt at a follow-up, neither John nor father could be found in the regional telephone books.

John experienced a catastrophic loss at age five, which he expressed in his analysis through working on past and present catastrophes, such as the assassination of Lincoln. At the time he tried to deny this, as did his family by not telling him, but he overheard accusations leading him to believe that adult males and babies killed mothers. He developed a chronic personality problem in which he inhibited his learning leading toward maturity, and expressed it in a provocative way with women, which annoyed them and kept them at a safe distance from his fantasied destructiveness. Although analysis allowed him to work through the fear that pregnancy kills women, the episode with the dog in his adolescence showed that he still was unsure of what caused the disappearance and death of creatures close to him. There was no indication during the analysis that he had any inner concept of his mother as a person, which may be one reason why his mourning was incomplete. As an adult, it is doubtful that he could overcome his fear of aggression sufficiently to be truly successful, and, if he married, he would be vulnerable to anxiety or depression during his wife's pregnancies.

A CASE OF FATHER LOSS AT AGE TEN

Bob was a much more complicated case. He was the younger of two sons by nine years. The long interval was due to mother's repeated hospitalizations for either depression or asthma. Maternal grandmother had committed suicide when mother was ten, on the same day an infant brother died, and mother had been placed in foster homes on numerous occasions. Nevertheless, she was considered the "strong" parent. She had some toxemia during the pregnancy with Bob, and he was a little premature, but was healthy except for bilateral inguinal hernias. The first hernia repair took place when he was four, and the second was delayed until he was eight-and-a-half by one of mother's hospitalizations. After the second operation he developed a school phobia, and was taken to see a child psychiatrist. This revealed that he had been allowed very close physical contact with mother, and that father carried him whenever he complained of pain, and allowed him to stay home from school. Father, whose mother had been severely mentally ill, was considered "soft" compared to mother. Both parents were in psychiatric treatment. The child psychiatrist recommended limiting the closeness with mother, and that father firmly support his return to school. At follow-up, about a year later, Bob was described as quiet and well behaved in school, was teacher's pet, but was teased by peers. As he was still anxious, intensive treatment was recommended. Arrangements were made for psychoanalysis in the summer just before he was ten. In the fall it was learned that father had had a lung resected for cancer, and he died three months after the analysis began. Under such circumstances, it is apparent that the treatment situation is pervaded by intense feelings of sympathy for a child undergoing such a loss.

Bob was seen in analysis for three years for a total of 350 hours. As so many of his problems preceded, or were unrelated to the death of his father, the material presented will be that most related to loss and mourning. He was an owlish little boy, expecting praise and reward for behaving well and trying hard. He accused others of being aggressive. Although no formal psychological tests were done, he did not seem unusually intelligent. He regressed during his father's final illness, wetting himself while waiting for a bus after the school principal told him he would have to be a man before his time, and once in the office when he blocked in making a winning move in a game. He played a great deal with clay, and formed two clay dogs who fought. After his father died, he combined the two into the shape of a man. He agreed that the dogs represented himself and his brother, and it was necessary to stop fighting and unite in order to keep the memory of father alive. For the next year he would stop other play and repeatedly go back to this figure, alternately destroying it and reconstructing it in a way he thought would strengthen it, like putting paper clips in the arms and legs. In this way he played out his anger at father for dying, and his wish to have him back stronger. He also changed the identity of the figure, from superman to a deep-sea diver, to a soldier, shifting from the ideal to the realistic. At the anniversary ceremony, mother reported that he cried. He did not play with the figure for another six months, and then decided to dismantle it. He evidenced some disgust at the clay that had softened around the paper clips.

Most of the analysis was involved with getting him to accept responsibility for his hostility, and trying to modulate his omnipotence. He saw himself as a poor little victim who should have the power of others available to him to make up for what was realistically a remarkable amount of bad luck. One piece of evidence that he was not helpless was his ability to come by himself on public transportation, with several transfers. His omnipotent expectations from others were expressed by his only half-joking expectation of presents ranging from an elephant to the Eiffel Tower, and his ability to get his brother to do his homework. When errors or imperfections were pointed out in some of the school projects he brought, he became sullen, but only expressed anger at home. As he was more outgoing with friends, and even took a position as a school crossing guard, termination was planned to coincide with his entry into high school.

He came in once a couple of years later when he was depressed about his school achievement. He said that his male physics teacher dropped out in the middle of the semester because of illness, and he had a rather strange female English teacher, but he knew how to handle her—obvious references to his experiences with his parents. Several years later when he was in college a vocational counseling service wrote with the patient's consent that he was having trouble with engineering, and they helped him shift to accounting. He did not respond to a recent letter offering a follow-up interview, but an accidental contact with his mother revealed that he is married and has two children, still of latency age, and is quite successful in business.

In contrast to John, Bob did show evidence of mourning. He never showed grief that could be directly observed except once when his mother called during his hour to say she was in the hospital. However, he regressed during the final illness, and symbolically worked on his internal representation of his father through the clay man. His mother openly told him about the impending death, and he used his brother as a substitute father. The difference might well be because of his age at the time of the death, as well as better handling by the family, and the help he received in analysis. As an adolescent he also showed his vulnerability to a situation such as the illness of a male teacher which reminded him of the death of his father, and had to deal after analysis with his unrealistic ambitions which required greater abstract ability than he possessed. So far, he does not seem to have suffered any effects in adulthood, but it is possible that he will have difficulty helping adolescent sons make realistic vocational plans. Of course, he might also be vulnerable to an anniversary reaction when he reaches the age at which his father died, or at some time suffer from the family bipolar disease. One can only hope that his analysis during a very crucial period will prevent such consequences of his loss.

AN ADULT WITH FATHER LOSS AT AGE NINE

Mr. A., who suffered the loss of his father as a child, showed the prolonged effects when he entered treatment at about age thirty. In particular, he showed significant difficulties with aggression, just like the two cases described earlier. He had done a great deal of reading in psychology, and had some previous treatment which had been helpful, but had not been able to affect his major difficulties at work or home. He entered analysis because of an almost paralyzing inability to complete tasks at work, marital discord, depression, and anxiety. In spite of these chronic difficulties, Mr. A. was able to function in his field of scientific endeavor, but at great personal cost. He had not been able to complete the formal training in his chosen field. However, he had a brilliant mind, was extremely verbal, and quickly showed understanding and adeptness with psychological concepts.

Mr. A. was the youngest of three children whose parents were in their late thirties when he was born. His two much older sisters lived and worked in a distant part of the country, and had little contact or influence on the family dynamics during his latency years. Almost the first historical information obtained in the diagnostic period was that Mr. A.'s father had committed suicide when he was nine years old, and that he had discovered the body. Mr. A. remembered the confusion and excitement of family and neighbors as father was taken to the hospital. He cried briefly, but was mostly bewildered by the events. Because of the nature of the death, there was conflict in the family over burial procedures, and he was not included in the arrangements. He was given some of father's belongings, and told by visiting relatives and mourners that he was now the man of the house. Mr. A. remembered feeling a mixture of sadness, confusion, and exhilaration. As the fortunes of the family declined, these feelings were replaced by anxiety, anger, and despair, while the confusion remained.

As the treatment unfolded, the complex relationships in the family were revealed. Mr. A. felt he had had an unhappy childhood, even though both parents displayed obvious affection toward him. His relationship to his mother was extremely close, and they spent long periods of time alone together. Mr. A. remembered with anger and resentment, that, at the same time, she was preoccupied to the point of intrusiveness with his bodily functions. Both parents were permissive, but would disagree on how to care for him or deal with his disobedience. His parents seemed intimidated by him, discipline and care could be erratic, and he grew up as a stubborn child who was difficult to manage. Not much affection was displayed by the parents toward each other, but it was clear that Mr. A. was cherished by each of them. He often slept with his parents, which he found both stimulating and anxiety producing. In the treatment it became clear to him that he must have seen himself as the center of the family, and simultaneously felt omnipotent and inadequate. He was startled on realizing that he tried to be the sexual *(or* object for each parent. In retrospect, Mr. A. felt that each *one* parent must have loved him more than they did each other. *parent*

Mr. A.'s relationship to his father was particularly ambivalent. They engaged in a number of activities which he remembered with pleasure and affection. However, he also remembered many times when father would break promises and tease him about his disappointment. The rage and frustration that he experienced under such circumstances were reported in the treatment, as well as wishes to beat his father. On occasion he actually had attempted to strike father. As he felt closer to the analyst, his difficulties over his aggression could be worked on in the transference.

As Mr. A. remembered and described a number of incidents that seemed to cluster around the time of father's death, it became evident that he unconsciously and at times consciously blamed himself. He connected his aggressive */✓* and antagonistic behavior to the suicide. When, as a child, he felt frustrated or belittled, he engaged in pranks that often caused minor injury to others or damage to property. He marred furniture, tripped people, and occasionally hit or kicked other children. One incident in particular stood out. After being told that a particular material in the house would not burn, he, being of a scientific mind, set forth to discover for himself if this was true. He used a magnifying lens to determine if the material could be ignited. The fire he succeeded in starting got out of control, and before it could be extinguished, damage had been done to the storage room where he had conducted his experiment. He now began to recognize the terror he felt of something destructive happening to him or to the analyst if he made progress in his treatment or his work.

In working over these episodes and his anxieties and fears, his conflicts over aggression and the persistent effect of the trauma became apparent. Other experiences during his growth and development contributed further to his guilt over success. On several occasions when he was learning well from admired men, and doing good work, something happened to these men. They were injured, became ill, or were transferred. This added to the belief that his success was destructive to others, and in particular, that his "scientific" success had been the cause of father's death, a last straw in father's difficulties.

The inadequate childhood mastery of aggression also contributed to Mr. A.'s difficulties in parenting his young son. As the boy grew and developed, it became clear that Mr. A. was identified with both the child and his deceased father. On the one hand, he was determined never to disappoint the child as he had been, while at the same time he became inconsistent and permissive whenever he became concerned that he might stir up anger in the child. While he was generally warm and caring, he also expected the child to feel and behave as he himself had, prior to his father's suicide, and was overly sensitive to issues of competition and power. At such times, he would feel as threatened by the child as he imagined his father had been by him. He could sympathize with his son's efforts to assert himself, while at the same time, he unconsciously feared that the boy would displace him and be the cause of the violent death that Mr. A. was sure awaited him. He often fantasied that he would die before he reached forty. These feelings became particularly strong as he and his son approached the ages he and father were at the time of father's suicide. These complex identifications and misidentifications produced several impasses in the mutual interaction between Mr. A. and his son. Discipline was a particular problem. He wanted to give his son a better start in life than he had experienced, so he would at times overindulge the child, and then overreact to the resulting aggression and impose severe restrictions on the boy's activities. His son, in turn, became stubborn, and began to engage in childish pranks that resembled the misbehavior of Mr. A. as a child. In a significant way, this repeated the parent–child inconsistency Mr. A. had been exposed to as a child. As the boy grew and developed, he did in fact, take on more and more of Mr. A.'s characteristics, which served to increase the mutual identification.

When the child entered preadolescence, Mr. A. was at a complete loss as to how to deal with his son's widening interests, and especially his beginning heterosexual activities. He continued to treat his son as a latency child, and the only secure way he had of showing his interest and affection was to offer the kind of excursions his own father had offered him. Lacking the adolescent experiences with his own father, Mr. A. seemed unable to switch and participate in his son's newfound interests and activities. It was as if he could be sensitive and alert to the needs for closeness, comfort, and encouragement in a latency child, but seemed at a loss in relating to a more independent preadolescent and adolescent boy.

It seemed clear that Mr. A.'s ability to parent had been seriously interfered with. This had three roots: one was the unresolved conflict over aggression that was also at the base of Mr. A.'s difficulty in pursuing his professional work.

Second was the pathological identification with his dead father and his young son which served to make Mr. A. unconsciously repeat the feared conflicts with his son, limiting his role as a parent, and affecting his son's growth and development. Third, Mr. A. also suffered in his parental function because he had missed the experiences and interactions with his father in the developmental phases beyond latency that would have given him the necessary varieties of experience useful in dealing with his son's struggles in the later phases of development.

DISCUSSION

These three cases give some indication about what factors might promote adequate adaptation to the death of a parent in childhood, as well as what might interfere. First, there is the need to impart accurate information about the death. Bob and Mr. A. both had this, so it is obvious that information is not enough. The experience of John demonstrates the long-term effect of distorted information, or concealing information. He not only had problems during each of his stepmother's pregnancies, but reacted in adolescence to the concealment of the death of a pet. Of course, he was the youngest of the three when his mother died, and people in the environment seem to have particular difficulty in finding appropriate explanations for preschool children. It can be concluded that older children find it easier to understand the death cognitively, but this also is not enough.

The second aspect for consideration is allowing the child to grieve. All three cases showed some initial grief, and Bob also grieved at a ceremony at the anniversary of his father's death. Both Bob and Mr. A. were encouraged to mature at a more rapid rate than normal, and this might have a tendency to cut down on the expression of grief. John was not encouraged to cry, but was rather allowed to remain immature, which tends to support denial. This latter tendency would also tend to be found more often in younger children.

Of course, children might react immediately to a death in other ways than showing grief. They might show denial, as John did, by distracting themselves, and becoming overinvolved in play. They might show various symptoms of regression, such as night fears, or, like Bob, wetting. There might be a generally depressed affect. Some children might express anger, although the direct show of anger is not common. John showed it by his provocative behavior with his stepmother, and Bob by his attack on the clay figure symbolizing his father. We do not think that the omnipotence so prominent in all these three cases was a result of the death, but more likely preceded it, because all three were, for one reason or another, especially prized children. It may relate to the later effect of feeling responsible for the death.

The most difficult area to study is the fate of the internal representation of the dead parent. This can be related to the more easily observed factor of providing an adequate substitute for the parent, for support and identification. Sometimes such a substitute is provided too early, interfering with the gradual giving up of the parent. Bob's play with his clay man can be considered a model, and he worked with this for a year-and-a-half. His brother was sufficiently older than Bob to provide a substitute that Bob could use. John had his paternal grandmother, and then a stepmother. He was unable to make full use of stepmother, probably because his internal representation of his mother was never really given up. It must have been deeply repressed, as little evidence of awareness of his mother was seen in analysis. Mr. A. apparently tried to find substitutes in teachers and other authorities, but basically had to become his own father, with all the difficulties previously described.

The late effects of the death of a parent in childhood vary considerably, depending on individual circumstances. Certain generalizations may be made from these three cases. Common to all was a difficulty in learning or working up to potential. This was particularly true of John and Mr. A., whose openly expressed hostility and omnipotence made them feel responsible for the death of their parent. Bob's hostility was more inhibited, but his omnipotence interfered with his choice of vocation. As far as is known, he had made the best adult adjustment. All three also showed their vulnerability to incidents reminiscent of the death, the boys in adolescence, and Mr. A. in adulthood. Although the boys could not be followed long enough to see if certain predicted problems occurred, the experience of Mr. A. indicates that, when the parent of the same sex is lost, there might be difficulties in parenting, and also an identification which would lead to the expectation of following the parent in death at the same age. One can only guess that the death of a parent of the opposite sex may lead to difficulties in later heterosexual relationships.

In summary, these cases illustrate various early and late effects of the death of a parent in childhood, and suggest various interventions to help such children, and at least partially prevent later consequences. It is comforting to know that, even if there are difficulties in adulthood, psychoanalysis can help such people mourn in a more adequate fashion.

Chapter 11

Construction and Reconstruction in a Case of Parent Loss

Benjamin Garber, M.D.

Mourning in children is a very complex subject about which much has been written and about which little is understood. While the understanding of mourning in the adult seems to have evolved as a sequential and relatively linear process, mourning in the child has remained an enigmatic problem due to the concomitant developmental complexities. Although there seems to be a consensus in the psychoanalytic literature that children usually need assistance in dealing with the loss of a parent (Furman, 1974), finding the optimum method of doing so has been elusive. Due to environmental changes, the immaturity of the psychic apparatus, and developmental shifts the optimum therapeutic approach with the child whose parent has died has been difficult to delineate. In those instances where the loss has occurred during the preverbal period, treatment has remained at best a nebulous undertaking.

This paper was presented to the panel on the Vulnerable Child at the American Psychoanalytic Association meeting, May 13, 1982, Boston.

With latency age children and older, whose development has been arrested as a result of their loss, the therapeutic stance seems more definitive. Usually the child is expected to engage in some type of mourning activity which may be in keeping with his developmental capabilities (Garber, 1981). Some latency age youngsters may indeed manage an adultlike mourning process while others will more than likely experience some type of partial mourning work which may have to be completed at some later period in their development. However, for those children who experienced the loss in a time frame that one tends to think of as prepsychological, it is reasonable to wonder about the therapeutic strategies. Although such youngsters may be suffering from arrests and fixations dating from the time of the loss, their ability to go back and recapture the genetic roots of such traumas may be impossible. Such limitations may be due to the immaturity of the psychic apparatus as well as certain cognitive deficits.

In *A Child's Parent Dies* (1974) Erna Furman addressing herself to this issue wrote: "In patients who experienced the death of a parent as babies or toddlers the stress appeared to affect basic aspects of their personality development. Our interest focused on several patients whose difficulties centered especially on interferences with developing ego functions" (p. 173).

Dr. Eleanor Galenson (1982), responding to the same issue from a therapeutic vantage point indicated that when a loss occurs before age three, the parents are not fully introjected. She illustrated this point with one of her cases who had lost a parent at eighteen months of age. As a result, her relationship with her doctor was not a transference but a primary relationship. Should the relationship be disrupted, she would then begin to mourn this primary relationship for the first time.

Dr. Justin Call (1976), at a panel addressing this very issue, raised the question as to whether the warded off grief as a result of early parent loss exists as an affect potential that must emerge in later analysis, or whether a different kind of reaction is present from the start.

The clinical material in this case was not the usual type of parent loss referral. Rather this was a situation in which a seven-year-old child was trying to assimilate a trauma which was preverbal (age twenty-two months) and in some ways the remnant from a time period before the child can report internal psychological states.

Steve was seven years old when his father first brought him for an evaluation. There were no specific complaints except for a history of intermittent enuresis and occasional temper tantrums. The main motive for referral was that Steve's mother died when he was twenty-two months old and his father wished to "check things out"; he was interested in acquiring an objective impression of how his son was getting along without a mother and whether he (the father) was doing an adequate job as a parent.

Steve's mother was killed in a car accident as the family was driving to visit the maternal grandparents. It was raining heavily at the time and there was a head-on collision with another car which skidded into their path. The father had a number of serious injuries, Steve's five-year-old sister was also injured, while his mother was killed instantly; she was twenty-six at the time. Steve was the least injured in the accident, he had a seizure the following year and was put on phenobarbital for a couple of years, but a subsequent electroencephalogram (EEG) was normal. Some of the crucial events and details in and around the accident as well as the subsequent adaptation to the trauma were missing. Even though the father said that he talked about it and could talk about it with his children and with the clinician, he was far more interested in discussing his son's enuresis, his school performance, which was excellent, and asking advice on how to raise his children.

There had been a succession of housekeepers to take care of the children, none of them overly satisfactory. The last one was an older woman who was very punitive with the boy for his bed-wetting.

Steve's parents were married for seven years prior to his mother's death. The marriage was quite stable and Steve's father described his wife as a wonderful mother and a great lady. There was a hint of marital difficulties several months prior to the accident but the family situation was described as good and stable.

Steve's father was a rather pleasant, outgoing, bright, and articulate man. There was an intensity and a surface businesslike manner which tended to obscure an underlying sense of warmth and spontaneity.

In his younger years the father was a rather lonely and unhappy child who was treated as an outsider. He kept his feelings to himself, and was seen as an eccentric as well as a poor student. In high school, he became more social with his only interests being material things and cars. Father was in therapy while in high school and apparently had a positive experience. In college he did quite well, received a degree in accounting, and entered his father's chemical business. There were many struggles with his own father who was seen as a rigid autocrat. Eventually he took over the business, expanded it, and was extremely successful in his work. Paternal grandfather had died two years earlier from a heart attack while the paternal grandmother had continued to function well and had been actively involved with Steve, and his sister. The maternal grandparents, who lived in a different city, had also been very interested in the children; they visited often, and Steve had spent vacations and part of the summer with them.

From father's history, it was not clear just what happened to Steve and his sister after mother's death. There was a brief hospitalization and the children participated in the funeral, but beyond that the subsequent period of adjustment of the family was fuzzy. Steve's father became very involved in his work; this necessitated frequent travel which the children seemed to handle well. Father was also involved with a number of different women, some of whom became very attached to the children and noticed that Steve seemed unhappy. They urged the father to seek professional help for Steve. Although father considered remarriage after recovering from his loss, the last few years he had enjoyed the role of a widower and playboy.

Steve's relationship with his sister had always been poor, as she seemed problem free, sociable, and very provocative with her younger brother. Although they complained about each other constantly, they seemed to get along better when father was away or when they united against a disliked housekeeper.

Steve presented himself initially as a rather small, appealing freckle-faced, restless youngster who in some ways appeared very mature. There was a certain bravado about him, mixed with sadness. Although he was able to tell the clinician with little emotion that his mother died, he did become sad and somewhat forlorn when he described his father, sister, and himself as living in a big, sad, and empty house. When the author sensed that Steve was telling him that something was missing, he brightened up and asked for help with math problems to figure things out.

He was very verbal, bright, and expressive and told the clinician, with his foghorn voice, about the fights with his sister, which he considered his biggest problem. At the same time, he mentioned that he and his sister talked a lot and sent secret messages to one another when their father was out of town. When the clinician asked Steve how he could be helped, he made up a word game in which one put together different sentences, which were: "the boy needs love," "the boy needs help."

The clinician started seeing him with some trepidation as it was not clear what he would be trying to help Steve with. Obviously he was in pain and indicated a need for help, so he must have had something in mind. Since he had no recollections of his mother, helping him deal with the loss and its significance at best seemed a rather nebulous task. At the same time, the clinician was the recipient of father's pressure and requests to help his son overcome the enuresis as well as constant demands for advice and guidance on how to deal with both children. In the beginning, the clinician had some serious misgivings about the therapeutic possibilities.

Steve settled into the treatment routine very comfortably, whether playing games or discussing his father's frequent business trips. His initial transference reaction was stimulated by a trip the clinician took during a winter vacation. Upon his return Steve was alternately curious and angry. He missed an appointment and then for the first time expressed mild curiosity about death, dying, and what really happens to people after they die. He talked about an uncle who had died a couple of years earlier, while his children still get money from him (presumably some kind of trust fund). He wondered how that could be. He also began to emphasize the frantic quality in his play and his verbalizations. Since he was going away for a week he was driven in a kind of semicontrolled frenzy of telling the clinician as much as he could and playing as many games as possible. Each time the clinician would mention the possibility of some anxiety about his death or the clinician's, it did not seem to have any impact on Steve's behavior. Only some time later did the clinician begin to realize that the activity had to do with a sense of something missing and an almost driven self-propelled need to fill a void.

The following spring he seemed to have a mild reaction to their latest housekeeper being fired. There were several episodes of anxiety at night, when his father was out of town.

During this period he was somewhat clinging to his sister; however, an attempt to connect this loss to previous losses did not prove to be very fruitful. He invited the clinician to attend a carnival at his school and seemed lost and remained distant when he was told this was not possible. Interpretations about his feeling hurt, disappointed, and anger did not have much impact either. Even pointing out that this might be his attempt to replace the missing parent did not have any effect. When the clinician was late on a couple of occasions he became anxious while sitting alone in the waiting room. It soon became apparent that Steve carried a number of items in his knapsack no matter where he went, whether to school, his sessions, or just to visit. The items varied from his baseball card collection, to stories that he wrote and books that he read, or might read.

During another trip that he went on with his father he told the clinician that he kept track of the times when he should have been at his sessions. He noted the time differential and was curious about what the clinician was doing at those times.

About a year after therapy started, for the first time he began to talk about his mother. This was stirred up once again by the clinician's anticipated vacation. He talked about an upcoming visit to the cemetery to see his grandfather's grave and mentioned in passing that his mother's grave was close by, so he would get to see it. He then wondered why his mother was not buried where her parents live. The next session Steve surprised the clinician in that he remembered his mother putting on a raincoat and going out for a drive in the rain. It was raining quite heavily when they were involved in the accident in which his mother was killed. When the clinician questioned his remembrance of this event and wondered what other things he remembered he dashed into a phase of frantic activity which lasted for the next several sessions.

After the clinician's return from a vacation, Steve became

preoccupied with death once again. His questions and thoughts on the subject ranged from the philosophical to the obscure. There were the usual curiosities about reincarnation and whether people come back to life as other people or as animals. He also wondered if a person committed a crime and died in jail would someone else have to complete his jail sentence. He then became curious about orphans in various movies and raised questions about what happens to the child if the dead parent comes back to life or did not die after all. Each period of questioning ended in sadness. Any attempts to relate these questions to his own history elicited defensiveness, anger, and intense complaints about having to see me. These episodes were interspersed with periods in which he was markedly curious about the clinician's life. When he was frustrated in the transference he became angry and occasionally stalked out of the office. When the clinician answered his questions and then tried to explore their significance, he kept complaining that the clinician really did not answer anything, nor tell him anything that he wanted to know. He went away on a trip during spring vacation, and upon his return he complained bitterly about having to see the clinician. He had no problems— except his hate for his sister and his resentment about seeing the clinician. With marked glee he elaborated a whole series of phantasies of killing the clinician, burning his office, throwing him out the window, and trying to convince his father that seeing the clinician was a waste of time and money. His anger was interpreted as a displacement from feelings about his father who goes away, and that helped temporarily. Since the clinician reminded him of his problems, especially the loss of his mother, seeing him made Steve feel worse. He experienced some excitement when the clinician interpreted his wish to set the office on fire so that he could put it out with his urinary stream. There emerged a sequence of phantasies, which appeared at night when he went to the bathroom, whose theme was a fear of being flushed down the toilet because he is such a "little shit." There were also castration fears, as symbolized by dreams of being bitten by alligators coming out of the toilet and robbers coming through the window to cut off his dangling feet. The anger persisted for the next couple of weeks, which he expressed via complaints about boredom, restlessness, and finding flaws in what the clinician did, said, or how he looked.

During one extremely frustrating session, in which he was alternately angry, sad, and tearful, he said that if his mother were still alive he would not be seeing the clinician now nor at any other time. The clinician was taken aback by this rather insightful comment and after some thought felt that he was probably right. At this point he calmed down and became sad and pensive, he then said that he really did not remember his mother. The clinician wondered if Steve thought what life would be like if his mother were still alive, in fact, the clinician also wondered what he thought life was like before she died and afterwards; and most importantly, did he wonder what his mother was like as a person. As he became preoccupied with these questions, he started to bring food to the sessions, as both he and the clinician noticed that it calmed him. It was then decided that his mother was an excellent cook and that she also enjoyed her food, as somewhere he heard and saw pictures in which she was overweight. When he went away for a few days he was able to tell the clinician that he missed him and then became especially sad when he remembered that it was the anniversary of his mother's death. Steve showed the clinician a scar from the car accident which actually was from a later injury. Steve "remembered" how beautifully his mother played the piano, and when he brought a book of short stories that he and the clinician read to one another, he "reminisced" about how she used to read to him. The tone of the sessions began to shift as he was excited when he and the clinician discovered something about how things were or might have been, but he would become melancholy and impatient when the clinician interfered in his elaboration of the past on flimsy evidence. Steve was full of questions about what life was like in the old days—the days of black-and-white television and radio serials. He became obsessed with "the good old days" and in this manner decided what movies, television, and radio shows his mother must have liked.

Since his mother came from a city in which they made baseball bats, he concluded that she must have been an avid baseball fan. So for a while he became preoccupied with current teams, but more importantly, with former baseball players and their accomplishments. His baseball card collection was huge.

It became apparent that his preoccupation with the past, his phantasies about his mother and their life together became the single most crucial element of the therapeutic work. The work became an amalgam of his transference reactions, sketchy information about his mother, his phantasies, and the clinician's understanding of development and how it is affected by the loss of a parent at a particular age. The work did not proceed in a linear fashion, but in fits and starts and at the most unexpected times. After a very productive session he said rather sadly that as soon as the clinician and he started to figure out how it used to be, he knew that he was not going to see him that much longer. In other words, the construction and reconstruction of the past ushered in the termination phase of the analysis.

Certain developmental milestones such as taking the bus by himself to the sessions, and going to overnight camp precipitated a number of anxieties about the clinician's death. He checked his age very carefully and compared him to his father, as he frequently worried about his father's death. After much questioning, he decided that his father did not remarry because he loved his wife so much. He and the clinician then reminisced about what birthdays were like when his mother was alive, as well as the kind of birthday parties he had after she died. This resulted in a string of meaningful memories about different housekeepers and what they were like.

He finally said how much he enjoyed playing table games with the clinician because he "knew" that his mother liked them since his father did not. That answered the clinician's puzzlement about his minor concerns as to who won or lost. At this time he also admitted how much he missed his sister who was away at overnight camp. They corresponded faithfully and he sat calmly as he had the clinician read her letters out loud, just the way his mother would have done.

Steve related a number of episodes in which he provoked fights with his father about his meals and the type of food that he ate. Steve and the clinician decided that he must have done something similar with his mother. His reaction was to leave a hoard of candy for himself in the office. He surmised that when he was younger he was like his mother, but as he became older he was more like his father, and now in some way, he might even be like the clinician. When his father had a party, Steve became curious about alcohol and what it does to a person (there was some question that the driver of the other car may have been drunk). He then explored the whole issue of blame for his mother's death as it related to his father's driving skills which he monitored conscientiously. He now understood why he was reluctant to go on father's sailboat, as they had been involved in a minor boating accident a couple of years earlier. During a time period in school when his teacher was replaced by a substitute he "remembered" that his mother was also a teacher and that she also liked working in the library. That is why he liked reading and collecting books. He remembered that one of the things that he liked about the clinician when he first came was that there were so many books in the office.

One of the more significant interactions occurred when his father left the country on a month-long business trip. Steve was very anxious; at first he kept charts, maps, and a calendar of his father's activities, which was helpful. One day he came in very exhuberant with a new book: it was a poem by Shel Silverstein (1976) called *The Missing Piece*. During the next couple of weeks Steve and the clinician read and reread this very poignant poem, looked at the pictures, and experimented with different verses and pictures. Most importantly, they understood the content and its profound meaning for Steve. It was the story of a something which was missing a piece and it was not happy, so it set off in search of its missing piece. The different adventures encountered in the search, the attempts at trying different pieces to fill in the place of what was missing, and eventually finding what looked like a perfect fit. All this is told with humor, charm, and directness. Meantime, Steve heard from his father and then he and the clinician tried to figure out what it would have been like if both of his parents had gone on trips as he grew older.

At this time Steve started to remember lengthy dreams. Some of the dreams dealt with driving big, fast cars on lonely country roads and it keeps raining. In one dream he gets put in jail for driving too fast, which he felt was not fair. We explored his feelings of guilt over the accident and his survival. He then responded by becoming hostile and provocative, leaving sessions early, and throwing things. We finally agreed that he was testing the clinician the way he must have tested his mother to see just how much of his badness could be tolerated. The temper tantrums were also a way of distracting father from his work and letting him know that all was not well. As the tantrums continued he realized his guilt feelings over the accident and the need to be punished. After he surmised the full impact of his rage at the clinician and his father for the accident, and being put in a position of suffering and atonement, he settled down.

There was another dream in which the clinician was

selling candy from behind a counter and it seemed he was about ready to fold up his booth, since he had sold all the candy and it was time to leave.

After this period his mood shifted once again, he became more subdued, and the activity level diminished. He talked a lot about school and complained about the trouble he was having with science, if only his mother was around she could explain it to him better than his teacher. But after some thought he concluded that probably she did not like science either, but was more interested in literature and art. Perhaps he may continue to have periodic difficulties with science throughout his school years.

As a date was set for the termination, he handled some of the sessions by sitting in the waiting room after the appointment began, and then would come in and pretend, as if the clinician did not know that he was there. Steve and the clinician wondered whether if his mother were alive perhaps there would be periods during which she would have preferred to be away from him and he from her. He then focused on his disappointment with his father who could provide all sorts of material things, while the clinician could provide some emotional things, or as he would refer to them as "missing piece things," but neither one of us could provide a mother.

During the last couple of months he was very low key with occasional flashes of excitement. Together the clinician and Steve did go back and do most of the things that they had done in the three years of treatment. Only they did them more slowly, thoughtfully, and deliberately. This is probably how his mother would have done it. On a couple of occasions he helped the clinician close up the office and then walked him to his train, but halfway through he would change his mind. He explained the change by a realization that he did not want to walk as fast as the clinician did, he would rather walk at his own pace. Our last sessions were spent in reading the poem, *The Missing Piece.*

And then one day it came upon another piece that seemed to
   be just right.
It fit! It fit perfectly! At last, At last!
And away it rolled and because it was now complete it rolled
   faster and faster.
Faster than it had ever rolled before.
So fast it could not stop to talk to a worm, or smell a flower.
Too fast for a butterfly to land.
Oh my, now that it was complete it could not sing at all.
Aha, it thought, so that is how it is.
So it stopped rolling and set the piece down gently and
   slowly rolled away.*

In clinical work in general, we work with derivatives and
telescoping of memories and affects from earlier emotional
states. This is a crucial element in any therapeutic undertaking, but in this case it was not enough. Almost from the very
beginning Steve and the clinician knew that something was
missing and Steve was hopeful that the clinician would
provide "it" while in turn, the clinician felt limited in his
ability to do so. The result was a consensus in which the
clinician decided to try and provide him with something and
he had the choice of rejecting or accepting it, but at the least
there was a choice.

When one talks of this mysterious something that is
missing, then the discourse tends to range from complex
metapsychological formulations at one extreme to philosophical speculations at the other. Neither one was quite appropriate for a seven-year-old child who was extremely unhappy.
It seemed that what he was missing, among other things, was
a sense of his own history and the continuity of some of the
events that shaped his very being; for this absence contributed

---

*Abridged from THE MISSING PIECE by Shel Silverstein. Copyright
© 1976 by Snake Eye Music, Inc. Reprinted by permission of Harper &
Row, Publishers, Inc.

to a sense of neediness, restlessness, searching, and expectation. Whether due to the immaturity of his psychic apparatus, repression of the traumatic past, or from an environmental conspiracy of silence, something was indeed missing in this child. He was determined, in spite of the clinician's initial interference and later with his help, to arrive at some kind of coherent story to help him understand and fill in his past.

When attempting to reconstruct the past, some analysts have stressed the importance of recovering via reconstruction the actual traumatizing events since their impact is different from that of phantasy (Greenacre, 1956). Others have suggested that one cannot recover the actual event since its meaning is constantly changing during development and it is subjected to the selective scrutiny of memory (Kris, 1956). Still other writers believe that the important element may be the analyst's provision of a new conceptual framework making possible new connections through which the patient can see himself differently (Loewald, 1960). In regard to the psychoanalysis of children, Kennedy (1971) has expressed an idea similar to Loewald's. She has suggested that reconstruction in child analysis functions primarily as a means of providing a conceptual framework for the child whereby he can understand his present dilemmas rather than being aimed at giving him a complete and true insight into everything that happened in the past.

Lopez and Kliman (1979) in their analysis of a four-year-old girl, whose mother died when she was nineteen months old, depended on an active effort at reconstruction of the past based perhaps on memories and things overheard, however vague they might be. However, this youngster was seen as a rather exceptional child with unusually developed visual memory skills. There may be certain children who respond to an early loss by recalling very early events, especially memories of the loss which are essentially self-generated rather than gathered through input from adults.

In Steve's particular case this was not possible—for he remembered nothing about the loss—yet he was searching and longing for something. So instead of attempting to reconstruct the past, one had to be created anew from its very beginnings. The work with this child involved more than putting words to preverbal experiences, it entailed the reconstruction of a plausible history of the patient who then tried to work it through. Ideally, such an effort then would allow for new relations, new beginnings, and new solutions to conflicts and problems. In a sense, it was an attempt to provide for him and create with him a history of his past that he could then build on, alter, and modify with changing developmental concerns.

What occurred in the treatment is similar to ideas expressed by Cohler and Weiss (Personal Communication, 1981) in which they argue rather convincingly that what occurs in an analysis is that the patient and analyst construct a history of the crucial events that shaped the analysis. In a sense, that is the only truth, for it can be validated and affirmed by both participants. However, before there can be a history of the analysis there has to be some semblance of history of the person himself.

It has often been demonstrated that historical accuracy is not significant for the psychoanalyst and only that which occurs in the clinical situation is important. In this situation the clinical data was enhanced by external events as well as by an appreciation of normal development and the impact of parent loss at a crucial time in the child's life. Such an imbrication of data from various sources made the construction meaningful, plausible, but above all syntonic with the developmental needs of this child.

As the treatment progressed, he became visibly calmer and more content in the office as well as outside. He was also able to relinquish the need for his sister and to some extent his dependence on his father for what was missing. Perhaps the ability to accept a substitute, which may or may not coincide with his idealized creation of what a mother should be, may become the next milestone or crisis in his life.

It would seem that during each developmental phase this child may have to go back and rework his life history. During each succeeding developmental stage he may need to step back and in a sense try to "refit" and to reconstitute the missing piece. Such a task is perfectly acceptable and reasonable for it seems that our work together was not really the end, but it was only a beginning.

Section V

The Parent Loss Project:
Adult Cases

Chapter 12

Activation of Mourning and Growth by Psychoanalysis

Joan Fleming, M.D., and Sol Altschul, M.D.

In this paper we intend to present clinical evidence (1) for phenomena associated with pathological mourning as an adaptation to object-loss; and (2) showing how psychoanalytic treatment activated the mourning process and facilitated resumption of arrested development.

This paper is presented as part of the work of a group of analysts at the Chicago Institute of Psychoanalysis studying the effect of object-loss in childhood on adult personality structure. This group research, called the Parent Loss Project, has been described in another paper (Fleming, 1963) which defines the special population of patients and the method of study. All the patients are chronological adults who have lost a parent by death in childhood. They are being treated by psychoanalysis, which offers an excellent method for observing the effect of various childhood experiences on the development of adult personality structure.

Reprinted by permission of *The International Journal of Psycho-Analysis* (1963), 44:419–431.

In the psychoanalytic situation childhood events are relived in the transference, and the vicissitudes of the ego's adaptation to the stresses of normal growth as well as to pathogenic experiences can be subjected to close scrutiny. Regressive and integrative processes become observable, and various developmental influences on the structuralizing of the ego can be studied through the testing of reconstructive inferences.

Our study has focused on the adaptation to loss of a significant object prior to maturity when the structure of the personality is more vulnerable to deprivation of an object needed to supply experiences essential for normal growth and development. In recent years there has been increasing emphasis on the importance of the object in the development of personality. This has been documented in both clinical and theoretical studies. Many authors have written on the function of the object in normal development, and others on the effect of object deprivation as an interference with the developmental process. Most of these studies have been made on the mother–child relationship in early infancy, on longitudinal studies of child development, or on institutional or foster-home placement as it affects the growth of children. Very few reports have been made of observations on adults who have suffered the loss of an important libidinal object during the formative stages of the child's development. One of these studies, conducted by Hilgard and Newman (1959), was an important stimulus to our own work. They investigated anniversary reactions in adult patients who had lost a parent in childhood and who, after becoming parents themselves, developed a psychosis.

In a preliminary report (Fleming, Altschul, Zielinski, and Forman, 1958), evidence was presented from the analyses of the first three cases in our series, which demonstrated a disturbed adaptation to the death of the parent. The immediate reaction was characterized by absence of grief at the time of loss, and denial of the reality was manifested in various forms. Efforts to adapt to the trauma resulted in uncompleted mourning work and what appeared to be a persisting immaturity. Patterns of immature behavior seemed to be correlated with the level of development achieved by each patient at the time of loss. In our preliminary report, very rough correlations were made with generally accepted descriptions of phase-specific behavior.

Since then, in a larger series of patients, correlations of adult behavior patterns with developmental phases point toward an arrest of the normal process, especially in the area of ego-object relations. A striking picture of immaturity in self-image and in the development of ego-ideal and superego structures is apparent. Reality-testing, impulse control, object-need, and self-object awareness are not adequate for adult functioning in the patients studied. These manifestations of ego deficiencies seem to belong to levels of functioning more appropriate to different stages of childhood development. We encountered many difficulties in attempting to make an accurate diagnosis of phase-specific behavior, as well as in formulating metapsychological concepts of age-adequate progress along significant lines of development. The recent work being done at the Hampstead Clinic by Anna Freud and her colleagues on profiles of development promises to be of great assistance in our investigation of adults (Sandler, 1960; Sandler, Kawenoka, Neurath, Rosenblatt, Schnurmann, and Sigal, 1962; Sandler and Rosenblatt, 1962; A. Freud, 1962).

It was with the first case in our series, a twenty-nine-year old woman who had lost both parents in middle adolescence, that recognition of these phenomena and their dynamics began to occur. The first clue was apparent in the failure of the transference to develop after the usual pattern. For some time this situation prevented our clear understanding of the patient's dynamics and the dynamics of the therapeutic relationship.

In the analytic situation, the defensive denial of the

reality of loss was manifested in two ways; first, by negating the significance of the analyst in present reality, and second, by insistence on repeating with the analyst the fictional relationship with the lost parent. This state of affairs produced a transference resistance which interfered with the establishment of a therapeutic alliance as a basis for interpretation and working through. The patient's defensive balance demanded that no relationship with a new object could exist, especially on a new basis, because it would disturb the protective illusion and require the patient to face the painful fact of parental death and to resume the mourning work successfully avoided up to this time.

When we realized that giving the analyst any significance in her present life meant to her the establishment of a new relationship that would force her to give up her fantasy that her parents were still alive, we began to see the fixation and its defensive function, and knew the therapeutic task was to break through the defensive denial of loss and to complete the work of mourning. The mourning process had to be set in motion before analyzable regressive transference neurosis could develop. In a number of cases we have observed, once the resistance against mourning has been overcome, the analyst becomes important not only as a transference figure but as a new object useful in new integrations.

In this paper we offer clinical evidence from the analysis of one patient to show: (1) how the defense structure she had built up in response to the trauma of separation and loss of her parents delayed the development of an analyzable transference in the first 270 hours of therapy; (2) how this serious resistance was broken through; (3) how the patient's investment of energy in a therapeutic relationship activated the mourning process with the recall of previously repressed memories and the experiencing of grief; (4) how, when the mourning for the dead parents had been partially accomplished with much of the guilt for the ambivalence resolved, the patient began to work through her adolescent sexual conflict, which had continued to exist for fourteen years on an early adolescent level; (5) growth and change began to occur with the achievement of insight into the denial mechanisms. Termination of the analysis reproduced the traumatic separation in the transference, but with a more integrated ego which could grieve and mourn for old losses and new separations without trying "to make time stop." Lastly, we would like to discuss the theoretical aspects of mourning derived from this case and how it correlates with the work of previous investigators.

CLINICAL MATERIAL

The patient, a twenty-nine-year-old woman, was an only child born in Germany, who separated from her parents at age fifteen. Her parents remained behind and were killed in the European massacre sometime around her eighteenth year. She entered analysis because of anxiety and depression, precipitated by failure to pass an examination in graduate school, and disappointment in a love affair.

In the early hours of the analysis, the picture unfolded of the adolescent quality of her twenty-nine-year-old character structure. These adolescent patterns and the typical early adolescent conflicts dominated the analysis. The preoedipal and oedipal material which comes into sharp focus in the usual analysis played a very subordinate role in this one.

However, since she was twenty-nine years old, it did not occur to either of us to think of her as an adolescent in her character structure until the analysis had gone on for some time, and the difficulties in establishing an analyzable transference became apparent. Even then we did not diagnose these difficulties as being born of the adolescent personality structure. The uncompleted mourning struck us first. The denial of the parents' death, the absence of grief for them, were observations which preceded the recognition of the extent and fixity of the persisting adolescent personality structure.

In the beginning of treatment, in what we later recognized as a characteristically adolescent attitude, the patient protested that she did not really need help—she was sure she could work out her problems by herself, although it might take longer. She felt that external circumstances were primarily responsible for her difficulties and insisted that everything would be all right if only she could have a satisfactory love affair.

In relating her history, she described her inability, up to the age of twenty-nine, to establish warm relationships with either men or women. She had few girlfriends her own age. With her aunt she was defiant and rebellious, feeling that the aunt was trying to dominate her as she felt her mother had tried to do. With men she carried on a buddy-buddy relationship even when she had intercourse with them. She tended to avoid any close contact except in her fantasies, but became easily hurt and felt rejected when men turned away from her.

Prior to the age of ten her memories were vague and meager. The patient was fixed on the few years just before and after the separation from her parents, which she described as the longest span of her life. During the whole analysis very few memories were recovered that belonged to the earlier period, although it is more than likely that this period of time predisposed the patient to this type of defensive character structure.

Her emotional tone at the time of the separation from her parents appeared to be typical of some adolescents with a conflict over sexuality. Her romantic fantasies, which were about imaginary men, were always kept secret. Later she rejected any idea of having a man for herself and depreciated women whose only task is to have children and be housewives.

She prided herself on her lack of breasts, her boyish figure, her masculine stride, and was considered arrogant, aggressive, and bossy by her friends. Keeping a diary was another pattern characteristic of her adolescence. She filled this diary with arguments between herself and her parents, and compared the need to write in the diary with "the need to have a friend to whom you can tell everything because after all there are some things that you can't discuss with your parents."

It was in this atmosphere that the separation took place. Little information was reported about the decision to separate or the events and affects surrounding the separation itself until much later when the process of mourning for her parents was far advanced. Letters full of arguments continued the old type of relationship with her parents which had existed in Germany. She did not hear of their fate until after the war, although after 1942 her letters brought no reply. When people sympathized on hearing about her parents' death, she felt guilty because of her lack of obvious mourning. In fact, she occasionally had the fantasy that if they did come to England she might have to support them, and this she did not want to do. In the last few years prior to therapy, any conversation which brought thoughts about her parents evoked tears.

One of the difficult problems was the resistance of the patient to letting herself be aware of her involvement in the analysis. She talked about being afraid that she would be overwhelmed if she became fond of someone, and said that her feelings about the analyst were amorphous. Continuing along this line, she expressed the idea that the treatment had become a nuisance: "It's silly to investigate some of these things; these are ideas I picked up in the course of my life and I just ought to shrug my shoulders about it."

Around the 100th hour came the shift in the patient's recognition of the analyst as someone of importance to her.

After being informed of the analyst's vacation, she had a dream of dying, being shunned and abandoned, and subsequently got depressed. When the relationship to the vacation was pointed out, she said she "almost had a desire to be taken care of." She thought of the analyst and then dismissed the thought. Shortly after this, she felt helpless and abandoned and, for the first time with any affect, began to talk about her parents. She began to realize that she was much more affected by their loss than she had thought.

Concurrent with her denial of the analyst's significance to her, she dreamed of her parents' being alive. In these dreams she was embroiled in arguments, trying to provoke them and feeling deprived. This seemed to support the defense of denial and to maintain the illusion of their existence. This illusion was continued in another form through the development of an affair with a married man. She acted out with him a fantasy of a relationship with an older man, and used it as a resistance against an awareness of feelings and fantasies about the analyst. As long as the patient was able to continue to confuse the analyst with her friend B., she was able to confuse both the analyst and B. with the image of her father, and so deny father's death. As she began to feel frustrated in the relationship with B. and to recognize a need to repeat frustrating experiences, she became better able to differentiate between the analyst and B.

At about the 270th hour, using this greater differentiation on her part as a wedge, a suggestion was made that she stop the acting out. It was felt that she could tolerate this prohibition because she had become a little more involved in the analytic relationship. The patient became depressed, but in response to a transference interpretation got some recognition of the struggle with her parents at age thirteen.

At this point, the 280th hour, she brought in a fragment of a dream, "I left the icebox door open and everything was defrosted. Things were beginning to spoil. I could not imagine why I had left it open." This dream seemed to indicate that the defense of repetition in fantasies was no longer as effective as before.

In the next series of hours, as the analyst became increasingly recognizable as an important figure in the transference, the grief associated with the loss of the parents came to the surface, but was pushed aside. The patient reacted to the second annual vacation with the idea that she would miss the analyst but that it was futile to talk about it.

After this vacation she expressed directly the feeling that she was beginning to feel toward the analyst as a child feels toward her father. Also in hanging up her coat in the office, she felt like an intruder and remembered arguments with her mother. She dreamed of her parents in Germany. They had gone out without her and she was in a rage. In association to this dream, memories of what the parents had been like returned. She wondered if father preferred mother. As this material unfolded it was associated with more grief. She remarked, "There are times when I wish my parents were alive and could see me now; it is agonizing to think that I will never see them again." She said at this point, "I've hit a new low," and reported a confused dream, "I didn't know where I was. I couldn't understand time." She compared this dream to one she had just before entering analysis in which she awoke one morning and couldn't get up because she "had forgotten her coordinates." In looking back this dream seemed to represent her fear of change, and an unconscious understanding of her problems, concurring as it did with her first step toward getting help for herself.

In relationship to feeling excluded and rejected in an affair, she wondered if this did not resemble some old feeling she had about her parents. When the analyst agreed, her response was, "I won't see them again, I'll never see them again." She began to cry and said, "I must have loved them. I never wanted to look at that." Then she wondered why she should have chosen that way to deal with her feelings about her parents— denial: "It's back to the death of my parents." This time the interpretation was made that as long as she could perpetuate the feelings of conflict with her parents, she could continue to reenact her preloss relationship with them and so continue to believe they were alive. In the 450th hour, on coming across a story of the War, the patient began to cry during the hour, with great affect, and asked, "Am I belatedly mourning my parents?"

At this point, longer in duration than in many analyses, the relationship in the transference had opened up and activated a grief reaction that had previously been repressed. The task, at this point, was the resolution of the mourning for her parents in addition to the resolution of the normal conflicts of adolescence. Both involved separation for the sake of growth.

In response to the third vacation, a shift in conflict appeared. The patient focused more on the wish to separate two people in contrast to her former fear of being abandoned.

Material in the hours dealt with envy of her mother's hair, and a desire to be more feminine. In a dream, she was in the middle between a man and a woman and felt squeezed out. She suggested it would be better "to walk with a woman on each side of the man," which was done. But she felt guilty because the man was holding her intimately. In association, she wondered if she ever felt this way about her parents, and then remembered the time when she got her own room. She felt both pleased and pushed out, "A feeling of suddenly finding out that you have grown."

This was very much the tone of her current life where she felt like a child on the fringe, and at the same time was able to act in a more feminine way with one of her male friends. Although she felt about to make a big jump, she still pictured herself in her fantasies with her parents hugging them and crying. She also had a fantasy of what it would be like to meet the analyst in ten or twenty years. Two events occurred concerning two friends she had known in London, where it was obvious to her that changes had taken place in them. She vigorously insisted that she herself was not going to grow. It was interpreted that she was having more and more difficulty in acting as if the world were the same as it had been when she was fifteen years old.

During the last eighteen months of treatment, there was an increasing elaboration and expression of the mourning process with recall of significant events related to the separation from her parents. Development of insight into her mechanism of denial was achieved, and with this achievement there was a more direct approach to her adolescent conflict. The patient no longer had to depreciate sexuality and competitive impulses. She began to talk about a man, C., with whom she had recently become intimate. She wanted the analyst to meet him, stating, "I, too can have a man."

As she worked through this conflict of wanting a man of her own and choosing between C. and the analyst, she talked about her parents in a different way. "At times I think it's a shame that I never knew them when I was grown and they didn't know me." Here is evidence of acceptance of their death and movement toward the conflicts of later adolescence, with a beginning of detachment of libido from the parental images and making it available for new objects. Some of this energy was attached to the analyst as she used the latter for a transference object to work out her adolescent struggle for emancipation and growth. Here, on the stage of a basic positive relationship, she acted out her adolescent rebelliousness with simultaneous fears of steps toward adulthood. She was feeling rebellious toward the analyst as she planned to move into a new apartment. She reported a dream of some teenage kids all behaving in a noisy, violent fashion, but she was different. She began talking about ending the analysis, but in no concrete way.

Much of the conflict at this stage of the analysis could be

described as the patient's efforts to grow. Steps were made forward, followed by retreat, refusing temporarily to accept the real changes that were taking place in her job, personal life, physical characteristics, and general sense of well-being. In association to her rebellious feelings toward the analyst the patient talked about her rebellious feelings toward her parents with a new insight that in a later stage of development one can see one's parents as people. She had never felt this, but had always taken them for granted.

The conflict about growth continued. It was associated with the expression of grief and increasing perception of the present-day situation. She felt deprived of her parents, but "I refuse to have their place taken." In association to a dream of a power struggle with her mother, she said tearfully, "I don't let my parents die." She began to think about the separation for the sake of her own growth as excluding the parents. Around the time of the fourth vacation, she reported a dream of phoning her father in London, but with the perception that he should be dead. On a vacation of her own, she felt desolate although rebellious. This feeling was associated with the fear that the analyst would not be there on her return. This was interpreted as her fear of the repetition of the real experience. Once she left her parents and had never seen them again. Her reply was, "I thought it would only be for two or three months. How could I get so fouled up? This business of being stuck somewhere without wanting to grow. I feel ashamed of it. It makes me feel inadequate, that I'm not able to cope with my problems better than by refusing to grow up." The reality of the danger in the European situation in 1939 came up. It was interpreted to the patient that she needed to separate from her parents to survive, and that they sent her away so that she could survive. Her associations were, "They must have been more aware of the danger than I. I have to live in the present, and I've never done this."

After the summer vacation, the patient informed the

analyst that she had put in motion an application for restitution from the German government. This was possible because she was accepting the fact of their death. She had a feeling of being on the fence and did not want to jump. She began to bring up the idea of approaching the end of treatment, but "I have some things to work out. It's not a problem of growing up, but it's accepting myself as I am. I'm still not satisfied. If I'm still not satisfied it's too bad. I could always look to the future as before. I kept myself happy by this. Maybe I'm just postponing the moment when I may not like some of these things." She began to have a growing awareness of the passage of time, and made the remark, "I've lost a lot of time—eighteen years."

There was, concurrently with this, a growing awareness of the analyst as a person. "You must have got a lot of pleasure out of fixing this room up. You like it and spend a lot of time here. I'm very pleased, we have something in common. I fix my room, you fix yours." This whole period of struggle about growth culminated in a dream. The patient made a point of saying she dreamed her parents were alive. She was away somewhere on a camping trip. Then she got a phone call that was from her grandmother. Grandmother was beating about the bush regarding some bad news. Patient knew it was about her parents. Grandmother did not want to tell her. She asked the patient on the phone to come back, and the patient said, "For Christ's sake tell me." She was in a panic—something had happened to her parents. Even in the dream she was amazed at her own feeling and was horrified when she learned that they had been killed in an automobile accident. She was grief-stricken even though she knew it was a dream, and she was amazed at the intensity of what she felt. When she awoke she said, "Good heavens, can you imagine such intensity of feeling so many years later?"

As the patient worked on the resolution of her mourning and her adolescent conflicts, the significance of the sense of danger previously experienced in the analysis became more apparent: namely, the importance of her guilt over her wish to separate from her parents, and the part it played in her need to deny their death which followed on leaving them. She talked about feeling guilty because of doing so well in her personal life and in her job. When the analyst remarked that she associated things going well with her to the loss of her parents, she replied, "I thought you meant that things were going well *because* I lost my parents." This she associated to a feeling of liberation. "It's a good idea at sixteen to separate from your parents," she said, but she was doubtful what she would say about it now because her separation was a "complete loss." But if her parents were alive this would limit her ambitions, and about this she felt guilty. At this time, the patient was concerned with the question, what is wrong with having loving or affectionate feelings toward the analyst or her father? At the same time she felt rage when she got no response from C., or the analyst, and remembered similar feelings toward her father when she was a small child. All this was related to thoughts of terminating the analytic relationship, which the patient compared to leaving her parents. She was afraid of being on her own, felt guilty about leaving the analyst behind, and had an increasing insight into the way in which she handled her fear and her guilt. "At some point when I left my parents there was something that was so unbearable, it stopped the clock. I couldn't keep the outward circumstances constant so I kept the inward ones constant." When the analyst remarked that it looked as if the clock was starting, the patient reported changes in her personal habits. She felt on her own now. She had the feeling that she had something to settle with the analyst, and remarked that as an adolescent she did not feel afraid. The analyst asked what she was afraid of repeating with him, and she replied, "That rings a bell, but what? Why was I stuck about feelings about father? It's O.K. for teens but why didn't I grow? Is the clock stopped? What was too painful? To avoid realizing that they were dead—did I have to stop everything?"

Under the pressure of guilt about termination, the patient retreated and again denied caring about people she might be leaving behind. "In due course I'll be leaving this city without caring the least about leaving anybody." But soon after this she began to talk about whether she was important to the analyst, would the analyst remember her? She felt she had grown beyond C. The analyst made a transference interpretation that she was repeating conflicts which existed before she separated from her parents, which had to do with the desire to surpass her mother. She was guilty about this and yet she wanted to be special. In a way she had been special because she was saved and they were not. Therefore she has to continue living over and over the conflict with her parents in order to master the guilt of her own survival and their death. The reaction to this interpretation was a wish to cry, "You hit it right. The guilt before separation—it's true, I wanted to be independent and I was not upset when I left them. When mother cried I was ashamed that I had no response." The analyst said, "But one of your wishes was to go away." Her remark was, "The final separation—there was a lot wrong with it, especially the way it occurred—it could have been such fun to go away and come home."

When the patient wanted to take a vacation from the analysis, the analyst questioned her motivations and wondered if it was advisable. Again she became rebellious, as if the analyst were holding her down and not giving her her freedom. This led to the recall of "After I left my parents, I was forever in rebellion. This is typical of teenagers but not of the thirties, or should not be, but I enjoyed it. I was proud of it. I resent talking to you. I was glad when I left home, I felt free. But I was guilty later when my parents were killed. Every time something comes up about being glad to leave, it adds to the feeling that it had not been nice of me. It's a shame that my parents couldn't understand me as a teenager, but I guess they were just human too." It was interpreted that she did not want to change but wanted to keep herself in this position because to grow and be free meant something destructive to her parents and also to herself.

After this she began to have a more realistic approach to what father and mother had been like. Specifically, she began to talk about father, wondering why he did not get out of Germany. Everyone knew that the end was coming, even when he left he did not really get out. Then she remembered a picture of mother at her prayers, "Several times I caught her crying. I used to be pretty upset, but it's likely I pretended not to know." The patient began to cry and said, "It's strange, I never realized that I loved my mother until this minute." She had a picture of mother crying and praying and wished that she could do something for her, as though it were now.

Following this, she experienced an important transference reaction. She wondered about the separation from her parents. "For it to have had such an effect there must have been some weak spots in the relationship with them. Is that right?" she asked. When the analyst said, "It sure is," she had a feeling the analyst was laughing at her for trying to make interpretations and feeling able to do what the analyst does. "Will I ever be able to stand on my own two feet again? It's funny that I added 'again'." She had the idea she was beginning to finish and realized she was afraid. She began to talk about giving up her own work and going into psychology instead. She was somewhat ashamed and embarrassed to talk about this. The analyst said she was talking about the same thing that he does, and that this was a problem never worked out with her mother, namely, being able to do the same thing as well or better. She continued to ruminate about feeling guilty about growing, "But I don't want to be an analyst," she protested. She then had a splurge of activity in which she functioned well but presented herself as afraid of finishing. She began to talk about the positive values of finishing—more time and money for herself. The analyst interpreted that she was afraid to face these feelings because of some idea that it was associated with destruction.

At this time she felt that the analyst had canceled some hours deliberately as a way of cutting down without it seeming to be so. The analyst pointed out her need to see this as being done surreptitiously. This would solve the conflict about her wish to leave the analyst behind and make it seem as if there had been no parting.

The problem discussed here becomes clearer in another dream about doodling. She had a piece of paper and a pencil—she was talking and doodling, "It meant something to you because you took the paper and looked at it. It was very valuable because at that session things became clarified without my having to do much about it. The doodle was more important than what I had said." The analyst remarked that he thought she had already made her decision and that she could not communicate it directly but only by the doodle. The patient said, "I wonder what it could be. The only thing is how much longer am I going to come here?" She felt blocked and frightened at this point, but when asked, "What date did you have in mind?" she said, "It's very close, maybe by the time summer is over. The time that actually occurred to me was when you go on your vacation. I never put a date on it before. I thought about it being at the end of the summer before but this time it's different."

When she continued to talk about separation from her parents, the analyst asked her about that date. She gave the date and compared it to leaving the Zionist farm to go to London a year later. Going to London really was permanent, but she wanted it to look like a vacation. The analyst remarked, "It sounds like the problem you have about leaving analysis. You feel guilty about the idea that you might never see me again." She said, "I've done this for years," felt sad, depressed, and began to talk again about finishing. When the analyst interpreted that if someone is out of sight they do not exist any more, she remarked, "Something occurs to me: it seems I got stuck when my parents and I separated and I didn't see them any more. After a certain number of years they ceased to exist actually. This was a shock. It seems as though I got fixed on this reaction and I react to everyone in this way; why should I unless I was guilty or felt responsible for what happened? I had a thought—it just hit now—they did it for me. They sent me to England by myself and I was better off materially than if they came with me." The analyst remarked that she felt guilty about the mere fact that she had survived. She said, "That goes for the money and survival."

The subsequent material had to do with the patient's denial and delay in facing the termination, and her associations and interpretations about the meaning of this. Of equal importance is the patient's participation in setting the procedure for termination. On June 3 the patient was informed that the analyst's vacation was to begin on July 15. Her reaction to this was, "It seems so soon. I just won't terminate then." She began to talk about "How do you finish? Do you come less frequently?" She did not want to decide because she would never be certain whether the analyst had approved. She wondered if she would be just as upset if she quit before the time to terminate. Her indecision about making a decision came up in association with the original idea of going to England. She realized that she had had quite a bit to do with it—her parents brought it up but she liked it since she was not the least bit eager to go to Poland with them. She wondered, 'Will I actually finish on the fifteenth?'

She came in on the anniversary of her separation from her parents all tired out and depressed. She was about to repeat the dawdling of the day before, "What do you do at the end? Do you throw a party? C. said, Take a bottle of wine to the hour'." The analyst felt the patient did not recognize the date and its significance. When he asked if she knew what day it was, she gave the date and remarked, "Good heavens, I didn't remember. Now I'm crying. That must be why I resented C. going home today."

This awareness enabled her to talk about the last day with her parents. She remembered them on the platform crying. She had no regret and felt terrible about this. It was necessary to change trains in Frankfurt and the officials were very disagreeable. When the refugees crossed the border, they were welcomed by a group of Dutch people, tea, food and great rejoicing. When she got to England she was confused and could not take care of her luggage. On this anniversary in 1957 she said, "I must have been remembering all of this yesterday without realizing it, and that's why I got up at 6 o'clock. I was thinking of father and mother, how old they would have been now. Father would be fifty-seven now. The last seventeen years have gone so fast—faster in memory than the first seventeen years. I don't remember, but this is sort of an anniversary—exactly eighteen years, or is it seventeen? I can't do the arithmetic! It's really eighteen."

She began to look more grown-up and feminine at this point, and continued to talk about terminating, "I can't visualize that this is the end. Yet it's going to be very soon. I'm not able to decide." She confused C. with the analyst frequently at this point, and it was interpreted that she was trying to avoid the intensity of her feelings about leaving the analyst. "I can't feel it's right—I should say, I can't feel it's wrong." She then talked about leaving England again, began to ruminate about a coat of her mother's and wondered whether it would fit her now. She talked about finishing in a month; "Maybe I will and then I'll just see you a couple of times." The analyst agreed with the wisdom of this procedure, which would in this way avoid a separation too identical with the separation from her parents.

Then came a long dream, indicating some integration of herself in time and in present reality. She was back in Munich with her parents. They left and called to her, "Aren't you coming?" She said, "I'm going to stay another day." Then she looked through the apartment, talked about the living-room with windows a little high, "I was surprised to be my present age in the dream but when I say this about the windows that might be how it would look to a child." Then she investigated the apartment and found a telephone which in reality they did not have. She wanted to call someone, but she did not quite know whom to call. Then she did not remember the number; "After all, it's been seventeen years." Then the dream changed and there was the idea that her parents were dead. She thought of looking up people who were still there. This was both pleasant and painful. She thought of some teachers, but they were old and might also be dead. Then she reported another dream, back in Munich, but it looked like London. She did not mind walking by herself after dark, but she was hungry. She talked to someone; German was spoken, but without any fluency on her part. There were lots of stands for snacks, but none seemed to have what she wanted. One had the remains of a sign in English, "It must have been from the war—an American hot dog stand, and I was annoyed that it was not there any more."

She felt this dream meant, "I was finally making my peace, a final step." She continued to talk about her guilt for leaving her parents. The analyst pointed out the termination was difficult for her because it looked as if she took all of her mother's talent by growing. She said, "I can't remember, but what I think seems to confirm this. I'm pleased to look like a woman. I want everyone to notice my weight, my legs, my waist." Then she talked about being surprised that the analyst took her seriously about the termination date. "The status quo is over, I can't postpone any longer. Treatment is beyond the point of usefulness, it's prolonging the dependence relationship that's no longer necessary. I've grown fond of you and the idea of not seeing you is going to be painful. Now I want to cry." She then talked about setting a definite time to see the analyst after she terminated, and the analyst agreed that they would make an appointment sometime in September when she returned from her vacation.

In characteristic fashion her next remarks demonstrated the persistent drive to keep a separation from the analyst as identical as possible with the separation from the parents. She said, "Do I kiss you good-bye? I presume I kissed my parents good-bye." People suggested to her that she ought to celebrate about finishing treatment. She said there was nothing to celebrate. The analyst remarked that there was some sadness. She said she ought to be able to answer yes, but she feels none, as if she must again repress her emotions. "It's foolish to cry or be upset because one is finishing. Everyone else reacts that it's nice and they're happy, and so it is in a way, but on another level I have nothing to celebrate. It's odd to feel this way about someone that you know in such a limited contact."

It should be emphasized that five or six weeks prior to the termination of the analysis was the anniversary of the first weeks in England and the period immediately following the separation from her parents.

She began to talk about what she would do in the last hour. Would she sit up? It would be difficult. The analyst pointed out how she wanted to make the last hour like all the others. She said, "Sitting opposite you I'd be tongue-tied. When someone you're fond of leaves you get upset. I'm sorry that it's coming to an end; I can't face it. It's only half real—it isn't true. It's absurd to be upset on leaving one's psychoanalyst. I've tried to make a joke out of it. Maybe there is a parallel between leaving my parents. There's something inevitable about this separation just as there is with parents and children—only mostly they're not quite so drastic. But this is inevitable, natural and right, so I have no right to be unhappy." The analyst agreed with her that there was a parallel between her feelings for the analyst and her parents, but the same thing was actually not happening. She was close to tears, and said, "What difference does it make?" The analyst pointed out that unhappiness was not all she felt. When she had said it was inevitable, natural, and right, there was some gratification in leaving. She said, "It's true, I don't feel it when I'm here, but it's uppermost in my mind when I'm away. Do I feel guilty?" She would like to know the analyst socially. Separation and breaking up in any kind of contact one has valued had always been difficult for her. She thought it would be difficult to imagine not liking the analyst.

Patient then returned to the question about making an appointment after she had finished. She wondered what she was afraid of. The analyst remarked, "You're not really sure you'll ever see me again." The patient's response was, "It looks like it," and was close to tears.

The last hour the patient came in and emphasized the convenience of not having to come any more. "It's your turn to talk now." She said she had learned a lot "but that is not the primary purpose of treatment; the rest, I feel, is intangible. It would be funny to mention to C. that this is the most prolonged relationship I've had. The word I wanted was the first mature relationship. How do you say good-bye? Do you shake hands? I should have brought flowers. As I was coming I thought this was the last time and I was glad. When I'm here it's all so different—it's mostly sad at the parting and some fear. It's easier to talk to you. It stops me from deceiving myself." Then she talked about teenagers growing up whether they want to or not.

At the end of the hour an appointment was made for the

last week of September, following the vacation. The analyst remarked that he had enjoyed working with her. They shook hands, the analyst wished her luck, and they said goodbye with some feeling of sadness on both sides.

When the patient returned in September she reported that she had "had a lousy summer." For two weeks she felt acutely bad and then the rest of the summer was generally miserable. She told about difficulties with C. till the last week when he was leaving town. This was interpreted as reliving the separation from her parents and wondering if the analyst would be able to survive the change in the relationship. "Even if I try to put you into a fantasy, there is no place for you." She had been thinking about her parents in the last three weeks, with sadness about never having known them as an adult.

Patient readily agreed to come a few times to talk the situation over. The analyst interpreted that what she called her relapse was due to a problem about leaving the analyst, that she could not allow herself to feel because she had fears of a total dissolution of the relationship with the analyst rather than a change. She said, "But separations were always permanent, like with my parents, and leaving London."

The patient felt better immediately after the return visit and had a dream about two men in which she had to make a choice. She chose the man associated with C. and not the one associated with the analyst. She talked about wanting to know the analyst in the future, but had no regrets in the dream about her choice. She felt much better about herself at this point.

The patient was impressed with the change in her feelings following these return visits. She realized that the interruption and return had been necessary in order for her to accept the change in herself. She said not to return would have left something undone. In the treatment her idea that learning and growing meant the destruction of her parents "became untwisted." "The way I handled it then was maybe the only way but not very good. This is a better way."

DISCUSSION

We have described the course of an analysis of a twenty-nine-year-old woman whose maturation was complicated by the death of her parents during her adolescence. This traumatic event had intensified the adolescent development task of emotional and social emancipation from childhood parental relationships. The mechanisms by which she adapted to this experience included denial of the reality of her loss and of the passage of time. This adaptive effort resulted in a prolonging of adolescent behavior patterns and a failure to complete either the mourning for her parents or the normal resolution of her developmental conflicts.

This arrested development and uncompleted mourning presented an unusually difficult resistance and distortion of the development of the transference neurosis. Our material confirmed what Anna Freud described in her article on adolescence (A. Freud, 1958). Here she pointed out how attempts to analyze an adolescent often met this kind of resistance, an inability to cathect the analyst and so to establish a basic transference from which the analytic work can proceed. According to Anna Freud, growth in this period normally requires a withdrawal of cathexis from the parent similar to what is required in mourning work, but so much energy is needed for this adolescent developmental task that not enough is available to cathect objects involving new levels of relationship.

In our patient, the demands inherent in the tasks of emancipation and mourning occurred simultaneously and required an integrative capacity which the patient did not possess. She managed to function well for fourteen years as long as the pressures for further sexual and social growth remained fairly constant. However, when life forces urged adult sexuality and career roles on her, adaptations to stresses of adolescence and to the trauma of parental loss broke down. At this point she was able to seek and eventually use outside help. Only after the repressed grief and ambivalence for the parents was mobilized through the repetition of separation experiences in the analytic transference could a new resolution to her adolescent conflicts be achieved. Analysis of the initial transference resistance activated the uncompleted mourning process and permitted the patient to proceed with her interrupted development. The most significant working through was accomplished in the experience of termination and consequently separation with emancipation from the analyst. The termination of this relationship differentiated him and the analytic experience from what had occurred with her parents, and freed her from the defensive fixation which had arrested the process of maturation in this patient. She was able to accept the death of her parents without ambivalence and guilt and to gain a new self identity with an orientation in present time.

Repression of grief has been described by* Helene Deutsch (1937). She explains the absence of expressions of grief or awareness of the feeling as the ego's defensive attempt to preserve itself in the face of overwhelming anxiety. Death of a libidinal object is experienced as separation from a needed source of supply, the loss of which threatens the self. The intensity of the danger depends upon the degree of helplessness experienced in the separation. The more immature the ego, the more needed is the object and consequently, more intense anxiety will be experienced

---

*Pollock, in discussing an earlier presentation of this material before the Chicago Psychoanalytic Society, pointed out that the developing transference neurosis is atypical not only because the patient cannot accept the death but because accepting the death unleashes the guilt and other ambivalent feelings associated with the object that is deceased.

as a result of the loss. Deutsch emphasizes the importance of ambivalence and unneutralized aggression present in the preloss relationship as a factor in determining the quantity of stress to which the ego must adapt.

In "Mourning and Melancholia" (1917a), Freud develops the concept of mourning as a process whose aim is adaptation to the loss of a loved object. It is a process which continues over a period of time, has stages in its operation, and a goal resulting in a modification of ego organization. He called this process mourning work, whose task is to shift libidinal cathexes from their attachment to the lost object and make this energy available for use in new relationships.

Partial and temporary separations from libidinal objects are experiences which from birth possess significance as activators of the adaptive mechanisms of the ego. To a large extent these separation experiences influence the rate and direction of growth, and play a part in organizing the developing ego structure. Thus the process of growth and maturation can be compared to mourning work in that every step toward maturation involves some adaptation to separation, and therefore some mourning work. In true mourning, however, the separation is total, whereas in normal growth the maturing separation more often involves detachment from an old pattern of relationship while the real object continues to exist and the step forward is in terms of change and giving up rather than losing something. Freud, in "The Ego and the Id" (1923), described this developmental process most succinctly when he said, "the character of the ego is a precipitate of abandoned object-cathexes and . . . contains the history of those object-choices."

Spitz (1957) and others have demonstrated that the presence of adequate objects is essential for the earliest organization of the ego. Many authors, A. Freud and D. Burlingham (1944), Benedek (1938, 1956), and others have described at length the importance of the mother as a part object, then as a differentiated object essential for the experiences which structure the child's sense of self and the ego's patterns of adaptation to reality. Meiss (1952), in reporting on a five-year-old boy whose father died when he was three, emphasizes the need for objects of both sexes when the integrative tasks of the oedipal period are at their height. She describes how her patient attempted to provide himself first with his own father through imagination and then with an actual substitute father in a transference triangle with her.

The disturbing effect of object loss on ego development has also been described by many other authors. Rochlin (1953), stresses the length to which the child's ego will go to make up for the deficiency caused by the absence of a needed object. In his case, the loss occurred very early in the little boy's relationship with his mother when his need for narcissistic sustenance from her was still paramount and even before his perception of her as more than a part object was well organized. His solution was to withdraw to social isolation but in contact with a symbolic object in the form of his mother's fur coat. She did not die but she withdrew from her son, and the substitute caretakers did not supply the experiences of emotional response necessary to change narcissistic libido into object libido. Rochlin emphasizes that withdrawal to the self is not enough when an externally existing object is needed by the immature ego. The needed object is strenuously sought for to prevent disintegration of the self. This may be accomplished at the cost of a rupture with reality (Freud, 1924). In "The Ego and the Id" (1923), Freud describes the "reinstatement of the object in the ego" in reaction to loss, and says that this introjection results in a modification of the ego.

In agreement with these and other authors, we felt that the failure to mature was largely due to the absence of a libidinal object whose presence was necessary for the ego's growth toward normal maturation.

In our preliminary report and in this case, it seemed to

us that two things had occurred as the immature ego began its work of adaptation to parental death. First, the loss of the love object was experienced by the ego as a danger to itself and reacted to with denial of reality, denial of the absence of the parent, and concomitant repression of affect. The second adaptive mechanism set in motion by this overwhelming situation seemed to result not only in absence of grief but in pathological mourning which could be described as prolonged and still incomplete at the onset of analytic therapy many years after the traumatic loss occurred. These defenses of repression and denial of perceptual reality, accompanied by fantasied continuation of the lost relationship, constitute the early stages of a normal mourning process. When prolonged, they absorb the energy necessary for growth and the establishment of new relationships in the present. Pollock (1961) has recently focused on the usual adaptive function of mourning work in bringing about new integrations after the loss of a significant figure. This contrasts with the adaptive function that resistance to mourning serves in the patient under discussion here.

Bowlby, in his recent series of articles on separation anxiety, has described observations of the sequence of behavior which commonly occurs when children between the ages of about twelve months and four years are removed from the mother figure to whom they are attached and placed in the care of strangers. These behavioral sequences have been termed by Robertson and Bowlby: protest, despair, and detachment. Protest is associated with the problem of separation anxiety, despair with grief and mourning, and detachment with defense and future psychopathology (Bowlby, 1960a,b,c, 1961).

These concepts of Bowlby's have aroused controversy as to whether these reactions can properly be termed mourning. The basis of the controversy is whether sufficient structural development has taken place in the still maturing ego for mourning for a lost object to occur, or whether this is simply a separation reaction to loss of a need-satisfying or part object (A. Freud, 1960; Schur, 1960; Spitz, 1960). These questions, of course, must wait further clarification of concepts of ego development and structure before a definitive answer can be reached.

Bowlby has also postulated that the term *mourning* should not be confined only to those cases of successful mourning (Bowlby, 1961). Using this broader definition, Bowlby's patients certainly are undergoing a mourning process, but a process which may become interrupted in a particular phase. This interruption may be an arrested state, as where the resistance against the work of detachment was especially demonstrated in our patient. The phase of protest and despair may be successfully managed, but the phase of detachment requires an integrative effort not always possible or in which the mechanisms used result ultimately in some form of pathology.

Our patient gave no evidence of any acute reaction, such as protest or despair, to the loss of her parents. In fact, she reported feeling no grief, much as Helene Deutsch's patients did (Deutsch, 1937). It would seem that the vigorous and lengthy denial of the loss certainly carries in it "protest." Moreover, upon the activation of mourning, despair was felt by the patient. "I won't see them again. I'll never see them again," and "I must have loved them. I never wanted to look at that."

Freud, in "Mourning and Melancholia," defines de-cathexis of the lost object and the freeing of energy for new objects as the essential integrative task. When achieved it brings an end to mourning. Our patient in the light of these definitions must be seen as unable to mourn successfully, but as continuing a pathological mourning process in that she could not accomplish the decathexis of the lost objects. Her failure resulted in incomplete mourning, and confirms the observation of Bowlby that the stage of detachment is difficult to work through. His findings (1961) indicate that serious psychopathology may appear during this stage of the mourning process.

Investigation of the mourning process in cases of adults whose loss occurred in childhood many years before coming under observation, offers a fertile field for the study of the normal and pathological aspects of this important experience. It is an experience which confronts the child with demands on his integrative resources that bring those specific stresses and corresponding adaptations into clear focus when observed in the transference repetitions of a psychoanalytic situation. Genetic reconstructions of the childhood vicissitudes of development and a given child's methods of adaptation become possible. The resulting personality structure can be correlated with the childhood trauma and its various dynamics identified. Such information is available otherwise only in long-term studies of a child while living through such an experience over a period of many years. Information from both types of studies should contribute valuable data for metapsychological concepts regarding the function of the object personality development as seen through studies of object loss.

CONCLUSION

The course of an analysis of a twenty-nine-year-old woman is presented, which demonstrates a form of pathological mourning; that of the defensive denial of the reality of the parental loss resulting in prolonged mourning and interference with successful maturation. This adaptive equilibrium persisted for fourteen years with a continuation of adolescent developmental conflicts and personality structure. Psychoanalytic treatment was able to penetrate the defensive denial, activate the interrupted mourning work, and help the patient to resume the growth process interrupted at age fifteen, with resolution of adolescent conflicts and new integrations. This complex of prolonged mourning and developmental fixation is discussed in terms of adolescent developmental tasks and in relationship to mourning, growth, and the pathological consequences of unfinished mourning.

Chapter 13

Report of a Psychoanalysis and Follow-up: Severe Emotional Trauma by Parent Loss at Seventeen Months, Consequences for Development, Formation of Borderline Syndrome

Henry Seidenberg, M.D.

The occurrence of early childhood parent loss by death provides psychoanalysts with an opportunity to study the consequences of catastrophic trauma on personality development (Fleming, Altschul, Zielinski, and Forman, 1958; Fleming and Altschul, 1963; Fleming, 1963, 1969; Altschul, 1966, 1968; Forman, 1966; Seidenberg, 1966). Settlage (1977), in writing about the borderline syndrome and narcissistic disorder, states:

> Analysts are thus engaged in a new effort at defining the pathogenesis, the pathologic formations and the means of treatment of narcissistic, borderline and psychotic disorders. The potential for such definition rests upon the precise correlation of traumatic experience during the first

years of life with the newly delineated phases of *primary psychic development* and the specific emerging developmental attainments these comprehend: self–object differentiation; core identity and the sense of self; autonomous and experientially based ego functions; early defensive and adaptive mechanisms and modes; initial control and modulation of drive and affect expressions; libidinal object constancy; initial capacity for one to one relationship [p. 806].

To add to the growing body of clinical observations which contributed to that precise correlation mentioned above, some segments of a psychoanalysis will be presented. This psychoanalysis describes the long-range consequences of the sudden death of father when the patient was seventeen months old, and the partially immobilizing depression of the patient's pregnant mother, a depression which persisted for approximately two to two-and-a-half years. The studies of the rapprochement subphase of the separation–individuation process pioneered by Margaret Mahler and her colleagues (Mahler, Pine, and Bergman, 1975) help clarify the patient's diagnosis, the nature of the psychoanalytic process, the results of treatment, and the patient's personality organization.

In addition, this chapter bears on the two hypotheses advanced by Fleming and Altschul (1963) which state that:

1. In *some* individuals, adaptation to the death of a parent in childhood results in an arrested development in ego-object relationships at a level achieved at which the loss occurred.
2. In *some* individuals, adaptation to the loss of a parent in childhood is associated with failure to complete the work of mourning.

The clinical data demonstrate that rapprochement subphase trauma led to (1) a partial arrestation of personality development characterized by the persistence into adulthood of rapprochement phase qualities and thus to the formation of a borderline syndrome; (2) the trauma led to a variation of the second hypothesis regarding incompleted mourning in that the long-range psychopathological consequences of paternal death and maternal depression at age seventeen months was clearly manifested by the patient's pathological mourning at age nineteen when her mother died. At seventeen months structuralization was incomplete and mourning was not developmentally possible; and (3) the trauma led to the formation of a severe resistance in the initial phase of the psychoanalysis which interfered with the development of the therapeutic alliance and of an observable and interpretable transference neurosis.

CLINICAL PRESENTATION

History

The patient, an unmarried, white schoolteacher, started analysis when she was twenty-nine years old. She was acting on the recommendation of a consultant to whom she had been sent after her psychotherapist terminated treatment. In fact, the reason for ending had been the therapist's inability to help the patient understand her massive sexual attraction for him which led to uncontrolled behavior in the session.

Without prompting, she told a hard luck story in which she blamed the world for her troubles. Her chief complaints were: (1) feeling upset all her life; (2) excessive stubbornness; (3) a homosexual tendency in that she stimulated herself to masturbate by looking at pictures of seminude women; (4) avoiding men entirely after years of heavy petting and refusal of intercourse. When the patient was nineteen years old, her mother died after a three-year illness with nephritis. Her father had died from acute peritonitis when she was seventeen months old. At that time her mother was pregnant and a girl was born six months after her father's death. The patient's mother reacted to her husband's death with a depression. She made suicidal threats which were taken seriously enough by a maternal aunt and uncle so that they renovated and enlarged their house to accommodate the patient's family. The families lived together until the patient was fourteen. Because of her depressiveness, the mother was unable to take care of both the infant and the patient. Consequently, the patient was often left in the charge of her aunt, while the infant's care was managed by her mother. Contact with the aunt was actively sought by the patient during her mother's frequent crying spells. Since the family was in poor financial condition, her mother took a factory job when the patient was four. Mother kept working for the next fourteen years. The patient resented her mother's leaving for work. In addition, she did not like being with her aunt, with whom she always fought.

Her achievement at school was adequate. No serious external events disturbed her until her brother, thirteen years older, left home to marry when she was fourteen. At this time she developed attacks of urinary urgency and intense fear of incontinence, which did not abate until well along in the analysis.

In adolescence, she had several crushes on boys who paid her no attention. Dating was infrequent and enjoyment was limited by tension over doubts about acceptability. She was very close to her mother and told her all.

A month after her nineteenth birthday her mother died. She reacted with fainting, anorexia, vomiting, weight loss, insomnia, and depressive affect. Though her higher education was interrupted by her having to help nurse her mother for a year, she went back to school after her mother's death and took a degree at a major Western university. Following graduation she went to a new city, and there experienced severe anxiety and depression. She left a menial job and fled to graduate school where, with the help of a counselor, she felt much better. After graduate school she held a series of jobs with only the first being commensurate with her training. There was gradual decompensation marked by trouble with her bosses, growing out of trends of compliance and defiant oppositionalism. Contact with girlfriends and with her family was allowed to attenuate. Relations with men were unsatisfactory. The usual ending came with her denouncing and driving the man away. One particularly troubling relationship was carried out entirely in fantasy. It was her crush on a radio disc jockey with whom she could establish no contact.

Course of Analysis

Initial Phase. Excerpted below are instances which attempt to give an impression of the quality of the first two years of the analytic process and how, in a special way, the patient resisted it, thereby warding off the formation of a workable therapeutic alliance and an interpretable transference neurosis. The clinical presentation includes a description of a session in which the interpretive process seemed to make a change which ushered in the type of therapeutic regression which then led to an observable and interpretable transference neurosis.

At first, the patient appeared as her stated age, but shortly after the analysis started, she cut her hair short, wore tennis shoes, bobby socks, and tended to look like a high school girl. The content of her speech indicated a fine intelligence. Her manner was urgent, pleading, and anxious to please. Affect was mercurial, varying from being soberly businesslike about fees to plunging abruptly into tears about her hating men and feeling guilty about this. Sarcasm was plentiful, and without further ado, she attacked the analyst for being "sunny without warmth" on the phone when she had called for an appointment. His first impression of her was that she was critical of others, driving them away, that she managed her guilt by provocativeness, that she was bossy and struggled to control the treatment situation.

In examining her reaction to the analyst not immediately explaining the patient's job in analysis, one gets some information about her malfunctioning sense of reality. In the first couch hour the analyst had wrongly assumed from her previous experience and education that she knew about free association. After five seething minutes of silence on the couch, she informed me that she did not know what to do. I then explained. Her first tantrum of the analysis followed, in which she reviled her former psychotherapist, her brother, and the analyst. The content was that men liked to make her miserable. This was interwoven with the following fantasies: (1) in which the analyst makes her speak and a fight breaks out between her and him; (2) in which she and the analyst are in love and live together in a very fancy apartment.

In the first one-hundred hours there were many indications of her attitude to authority centering around the defensive maneuvers of feeling criticized and attempting to provoke limitations from the analyst. She experienced him as a woman boss who was critical and laughing at her for her pseudosexual behavior, and that he was also the man in her romantic fantasies, but the patient showed no insight into the way she used his image in fantasy.

The analyst's attempts to inquire into her defense of feeling criticized led to her lifelong reaction of temper tantrums. Here she was reproducing behavior without analyzing. This was an early manifestation of the special resistance against the gradual and orderly formation of a regressive transference neurosis.

About seven months into the analysis, the situation became particularly stormy. Her provocativeness and temper tantrums in the sessions increased. A brief example follows. One day she began a session saying, "I see you have a haircut." The analyst responded with silence. In the rest of the session she alternated silences with crying and screams of accusation that she felt let down after being seduced by the analyst's smile of greeting. This was a typical session. At times she would rage at the analyst for twenty minutes seemingly without drawing a breath and leave early, slamming the door in fury. She failed to appear for her appointments and claimed it was the analyst's fault. She dreamed of women being enslaved for sexual purposes by the Russians and she expected to be dropped from analysis.

Further evidence of the immature functioning of her ego appeared in the splitting of the transference. She engaged as her general practitioner Dr. W., a woman who the patient knew was acquainted with the analyst. After developing a crush on Dr. W., all good came to be embodied in her and the analyst stood for all bad. Not long after, the patient persuaded Dr. W. to perform an optional appendectomy and cystovariectomy. Attempted analysis of motivation produced obstinacy.

It was very difficult to see through the resistance. The analyst could not understand what was being repeated, what was being defended, what he represented, and what were the unconscious fantasies clustering around her image of him. Here it could be surmised that a special type of resistance was being encountered which made this analysis different from many others in which the transference neurosis gradually formed and was relatively observable as it took shape. Early behavior was being reproduced. The patient could not recognize this, and as a result no recall followed. A state of severe resistance prevailed in which old fantasies and especially old behavior were being repeated. This resistance was not interpretable until it could be diagnosed, and even then the patient was refractory to interpretation for a long time until her denial of reality could be reduced.

As the above storm blew over, she brought family photos for the analyst to see. At this time he conjectured to himself that she was testing him to see if he would scorn her as she felt her brother had when she had reached out to him. Later on, the analyst could see that this was one act in a series given to reproducing an aspect of her relationship with her mother. On other occasions throughout the first two years, she brought in accomplishments such as her knitting, sewing, and architectural floor plans. She requested that the analyst examine them. These acts reproduced behavior identical with that of her mother. After fourteen months of analysis, near the time of the anniversary of her father's death, the transference configuration was both dyadic and triadic. In the triad she experienced the analyst as the rejecting brother, and Dr. W. as the kind mother. Below this was the dyad in which the analyst, as mother, thought of her as trash. In her associations trash was equated with menses which, in turn, stood for having no penis. This offered an explanation for her feeling that mother was not interested in her. She recalled mother's telling her that she would have sacrificed any one of her children to have father back. This contributed to the rise of the patient's childhood fantasy of wanting to be father to make mother happy, and then be the one closest to mother. In telling the analyst this for the first time, the patient seemed to be in a trancelike state. She said, "Now that he's gone, she [mother] belongs to me." The patient awakened and said, "She's dead, too—a fantastic experience."

Then followed two weeks of rage which may clarify her early relationship with her mother and which provides us with another example of the atmosphere of this analysis. The apparent stimulus provoking the rages was the analyst not granting requests. For one, he could not shift all her hours in the foreseeable future, nor did he turn off the air conditioner in another hour when she asked, until the room had cooled. Her behavior was a mixture of silence and shouting frenzy in which she upbraided him, stormed out of sessions early, had insomnia, and at times curled up on her side on the couch.

She seemed to be a very young child kicking her heels on the floor as she wept. Because this was at the time of the anniversary of her father's death which coincided approximately with her mother's depression and the birth of her sister, the analyst interpreted to her that the tantrum was her way of reliving the preverbal time when she may have felt that her mother no longer cared for her since her sister had come along and/or because mother was so wrapped up in her own loss. The patient dismissed the sibling rivalry aspect of the comment, but received the second part with a stab of pain.

Responding to this reconstructive interpretation, she described what she had been told of her mother's depression in which the latter cried for eight months, and made suicidal threats that were taken seriously. Also she told of her fright and anger at the analyst because he might die since he had a cold. With the process of differentiating past from present set in motion, she observed that her behavior of the previous weeks was a repetition of behavior only with her mother, that her mother was the only one whom the patient trusted enough to be irrational with and that in these reactions she was always hoping that mother would let her know that the child was liked. This showed an aspect of the progress made in the treatment in that she began to see how she was responding to the memory of her mother in the shape of the analyst. Gradually the strengthening of the patient's perceptual abilities permitted her to differentiate between the object representations of her mother and of the analyst. This differentiation made recall easier and made for less defensive reproduction of the past.

As the second year of analysis finished, the underlying theme of the deserted child appeared in her depression and insomnia which were responses to the analyst's vacation. She discharged the tension by acting out with her former therapist. One night when he was in town for a convention, she manipulated a situation by which she managed to sleep in his hotel bedroom after he had left it, not intending to return that night. Romantic fantasies of a mad social whirl with her brother developed as a visit from him approached. She felt like she was growing up, but was frightened.

At this point in the analysis, around the 360th session, the development of her powers of discrimination between representations of objects allowed her to begin to see the equivalence between brother and analyst. The investment in brother appeared to be libidinal accompanied by frightening pregnancy fantasies. Ambivalence marked her involvement in the mother-image in which the hated woman, a displacement from mother, was her sister-in-law.

Several more characteristics amplify the description of the type of resistance that had to be dealt with.

She dreamed of masturbating while lying on the analyst's couch, using pictures of nude women to stimulate her. As she dreamed that she was masturbating, a woman tried to get in. With her previous therapist she said that she actually did masturbate on his couch. However, at this point in the analysis her masturbation was via verbal equivalents. She flooded the sessions with polymorphously perverse fantasies such as men urinating on her genitals. She imagined affairs and pregnancy. But she did not pause to examine her associations. She was lost in and enveloped by the reproduction. Nothing was heard of what the nude woman in the pictures suggested to her. Nothing was understood about her ideas of the breast and nipples which attracted her so much. Little was learned of the object-relatedness of the fantasies and of her ideas about her own body and its sensations.

Her response to the analyst was that she felt that he did not want her. Feeling unwanted by mother, in accord with her tendency to split the transference, she went to the accepting mother, Dr. W., her general practitioner, to ask questions about her body. Temper tantrums occurred. Through the storm she cogently remarked, with evidence of a beginning observing ego function, "I feel that what I'm repeating here is the same nagging inquisitiveness as with mother."

The examples show again the patient reproducing behavior from her relationship with her mother. In the reproductions she related to the analyst as though he were her mother. She did not talk about her feeling or perceiving him as if he were her mother. For her he *was* mother, and as such she resisted observing and understanding the significance and purpose of her behavior, until toward the end of the above episode when she made her telling observation.

Another way in which she reproduced her relationship with her mother with the analyst was in bringing things to show him. She brought family photos and the indications were that she wanted him to be one of the family. In one session she wore a dress which she had just finished making. Sitting on the edge of the couch, she pointed out various aspects of her skill, including turning up the hem to show me how she had lined the dress. One of the elements, among others that shined through here, was that of the teacher's pet. Winning mother's commendation had been important to her.

In the 360th session, further progress was made in dealing with this type of resistance. Some of this session will be reported to show how the analyst attempted to bring home to her the inappropriateness and purposiveness of this major life pattern of which she was now barely aware and with which she resisted entering a working alliance and developing a regressive transference neurosis.

In this hour she showed the analyst a procedural manual which she had written for her job. It had occupied and preoccupied her for five months. Her feeling was that it would establish her in the eyes of her superintendent not only as being unusually competent, but as being different from her coteachers. With expectant pride and hesitance she offered him the manual for examination. As with other offerings, the analyst examined the manual. Then he handed it back to her and said, "Well, this certainly represents a lot of work on your part and I can see why you would be proud of it, but let's not leave it at that. Now tell me why you're moved to show this to me."

She replied, "It's what I was talking about yesterday. I used to beg mother to come to school to share with me so I could show off to her. I do with you what I did with my mother in being teacher's pet—this is why I show you the manual." The analyst answered, "It seems to me that in this and in many other things you've been repeating the essence of your relationship with your mother here in treatment with me. As with her, you see me as moralistic, critical, judging you as right or wrong; you question me persistently as you did her, and you desire to be admired as a pet." Then she said, "Yes, you're right, because the feeling I'm getting now as you talk to me, which I realize is unrealistic, is that you are criticizing me, just in the same spirit in which mother used to talk to me. You don't criticize; you stick to analysis and hold things up for me to analyze." The analyst then said that repeating the essence of the relationship with her mother with him must have some protective purpose. She did not see what he meant. He told her then that she behaved in this way with him "in order to keep your mother alive."

She reacted by saying that he had hit a nerve when he had said that she was trying to keep her mother alive. Silence ensued. In a moment she began to weep softly. "I'm not crying because I'm mad at you. I'm crying because you're so right. Suddenly I see my relationship with my mother was the only real thing that I ever had, and I always fought to keep it. You said that I was trying to keep her alive. These are the very words I could have used in the last month of her life. I tried, in my mind, to keep her alive because in actuality I could do nothing else." She then told of the frustration of seeing her mother die of nephritis: "I tried to encourage her and keep her optimistic." Then came a long detail about mementos of her mother. These mementos, valuable as they were, were not considered to be crucial to her; what was more important were the images and memories of mother which yet were so alive. She cherished her mother's memory, for though she felt mother had made her sick, still her love and warmth had given her strength.

The patient went on to say, "I'm crying now because I understand what you mean. Today you're right, and it doesn't go over my head for a change. Maybe now I'm turning to my mother in the presence of you to help me get well. This was the only place I knew of to go for safety, and so when I came to you I had to see you as her."

"Mother could be proud of me because I accomplished such things as college, but I did nothing with it. Now I'm turning out work and I'm proud of it. I brought the procedure today because I'm going to show it to Miss A." (an older woman who worked in the same place as the patient, and also had a part-time job in the analyst's office building). "I've shown it to Mrs. B." (an older fellow employee). "I guess I treat many people as though they were my mother."

We then talked about how she treated others as she felt mother treated her. This was expressed by a you-follow-the-rules-or-else attitude. The point was made that by the process of identification she had another way of keeping her mother alive.

Midphase

As the analysis progressed and dealt with the preoedipal developmental hardships with mother, analytic work was also done on the triad of patient, brother, and her rivals for him—mother, brother's wife, and his two daughters. She had reacted to his marriage when she was fourteen with severe disillusionment. Her attachment to him was ruptured; she experienced conscious jealousy of her sister-in-law, and after two nieces were born, she had a very active fantasy system in which she saw his two daughters as her own. The disillusionment, jealousy, and rivalry which persisted were greatly relieved by the analysis. As this work was done, the deeply ambivalent and guilt-laden relationship with mother came into continuing focus. Much was done to relieve the splitting tendencies. She came to understand how she used Dr. W., the woman general practitioner, as a good mother who supplied her with pills which gave her temporary relief from depression. But she never completely integrated the split mother imago. Though she became less hostile to the author in the preoedipal mother transference, she found other "good" mother images to supply her after the end of the analysis and after Dr. W. became unavailable.

Around the 650th hour, the patient's associations indicated a growth in structure. This growth in structure was manifested by a shift toward more internalized conflict and guilt over sexual gratification and away from guilt over gratification of dependency needs. A change was observed in which the patient's personal relations were characterized by an emphasis on triadic object relationships and away from diadic, anaclitic, and clinging–possessive relationships.

To illustrate the above, a condensation of about twenty hours is presented. The patient dreams:

> My sister has a bed to herself. I am infuriated. I had to sleep with my brother and sister-in-law. I was next to the wall, brother and his wife were together. I thought that my brother and his wife would hate me for sleeping with them.

In her associations, she compares herself unfavorably to her brother's two daughters. She expresses a wish to get rid of her sister-in-law. With growing insight she says, "I'm beginning to see how much brother meant to me. When I want to hug you, I feel it's brother."

The triadic theme continues as she associates to another

dream. In this dream the patient and two friends are talking about homosexuality, feeling queer and worried about it. In her associations she reports insomnia, guilt, and anger. She fantasies dying of nephritis. The analyst comes into her private hospital room and she says, "It's okay to have intercourse because I'm dying and can't conceive. You told me how much you cared for me, kissed me, and then intercourse takes place." With humor and insight she quips that her associations sound like a pun, "I'm dying to have intercourse. I dream about homosexuality to protect myself against my sexual fantasies about you." She considers further the dream about being in bed with her brother and sister-in-law and recalls that her nieces were in bed, too. This suggests to her that she crowded the bed so that no sex play could occur and thus help her fight her impulses to do away with all the women around her brother and have him for herself. Later, as she recollects further the dream of being in bed with brother and sister-in-law, she sees herself in the middle.

As stated above, the patient's structural improvement can be formulated along the lines of increasing conflict awareness and engagement in triadic object relations in fantasy and in actuality. Early in the analysis, the patient did not experience conflict. Then her attitude was marked by the stance of having the right to wish for what she wished for and being hurt because she was unfulfilled. Now the wish generated conflict, guilt, and depression and was available for working through in her fantasy life with consequent growth in insight and diminished hostility toward persons close to her. The process of internalization had been reinforced.

The improvement in her social relations is illustrated by the patient's description of an afternoon spent with her brother and sister-in-law who visited her. This visit took place in the patient's apartment. She had just left a dormitory living arrangement and was living in her own home for the first time in her life. Thoughts of terminating analysis occurred to her. The analysis was now in its fifth year. She had not seen her sister-in-law for seven years. To her surprise, she enjoyed her sister-in-law. The patient described with pleasure the sister-in-law's cordiality and kiss of greeting. With manifest delight, the patient recounted how relaxed and charming she was as hostess and how at ease she put her sister-in-law.

In the patient's words: "I'd always thought she was a phony and a liar, but I sensed no underlying hostility in her today; she was sincere. I was relaxed. They liked the apartment. She seemed kind. Yesterday I felt things were solved. I felt like an adult with them."

The patient's emphasis on the improvement in her relationship with sister-in-law as accountable to the observation that she detected no hostility in her sister-in-law posed a problem in diagnosing the level of her structuralization. There was evidence that the patient had changed. Earlier in the analysis if the analyst inquired into the motivation for her asking a question, or if he asked for associations to the question, or if he responded with silence to a question or to a request, a mighty storm would follow with her screaming, cursing, and stomping out of the room, slamming the door. At this stage of the analysis, her struggles with the analyst and others went on inside her and she felt dread and remorse. Earlier on, she had reacted to others as though they were external prohibiting forces, specializing in frustrating and rejecting her. To deal with these prohibiting forces she was defiant, negative, and oppositional. She claimed always to be the victim. Now the oppositional trends had been modified to "I must limit myself" or "If I want something, I must work for it." With her awareness of conflict within herself, she was also aware that there were alternatives. At this point in the analysis, instead of approaching sessions with a sense of storming the fortress, she sensed dread and remorse, a sense of guilt. However, her not fully acknowledging her contribution to the hostility between her and her sister-in-law indicates that structuralization was incomplete and vulnerable. The preceding description of the course of the analysis demonstrates the structural changes which may occur in a person. This patient showed many borderline qualities at first. With treatment she proceeded from the borderline organization characterized by temper tantrums, disturbances of evocative memory, severe separation, and ambivalence anxiety, to the organization of a narcissistic personality disturbance requiring mirroring and idealization for self-esteem regulation, through to the organization of a well-structured psyche experiencing conflict awareness and guilt in the complexities of triadic interactions. However, the stresses of life often found her vulnerable and thus regressing to levels of rapprochement crisis development with recurrence of the cognitive failures; that is, impairment of evocative memory, object constancy, and affective and control regulation disturbances. This was the basic personality organization to which the catastrophic trauma at age seventeen months predisposed her.

Termination Phase

The plan to terminate the analysis was first alluded to by her when she was able to leave the dormitory for an apartment. But the decision was made primarily by the analyst about fifteen months before the sessions stopped. Treatment had been going on for about five-and-a-half years. The analyst's reasoning took into account the extent of her improvement and the pattern of her resistance. On the side of progress, it was observed that she had made great strides in changing her relationship with her brother. What had been hostile and distant became a mutually gratifying friendship. Their contacts became frequent. The overt hatred, jealousy, and envy of her sister-in-law ceased. Her nieces, who had been the center of her envy because she had wanted herself rather than her sister-in-law to have given birth to them, became a source of interest and pleasure. Sister-in-law and she were at peace. The patient's brother, whose inclinations were always friendly and supportive, now was able to help the patient through guidance, counseling, and affection. In addition, symptomatic improvement was noted. Anxiety over loss of ordinary control disappeared as did an elevator phobia and other evidence of tension such as wet palms. Structural changes could also be seen in that she could observe her hostility, contain it intrapsychically, and process it, leading to a diminution of self-punitive tendencies. Self-object differentiation improved as did reality testing.

On the other side, she still had many problems in dyadic object relations. Controlling hostility toward maternal men and women was difficult. She often did not differentiate, but saw them as frustrators of her desire to be reassured that she was valued, desired, and considered worthwhile. Her object constancy was flawed in that ambivalence was characterized by swings more toward hostility than toward love, and consequently she lacked the confidence of being able to maintain the image of the nurturing person. Naturally, this produced a tension state which undermined the smooth and effective function of her ego apparatus; her mood was unstable and often moved toward painful depression felt at times as self-punitive and at others as empty. Insomnia and vomiting were frequent. Splitting of the maternal object representation was constant. It had resisted analysis. Separation anxiety was ever present.

The transference fantasies were both dyadic and triadic. More often the dyad was in focus. The splitting and separation anxiety were presented in the transference regression. Dr. W. was still, after five-and-a-half years of analysis, the good mother who gave pills for weight reduction and depression, while the analyst was the bad mother who did not value the patient and subjected her to separation anxiety by his emotional unavailability. The analytic sessions were a visit to mother in a continuing attempt to gain reassurance that she was desired and thought to be worthwhile. As the patient put it, "I don't want analysis. I want you." The visits with the analyst prolonged the idea that mother was not dead; the analyst was mother incarnate. Often she did not differentiate between analyst and mother. Though there had been improvement in this regard, there was a fixity to this complex. Insofar as the visits were accompanied by the hope that analyst would reassure her that he was the hoped-for accepting mother who understood ambivalence, allowing her to feel heightened self-regard, the analysis was repeating (and had been despite continuing interpretation) a pattern of qualities characterizing the rapprochement subphase of the separation–individuation process.

Thus the decision to terminate was based on the hope that this pattern of resistance would be interrupted or ameliorated by continuing interpretation during the termination phase in combination with the improvements in structure formation which had already taken place and had led to changes in triadic object relations; namely, relatedness to brother, sister-in-law, and nieces.

The analytic work over the last fifteen months of the analysis touched on several issues. Briefly, she had the experience of having sexual intercourse for the first time. It was with a man fifteen years her junior who was not a social peer. The intercourse was neither arousing nor gratifying, nor was it marked by altruism and object relatedness. This particular relationship foundered on her demanding to be mothered.

As she contemplated never seeing the analyst again, she felt she was developing the same disease that had killed her mother. If analyst–mother were no longer to be available, then she would herself become mother and thus forestall mother-loss foisted upon her through termination. She had a dual view of the analyst. As evidence of her growth she could see him as a person who worked toward her well-being. On the other hand, he was the mother who had deserted her before and would again. In her personal relations as in the analysis, she was mainly motivated by the desire for reassurance that she was valued. She gave no consideration to the requirements of developing the relationship. In the analysis, though the need for reassurance was paramount, she did take steps toward self-observation. She had been complaining continuingly of not getting what she wanted from the analysis, but she could not give it up. The analyst explained to her: "As you have said recently, you want to come for life because I am mother for you, but this no longer works for change; you tie up much energy in repeating here your relationship with mother. From now on, the change has to come from you."

She felt rejected and sobbed that she could never trust him again. This attitude over time alternated with comments from her about her improvement; for example, "Look, I've finally gotten to the point where I can save all of my feelings for the analysis and I don't expend them on ventilation with others. It's better to face it by myself and save it for here. . . . I have to face reality. If you think it has to end, I have to face it. I've been living in a cocoon. This is not as bad as when I left Dr. X." (upon leaving her former therapist she had a depression with vegetative signs and symptoms). "I'm just not that depressed any more. I can't find the old depression." She then associated to a dream in which she could not tell me what time it is. Her comments were: "The dream shows my confusion as to time. I've got to pull myself together. I said that I didn't want to grow up; this is negative, but I do feel the positive side creeping in. I wanted to get all the rot out of me before growing up. Yesterday with you I lived as though you were still my mother."

Much of the patient's analytic work through the oscillation of her moods over the next year focused on facing the termination as a death. However, she did not put it so much in terms of the recognition of reality of loss as though she were a mourner, but she experienced the process as "tearing myself away from mother . . . I've been helped, but I want to be cured," was the way she compromised her unfulfilled claims on the analyst with her sense of accomplishment.

She faced the disillusionment that analysis did not return her to her fantasies of the beautiful days before father died. Once again she worked through her disappointment in not having a child by the analyst. Ambivalent swings were wide; for example, "I am weaned and I am optimistic" versus, "I'll let people know that you were my analyst and they will know what a failure you are." Insight came to her about her use of alcohol. She saw drinking as feeding herself while mother fed her sister.

Her difficulty with object constancy and evocative memory was well illustrated as the analysis drew to an end. She tried to master the idea that leaving treatment and leaving the analyst was not death. She struggled with, "But if I don't see you, you don't exist for me, so you're dead . . . but I'll be thinking about you and that's like hanging on to mother. *Will I remember your face?*" Mixed with grief and dismay over the ending of the analysis were many statements about the benefits of saving money and time, and having energy to invest in work and friends.

Follow-up

Three years following the termination of the analysis, the patient agreed to volunteer for a follow-up study done by Dr. Nathan Schlessinger. His report to the author follows:

Summary of Follow-up Study on Ms. A. Ms. A. was seen for six sessions at weekly intervals. She described a narcissistic withdrawal with emphasis on gratification in fantasy as the solution to termination of the analysis. Her contacts with her analyst had continued intermittently. In the initial interview, she presented a generally miserable view of her life in which drinking made her day complete. She spoke of her preference for privacy and loneliness. Mainly, she lived like a hermit, taking no phone calls at home and spending the weekend in bed or reading. She projected a clear view of herself as a mistreated and suffering child with accompanying anger.

After this initial bleak description of herself and her life, she described her circumstances more insightfully. She remained in an analytic frame of mind with some capacity to achieve insight. Her symptoms seemed regularly related to separations. It was as though she had determined not to separate from her analyst. (She felt that termination was his idea and that he wanted to get rid of her.) The recurrence of symptoms was related to what she took as an involuntary separation. She had used Dexamyl and alcohol during her analysis. After her analysis was over, drinking became regular and habitual at night after work. Drinking permitted her to attend to unpleasant chores at home and facilitated her fantasying. Drinking is her life. It is communicating with mother. She spent a lot of time pouring over her checkbook, as she paid off her debt to her analyst. He had been like a good Samaritan. The payments were a continuing bond with him. As long as she had her fantasies, she was in great shape, ready to conquer the world.

At the conclusion of the follow-up sessions she was quite depressed. She had thought of them as a renewal of her treatment. She expressed her anger in the form of feeling like a charity case, who never got a full analysis. The follow-up analyst suggested that she was reacting to the end of the follow-up sessions with anger, too, and expressing it in depression and symptoms as well as a maintenance of her analysis in fantasy. She recognized that whether she ever tackled her problems in reality depended on her own motives, that generally she was content to make do at work and enjoy her alcoholic reveries in the evenings.

About five years post-termination, Dr. W., her female general practitioner became unavailable, and she changed to a male internist. The male internist, whom she saw regularly for several years, helped free her from her drinking through his support, combined with prescribing Valium. However, when the doses of Valium became excessive, and when her entreaties for support became inordinately urgent, he suggested that she turn to someone else for treatment. It was then that she turned to the author for advice. He referred her to the outpatient department of a local hospital.

When the patient started to work with a woman guidance counselor at the local hospital, it was now ten years after termination. Two letters from her arrived within one month of each other. The first was a closely written, twelve-page letter.

At first she wrote about her treatment at the clinic. Though she made it clear that she did not want counseling, she agreed to see both the woman counselor *and* her internist on a monthly basis, for counseling. Thus she would be seeing two different therapists every two weeks (shades of the split mother transference).

She brought the author up to date regarding her relationship with her sister, twenty-three months younger. The patient had decided to break off the relationship, knowing from her work in analysis that her sister was a mother imago. Her understanding was that she was going through a teenage rebellion. Considering that her aunt, a beloved cousin, and her brother loved her, she did not need to maintain the hostile relationship with sister. With her brother there was a continuing gratifying interaction. They spoke frequently by long-distance phone. Their freedom of expression surprised her. When he told her how much he had worried about her, she responded by telling him that deep inside she was as hard as a rock, but she omitted mentioning how much pain she felt.

Then she went on to describe her envy of the author because his appearance had not changed in sixteen years. Her hatred toward him was stoked when her woman counselor mentioned how nice he had been on the phone. She completed this paragraph with "Ambivalence is a real joy. Ugh!" She continued:

> I think you will be happy to hear that since I stopped drinking I am finding analysis not only useful but available. Occasionally I actually analyze a dream. Haven't been doing it much lately, though. But when it started, it just started and then, all of a sudden, I realized I was doing it. Sorry I didn't also do it at the right time—more sorry for me than for you about that.
>
> Then, occasionally, an insight almost knocks me over. (I do work at figuring out a lot of things, but I'm talking now about the big ones that I don't realize I have been working up to.)

Her letter describes her understanding of the anxiety and weepiness which came with a request from neighbors to cat-sit over a weekend. First she wept for her mother because both she and the mother had shared a deep love for their cat. Second, she realized that she was made anxious by assuming a position of responsibility to someone. That responsibility would threaten her with the likelihood of intimacy, which would require her to give to the other. Also, the other might take her autonomy away. Thus, all her relationships had to be either casual or over the long-distance telephone.

The patient continued the letter by describing how draining she felt responsibility to be. Because of this, she had no pleasure in work and experienced chronic instability in employment. She explained the problem of responsibility as being related to her being burdened prematurely with responsibilities around the time of the mother's chronic illness and death, that this interrupted her normal progression from late adolescence to early adulthood. She continued:

> So I think you can see that the analysis is still working and I do know I never would have been able to hang on without it. I was unrealistic about what it could do, but I have never found that I want to thank you more than I can say. I am grateful for it and wish I could have put more into it. I am grateful that it is still working and am rather excited about seeing where it will lead. Growth can be both horrible and wonderful. I do thank you and sometimes wonder where I would be without it.

Then the patient gives us further insight into her immature and impaired capacity for personal relationships. She describes in great detail her friendship with two men. The first was an intercity bus driver whom she came to know three years after the analysis when she regularly visited a relative who lived along his route. She now agreed with the analyst's interpretation given during a follow-up visit that the bus driver was a mother imago for her rather than an uncle. Most of their relationship was conducted by phone. She had many fantasies of sexual intercourse with him, but nothing ever occurred.

The patient ended her follow-up letter with a lengthy, detailed description of a man she "picked up" on a cross-country train trip. He was about twenty years her senior, a distinguished physician of high administrative and academic rank. She phoned him once or twice a year. Though she had seen him only once after the original meeting by "working my way from the back door of his hospital right into his office," she wrote about him in a way indicating great personal familiarity and knowledge of his family. Four years after their second and last visit, she wrote, "It takes me about six months to come down out of the clouds after I have seen him." She had seen him only twice, but wrote as though visits were frequent.

Her letter described a fantasied relationship with him that was the product of her wish to be part of his family and have him for a parent–spouse–lover. Time and reality testing were distorted. She wrote as though they are in constant, mutually desired relatedness, but there were clues that he was trying gently to fend her off and point out that she was mistaken in her assumptions about him.

She ended with: "I really wanted you to know about these two men and how long these things have lasted. I'm not sure why they last, perhaps because I show interest in them."

Several years later the patient phoned to tell the author that her aunt had died. The patient was managing the loss well. She had had periods of heavy drinking and unemployment since the letter quoted above. The author has not heard from her in about eight years.

DISCUSSION

The tragedy of father loss at seventeen months, combined with maternal depression, provides us with an opportunity to study the long-range effects on the development of psychic structure caused by severe trauma occurring in the rapprochement subphase of the separation–individuation process as described by Mahler and her co-workers (1975). In examining the data of the analysis presented above, we note the patient's incomplete structuralization and consequent vulnerability, and we are led to consideration of states of severe psychopathology encompassing configurations such as the borderline syndrome and narcissistic personality disorder. In addition, the hypothesis of Fleming and Altschul (1963) regarding the effect of parental death on personality development and mourning must be studied, and finally, the severe psychopathology leading to changes in the psychoanalytic process encountered in treating such a patient must be accounted for.

DIAGNOSIS

In *The Psychological Birth of the Human Infant,* Mahler, Pine, and Bergman (1975) write that in the rapprochement period, while individuation proceeds rapidly, the child "becomes more aware of his separateness and begins to employ all kinds of partly internalized and partly still acted out coping mechanisms in order to deny separateness. One of the frequently observed coping behaviors is the toddler's insistent claim for the mother's attention and participation" (p. 228). With mother's unavailability because of shock, grief, and depression, in the patient presented, we can begin to see why developmental mechanisms leading to ego autonomy were impaired.

The authors cited above write:

> The junior toddler gradually realizes that his love objects, his parents, are separate individuals with their own interests. He must gradually and painfully give up both the delusion of his own grandeur and his belief in the omnipotence of his parents. The result is heightened separation anxiety and disidentification from, as well as coercive dramatic fights with mother. This is the crossroads that we have termed the *rapprochement crisis.*
>
> In some children, however, the rapprochement crisis leads to great ambivalence and even to splitting of the object world into "good" and "bad," the consequences of which may later become organized into neurotic symptoms of the narcissistic variety. In still other children, islands of developmental failure might lead to borderline symptomatology in latency and adolescence [pp. 228–229].

In this patient's analysis and follow-up are revealed examples of chronically repeated derivatives of the rapprochement subphase and crisis. Instances of separation anxiety are often encountered, stimulated by vacations, brief interruptions, and those separations due to the patient's alienation from family members, friends, and the analyst because of her temper tantrums. Evocative memory (Fraiberg, 1969) was undermined by separation. She could not be sure that she would be able to see the needed and desired object in her mind's eye were she separated from it. Consequently, during summer vacations she desperately required knowing where the analyst was so she could write to him, even if he did not answer, and thus bolster the inner experience that he still existed. The same is exemplified in the description of her anticipation, described above, that termination of the analysis would be accompanied by her inability to remember the analyst's face. The coercive fights with mother are well documented both in the patient's history and in the frequent temper tantrums in the transference within the psychoanalytic situation, which led to fantasies of vengeful rage attacks against the analyst. Often in this patient we observed that splitting of the object world was an outstanding quality of both the analytic transference and of her major relationships. The splitting resisted repeated analysis and was evident in the long-term follow-up data.

Further impairment in her primary psychic development is noted. To pick a few instances from her life: (1) the fragility of her capacity to differentiate self from object imagoes is suggested not only by her uncontrolled transference readiness (i.e., her easily mobilized tendency to regress to infantile imagoes), but also by her response to major life events such as the loss of her mother when the patient was nineteen. Her response was not only grief but the mourning process itself was overwhelmed by a melancholia in which she was disabled by depression characterized by severe vegetative signs such as anorexia, vomiting, weight loss, and insomnia and a painful sense of emptiness. This was repeated when her two psychotherapies were terminated. Self and object were not differentiated. As a result, loss of object was experienced as a severe loss of self and self integration. (2) That core identity and sense of self were not firm is shown not only by much of the foregoing, but is further demonstrated by the lonely, seclusive weekends in which she was lost in drinking and in a sense of merger with her unremembered father, whose existence was suggested to her by the orange light of the sunset, the time when she was told she would wait at the window for his daily return from work. (3) Basic ego functions such as symbol–object differentiation and reality testing were impaired. Instances of delusion formation are seen in her belief that there was mutual love between her and a disc jockey at a radio station who would never acknowledge her calls. Her belief in the investment in her by the bus driver and the prominent physician was also delusionlike. (4) Libidinal object constancy—it is in this regard that we observe a serious failure to attain a developmental objective. This patient's libidinal object constancy remained incomplete. (5) The pervasive splitting in which she separated the good from the bad representations of love objects persisted into adulthood. Ambivalence continued to fluctuate from one extreme to another, and depression in which she turned aggression against herself was an enduring quality. She was not able to mourn the loss of her early childhood mother because the loss occurred at a time when her structure formation was not equal to this integrative task. As a result, when her mother did die prematurely as the patient entered adulthood, she was not able to mourn, but became depressed instead.

The patient presents a clinical syndrome of severe developmental disorder. Because of the disturbed functions of her love objects and because of the sequellae of the rapprochement trauma, the patient's structuralization and dyadic and triadic object relations were impaired. Thus, there is a strong suggestion that the clinical syndrome observed during the psychoanalysis was not regressive but rather the manifestation of primary psychic development impairment deriving from rapprochement crisis arrest.

Kernberg, in *Borderline Conditions and Pathological Narcissism* (1975, p. 44), sees the borderline personality organization as consisting of:

1. Symptomatic constellations such as diffuse anxiety, special forms of polysymptomatic neuroses, and "pre-psychotic" and "lower level" character pathology;
2. Defensive constellations of the ego based on ego weakness and a shift toward primary-process thinking on the one hand, and the other specific primitive defense mechanisms (splitting, primitive idealization, early forms of projection, denial, and omnipotence) on the other;
3. Pathology of internalized object relations;
4. Instinctual vicissitudes; namely, a particular condensation of pregenital and genital aims under the overriding influence of pregenital, aggressive needs.

Reviewing the clinical data with Kernberg's criteria in mind, we observe a syndrome of qualities which strongly suggest that the patient's personality was organized along the lines of the borderline. She suffered from chronic, diffuse anxiety and phobias related to her body. She feared she would lose control of her bladder. The thought that she would be looked at made her avoid social situations. Hypochondriasis was important and with it were paranoid trends. She was strongly dependent on alcohol and drugs. From a structural point of view, there was impaired anxiety tolerance and lack of impulse control. The attempts to maintain lost objects such as the depressed rapprochement phase mother imago and the dead, late adolescent mother imago led to regressions toward primary process thinking as manifested by transient delusional states in which she routinely, on lonely evenings and weekends, played imaginary double solitaire with her mother and believed for the moment that mother was alive. Finally, the pervasive appearance of splitting, an essential defensive operation of the borderline personality in which introjections of opposite quality are kept apart, lends further support to the suggestion that this patient's personality organization was borderline.

Further differential diagnosis requires consideration of Kohut's (1971) delineation of the syndrome of the narcissistic personality disorder. Gerald Adler (1985), in his monograph *Borderline Psychopathology and Its Treatment,* writes that there is a continuum from the borderline to the narcissistic personality disorder. This notion seems helpful in organizing one's diagnostic thinking about the patient under discussion. It would appear that the most predominant organization presented by the patient was that of the borderline. Her regression took her to states of function leaving her more seriously impaired than a patient with a narcissistic personality disorder. With treatment and improvement in organization, issues of self-esteem regulation came into sharper focus. Narcissistic transferences were experienced throughout. They were both of the idealizing and mirror varieties. More often than not, the required self-object function was for holding–soothing and reassurance that she belonged to mother and that abandonment was not imminent. The self-object function bolstering self-esteem with a resulting sense of cohesive self, when observed, was accompanied by the urgency associated with the holding–soothing self-object function and tended to come into focus later in the analysis. Regressions bypassed the self-esteem self-object functioning and stopped at the era where the child seeks the rapprochement self-object mother to deny separateness.

Thus it appears that the trauma of father loss by death provoking a significant depression in the mother during this patient's rapprochement subphase led to an arrestation of personality development marked by rapprochement crisis qualities. The disruption of primary psychic development led to the formation of a borderline syndrome and to an impairment of the capacity to mourn.

PARENT LOSS HYPOTHESES

This brings us up to a point where we may consider the work of the Parent Loss Project of the Institute for Psychoanalysis of Chicago. As cited previously, Fleming and Altschul (1963) advanced two hypotheses regarding parent loss by death. Amply illustrated by the above case presentation is the first hypothesis that death of a parent in childhood results in arrested development in ego-object relations at a level achieved when the loss occurred. In effect, the loss at seventeen months of age was a double loss, father by death and mother by depression. The arrestation led to a personality organization characterized by lifelong qualities of splitting, temper tantrums, a basic depressive response, separation anxiety, and severe fluctuations in self-esteem accompanied by swings from delusions of grandeur to painful states of impotence. Because of this, the patient was not able to develop a firm state of object constancy by moderated ambivalence.

The second hypothesis of Fleming and Altschul states that the loss of a parent in childhood is associated with failure to complete the work of mourning. Many elements of the foregoing discussion lend themselves to the support of this hypothesis. Recognition of the reality of loss with subsequent reinvestment of interest in other personal objects and activities was not the usual process for her. As previously stated, her first losses occurred prior to a level of structure formation equal to the integrative task of mourning. Later losses demonstrate her incapacity to mourn by virtue of ego pathology. When her brother left home (she was fourteen) she had temper tantrums and expressed lasting hatred toward brother and sister-in-law. When mother died, and the patient was nineteen years old, mourning did not follow but she became clinically depressed, and though she was able to complete her education, she remained vulnerable to collapse of those internalized functions by which we parent ourselves, leading her to return home soon after she had set out on her own in a distant city. Separation from two psychotherapists led to clinical depressions. Termination of analysis, though begrudgingly and severely resisted, did not lead to depression. Loss was faced, and she mobilized her resources to work, established new and better living conditions, and socialized on an adequate level. However, the follow-up studies show that serious social and intrapsychic incapacities made their reappearance and remained with her. A general evaluation of her response to loss shows that the mourning process was not straightforward, but was often replaced by depression. This interfered with her integrating the recognition of loss and reinvestment of her energies.

PROBLEMS OF RESISTANCE
AND INTERPRETATION

The clinical data presented provides an opportunity to examine the observation that in some cases of traumatic parent loss in childhood, the initial phase of the analysis is characterized by a special resistance which interferes with the formation of a therapeutic alliance and with the development of an observable and interpretable transference neurosis.

Such an observation was made by members of the Parent Loss Research Workshop of the Institute for Psychoanalysis of Chicago studying the effects on personality development of the death of a parent in the formative years (see chapter 12). One finding was that the psychoanalytic process was marked by unusually severe resistance and distorted transference development. It was understood that these patients were reproducing the preloss parental relationship, either in fantasy or in behavior with a present-day substitute. The reproduction served to maintain the illusion that the dead parent was still alive.

It was hypothesized that this aberrant process in the psychoanalysis was the result of the attempt to cope with massive anxieties provoked by untimely separation and was a lingering effect of the consequent attempt to adapt to the loss. It was further postulated that in adapting to the loss these patients, though perceiving the reality of the absence of the parent, denied the emotional meaningfulness of the loss. They showed signs of incompleted mourning and the structure of their personalities suggested that self and object representations were those which corresponded to the developmental levels expected at the time of loss. Adaptation by incompleted mourning and an arrest of a segment of ego development staved off the affects resulting from object loss and its recognition, the demanding integrative task of mourning, and potential states of psychic disorganization, such as depression and severe regression. This variety of adaptation in the segment of the psychoanalysis described demonstrates complications in the psychoanalytic process. Because the subject of adaptation to loss is broad, this section of the discussion will deal only with the issue of resistance in the psychoanalytic process and how a beginning was made in resolving it.

The resistance which made this psychoanalysis different from the usual, consisted of a system of fantasies representing an ongoing internalized relationship with the lost maternal object. The relationship was repeated in two ways, each supporting the illusion that mother still lived. The first way was reminiscent of a young child deeply absorbed and talking to himself in his play. For the moment, he believes in the reality of his fantasy. In this manner, the patient played solitaire and had long imaginary conversations with mother as they had when both had often played double solitaire. Through this kind of play the patient could believe in the illusion that mother was alive and deny the meaningfulness of loss. The second way of reproducing the internalized relationship with the lost mother was in transference activities with members of the environment. These activities, with a quality of serious playacting, repeated segments of behavior with mother. The image of mother was superimposed on and undifferentiated from the percept of the environmental personal object; the reality of this current object was denied, and the illusion that mother was alive continued. This was done out of intense need for the mother who was felt to be lifesaving. Important only was the feeling of the presence of mother.

These transferences preexisting treatment were repeated with the analyst as the target from the very beginning of the analysis. The transferences functioned as resistance in the analytic setting as they had done in previous settings. Before analysis they had served to deny the meaning of people in reality; now they served in the same way as an obstacle to the patient's awareness of (1) the analyst's reality as analyst, and (2) the goals of the analytic situation. Consequently, the therapeutic alliance was impaired. This alliance was necessary as a foundation for the analysis of these preanalytic transferences. Analysis of these distortions of present reality had to precede an interpretable transference neurosis.

This state of affairs differed from the usual analysis in which there are, at the start of treatment, better defenses for impulse control and better reality orientation. In the analysis of the less disturbed patient, we see a realistic awareness of the strangeness and strain of starting treatment; as transferred patterns of communication, behavior, and defense appear the analyst's role is not lost sight of. Therapeutic regression is controlled, and the resistances are against experiencing the anxiety of this regression and not against the mutual purpose of discovery and insight.

But in this case, impulse control and reality orientation were severely disturbed and the need for the mother was so great that the analyst's treatment role and the purpose of the analytic work were not appreciated. Immediately, transferences were produced which were aimed at "living" with mother, at gratification of object need, and they served to resist insight. As such, the clinical situation was neither readily diagnosable nor amenable to interpretation.

Resulting from this kind of resistance was (1) a protection against the pain of recall and recognition of the meaningfulness of loss which would lead to grief and the demanding task of mourning, and (2) a protection against the severe regression and depression which might follow recognition of loss.

During the first two years of the analysis, the following line of interpretation had been developed: as the first year of the analysis concluded, the analyst began to see a pattern. He interpreted it to the patient as behavior reproducing the past. Then, later, he added that it was repeating behavior with her mother. Finally, as the initial phase of the analysis drew to a close, the interpretive line was extended to explain this behavior on the basis of her need to maintain the illusion that her mother was alive.

EFFECT OF INTERPRETIVE WORK

The major resistance of keeping an internalized relationship with her mother going without observing it had been interpreted. The effectiveness of the defense of denying the meaningfulness and reality of loss had been lessened. This, in combination with the growth of her cognitive function in the previous two years, resulted in a reactivation of the incompleted mourning process.

The analyst's words, *in order to keep your mother alive,*

confronted her with her inappropriate behavior because she knew her mother was dead, but she did not want to believe it. Having to face the meaningfulness of this reality she then experienced loss. Then, in true mourning work fashion, she recognized that she kept her mother alive by means of reproduced behavior in transference activities and with a system of fantasies isolated from the external world. It was with this system of transference fantasies that she resisted the formation of a regressive transference neurosis by repeating instead of remembering. Also, this system, in diminishing her appreciation of the analyst's realistic role, impaired the functioning of the therapeutic alliance. Following the above interpretive work, the working alliance improved and the more usual defenses against the transference neurosis began to appear, as did the transference neurosis itself.

DYNAMICS OF THE RESISTANCE

The major dynamic activating the clinging to mother was the need for an object. This followed from the patient's impaired ego state of faulty control functions, ineffective reality testing, splitting, and vague self–object differentiation. The fantasies of mother and the transference activities provided her with a selfobject or transitional object which, although illusory, was able to sustain her minimally through the travails of libidinal frustrations and the above noted ego malfunctioning.

In the analyst's provision of such an object via the parameter of gratifying her demands for belonging, implied in her bringing photographs, knitting, sewing, and job projects, the self–object differentiation necessary for a thera-| ✓ peutic alliance was fostered. As this was being done, reality testing was also being aided by the gradually increasing pace of the inquiries into her motivations, which, later on in the analysis, was combined with the frustrating of her demands.

CONCEPTUALIZATION OF THE TRANSFERENCE IN ITS RESISTANCE FUNCTION

Prior to the conclusion of this phase of the interpretive work described earlier, the patient clung to the fantasy that mother was alive because this illusory object was felt to be lifesaving. For her, a relationship with a present-day person was an opportunity to externalize on the new object wishes, fantasies, conflicts, and behavior relating to the old object representation of the mother. This is the essence of transference of past imagoes onto a present figure. In most instances, object need is not so imperative, the ambivalence conflict is not so intense, and reality testing is better. Then transference occurs in such a way that a patient can observe the superimposition of the externalized introject on the new object and simultaneously differentiate the two. The patient could not make this differentiation, and the transference was not usable or interpretable in the usual way. The image of the mother of childhood and adolescence coalesced and was preserved, and prevented the establishment of new relationships which were a threat to old internalized relationships.

In the analysis the same situation occurred. Transferences to the analyst formed as they had with others prior to treatment. These transferences were resistances from the start against the analytic process and in behalf of the preservation of the introject. To see the analyst as therapist in reality and to experience and observe him as a target for her transferences, thus introjecting him as an internal image, would have forced her to shift energies and partially decathect the mother introject, and would have threatened her with the consequences of loss.

This describes what happens as the analysis of a transference neurosis is worked through. In the process there is a partial decathexis of the parental introject and a cathexis of a new object. In the treatment described here, her need for and ambivalence regarding mother had to be lessened before she could give credence to the analyst in reality or as the focus around whom the elements of the therapeutic alliance could form, to be followed by an analyzable transference neurosis. The interpretive process, in reducing her denial of loss, interfered with the dialogue with mother. Interpretation led to a decathexis of the internalized image of the mother. As the transference was interpreted, its resistance function was diminished, and her ego was forced to send out considerable quanta of object libido taken from her investment in the archaic mother introject. It was then invested in an object relationship with the analyst. Up to this point her investment in the analyst and in her mother was undifferentiated in her mind. After the interpretive work took effect, the patient could then differentiate the analyst's image from that of her mother, and see him both as analyst and as mother image. Thus, from the process of gradual deinvestment of the archaic mother introject the patient could begin to see how her behavior toward others had been deeply influenced by her relationship to an unconscious image of her mother.

SUMMARY

The profound and lasting consequences on personality development caused by severe emotional trauma at age seventeen months have been presented. The instance described concerns the loss of father by death and of mother by reactive depression.

I have attempted to add one case to the body of literature citing a traumatic instance and its sequelae of interruption of normal primary psychic development so that theories of personality development may be clarified.

Striking in this case is the correlation between characteristics of the patient's personality seen through childhood and adulthood which match the description of the rapprochement subphase and rapprochement crisis, in particular as described by Mahler and her co-workers. Pathogenesis of a borderline syndrome as deriving from rapprochement subphase trauma is strongly suggested; this is the specific phase wherein trauma may lead to the borderline syndrome.

In addition, it supports the claim of the Parent Loss Research Group of the Chicago Institute for Psychoanalysis which states that parent loss and its traumatic consequences lead to arrested development and distorted structuralization in certain sectors of the ego and ego-object relations. The author understands this case to be a variation on the second claim of incomplete mourning. The mourning in the first instance of loss at seventeen months is not an issue because of age and structural inadequacy. However, the resulting psychopathological structural distortions led to an incapacity to mourn adequately later in life as seen in her acute depressive response to mother's death at age nineteen years and to the chronic incapacity to integrate it. The analysis presented also illustrates the nature of the resistance to the psychoanalytic process which is associated with arrested development and incompleted mourning, and how an attempt was made to analyze this resistance. Also, the presentation demonstrates the influence of this analytic treatment in the development of the patient's personality structure, though it was always vulnerable to regression. Finally, a brief historical note may be in order. This patient was treated in the era before the recent advances in development theory, object relations theory, and theories of the self. These theories have led to various approaches to the treatment of the borderline syndrome. Consequently, more therapeutic options are available now than when the described psychoanalysis began. However, the clinical observation remains that this modified psychoanalysis led to structural changes in this patient burdened by a borderline personality organization. Since the structural changes left the patient still impaired, we must consider adding to the psychoanalytically informed method of interpretation and defense reduction an approach which combines with the foregoing and provides for treatment of a long-lasting relationship without a fixed, ineluctable termination, but instead uses multiple interruptions over the patient's lifetime.

Chapter 14

Preadolescence and Early Adolescence: A Reconstruction

David Dean Brockman, M. D.

Pluck from the memory a rooted sorrow,
Raze out the written troubles of the brain, . . .

Macbeth 5.03.41–42

INTRODUCTION

Psychoanalytic knowledge about preadolescent (Sullivan, 1953) or early adolescent development comes from three sources within the field: direct observations, analytic treatment of the ten to thirteen or fourteen-year-old (Miller, 1978), and reconstruction during psychoanalytic treatment of adults. Even though data from this period is often silent in the analysis of adults (A. Freud, 1958; Isay, 1975; Feigelson, 1976), a unique opportunity was provided in the analysis of an adult man who had lost his father at age eleven. At the

351

outset, this thirty-six-year-old man's behavior in many ways resembled that of a youngster. He described himself as "having sprung from childhood into a childish adulthood." He felt "frozen in childhood like a pruned and dormant tree ready to be transplanted to acid-free soil." In a manner of speaking, his personality was arrested at the preadolescent level of development. However, there was ample data from the analysis that there were oral, anal, and oedipal fixations which complicated the clinical picture of an arrested personality. Preadolescent behavior is characterized by regressive pregenital and narcissistic features. The author will demonstrate with clinical data certain preadolescentlike qualities which correlate with what is described in the literature about preadolescence.

The pretreatment historical data confirmed the findings of Fleming and Altschul (1963), Altschul (1968), and Fleming (1972a, 1972b). There was massive denial of the loss, delayed mourning, and interference with further developmental growth. A mourninglike process had been mobilized in this man but these effective stirrings were of limited usefulness to him, and, most importantly, served as an initial transference resistance which had to be interpreted first. However, analysis of this resistance activated the stalemated mourning process, releasing an arrested personality which was followed by developmental changes into more typically adolescent phase conflicts (Blos, 1962) and from there on into adulthood.

In order to provide a general framework for understanding the clinical data of this patient, a summary follows of some aspects of the preadolescent phase as described in the pertinent psychoanalytic literature.

Of crucial importance in understanding preadolescent development is the degree to which latency age achievements have been consolidated (Blos, 1958). Blos's (1970) criteria for the consolidation of the latency phase may be summarized as follows:

1. There is greater ego expansion and greater ego autonomy due to new identifications which replace earlier object dependencies.
2. Self-esteem regulation is relatively freed up from external environmental influences—the child is more capable of sustaining a reasonable balance in self-esteem regulation.
3. As the child expands mastery over himself and objects, there is an increase in social adaptation and social anxiety diminishes.
4. Skill and competence, perseverance and ambition become systematically articulated into normative activities as taken up through games, school, hobbies, and chores.

The onset of puberty proper is presaged by beginning changes in the physiological maturational processes while psychologically it is a developmentally stressful phase of major proportions (Hamburg, 1974) which is characterized by an impoverishment of coping skills. Variations in ego strength or weakness lead to specific areas of vulnerability (Murphy and Moriarty, 1976). The gap between fantasy and reality is narrowed (Kaplan, 1977). Rapid shifts of narcissistic cathexis from one body part to another and from objects to body parallel swiftly changing moods reflected in frowning, grinning, pouting, or scowling (Kestenberg, 1980). Languid stretching or sprawling while talking endlessly on the telephone to friends express increased instinctual tension as well as a regressive relaxation or inertial type of boredom. The neat, educable, and adapted latency child is now sloppy, more difficult to control, and less educable (Brownell, 1977).

These changes are not uniformly manifested in children of this age group because of marked variations in terms of age of onset and rates of growth (Beiser, 1980), and developmental age doesn't necessarily coincide with chronological age (Tanner, 1959). Pubertal changes seem to be occurring earlier in both boys and girls, and the gap of two to two-and-a-half years between the sexes appears to be narrowing (Kestenberg, 1980). Menarche in girls and the first ejaculation in boys are used as general guideposts to mark the onset of puberty, but there are indications of physical as well as psychological changes earlier than these dramatic events. Detectable increases in the gender specific gonadotropic hormones (Frank and Cohen, 1979; Kestenberg, 1980) are responsible for the specific maturational changes associated with puberty; that is, the growth of the internal and external reproductive organs and the secondary sex characteristics of the body.

Also, physical growth is strikingly uneven, since many individuals experience sudden, disturbing spurts of growth, particularly of the trunk and extremities (Tanner, 1972), which are difficult to integrate into a cohesive mind–body–self–image. In certain special instances, complicated athletic and gymnastic achievements are sometimes possible, but more commonly there is an exquisite sense of touchiness, fidgetiness, and awkwardness (James, 1908). For example, at the ends of elongated extremities, hands and feet feel strange and distant. Alice, in *Alice in Wonderland,* refers to her feet as though they are located at great distances.* As the center of gravity shifts to lower down in the pelvis in girls and an equivalent broadening and strengthening of the upper girdle in boys, it is not unusual to observe much confusion about

---

*"Curioser and curioser" cried Alice (she was so much surprised that for the moment she quite forgot how to speak good English; "now I'm opening out like the largest telescope that ever was! Goodby feet." (For when she looked down at her feet, they seemed to be almost out of sight, they were getting so far off.) "Oh, my poor little feet, I wonder who will put on your shoes and stockings for you now, dears? I'm sure I shan't be able! I shall be a great deal too far off to trouble myself about you: you must manage the best way you can— but I must be kind to them" thought Alice, "or perhaps they won't walk the way I want to go! Let me see: I'll give them a new pair of boots every Christmas."

body–self boundaries in relation to the environment. There
is much excitement, too, amongst this group about body
changes visible in the budding breast development in girls,
and in both sexes enlargement of and sensitivity of the
nipples and areolae, the appearance of pubic hair in both
sexes, and facial hair in boys. In boys the penis and especially
the testicles enlarge in weight and volume (Bell, 1965),
become pigmented, and very sensitive. Embarrassing erec-
tions and nocturnal emissions occur without warning at most
inopportune times and are not usually connected to organized
object-related fantasies (Scharfman, 1977). In boys there are
the well-known uneven changes in voice timbre and pitch.

There is much fantasying about and anticipation of the
future. Excitement about all these changes is comparable to
the first efforts at emancipation from parental ties in early
childhood, especially the practicing subphase of separation–
individuation. Feelings of unworthiness, inferiority, and
discontent are opposed by a sense of specialness and unique-
ness (Harris, 1976) reminiscent of infantile grandiosity; for
example, the expansiveness of the two-year-old and the
fearlessness about the world of the four-year-old (Greenacre,
1975). Early omnipotent fantasies are revived, in part due to
the young person's inability to meet the social and economic
responsibilities that would be involved in responding to and
acting on increased sexual and aggressive drive derivatives.
In fact, puberty makes the threat of incest more of a real
possibility. Another reason is the rapidly accelerating cogni-

---

And she went on planning to herself how she would manage it.
"They must go by the carrier" she thought; "and how funny it'll
seem, sending presents to one's own feet! And how odd the
directions will look:

> Alice's Right Foot, Esq.
> Hearthrug
> Near the Fender
> (with Alice's love)."

tive development of psychological-mindedness in middle childhood which results in abilities to make insightful inferences about adults, and which inevitably result in painful disillusionments and disappointments in the idealized parents (Barenboim, 1977). In terms of this disruption of narcissistic equilibrium, there is increased vulnerability or sensitivity to slights and reverting to infantile grandiose fantasies of becoming a world conqueror or savior. On the other hand, a certain studiousness develops along with an interest in politics, art, music, science projects, models, the working of machines, and so on, as transformations of narcissism and sublimations of drives.

With all these changes, there is now an opportunity for a restructuring of the total personality, including the ego, superego, and ego ideal (Blos, 1974), which Blos calls "a regression in the service of development." Drive diffusion and drive dedifferentiation serves as a "springboard for a progressive reintegration of pregenital and genital drives" (Kestenberg, 1980). At the onset of preadolescence, there is a beginning dissolution of some of the psychic structures which were established during prior phases of development. Self-cohesion is lost and a kind of disequilibrium takes place resembling an identity diffusion (Erikson, 1959) characterized also by confusion about sexual identity and sexual roles. Bisexual body identifications contribute to body image distortions (Harley, 1971). There is much confusion and misinformation about sexual functioning or reproduction.

Reactivation of the Oedipus complex is associated with a loosening of the repression barrier and increased vulnerability to regression (Frank and Cohen, 1979) which allows for the reappearance of component instinctual behavior (oral and anal) which has never undergone expectable developmental transformations. Thus, in general dynamic terms, there are alternating progressive–regressive movements, and structurally speaking there are integrative–disintegrative or cohesion–fragmentation sequences. Reaction formations are reversed and the consolidations of latency are dissolved (Wieder, 1978). The dynamics of this phase have been summarized recently by Blotcky and Looney (1980), but Anna Freud's (1965) description remains a classic:

> At this time, changes in the quality as well as the quantity of the drives and the increase in several primitive pregenital trends (especially oral and anal) cause a severe loss of social adaptation, of sublimations and in general of personality gains which have been achieved during the latency period. The impression of health and rationality disappears again and the pre-adolescent seems to be less normal, and often appears to have delinquent leanings [p. 163].

Blos (1958, 1970), however, believed that "only with the boy, is it correct to say that the quantitative increase of the instinctual drives during pre-adolescence leads to an increase in an indiscriminate cathexis of pre-genitality," which agrees with Helene Deutsch's (1944) view that the female preadolescent normally turns toward reality and attempts to adapt herself to it. Selma Fraiberg (1955) and Martin James (1964) emphasize the fear of emotional surrender in both sexes and especially in boys, the fear of the phallic mother. In fact, Blos (1958) considered the phase specific conflict of the male preadolescent to be castration anxiety in relation to the phallic mother which is defended against by a homosexual retreat. Boys are especially uncomfortable in accepting affection from their mothers. A. Bell's (1961, 1965, 1968, 1970) explanation for the passivity so frequently observed (Beiser, Personal Communication) in prepubertal boys stems from an earlier preoedipal helplessness and powerlessness to control retraction of the testes. Early object loss of breast and feces promotes a feminine identification with the powerful and creative mother; for example, fantasies of having breasts and bearing children. This early anxiety is the forerunner of phallic castration anxiety (Bell, 1965).

The developmental tasks of preadolescence from a Piagetian point of view have been outlined by Thornburg (Ryan de Brun, 1981). Piaget (1952) described the typically exuberant thoughts and fantasies of the preadolescent which are related to a native creative imagination but adaptation is actually hindered because thinking processes are still closely connected to autistic imagination. Piaget regarded pre-adolescent thought processes as an intermediate link between prelogical and logical forms: "Several disparate images melt into one" and "qualities belonging to one object are trans-ferred to another" (p. 158). He called this form of thought "syncretistic thinking." He noted that preadolescents enjoy word games and prefer a punning type of humor, as did the patient described below. Piaget's main contribution, how-ever, was that formal operations or abstract thinking (Basch, 1977; Barenboim, 1977) begins in early adolescence, but in the author's opinion, is not completed until well into adult-hood (Dulit, 1972).

Obsessive–compulsive traits and habits appear in some preadolescents as an exaggeration of latency behavior along with magical thought avoidance and observance of rituals. Preadolescents rarely if ever (Beiser, 1980; Sklansky, 1980) engage in true psychoanalytic therapy because of limited capacities to introspect and free associate. Sklansky (1980) outlines the parameters that must be introduced to sustain a viable therapeutic enterprise. In the main, though, technique is determined by and adapted to the level of ego organization achieved and receptivity to interventions (Wieder, 1978) and certain special forms of resistance (Brody, 1961).

CASE HISTORY

Mr. L., a thirty-six-year-old bachelor veteran, entered analysis while actively researching his father's life in an all-absorbing fashion. The analyst noted that he seemed to have such a head of steam up he just couldn't or wouldn't settle for a short trip. He was the oldest of four children, with a brother thirteen months younger, and two sisters, four and six years younger. The father had died at age fifty-two of a brain injury when the patient was eleven. He sought psychoanalytic help for an inability to sustain a heterosexual relationship and a form of impotence—retarded ejaculations. He was confused about his identity or sense of self. Some quotes have been taken from his associations during the early sessions to illustrate how he viewed himself. "I see myself . . . as not yet settled or [having] found myself"; "I deny aging and I don't feel the passage of time"; "Twenty-five years have gone by and I'm still living in limbo"; "Sometimes I don't know who I am versus who he [father] was. I even adopted his signature and use the same bank"; "When I learned he didn't get married until he was thirty-nine I felt I could wait until then."

He was unable to advance himself in a career and he fantasized about entering his father's profession. He was chronically depressed and frequently awakened with panicky dreams. Also, he misconstrued real noises in the alley as violence being done. Once he experienced a hypnogogic hallucination of a dark and menacing figure in his room. Incidentally, he kept a large, life-sized portrait of his father under his bed. He was aloof and formal. To authority, he was rigid, stubborn, and defiant, which was posturally displayed by the stiffness on the couch early in the analysis, and in the initial contact by the military style of widely planted feet and the jaunty angle of his chin. On the way in and out of sessions, he looked at the analyst searchingly and longingly. Embarrassed giggles appeared when his appointment followed that of an attractive woman. He looked strange in a coat too large and a hat more appropriate for an older man. At first, he tried to engage the analyst in his physical concerns—his colds, allergies, and chronic constipation. This latter symptom epitomized his anal fixation, which was amplified in his detailed descriptions of his evacuations, gas passing contests with his roommates, withholding emotional involvement with others, and in the early transference relationship with the analyst. On the other hand he was passively compliant, which hid his unconscious wish to be relieved of his emotional "impaction" by active interventions from the analyst, just as his father had done with enemas to relieve fecal impactions. Early on in the analysis when the analyst pointed out how involved he seemed in mythologizing his father, he went home to have a large evacuation, which he experienced as a sense of emptiness, "as if I had lost something vital." Soon thereafter his bowel habits assumed a regular pattern—at 9:30 in the evenings, which dramatically coincided with the last hour he saw his father alive and emphasized the rather primitive identification with his father. Bowel movements were then regularly accompanied by a slight tearing or moisture in his eyes which he associated to losing somebody and feeling empty.

Two major events had coalesced to crystallize his motivation to seek analysis. First, he was shocked to be overcome with tears when his girlfriend announced a two-week vacation. Second, he received a note from his uncle that the father's ashes had been buried. In an all-consuming campaign he began to collect biographical data about his father for a scrapbook in a kind of searching or yearning for the father (Bowlby, 1980). He interviewed father's old friends, business acquaintances, and the doctor in attendance at the last illness. He discovered the father's birth certificate had been altered to make him seven years younger and that he had changed his name to suggest a particular ethnic origin. Whenever the patient saw the family name in print, he almost "believed" his father was still alive. He had dreams and fantasies that father would actually reappear.

He described in glowing, romanticized terms how his

father had been a renowned university professor with an enviable reputation, and later on a successful businessman. Mr. L. assumed he would be successful if he associated himself with successful men, but he merely became an efficient, trusted, and diligent assistant. He felt he was blessed with an unfilled destiny—vague and unformed in his mind—a kind of indestructibility or immortality. For example, he engaged in death defying sports such as mountain climbing, and unconsciously chose his father's favorite sport—white water river rafting. Twice he almost drowned, but his unrealistic view of danger was merely augmented and intensified.

While afraid to assert himself with male peers (e.g., allowing opponents to win in disputes with them), he easily attached himself to older father surrogates. There was a close relationship with an older man who served as mentor in personal matters and career interests. While seeking advice from this friend and other men, he strongly resented being told what to do. In the past there had been a succession of father surrogates. There was the choirmaster who expressed sympathy at the time of the father's death. "Feelings welled up inside and there was moisture in my eyes, but no tears came." In high school when a teacher took a liking to him his failing status dramatically shifted to top grades and an identification which was later fulfilled in becoming a high school teacher. A similar identification with a retired army officer–scout leader led to his becoming active in scouting for many years.

When not seeking out father surrogate relationships (Esman, 1982) he was usually a loner, though he yearned for a close personal relationship. During these times exuberant fantasies of inventions or owning a manufacturing business occurred. One such fantasy from preadolescence was about hydroponic farming, and more recently improving international food production through the creative use of new fertilizers. For many years, he collected information on tent designs and made drawings of a collapsible tent he would market, but was dismayed to learn that one such tent had already been used on the Hilary expedition to Mt. Everest. He treasured a crossbow he had made at age fifteen, and like a boy hid the trigger so no one else could use it.

He imagined himself the father sitting in the father's chair at the table carving the meat, but he couldn't integrate the memories of a tender sympathetic father with those of the raging, violent, drunken father. To be like father or identifying with him meant literally becoming his father, whom he saw as an unintegrated, ruthless competitor, and a helpless alcoholic dependent on his wife. He saw his three younger siblings as more mature and successful than himself. He could not behave as the oldest brother to them, nor as his mother's adult son assuming certain responsibilities. To be tenderly affectionate toward his mother frightened him and meant he was weak and effeminate. On occasions he telephoned her with sadistic practical jokes to forcibly separate himself from her. He saw his troubles with the women he dated as being fixated at an immature level, since he was unable to commit himself to any one of them. However, he was unable to change his behavior. It was easy enough for him to initiate the relationship with a woman, but he felt "frozen"—"I just sit and do nothing. I am standing still with the world going by. I'm like a fish out of water and afraid of getting in—a kind of paralysis mountain climbers get—they freeze." He perceived himself as smaller than his girlfriend. However, his belief in his youthful appearance was shaken by observing his graying temples.

Sexual and aggressive drive impulses were under severe control and self-expression in either area was accomplished but sporadically, and with much conflict (Gadpaille, 1978). He desperately wanted to win in tennis but, as noted above, often gave in to defeat by inferior players. Masturbation was repressed and its reappearance was delayed until twenty-five years of age.

The early phases of the analysis brought out the history that the father had taken over the care of the patient at four months when the mother's milk dried up with a second pregnancy. When the baby was reluctant to take the bottle, the father is said to have forced the bottle. The father made all decisions regarding child-rearing practices. A Swedish nurse was hired to carry out his rigid rules and regulations. Rocking or playing with babies for soothing or comforting was prohibited. When Mr. L. showed an early preference for left-handedness, his hand was slapped. He didn't walk until more than two years of age. The father was also intimately involved in toilet training. Daily evacuations were commanded right after breakfast and enemas were administered to ensure regularity. The father demanded that the bathrooms be washed down daily with Lysol because of his germ phobia emerging from the fact that *his* mother and several siblings succumbed to typhoid fever when *he* was three. Mr. L. remembered being a balky and uncooperative child who provoked his mother into anger. He saw himself as a retentive person, hoarding his father's books and furniture. He acted this out when he forgot to pay the first month's bill. He apologized with a note saying that it was an "anal slip." He was preoccupied with anal things. He dreamed of picking up feces floating in the river. He was balky at work, procrastinating with assigned tasks. In first grade, he had been sullen, angry, and withdrawn, and clung to his teacher. Photographs from this time showed him with a worried, withdrawn look. It was around this time a second sibling (sister) was born, and the thirteen-month younger sibling (his brother) contracted scarlet fever. The father became more involved with the sick child and even more turned his attention to Mr. L.'s second sibling, a sister. Fantasies recovered from this period consisted of soaring in space in balloons or rockets and babies dropping out of the air like baby mice. His self-image in latency was bisexual in nature—male and female characteristics were stuck together as though made of dough.

Thus, the clinical picture that emerged early in the analysis was of a compulsively compliant man who produced a wealth of significant psychopathological and historical data but who was largely engaged in an entrenched unconscious resistance to the development of a meaningful or useful transference relationship with the analyst; that is, until the seventh month, by which time he had formed an attachment to the analyst, and cried uncontrollably because of a brief interruption in the therapy. However, he was unable to sustain contact with his repressed and split-off affects after the analyst returned. On the first anniversary in the analysis of the father's death there was again some grieving and some awareness of anger toward father and the analyst in the transference. Dreams of confronting authority figures and winning out in a triadic rivalry appeared, which led to guilt, a need for punishment, and a homosexual transference regression. This sequence was repeated many times in the first year of the analysis. He denied feelings about separations, but the first sign of a breakthrough came at around the end of the first year of analysis when he admitted that each evening he walked past the analyst's office building to look up to see if his windows were lighted. When confronted about how much the analyst must mean to him and how much Mr. L. missed him during interruptions, he sobbed and associated to how he had sought out his father in various places and relics—in truth, to keep him alive. He shifted to a passive relationship with a series of phallic women. He played adolescent games with his girlfriend by jumping out from hiding places to scare her, and attempted to pass a grape into her mouth as he kissed her. He saw his angry negative feelings in the transference "as radiating outwards like a skunk—I'm burning inside and it goes back to the point of memory. I was made to hold my feelings back, it pervades my entire life, it's a sinking feeling that I'm so angry at you because I thought I had to be so lovey-dovey." "I've always sought warm mothering relationships with both men and women—I'm angry at you for not giving it to me." "I imagine sex with women who are warmly involved with me—these are the fantasies I had in order to achieve orgasm." In his relationship with the analyst he was a stickler for protocol and attempted to control him with it; when the analyst couldn't be manipulated Mr. L. got angry and fantasized defecating on the couch.

He returned to visit the family's home where he had last seen his father alive. Interruptions of a day in the weekly analytic schedule, and even more so weekends, brought more sadness and grieving.

As his fears of being swallowed up by the phallic mother in the transference lessened, he felt closer to the analyst and was more sexually active with different partners. He fantasized about marriage, fatherhood, and giving up his roommates. On the radio he heard an aria from Handel's *Messiah* ("For unto us a son is born. Unto us a child is given.") which brought tears to his eyes as he imagined how his father must have felt when he was born. He began to regard his father's personality more realistically and objectively. "I can't have my father and you as my father. I guess I am willing to give up my hold onto you as father. I can't cling to you as father because you don't give me what I want—and knowing that really helps! . . . I never realized I've lived this way for so long. I got used to it—like sinus pain. I didn't know how much relief I could get."

After he proposed marriage to his girlfriend he "felt a great sense of calm." "I feel bigger, older, stronger, and dealing with you person-to-person. I'd like to compete with you in some kind of game, one I can play well and not get so afraid that I'd fold up or stop fighting to win. . . . I never had a chance to express my hatred for my father after he died . . . just apathy and withdrawal. I'm afraid if I'm active I'll have to face the possibility of death—separations in a way mean death." He was struck with how openly the subject of death was dealt with in a movie, *All the Way Home,* based on the novel *A Death in the Family* (1957), by James Agee. "If I commit myself to someone, then I have to face the possibility of losing them." When the analyst didn't object to his proposal of marriage he felt the analyst's silence meant he didn't care about Mr. L. and supported it as a prelude to prematurely terminating the analysis.

Just before the wedding, the mourning process was intensified. To him it meant losing forever his infantile, childish self, and, in the transference, his relationship with the analyst as the restored father which was being split off and attached to the wife. It was a very emotionally moving experience for him. Upon his return a few days later he was angry with the analyst for letting him get married to a woman he now saw as phallic and castrating. He was reluctant to grow up. "What has to die is the feminine involvement with you"; "I've been used to dealing with a dead man. It's different to shift to a live person, but I like it and it feels good to be beginning to shape up."

As a result of mourning his father, work began anew on the mother transference. He recalled a recurrent dream of being in the darkened basement of the family home where he huddled in fear as a woman's footsteps came closer and closer. Here was condensed his fear of the phallic mother who had stood up to the powerful father. Her strength of character was revealed when she had secretly rocked him as a baby when the Swedish nurse was off-duty or out on an errand. She had single-handedly driven the family limousine to a relative's farm overriding the father's ultimatum to never take them there. Mother currently held an executive position with a department store.

Sexual games in childhood, with his younger sisters

dancing around nude and lying down together back to back, merged in late adolescence with a very strong attachment and involvement with his youngest sister. After returning from service in World War II he moved back in with his mother and reluctantly moved out at her urging eight years before starting the analysis. He recalled that he hung onto the fantasied hope of growing up to be like his father so he could then get back to his mother to have her for himself.

A flourish of adolescent behavior followed. A boyish, defiant rebelliousness was matched by pedantic bossiness at work. He tried to compete with the analyst in racing to the men's room. He was now more openly aggressive and competitive in games with his male friends, yet he was flippant and hesitant with women. He fought with his wife over her presumed intrusiveness and entertained sexual fantasies about other women that possessed all the characteristics of adolescent masturbation fantasies. He viewed his wife more as a mother than as a spouse. He had recurrent dreams about phallic women and sexual intercourse with his mother. He felt his mother had emasculated him and to get even he'd show her—and the analyst in the transference—how she'd failed with him, even if it meant becoming a failure to himself. "It's strange what I'm putting my wife through when I know she's nothing like my mother."

The unconscious reasons for his anger were reconstructed in the analysis: not only was he replaced by three siblings, but his mother had to repeatedly leave the children at home to go help her husband sober up for board meetings in some distant city. He experienced her as sexually stimulating (e.g., once in adolescence she applied Sloane's liniment to his legs after a sport event; he was afraid he'd get an erection). She regularly came into the bathroom when he was there. He described how overindulged and overfed he had been since infancy. There were piano lessons, dance lessons, and he was driven to school by a chauffeur. He felt he could achieve autonomy only by being obnoxious and cruel with his mother, his wife, and, in the transference, by flooding the analyst with many convoluted dreams with multiple themes and conflicts. Fantasies of freeing himself from his dependent relationship to the phallic mother were followed by castration dreams. He recalled as a child he felt too little, weak, and inferior to compete with his father for his mother's affection and love. He repeatedly created the triangular situation with his wife's former boyfriend to test out her love as well as motivate himself to win her again. He felt competitive with the analyst in analyzing his dreams, he made derogatory remarks about doctors, and felt more confident in himself, but then dreamed of being gored by wild pigs, shooting himself in the groin, "scrimshawed" and ripped open from a knife inserted in his rectum. He fantasized arguments with the analyst and his boss and dreamed of taking his brother's wife and the analyst's wife for himself. He was defiantly late. When Mr. L. dreamed of killing the analyst he associated to feeling stronger at the analyst's expense. "You stand in the way of having my wife or my mother." He dreamed of using his crossbow on the analyst and argued with a doctor from the south about the poll tax, but then he dreamed of a snake biting him on the penis and both arms were cut off. Concomitant with these oedipal fantasies and castration dreams he was able to be more freely and openly affectionate with his mother. A fantasy from preadolescence was of murderous rage while throwing lead soldiers into an incinerator. Another fantasy, with oedipal meaning, was that he would grow up to be like father without all his shortcomings so as to win his mother. He acted out his defiance by coming late. He got excited about manufacturing baby formula for hospital nurseries, but panicked when his wife broached the subject of having a baby. He connected his panic up with his impotence symptom. "I lost myself in a fantasy world where I didn't feel this impotent rage at being stimulated by mother and her walking away from me."

Over a series of sessions (hours 450–460) he spoke of feeling less hostile, brittle, or critical and expressed warm, affectionate feelings, but he retreated back to feeling uprooted and pursued by a phallic woman. Dreams of murdering his adversary revived his passive–submissive homosexual posture in the transference. Interpretation of the transference meaning of these dynamics led to recollection and reconstruction of his childhood theory of childbirth through the anal canal. "I thought if I could make myself female I could hold onto my father." He recalled that several years previously he had experimented once with anal stimulation by inserting a candle into his rectum, but got no real pleasure from it.

Thoughts of fatherhood, acting his age, and termination forced a retreat to feeling "I'm a bystander watching a love affair between my baby and my wife standing for my brother and my mother. I resist fatherhood more than husbandhood." He avoided sexual relations with his wife to irritate her—to gain distance. He remembered years ago reading in the popular press about sibling rivalry, but was unaware of any feelings; now he was aware, and, to top it off, the expected date of the delivery of their first child was close to his brother's birthday.

The second anniversary in the analysis of his father's death stirred up little of the former psychopathological reactions. Instead, he felt a sense of "liberation" and "freedom," and demonstrated that he could be tenderly affectionate with his wife, but tough and aggressive at work.

Again with thoughts of termination and his parents' wedding anniversary, he dreamed of visiting the family home, "to pick up my life and move on—it was as though my life stopped back there—all the intervening time was aimless wandering. My behavior now reminds me of when I was nine, ten, eleven. I'm mad because I couldn't control my father and he seemed so unconcerned about me. I realize that idealizing you was a rationalization for not growing up."

He was sad when his wife had a miscarriage, but he felt more relieved of the responsibility of becoming a parent too soon. This signaled a surge toward autonomy: he saw himself as stronger, thought of leaving the analyst, and more promptly responded to his sexual urges. "It's a little scary, though, it's like picking up the phone and someone has already dialed you— being suddenly connected is scary." This sort of fear of sexual excitement and heterosexual involvement is suggestive of how he might have experienced the sudden increase of the sexual drive in puberty. Thoughts of eliminating his defensive stance of a frustrated, sullen, angry, withdrawn, and passive person produced a dream of a snake with a woman's head disappearing into a hole. Thoughts of termination led to hypochondriacal preoccupations— how could the analyst throw a sick man out on the street? Almost in the same breath he announced he was looking for a new job, ending the analysis, had thoughts of becoming a father (Kestenberg, 1981), and of genuinely loving his wife. He reported a "creeping sense of well-being— some ups and downs, but the peaks and valleys aren't as noticeable. The past seems less in control of me. I'm not turned toward the past, and I'm not backing into life anymore." Mountain climbing again offered an apt analogy. "I'm lunging foward to get over the last bit of incline— you won't have to push or pull me across— the last step is mine."

When he dreamed of being at a funeral but without his shoes, the analyst remarked he seemed ambivalent about leaving since he needed to get his walking shoes on first. He was touched by the movie *The Pawnbroker,* in which an emotionally frozen-up man's outer shell was pierced when his protegé was killed. In this same connection he recalled his parents had broken into his room, when he was nine-and-a half or ten, while he was lying on his bed with an erection.

As he contemplated termination more willingly and seriously, there were regressive retreats of ignoring his wife, having drinks with an old girlfriend, and some of his pre-analytic personality returned. There were recurrent dreams of exhibiting himself or viewing a woman exposing herself.

There were repetitions of the same cycles of progression toward autonomy and regressive retreats. He recalled with fondness memories of a train trip with his father and brother to Yellowstone. He made plans to resume playing the piano with real interest. He dreamed of the family house being torn down and he threw out a number of books from his father's extensive library. He dreamed of driving a silver spike through a man's heart. But at the same time he was proud of his father's accomplishments, what he did for social improvement, such as his contributions to solving labor-management problems.

The third anniversary of his father's death during the analysis was accompanied by some sadness and he felt more strongly identified with his father's aggressiveness and self-assertiveness. He felt kinder to his wife; for example, in the final session he reported a dream of a boat ride in which he was buffeted by a fast current and other hazards, but he made it safely to dry land. "Not all hearts and flowers—I've still got things to do—it's like a rebirth—lot of hard going, but I feel a calm, peaceful inner security. My energies are more in control and channeled. I'm closer to mother but not shackled to her. I feel a certain kind of sadness, not depression, mixed with joy." Thus ended an analysis of 669 hours, covering a period just short of four years.

Seven-and-a-half years later, he returned for ten sessions, extending over a two-month period. His wife had suddenly left him and the children at a resort. She was fed up with his old symptoms of passivity, delayed orgasm, and emotional withdrawal from her. This symptomatic regression had been precipitated by his mother's sudden death and his mother-in-law's suicide attempt. He was unable to complete the reactivated mourning process on his own. However, with a burst of creativeness, he had composed a poem about his mother somewhat reminiscent of Gray's *Elegy*. He was confronted with fears of his own death and a rising up wish to join his mother's spirit. The threat of losing his wife sent him to seek help in working through the mourning process. He then recalled the joy and anxiety of the previous termination.

SUMMARY AND DISCUSSION

Mourning Process

To grieve and mourn (Pollock, 1961) adaptively and successfully, an intact ego and a consolidated personality are necessary (Wolfenstein, 1966). Mourning was not possible for this man when he was an eleven-year-old because he was already in a preadolescentlike state of disequilibrium. Some brief expression of grief had occurred at eleven, but it was quickly repressed since there was much ambivalence about his father. When the analysis began, his labile affects were strictly controlled by rigid defensive operations. Motorically, he lay stiffly on the couch and his carriage and gait were rigid and military in style. He was aloof, formal, and inhibited. During sleep, further evidence of ego disintegration, failure of repression, and erosion of reality testing function were observed in his frequent panicky dreams, hypnogogic hallucinations, and misconstruing real perceptions from outdoors. His researching biographical data about his father was a hypercathexis that dynamically served the aims of resistance (Forman, 1983) to prevent the emergence of a utilizable and interpretable transference. At best, it represented a transference readiness, and in another sense, it was a defensive idealizing of the analyst and his employers to reshape his poorly formed sense of self and identity. The deepest meaning, however, was to keep his father alive. At times he almost "believed" he would meet up with his father, indicating a split in his awareness of the reality of his father's death. A similar interpretation applied to his repeated visits to the spot where he last saw his father alive and mythologizing his father's memory. An innocent enough comment about this broke through this fragile and defensive pseudoidentification which he experienced as though he had "lost something vital," and his bowel habits changed dramatically to that selfsame fatal hour. He attempted to restore his father in his relationship with the analyst by looking at him searchingly and longingly, but most particularly by his ploys to engage him in his physical ills and constipation symptom, a regular part of the past relationship with his father who had frequently administered enemas. The underlying passive, feminine, receptive homosexual, or negative oedipal meaning of these maneuvers was brought out and interpreted. He was especially afraid of women because he saw them as phallic and he experienced physical and psychological intimacy with them as castrating. He was afraid to compete or assert himself with men too, because he needed the emotional support of men as kind, loving fathers against the feared, overpowering women. He lived with several male roommates in a perpetual adolescent fantasy of never growing up and reinforcing each other's immature personalities. He counterphobically disavowed his own vulnerability to physical dangers by engaging in death defying sports which had been father's interests too. Identifications with other men and their interests, vocational or avocational, were globally incorporated and had none of the characteristics of truly constructive identifications. Two such "identifications" mentioned in the case history were merely superficial detours in his quest for a permanent and solid career goal of his own. Identification with his father was full of conflict and polarized memories: a cruel, punitive, raging drunken father contrasted with images of the tender, loving, indulgent father, and the helpless alcoholic dependent man unable to control himself.

The first indication of a mourning process in the analysis (seventh month) appeared when he experienced acute grief over a brief interruption in the treatment, thus indicating a meaningful transference to the analyst was beginning. This was the first real evidence of a hypercathexis of the lost object as transferred onto the analyst. Checking the analyst's office windows each night indicated a solid settling into a mourning process. Affective discharge was more convincingly real and sustained, especially when precipitated by various interruptions in the analytic schedule (e.g., vacations, his wedding, and the anticipation of the formal termination of the analysis).

The most important result of the reactivation of the mourning process in the context of the analytic relationship was the unleashing of an arrested personality. Characteristics of preadolescent behavior gave way to more adolescent phase specific conflicts. He internalized a consistent analytic self-observing function which strengthened and consolidated those reality testing functions of his ego. A solid, secure sense of a masculine self-image emerged, which contained both tenderness and aim-inhibited affection toward women. Aggressive action in business situations as well as in relationships with his male friends grew stronger as his castration fears, associated with competing with authority figures in the external world and in the transference with the analyst, diminished. A solid sense of fatherliness emerged too (Kestenberg, Marcus, Sossin, and Stevenson, 1982) as an integration of basic constitutional elements with new psychological growth during the analysis.

His rich and exuberant fantasy life, which had closely resembled preadolescent fantasies and was disconnected from practical or realistic means to bring them to fruition, were now connected to newly discovered capacities to be effective. The grandiosity of the preanalytic period also abated.

While loss of the father at age eleven was the central traumatic event in this man's neurosis, there had been preloss issues associated with the father's problems with alcoholism, the parents' arguments over the father's drinking habit, and the family's enhanced ambivalence and disillusionment regarding the father. Earlier still, had been maternal deprivation experiences in the oral period associated with the father's rigid control over child rearing practices, but most particularly his attitudes in the anal period which reinforced fixations in the patient at that level of libidinal development. Subsequent development in this man was distorted by the oral and anal fixations which interfered with the phallic and oedipal phases (Dewald and Kramer, 1976). The trauma of the father loss was a further complication. Throughout this man's early childhood, major disruptive experiences interfered with the development of internal regulatory capacities to modulate arousal, excitement, and affects, as demonstrated in his various symptoms of anxiety, sexual dysfunction, and so on. The construction of the preoedipal period (Blum, 1977) raises the interesting probability that these early fixations would have been present regardless of a father loss. After the father's death, he felt forced into prematurely assuming an adult role which he felt totally unprepared for. He was told he had to be mother's "little man." He was not free nor could he rebel like his younger brother had done. These traumas had a cumulative effect on the development of this man's personality in adolescence. The mother's ambivalence about the father continued after the father's death in her interpretation of masculinity to the patient.

Sexual development had been retarded. His first ejaculation had occurred soon after father's death. It was a nocturnal emission associated with a dream about going faster and faster downhill in a car without brakes. Active masturbation leading to orgasm was delayed until twenty-five years of age. Dreams recovered from the early adolescent period were typically

CHILDHOOD BEREAVEMENT AND ITS AFTERMATH

stimulating dreams of being seduced by sex-starved Amazon women whom he was helpless to resist, but his perception of women as phallic and castrating induced terror in him (Blos, 1962, 1976, 1980). Analytic reconstruction (Blum, 1977, 1980; Glenn, 1976; Greenacre, 1976; Curtis, 1982) led to the recovery of a memory from childhood of remaining in the darkened basement of a house which the family had inspected in anticipation of purchasing it. The rest of the family had left the house only to discover later he was not in the car with them. One memory from age nine-and-a-half or ten was of his parents breaking into his locked room while he lay nude on the bed playing with his erect penis. His fantasy was about a scene he had seen earlier of the maid putting on her stockings and her breasts hanging down. Her perused his father's library for pictures of nude women. There was ample evidence for trauma in sexual overstimulation from the childhood history and his fantasy life in which he viewed a woman undressing or he exhibited himself. Before analysis he had dealt with it by turning passivity into actively teasing women to think he wanted intercourse, but he would sadistically withhold sexual intimacy and gratification.

As preadolescent fears of the phallic castrating mother gave way to the analytic work, he entered into a period with triadic transference meaning. Castration anxiety forced a regressive retreat into a negative oedipal stance which angered and humiliated him. Regressive–progressive cycles followed with increasing confidence in a capacity to engage in an assertively competitive transference relationship with the analyst, which he also applied to his business contacts and social friendships. He then proceeded to integrate a healthy attitude about sexuality into his personality.

Chapter 15

Two Defenses Against the Work of Mourning

Max Forman, M.D.

INTRODUCTION

We have found in the adult patients who sought treatment with members of our group that the child's ego was unable to accept the full emotional impact of the reality of the loss of a parent (Fleming, Altschul, Zielinski, and Forman, 1958; Fleming, 1963; Fleming and Altschul, 1963; Forman, 1966; Seidenberg, 1966). As children, these adults could not complete the mourning process.

In the study of adults who are in mourning, one response to the awareness of the reality of the loss is an attempt to hold on to the representation of the object by hypercathecting it. Missing the lost object is so painful that the fact of the loss is denied momentarily and we feel united or connected to the object. The truth, however, dawns on the mourner and he dissolves in pain, anguish, and grief. This initiates a prolonged process of repetition and bit-by-bit withdrawal of libido from the lost object. It leads to a gradual decathexis of the lost object (Freud, 1917).

377

Children also adapt to the awareness of the loss and the grief by hypercathexis of the lost object and denial. However, instead of just being a temporary adaptation, the child may adapt by solidifying the hypercathexis of the lost object and reinforcing the denial. These adaptations to the mourning process may then become permanent structured defenses and resistances against the progressive work of mourning, and thus become fixated.

In general, the defenses involved are denial of the meaningfulness of the loss and persistent attachment to the lost object. A major form of the manifestation of these defenses in the analysis is transference to the analyst of aspects of the dead parent in an attempt to preserve the attachment to and the meaningfulness of the lost object. A second basic defense is identification with aspects of the dead parent. Introjection of the lost object, which will be described in the patient below, is a variant of such identification.

In addition to incomplete mourning, another major sequelae of parent loss by death in childhood is arrested development of the ego, corresponding to levels achieved in the self and selfobject representations at the time of the loss (Altschul, 1968). In the patient described below, the forms of arrest and immaturity are described. The patient's intense need for the preservation of the lost object shows how essential the child felt the supplies of love and self-esteem were. The child felt that she would be overwhelmed and unable to survive without the presence of the lost object. Thus, she unconsciously went to great efforts to preserve the attachment.

DATA FROM THE ANALYSIS

The analytic data is selected to describe the material relevant to resistances and defenses against the work of mourning. The data is organized under four headings, and chronologically, as it emerged in her analysis: history, denial in fantasy, introjection of the lost object, and the transference neurosis.

History

Karen is a twenty-four-year-old Catholic mother of two children. Her father had died suddenly of pneumonia when she was six years old. She cried for one day and did not think she had missed him. This is the typical history of the brevity of grief and mourning we see in adults who come to us for analysis or therapy. Karen suffered from an obsessive–compulsive symptom neurosis. She complained of pain in her throat and the back of her neck and was undecided as to whether to give in to the compulsion to take an aspirin. She obsessively feared the death of her husband and child unless she made the right decision about her pain and whether to take the aspirin.

Karen had strong feelings of inadequacy and immaturity. She related childishly to her husband through bidding for sympathy and avoidance of intercourse. All of her relationships were shallow because her inner fantasy life predominated over reality.

Her neurosis was precipitated at age nineteen when, during her engagement, she was about to have intercourse with her future husband. She became extremely anxious, interrupted the act, and soon thereafter developed obsessional and compulsive symptoms fearing for the safety of her mother and her future husband. After marriage, she did not permit intercourse for four months.

As stated above, her father died suddenly when she was six years old. "I don't think I missed him," she said. She had a few memories of his making a fuss over her appearance, her dresses and her long, curly hair.

In childhood she recalled her mother as a cross, angry, critical woman. Her history reflects a maternal inconsistency over the issue of control of drives: in some areas extreme overcontrol and in others permission for excessive stimulation. The patient slept in the same bed with her brother until age four and with her mother after her father's death, for four years. From the ages of six to eight she was exposed to her overtly seductive and senile maternal grandfather. When the patient was ten years old, her mother remarried. Karen had witnessed much of the hand-holding type of courtship for the three years prior.

Denial in Fantasy and Resistance to Accepting the Reality of the Loss

Karen made immediate use from the first hour of a vivid and active fantasy life. She talked openly, with tears and conflict, about her wish to attract and impress the analyst. She felt that she had been in love with her previous therapist. She said: "When I went there, and when I come here, I dress up for something real important; it's like dressing up for a date, as though this is something big. I feel that I missed so much." She cried and then continued, "I feel that I am trying to make a good impression on you. I feel very glamorous lying here." In subsequent hours, Karen became aware that she was always flirting with men in her imagination. As time passed, it became clear that this exhibitionistic fantasy was very triangular, repetitive, and almost dreamlike. She always imagined that she was preferred by the husband of another woman and that the wife disapproved. The men and women were always interchangeable.

In the twenty-fourth hour, the meaning of this fantasy was elaborated by a very vivid memory of a repetitive form of doll play at age ten when she said:

I was a man, this doll was a girl. It was always a love story in bed and I was very excited. I put my head under the covers and kissed it passionately. I thought of my father and pictured him in Heaven, that he could see me. I associate him with God. He is more real to me than God. What would happen if I died and I would meet them?

She referred here to her father and aunt. She went on to describe how in the doll play she felt that her father and aunt were critical of her. She says, "sometimes I think I hate my mother. I have the feeling that I just exist and have no real interest except in my fears." It is quite significant that, in relating the fantasy, both at present and in childhood, her father was still alive for her.

Evidence for this denial was widespread. She resisted any change in her self-image and denied the reality of being an adult. It was hard for her to believe that her children belonged to her and she claimed to have no motherly feelings. The fact that the transference was a form of the same doll play became quite explicit. She thought of herself as a movie actress and wanted to attract the analyst, but feared being laughed at. Such thoughts demonstrate the strength of her fantasies and how real they were for her. They represented an acting out in fantasy of her wish to be her father's little doll, as in the doll play described above.

This defense of denial in fantasy was the substitution of a vivid fantasy in an attempt to deny the loss and the affective reaction to it. For with it, she tried to make herself happy and avoid any grief and depression.

In reaction to the first Father's Day in analysis (Hilgard and Newman, 1959) this defense was spontaneously broken through when she became depressed. In line with a wish to think of herself as a child, she went to the Children's Mass. She suddenly realized her mistake. She was not a child and she felt awful. She wanted to die, for she felt much too big and awkward standing with the children. Reporting her experience as if it were a new insight, she said, "Yesterday it flashed through my mind that my father was dead."

The fantasies toward men in a triangular setting are described as part of the same defense. A major aspect of the resistance was the quick and ready displacement from one male object to another to deny the reality and the frustration. Instead of individual, unique relationships with real men in reality, Karen had one repetitive relationship with illusory men in her fantasy life. Because this relationship existed in fantasy only, it did not require the participation of another person. It could be, and was, any and every man, be it brother, grandfather, stepfather, brother-in-law, father-in-law, husband's friends, the delivery boy, or the stranger in an elevator. All of these men she unconsciously imagined looked at and admired her. She imagined further that each of these men was married, that each preferred her to his wife, and that each wife knew and disapproved of the relationship. The widespread use of these extra-analytic transferences and the analytic transference from the first hour on the couch is described as evidence for the fact that the patient began her analysis in a state of a highly developed transference resistance.

Introjection of the Lost Object and
Resistances to Withdrawal of Libido From the Lost Object

A series of analytic episodes is presented as evidence for the introjection of her father's penis as an initial response to her father's death (Abraham, 1924; Fenichel, 1945). The material includes obsessional symptoms, a defensive cough and laryngitis, dreams and associations, fantasies, childhood memories, transference behavior, and a distorted reaction to a recent funeral.

Early in the analysis, the patient's obsessional fear of taking an aspirin to relieve the pain in her throat and the compulsion to feed her children supplemental foods were understood and interpreted as wishes to receive something orally from the analyst. She subsequently developed acute laryngitis and a cough as a defense against talking, in an attempt to preserve her fantasies. A dream of a black hat led to associations of a funeral and a death and to the realization that she was afraid to talk for fear of spoiling the fantasies of being special to the analyst. She said, "I have the feeling I want to *re-create* something. It has something to do with the feeling when I come here." In the analysis, the patient made frequent references to the analyst's penis; how important it was to her and how unique she thought it to be. She talked about his penis as if it were separate and apart from him, as an object in its own right. She reported a dream in which a girl is stealing a coat. Her associations and the material could be seen as representing her wish to steal the analyst's penis. She went on to associate to the analyst as a guardian who watches over her and is interested in her, and expressed in the fantasy that, "You are really interested in me because you love me . . . this gives me so much enjoyment in coming here because I keep this feeling alive, even though I don't get any encouragement from you. I keep hoping that you'll make a pass at me or something. All of a sudden I feel very ridiculous. I don't like to talk about that fantasy." Thus, at the very end of experiencing the fantasy, reality impinged and she became aware of its inappropriateness.

Memories from childhood emerged. She remembered sitting at the supper table and recalled her real father shouting at her and her brother. She recalled the analyst's explanation of her feeding her children as a substitute for satisfying her own wishes. She then recalled that some time after her father's death she and her brother ate bread dipped in water and sugar. Later she would call this food "the staff of life." In the associations she also spoke of the analyst's penis. Memories of her father's wake returned and fantasies of being admired as a cute girl by everyone present. In the transference, she relived the childhood experience of eating fruit after school while idling away the hours daydreaming, instead of doing housework for her mother who was at work. This experience was intensely pleasurable, though always followed by her mother's scolding. Now as an adult, eating fruit after her sessions and idling away the time proved to be an empty experience.

Karen associated to an experience of attending the funeral of a married man. In her sympathy for the man's wife she imagined the wife's grief: "It's like his penis belonged to her personally, as if that alone was the most important thing about this marriage; that that is where the union comes in. Not that she's holding it, but the feeling she has about it is so strong that it couldn't be cut off." The patient in this sympathy described the way she had responded to her father's death unconsciously as a child by oral introjection. For the first time she recalled the day of her father's funeral, crying and hanging onto her father's trousers which hung from a doorknob in her house. She began to tear here.

Further clinical evidence is presented to describe the breakthrough of the oral introjection by interpretation of her behavior as a fear of remembering a disappointment in the past. Karen thought of herself as a child, avoided showing her emotions for fear of being laughed at, and was bold in fantasy only. She fantasied with pleasure about the analyst's penis. She imagined holding it with pleasure. She tried to maintain her self-sufficiency and denial of needing help. However, in her associations themes of loss and fear of disappointment began to emerge.

Her behavior was interpreted as fear of remembering and repeating a past disappointment. Her reality testing of the transference situation and the interpretation led to further undoing of the hypercathexis of the lost object as evidenced by two dreams dealing with the death of her father. In the first dream she reported that her stepfather had died and "all of a sudden" she experienced in the dream a great sense of loss and a wish for him to come back. She associated further, "This must be my real father and it makes me think of strong feelings of love and warmth I have for you. Maybe I think of you as my father." The content of the other dream had to do with attending a wedding with her mother. In the dream she saw herself wearing a black corsage and saw a black ribbon hanging up in the air. From her associations the black corsage was seen as representing her grief and sadness experienced at the wedding of her brother and that of her mother and step-father. She associated to the cardinal's hat. The black ribbon hanging high in the air was a representation of her father's penis and now could represent the unattainable analyst.

The behavior of self-sufficiency in the fantasy of possessing the analyst's penis was interfered with by interpretation. With the fantasy no longer tenable, the libidinal transference to the analyst per se as father developed. This was associated with increased awareness of the absence and death of the father, symbolized in the dream by the black ribbon and the manifest content of the death of a father figure.

The analyst's reconstruction of this part of the mourning is that these episodes represented an initial step of oral introjection of her father's penis and were used to adapt to the loss by internally preserving the phallic part object. This type of fantasy, oral incorporation or introjection of the lost object, is described by Abraham (1924) and Fenichel (1945). As was seen, she wanted to enjoy the analysis as much as possible by pretending to possess the analyst's penis and love. In this way, as a child, and now in her analysis, she had kept the illusory father in a fantasy which functioned as her "staff of life" and thereby had resisted the process of decathexis. The defense is in the service of protecting against the impact of the lost object representation. Normally, mourning would proceed to the step of withdrawing the cathexis gradually. However, in this instance, as the evidence above reveals, the child's initial adaptation became a structured defense to avoid any further decathexis and feelings of loss.

The two defenses, denial in fantasy and the introjection of the lost object, were both manifested in the analysis as transference resistance. When they were worked through, the oedipal transference neurosis proper began to develop. It is evident that the denial and the hypercathexis of the lost object functioned as defenses simultaneously against mourning and against the development of a regressive transference neurosis.

The Role of the Transference Neurosis in Relation to Mourning

The regression to the transference neurosis provides evidence for a further step in mourning in the patient's increasing ability to distinguish between the father as a whole transference object, as a partial phallic object and the analyst as such.

As repressed material became conscious and the patient experienced sexual wishes and frustration in the transference, she recalled memories of frustration and feelings of hopelessness with her father, stepfather, and grandfather. Fearing the loss of all her satisfying fantasies, she reported a dream: "You and my father were there. I kept confusing the two of you . . . the idea of needing you and wanting you so much makes me think of changing from an adult to a child; like the difference between an adult and a puppy." Now the analyst was experienced and perceived as a total object and as a spearate person from her father. She went on to say, "I like to think of my own father and how he would love me if he were alive, because I really belong to him. I think I missed something not having a father . . . the idea of his coming back to life is the way I try to revive something here. It's the way I try to excite you, the way I didn't excite my father, but the desire was the same."

The negative transference neurosis with intense murderous wishes toward the analyst as father was relived in the analysis. The unconscious guilt for the fantasy of having killed her father, the magical omnipotence, was reconstructed and interpreted. She reacted with positive feelings for her children and a wish to have the ability to make friends. She looked at the picture of her father at times. Much more sadness, crying, and depression occurred. She began to differentiate more clearly between her husband and father and her analyst and father. She experienced intense wishes for the analyst to be at her house and to watch over her like in the doll fantasy of having her father in Heaven. She said: "It makes me think of a fantasy world I create for myself to escape all the pain of this one and I see my father in this other world." Dreams of the end of the world began to appear, representing the end of her transference fantasy world.

Karen described the function of the phallic introject and thereby revealed evidence also of the degree of advancement of the decathexis of the lost object. She said: "Maybe something about my father never really did leave me when he died. . . . He used to be a voice inside of me telling me what to do, like setting a table. Maybe it was my own voice. The voice inside me disturbed me very much. I just felt like he had to be there. I couldn't be all by myself because I didn't feel confident enough." She cried softly.

These attitudes and feelings which Karen projected to the analyst from the internalized introject represent some of her developmental needs as a latency girl, for a positive ongoing relationship with her father as a very crucial source of self-esteem, confidence, recognition, and protection. Thus, there were at least two motives for the maintenance of this introject: (1) As a needed supply of self-esteem; and (2) as a defense against the mobilization of affects of mourning.

DISCUSSION

Let us look back over the defenses against mourning. The first major defense of the analysis was a denial in fantasy (A.

Freud, 1936; Altschul, 1968). This was manifested by the fact that the patient immediately involved the analyst in a vivid fantasy life in which she imagined herself as glamorous and attractive. Memories from childhood soon provided evidence that these fantasies represented a continuation of doll play from childhood. She had made passionate love to a doll, playing out both roles—her lost childhood self and her dead father. During the doll play, she had felt that her father was in Heaven watching her. The importance of a hereafter and Heaven, to deny the reality of death, was very much part of her Catholicism. In childhood, she had pretended that her father was alive and in the doll play she had felt loved and admired by him. As an adult, in analysis, she played at being admired by the analyst in the father transference, and wished to be a glamorous doll for the analyst.

On the basis of history and reconstruction she reacted to the death of her father with a short period of grief which she defended against by erecting the defense of denial in fantasy as an initial step in mourning. The content and form of the defense derived from an oedipal wish to be admired by her father, a wish consistent with her level of development at the age of six, the time of the loss. The defense represented a wished for relationship to the lost object, a *fantasy* of an object relationship with her father. The doll play did not consist of actual memories of the father. By persisting in this defense, she maintained the illusion of a relationship with him. Until the defense was broken through, this illusion was reflected in her childish attempts to keep herself happy with this fantasy, in order to avoid further grief, depression, and other affects of mourning. She unconsciously tried to pleasurize her pain.

The second defense took the form of an introjection of part of the lost object. In the analysis, this was manifested by the resistance to talking about how special she felt to the analyst and how strongly she wanted and expected the analyst to attack her sexually. In the transference she wanted the analyst to make love to her just as she had herself made love to the girl doll by pressing her body against it. On a deeper level, it was seen that the patient had an unconscious fantasy of possessing her father's penis. A reconstruction of material revealed the origin of the defense was an introjection of her father's penis as an initial step in reaction to his death. In the analysis, like the denial in fantasy, this defense was in the service of keeping the patient in a state of childish pleasure, excitement, and happiness by creating the illusion of a strong tie to her father through the fantasy of possessing his penis. By this method, she protected herself against remembering her sexual wishes toward her father and the associated affects of pleasure, pain, frustration, and anger, and against experiencing the gradual emotional separation from her father.

We can reconstruct the unconscious fantasy that she could not live without her father. The importance of the parent in childhood is so great that some children believe they are unable to survive without the parent. Therefore, the child, and then the adult, tenaciously cling to the transference representation of the lost object and to the identification with it. The interpretation and working through of the defenses are essential to diminish the denial and transference attachments.

As was mentioned earlier, the persistent attachment also is an attempt to maintain a fantasy supply of self-esteem and confidence. These defenses are an attempt to preserve the past. As the defenses yield and the denial of the traumatic impact has begun to be experienced, the transference neurosis emerges. In this phase, the patient can more intensely mourn the loss of her father. She becomes increasingly attached to the analyst as her father. She wants the analyst to replace him. She seeks to gratify both infantile oedipal wishes for love and sexual fulfillment, but also functions from the analyst to build up self-esteem and to reopen her arrested development. In the transference and in the dream she becomes like a puppy dog. She wants to be dependent, close, and loved as the favorite child. She wants the analyst to come to her house and watch over her as if he were her father.

Extensive interpretations and reconstructions of the meanings of her transference to the analyst are necessary for the patient to become more mature and freer of symptoms.

Chapter 16

The Mourning–Liberation Process and Creativity: The Case of Käthe Kollwitz

George H. Pollock, M.D., Ph.D.

My prior research on the mourning–liberation process and the changing psychological meanings of significant figures throughout the life course (Pollock, 1975a,b, 1978a,b, 1981) has now expanded into a more focused approach on the relationship of psychopathology, the creative process, and the creative products. In the following essay, using the life course of a well-known artist as a clinical illustration of my thesis, I hope to discuss various considerations which may be

This essay is dedicated to the memory of our esteemed colleague, friend, teacher, and psychoanalytic researcher, Joan Fleming, whose work on childhood parent loss opened up an area of research at the Chicago Institute for Psychoanalysis which we are carrying forth. This work initially appeared in *The Annual of Psychoanalysis*, Volume X (New York: International Universities Press, 1982), and is reprinted with permission.

Supported in part by Anne Pollock Lederer Research Fund of the Chicago Institute for Psychoanalysis.

of clinical importance as well as applying psychoanalytic principles to aspects of creativity.

The longitudinal study of a life— be it through biography, autobiography, or diaries and other personal accounts—on occasion allows us to suggest some reasons for the outcome which is known. As such, we have a "follow-up" study where reconstruction is the method used to arrive at conclusions. At times these reconstructions are aided through the use of reported dreams and associations, and in fortunate circumstances one can even obtain data that suggest the presence of repeated transference phenomena. The study of a life course is not the same as the report of an ongoing psychoanalytic therapy, but it still has its value, and one can avoid the difficulties associated with issues of confidentiality and privacy. This is especially important when one studies very creative people who are easily identified. Since case histories are mainly used as illustrations and examples, the use of biographical narrative can serve this purpose.

Among twentieth-century artists, Käthe Kollwitz occupies a unique position as a latter-day champion of social justice and peace. For many, the German sculptor and graphic artist loosely identified with "expressionism"* is not only a symbol of opposition to war, but the courageous human being who spent her adult life fighting for the underprivileged and the oppressed, for helpless men, women, and children alike. The art work that represents the medium of her crusade is highly valued, and, by now, well known throughout the world. For psychoanalysts, Kollwitz's life takes on a significance that extends beyond her formal accomplishments: she is the successful female artist who, at

---

*Because Kollwitz's work is dark in spirit and style and was by and large rejected by the "establishment" of her time, she has been labeled an expressionist. In fact, the label is inaccurate. Although her art bears a certain affinity to the work of the expressionalists, Kollwitz never gave allegiance to any purely expressionist group or doctrine (see Kearns, 1976, pp. 139–140).

one and the same time, was a devoted wife and mother, a major creator whose life pattern might well lead us to question traditional formulations about the relationship between artistic creativity, femininity, and maternity (Greenacre, 1960; Nochlin, 1971).

In this paper, I wish to explore the complex interrelationships between Kollwitz's artistic productivity and her successful familial adaptations by focusing on that crucial aspect of her life that invites psychoanalytic scrutiny: her lifelong involvement with an unresolved mourning–liberation process that fueled her artistic productivity. For Käthe Kollwitz, we shall see, a lifetime of mourning was mobilized on behalf of her creative activity.

I

Käthe Ida Schmidt was born in the East Prussian industrial city of Königsberg on July 8, 1867, the fifth child of Katherina Rupp Schmidt and Karl Schmidt. Two of the Schmidt's sons did not survive, having died before Käthe's birth. This fact unquestionably bears on Katherina's inability to display affection toward her surviving children. However devoted a wife to Karl and mother to Käthe, Konrad, Julie, and later Lise (born three years after Käthe), Katherina's undemonstrativeness was probably a manifestation of the depression pursuant to the deaths of the two older sons. We would now attribute this apparent depression to an unresolved and possibly pathological mourning process for her dead children. As a child, Käthe took note of her mother's reserve and appeared to regret it. In fact, Käthe remembered little else about her mother during this period of her life. One striking exception is the memory she recorded in her diary about her ninth birthday:

> I received a set of skittles as one of my birthday presents. In the afternoon, when all of the children were

playing skittles, they would not let me play—I don't know why. As a result, I had one of my usual stomach aches. These stomach aches were a surrogate for all physical and mental pains. . . . I went around in misery for days at a time, my face yellow, and often lay belly down on a chair because that made me feel better. My mother knew that my stomach aches concealed small sorrows, and at such times she would let me snuggle close to her [in Kearns, 1976, pp. 2–3].*

A younger brother, Benjamin, was born shortly after this time. Käthe's recollections again centered on her mother's physical unresponsiveness to her new sibling. When Benjamin was one year old, Käthe recollected,

We were sitting at table and Mother was just ladling the soup—when the old nurse wrenched open the door and called out loudly, "He's throwing up again, he's throwing up again." Mother stood rigid for a moment and then went on ladling. I felt very keenly her agitation and her determination not to cry before all of us, for I could sense distinctly how she was suffering [p. 3].

Benjamin died of meningitis shortly after this incident, the very illness that had taken the Schmidts' firstborn child, Julius. Käthe wanted desperately to comfort her mother at this difficult time, but found herself unable to approach the stiff, aloof woman with "that distant look of hers" (p. 3).

The theme of the dead child and the living but deeply grieving mother would later occupy a significant place in Käthe Kollwitz's art. Already in childhood, the impact of Benjamin's death and Katherina Schmidt's ongoing pathological mourning made Käthe fearful of losing her mother:

*The quotations from Kearns (1976) are published with the permission of The Feminist Press, Old Westbury, NY.

I was always afraid she would come to some harm. If she were bathing, even if it were only in the tub, I feared she might drown. Once I stood at the window watching for Mother to come back, for it was time. . . . I felt the oppressive fear in my heart that she might get lost and never find her way back to us. Then I became afraid that Mother might go mad [p. 4].

Käthe never saw her mother break down, but she noted in her diary that whereas Katherina "never surrendered to the deep sorrow of those early days of her marriage, it must have been her years of suffering that gave her forever after the remote air of a madonna" (H. Kollwitz, 1955, p. 18). This air of maternal remoteness was frequently more than Käthe could stand:

> While Katherina Schmidt never cried, tender hearted, nervous young Kaethe did, often and violently; some of her roaring and kicking tantrums lasted for hours. . . . Perhaps Kaethe's childhood fits were unconscious expressions of her mother's pent-up rage and grief. But in later years, Katherina Schmidt's stoicism appeared in Kaethe herself—and in her many images of mothers [Kearns, 1976, p. 4].

From a psychoanalytic vantage point, it is plausible to suggest that young Käthe was angry with a mother who had not been able to give her the love and warmth to which she felt entitled. The daughter's early years were filled with cheerless days; from the outset, her life seemingly revolved around death, unresolved mourning, and controlled anxiety. Years later, Käthe's identification with her mother would be actualized in a concrete way when her own son and, later, her firstborn grandson were killed in the two world wars. Grieving mothers, frightened children, death and oppression—these were the life themes that were rooted in Kollwitz's life but gain expression in her art.

But Käthe's inheritance from her parents was hardly restricted to the dire subject matter of her etchings and sculpture. Katherina Schmidt was the daughter of a nonconformist religious leader who had suffered much political abuse; Katherina consequently grew up in a household of religious, political, and social liberality, although her strict religious training emphasized sincerity, seriousness, and truth. That Käthe's mother also possessed artistic interests and talents is "indicated by the successful copies of old masters with which she decorated her home" (Kearns, 1976, p. 5). After the birth of her children, she continued to read Shakespeare, Byron, and Shelley in the original English, even if Käthe rarely saw her reading and never heard her discuss what she read.

Käthe's artistic inclinations received further impetus from her father, Karl Schmidt. A lawyer who became discouraged with the conservative political climate of Bismarck's Prussia, Käthe's father had become intrigued with the ideas of Marx and subsequently joined the German Social Democratic Workers Party. At this juncture of this career, "Having joined the SPD, he knew it would be moral and political suicide to attempt to practice law in right-wing Prussia. He turned to the art of stone masonry and in time became an expert house builder" (p. 8). Thus, while Käthe's identification with her artistic mother may have steered her in the direction of graphic art work, her identification with her manually skilled father may well have played a role in her later sculpture.

It should be noted that the values of her father and maternal grandfather provided the basis for her own political and social ideals, even as mourning came to play a crucial role in the subject matter of her creative activity. Karl Schmidt, unlike many authoritarian Prussian fathers, was an idealist who taught his children through example and guidance rather than force. He encouraged his three daughters to aspire to roles other than those of wife and mother, and he placed particular emphasis on artistic work involving the use of one's hands. Both Käthe and her younger sister Lise showed gifts in drawing very early.

An interesting episode in Käthe's early development concerns her crush on the boy upstairs; in her diary, she describes the "refreshment" of kissing him. When this friend, Otto, unexpectedly moved away and their "love" was ended, Käthe was quite upset. Like most preteenagers of her day, Käthe was greatly confused by sex, love, and reproduction, and her parents did nothing to enlighten her on these topics. She went to her mother daily during this time, timidly trying to share feelings and get answers: "But she said nothing at all, and so I too soon fell silent" (p. 12). Owing to this silence on sex-related topics, Käthe continued for many years to feel ignorant and guilty about her own sexuality.

II

Käthe Kollwitz's artistic talent was already manifest at the age of eleven, when a drawing of her younger sister Lise won her father's admiration. Karl Schmidt appreciated his daughter's precocious talent and encouraged her art work; he believed she was destined to become a successful painter, one who would "not be much distracted by love affairs" as she "was not a pretty girl" (p. 20). Käthe's early efforts to please her father were intensified when he voiced similar expectations for her younger sister, Lise. Indeed, it was the threat posed by her sister's own artistic ability that fostered Käthe's single-minded pursuit of her art; she was inspired "to ask for drawing lessons before Lise might think of asking" (p. 21).

At the same time as Käthe demonstrated an early prowess at drawing, she formed her initial identification with the cause of German socialism. Indeed, at the very time she began drawing, she was drawn to poetry, and, especially, to Ferdinand Freiligrath's *The Dead to the Living*. In this poetic testimony to the ill-fated Prussian revolution of 1848, Freiligrath had the voices of various slain revolutionaries summon the survivors of the revolution to arm against profiteers and decadent monarchs. Like her left-wing parents, Käthe identified with the 200 martyrs of March 1848 who had been killed by the Kaiser's militia. Her affinity for socialism broadened in early adolescence when she began art lessons with the Königsberg engraver, Rudolf Mauer. It was at this time that she met her future husband, Karl Kollwitz, and his sister Lisebeth, two orphans then living with a family in Königsberg. Karl, a friend of Käthe's older brother Konrad, was also a supporter of Prussia's Social Democratic Party. Käthe was drawn into the political discussions of the two boys; in time, her conversations with Karl turned from socialism, revolution, art, and medicine to free love and marriage. Three years later, in 1884, Käthe accepted Karl Kollwitz's engagement proposal. As it turned out, the engagement would be a long and difficult one. Fearful that this early engagement would inhibit his daughter's future artistic career, Käthe's father determined to send her away to art school where she could reconsider her engagement to Kollwitz.

Käthe's ensuing stay in Berlin furthered her commitment to the cause of socialism. Her brother Konrad, who had made the acquaintance of Friedrich Engels, took her to the cemetery where the 200 slain workers of March 1848 were buried. The graveyard made a deep impression on the young girl; one wonders if, at a deep level, she connected the deaths of her three brothers with the martyrs of 1848.

Käthe's art studies in Berlin and subsequent continuation of her painting back in Königsberg could not forestall the inevitable. In 1889, she finally accepted Karl Kollwitz's engagement ring. Her father, once more alarmed at the prospect of her marriage, sent her away for additional art studies, this time in Munich. At the progressive Munich Academy of Art, Käthe wrestled with the question of marriage *and* art versus marriage *or* art. After much soul-searching, she determined to commit herself to both roles, despite her father's opposition and the resistance offered by the community of women artists to which she now belonged: "The women art students considered marriage an act of betrayal, for it meant abandoning their artistic work. . . . It was impossible for a woman to be married and an artist" (Kearns, 1976, p. 41).

Käthe's artistic progress at Munich is noteworthy for her definitive shift from painting to etching and drawing. The shift followed her reading of Max Klinger's *Painting and Drawing* (Kearns, 1976, p. 47). In this essay, the author propounded the theory that drawing entailed a freer relationship to the presentable world than painting. Confronting Klinger's ideas in the context of her continuing difficulties with the use of color, Käthe realized that etching and drawing were the natural media for the expression of her talent. Psychoanalytically, one may further speculate that her turning from painting, at a deeper level, represented an attempt to withdraw from the mother who *did* paint. Käthe's current doubts at the time about the advisability of marrying Karl are perhaps consistent with this speculation. Thus, at the very time she abandoned the artistic media associated with her mother, she wondered anew if engagement and marriage would oblige her to give up the free life of the artist to which she had grown accustomed.

Ultimately, Käthe remained true to the outcome of her deliberations at Munich and opted for marriage. Her biographer Kearns suggests that the decision represented "a rebellious act necessary for her emotional and artistic growth" (p. 57). She is referring, of course, to her need to free herself from the father whose intrusive presence in her life and work had by then grown oppressive, the father who had still not ceased pressuring her to become a painter but not a wife. But there were additional reasons for her decision to marry Karl Kollwitz. The young physician had been offered an attractive position in Berlin involving the new plan of social and medical insurance introduced by Bismarck. To Käthe, marriage to Karl would not only permit relative independence from her father, but would make available to her the active intellectual and social life of Berlin. Understandably, the prospect of being a physician's wife in Berlin appealed to her considerably more than the prospect of remaining a single woman in provincial East Prussia. We can thus appreciate the overdetermined basis of Käthe's decision: marriage not only offered her emotional and creative freedom, but social and economic security in an exciting city with a man whose social, political, economic, and philosophical ideals she shared.

Käthe and Karl were married on June 13, 1891; Käthe was twenty-four at the time. They moved into a flat in a working-class section of North Berlin (now East Berlin). They would remain at this residence for the next fifty years, moving from floor to floor within this corner tenement building. The marriage began on an auspicious note: both Karl and Käthe pursued their respective professions independently. Karl had known that Käthe would not abandon her work on marrying him; he not only endorsed her artistic aspirations, but proved a devoted, kind, and optimistic partner who balanced his wife's alternatingly introspective, depressive, and assertive tendencies.

III

During the autumn of 1891, Käthe became pregnant and in May 1892 she gave birth to a son, Hans. The child was born in the apartment at the very time Käthe was working on a greeting etching that would mark the occasion of the child's birth. She soon began to use Hans as a model, ultimately making at least eighteen studies of her first son (Kearns, 1976, p. 64).

On February 28, 1893, another important event lent impetus to Käthe's search for her artistic subject matter. This was the date on which she attended the premiere of Gerhart Hauptmann's play, *The Weavers*. Despite a Berlin police ban on all public performances of the play, it premiered nonetheless. Käthe Kollwitz had special reason for being in attendance: she had met and dined with the young dramatist when she was an art student in Berlin some years earlier. Hauptmann's *The Weavers* told the story of a group of Silesian peasants turned linen weavers who, some 50 years earlier, in 1844, had revolted because of low factory wages and wretched living conditions. Käthe strongly identified with the emotions of the weavers and was so moved that she began work on her graphic series, *The Revolt of the Weavers*. She spent the next five years creating and perfecting the six frames of the series: (1) Poverty; (2) Death—a weaver's child dies of hunger; (3) Conspiracy—the weavers plan to avenge their child's death; (4) Weavers on the march to the home of the factory owner; (5) Attack—on the owner's mansion by the weavers; and (6) The End—the revolt is over, as are the lives of some of the protagonists.

This noteworthy graphic series, involving working women as well as working men, presents the death of a child as the force that drives the workers to revolt. In so doing, it returns to an early artistic theme that has significant roots in Kollwitz's childhood. I have already observed that two of Käthe's brothers died before her birth whereas her youngest brother, Benjamin, died during her childhood. The Kleins (Klein and Klein, 1975) have noted that:

> [M]emories of Benjamin's illness and death were deeply stamped on Kaethe's mind. As a mature woman and even

> in her old age she recalled how she had ached with love and
> pity as her reserved mother had grieved silently for
> Benjamin. . . . Kaethe was tormented by feelings of guilt
> because of a strange circumstance that had occurred at the
> time of Benjamin's death. Her father had wanted his
> children to have worthwhile playthings and had given them
> large building blocks. . . . From these Kaethe had built
> for her own use a temple to Venus. . . . She was playing at
> worship in this temple when her mother and father, quietly
> coming into the room, had told her that Benjamin had
> died. Kaethe was terror-stricken. God, she thought, was
> punishing them all for her sacrifices to the pagan deity
> Venus [p. 6].

Since Käthe apparently held herself responsible for Benjamin's death, one might ask if this sense of responsibility
did not also mask her guilt at having survived the brothers
who had died before her birth. Although direct data are
unavailable, it is important to note that Käthe probably
reacted to Benjamin's death in a variety of ways. She was
guilty, she was frightened, she had feelings about losing a
little brother, and she also was very upset with the additional
depressive–pathological mourning responses of her mother
and father. The loss of a sibling when one is a child can give
rise to many concomitant responses. Survivor guilt in relation
to childhood sibling loss through death is especially not
uncommon (Pollock, 1978a).

In 1896, Käthe bore her second son, Peter. Following his
birth, she finished *The Revolt of the Weavers* and then
traveled to her sick father to present him with her first
graphic series; she dedicated it to him on his seventieth
birthday. He was overjoyed at this testimony to Käthe's
ability to integrate successfully the roles of artist, wife, and
mother. Kollwitz's series was subsequently nominated for
the prestigious Gold Medal Award of the Great Berlin
Exhibit of 1898, but Kaiser Wilhelm II vetoed the nomination,
possibly because of his opposition to "socialist" art. A year

later, however, she was awarded the Gold Medal, a prize conferred on her in 1899 by the King of Saxony. In her thirty-second year, Käthe Kollwitz had become one of the foremost artists of her country.

Over the next few years, Kollwitz produced various revolutionary works dealing with the French Revolution and the Peasant War of the sixteenth century, along with a number of works specifically dealing with women and their active role in fighting tyranny.

When Käthe's elder child Hans became seriously ill, her preoccupation with the theme of the dead child surfaced with new and alarming intensity. Both she and Karl tended the sick child through the night:

> "Finally, in the middle of the early morning, at three A.M., my husband said, 'I think we've won him back.' . . . During this night an unforgettable cold chill caught and held me: it was the terrible realization that any second this young child's life may be cut off, and the child gone forever. . . . It was the worst fear I have ever known."

> Months later, the long moments of this night would return to her; she would relive the awful knowledge of mortal—and parental—helplessness. At last she confronted Hans' touch with death in the creation of *Frau mit totem Kind* [Woman with Dead Child]. Though Hans had been its inspiration, she used Peter as a model for this piece.

> "When he was seven years old and I was doing the etching *Mother with Dead Child*, I drew myself in the mirror while holding him in my arm. The pose was quite a strain, and I let out a groan. Then he said consolingly in his high little voice: 'Don't worry, Mother, it will be beautiful, too' " [in Kearns, 1976, p. 87].

The finished etching was so expressive and painfully real that viewers seeing it felt the pain of the bereaved mother, although Kollwitz had to that point not lost a child. Interestingly, although she loved her sons, Käthe was undemonstrative toward them; like her own mother, she was unable to display physical affection.

Even as she received acclaim from all quarters and even as her family grew and prospered, Käthe's sobering concerns were ever present in her works. Her drawing *Raped,* the second of the series on *The Peasant War,* for example, is one of the earliest pictures in Western art that depicts the female victim of sexual violence sympathetically. In *Portraits of Misery,* we find moving portrayals of working-class women fainting from hunger, a woman mourning an infant's death, wife abuse, an elderly woman begging, and a pregnant woman knocking on a doctor's door, her head bowed low in shame. Her drawings for *Simplizissimus,* the progressive Munich magazine, dealt with similar themes. In 1910 she sketched *Death, Woman and Child*—the theme to which she continually returned even before she experienced the tragic losses of her adult life. *Run Over,* another work of 1910, depicts a scene of simultaneous horror and grief as parents rush to save their baby's life. Even as she matured technically, Kollwitz remained anchored in the theme of death, particularly as it involved women and children. It was a tragic quality of life that "gave Kollwitz her creative cutting edge" (Kearns, 1976, p. 119).

Käthe's worries about her sons—their health and their future— certainly fueled her work, but the underlying animus of her obsessive preoccupation with the theme of a child's death, I believe, stems from the deaths of her brothers and her attempts to work through the feelings associated with these losses. She was naturally driven, in this same connection, to work through the loss associated with having a mother whose own unresolved mourning had pervaded her entire personality and interfered with her ability to care for her children.

At the turn of the century, when Karl's sister, Lisebeth, died of tuberculosis, both Käthe and Karl became even more concerned about the health of their son Peter. He was constantly afflicted with upper respiratory illnesses, including coughs. One winter they went to the length of sending him to a sanitorium to facilitate his recovery and avoid further complications. Around the time Käthe's sons began leaving home for extended periods—Hans to attend the University of Freiburg and Peter to work as a farmhand in the fields of Poland—she began to explore the possibilities of working with stone and clay; this period marked the beginning of her work in sculpture. Käthe's experimentation with a new medium may have been partly in response to her apprehension over the lengthy absences of her sons, but an even more significant influence on her art at the time was:

Menopause—or her expectations about it—[which] affected her personality and work even more dramatically than did aging. For the first time in her career, due to irregular menstrual periods, she experienced immobilizing insecurity about her work. The irregularity unsettled her, and she railed against it. She recorded in her log:

"This is the second time I have destroyed work which required weeks to create. I felt almost driven to do this when I got my period and didn't know or expect I was getting it. The next day I found that menstruation had been the reason for my destructiveness. I and probably most women suffer similar pathological pressure during menstruation." She was used to obeying her will rather than her body. . . .

She feared that the changes in her body would sap her physical energy to the point of ending her creativity. A deadening mood of futility and depression overwhelmed her. Nothing engaged her usually alert intellect and social conscience for a significant period of time [p. 123].

In her ensuing fears of a hysterectomy and a thyroidectomy, she found "the deep faith within [herself] lacking" (p.

24). She had come to believe that her sexuality, as manifested in her ability to produce children, was tied to her artistic creativity. In this respect, Käthe's views opposed those of both her father and her female colleagues. She believed that creativity paralleled procreativity, holding that if the latter biological capacity was not present, creative work itself would be difficult if not impossible. Of course, we cannot ignore the symbolic meaning of menopause—the cessation of menses. To a woman as sensitive to loss, change, and abnormal mourning, it is quite conceivable that the vulnerability to abnormal mourning would be exacerbated at the time she was threatened with the loss of her uterus, her thyroid, and her ability to bear children, along with slackening ties to her growing sons. Her self-portraits of this period, in her mid- and late forties, reflect her doubt, anxiety, weariness, and grief. In one dated 1911, she appears to be in pain.

With the outbreak of war in 1914, Käthe Kollwitz was overcome by melancholy. Hans joined the army and Peter, barely eighteen, also wanted to be a soldier. After many unsuccessful attempts at dissuading him, the sad parents watched him volunteer for service. Käthe worked as a cook and cafeteria helper in a kitchen that fed large numbers of the unemployed, particularly destitute mothers and children. In her diary (H. Kollwitz, 1955), Käthe wrote about the young men who would die in the war. On October 22, 1914, she received the news that Peter had been killed in Belgium. She would never recover fully from this loss, the ultimate actualization of her lifelong psychological vulnerabilities.

Slowly, over the following months, Käthe began to achieve a partial resolution of her bereavement. Significantly, her progress was heralded by successful attempts to derive inspiration for her creative undertakings from Peter's death. She summoned his presence to help her in this work—work, she believed, that Peter had been denied the opportunity to do himself. After months of agony, she returned to her art:

"She found in Goethe's 'seed for the planting must not be ground' the moral, philosophic and emotional basis she needed as a mother and an artist to continue living and working" (Kearns, 1976, p. 135). Struggling with an artistic promise that, with the death of her son, could no longer be fully realized by him, Käthe Kollwitz began to cultivate the seeds of a talent that she feared would die with her menopause. Her renewed creative activity not only signaled a partial resolution of her bereavement; it further signified a liberation of "energy" through identification with the child who might have been creative if he had lived. That these dynamics should characterize Käthe's reaction to Peter's death is hardly surprising: shortly after his eighteenth birthday, the son destined to be a victim of the war had decided to continue his art lessons and become a painter. By identifying with Peter, the artist who might have been, Käthe Kollwitz dealt with her crushing loss in a creative fashion.

In the winter following Peter's death, then, Käthe Kollwitz began to create for her dead son. In the process, she not only memorialized Peter, but mobilized her own creativity by infusing her personal grief and pain with social consciousness. She decided to create a memorial sculpture that would simultaneously be for her fallen child and for all the young soldiers whose lives had been sacrificed. Predictably, designing the memorial was easier than executing it:

> As a mourning mother she was as yet unable to make her deep private suffering public. As an artist, however, she was obliged, ultimately, to reveal her emotions— as she always had— before the eyes of strangers. As she began work on Peter's memorial, she experienced great conflict between her "self-expressive" self and her "objective" self. . . . This trial, reflecting the struggle, rather than the harmony, between her "masculine" and "feminine" selves: the vulnerability, the intense feeling, the passion are there, but so overwhelming that she is unable to

objectify and create a work in which passion is controlled by skill [p. 136].

In 1916, Kollwitz executed a composition, *The Widow,* in which a pregnant working-class woman, gaunt and harried, stands, nearly full length; her large-knuckled hands, cupped as if to hold and embrace, reach out limply in empty space. The woman is shocked and despondent in her mourning; the woman is Käthe Kollwitz, grieved at the loss of her son. The despair in her artistic creation is her own, and yet she had conceived the creative product within herself and is able to deliver it as one gives birth to a baby. Although this is my interpretation, the appearance of the female figure represents a composite of Käthe and her mother. It is my contention that Käthe's many self-portraits are augmented by the graphic and other art works which show painful and frightening affects, and which reflect her state of feeling. Her entire artistic output can be understood as the attempt at creative expression of her, in the main, very upsetting feelings.

In a comparable way, Käthe was highly motivated to work on Peter's memorial; in time, the memorial changed from a sculpture of Peter himself to a relief of mourning parents— prototypically, Käthe and Karl Kollwitz. I believe the change occurred when her personal mourning proceeded to a newer stage of integration of her loss—she wished to use her creativity in the service of peace. Her ability to be liberated from her great private disruption helped her to work toward a more universal expression of what the death of all young men killed in war brings forth. The memorial would constitute a monumental headstone for the entire cemetery where Peter was buried. It was the largest work Kollwitz had ever planned, and she accepted the fact that years of work would be needed for its completion. In her execution, she constantly "strove for greater simplicity, to distill the human form to its most basic, expressive features and lives. . . . All her working time was concentrated on the memorial, and she often prayed that she would not grow old and infirm before she finished it" (p. 149).

The war ended in 1918, and the resulting political turmoil in Germany ultimately resulted in the establishment of the Weimar Republic. Under the Republic, Kollwitz became the first woman elected to full professorship at the Prussian Academy of Arts. In the large, fully equipped studio that came with the appointment, she drew a picture of huddling protective mothers who hear the death knell of poverty and war that threatens their children. This picture, *The Mothers,* embodies Kollwitz's conviction that children sustain their mothers' lives and not vice versa. It might be taken as a pictorial representation of the basis for Käthe's own resurgence of creative energy, i.e., the fact that, through Peter's death, her capacity to create once again reaffirmed itself.

But this plausible interpretation could easily belie the fact that Peter's death, aging, and the war itself had indeed taken their toll on the artist. She became fatigued, passive, and increasingly introspective. Her politics in the postwar years stressed faith in gradual change rather than violent revolutionary programs; Peter's death led her to renounce all war. Increasingly, she became an "independent" socialist whose artistic and emotional support of communists in Russia and Germany always stopped short of political advocacy (Kearns, 1976, p. 168). Beginning in 1917, she began to produce a series of woodcuts called *War.* The seven resulting productions constituted an impassioned protest against the gross senselessness of war, especially in the form of a woman's outrage. She finished the series in 1923 when inflation and hunger were rampant in Germany. This economic situation, in turn, provided the stimulus for a series of woodcuts on *Hunger, Vienna is Dying!, Save the Children!, Abolish the Abortion Law!.* In 1924, she designed Germany's

Children are Starving, and lithographed two posters, *Bread,* and *Never Again War!.* The 1920s were Kollwitz's most richly productive period. Her son Hans had by this time married and fathered a son, Peter, along with twin daughters. Käthe's three grandchildren were a great source of pleasure to her.

In June 1926, Käthe and Karl Kollwitz traveled for the first time to Roggevelde, the World War I cemetery where Peter was buried. After the visit she sculpted the Mother and the Father for the memorial and was able to visualize how they would stand in the graveyard. It had taken her many years to plan, deliberate, even incubate her ideas about the sculpture. It may be that only through her mourning of eight years was she able to be sufficiently liberated to begin actual work on it. In 1928, Kollwitz was promoted to become the first woman department head of the Prussian Academy of Arts. She taught the master graphics class and was on full-time salary; for the first time in her life, at the age of sixty-one, she received a regular income.

The economic crush of 1929 helped the Nazis rally over six million voters. Angered by the Nazis' use of brute force to suppress a workers' rally and alerted to the imminent political danger they represented, she created a drawing called *Demonstration.* Feeling a sense of apprehension because of developments in the political arena, her concerns turned to her grandson, Peter. On April 22, 1931, seventeen years after Peter's death, she unveiled the sculptures for the *Memorial to the Fallen* at the Prussian Academy. Over these past seventeen years she had been able to create artistically at the same time as she had attempted to work through the mourning–liberation process occasioned by her son's death. She would never complete the process, but the memorial signified her progress toward this end and simultaneously ensured that Peter would not be forgotten. Her memorial to her dead son involved a new medium— sculpture— and one can thereby see her triumphant recourse to sculpture as the product of a further creative shift set in motion by Peter's death.

Kollwitz's memorial sculptures are powerful statements of a personal loss that had come to symbolize and memorialize all the losses occasioned by war. In 1932, the sculptures were converted to granite. Fearful that agents of the political right would deface the memorials prior to their installation, Kollwitz arranged expense-free shipment to the Roggevelde cemetery after protracted negotiations with the German Republic, the German national railway, the Belgian government, and the board of the Brussels cemetery. Karl and she then journeyed to Roggevelde to direct their placement. Once installed, the figures cast a living spell of love and grief over the entire German cemetery, silent bereaved guardians of the young soldiers laid to rest there. At Peter's grave, Käthe paused, but when she came to the granite mother, whose face was identical to her own, she bowed low in sadness, wept, and stroked the stone cheeks.

When the Nazis assumed power in 1933, they demanded that Kollwitz and Heinrich Mann resign from the Academy of Art; the two artists had signed a manifesto calling for the unification of the political parties of the left. Käthe proceeded to suffer governmental derogation but never outright censorship until 1936, when the Nazis closed the last museum in which a few of her pieces could still be found. She never again saw her work on public display. In 1934, she began a series of eight lithographs on the cycle *Death.* Her sister Lise had once remarked that Käthe had carried on a dialogue with death all of her life; in this last series, the artist interpreted eight different "conversations" with death in profound fashion (Kearns, 1976, p. 210). In the final work, *The Call of Death,* we see the artist herself, aging and sexually undifferentiated (Fig. 1).

On July 13, 1936, two Gestapo officers called on Käthe

Figure 1.
The Call of Death (Self Portrait) by Käthe Kollwitz. Courtesy of the Art Institute of Chicago; gift of Mr. and Mrs. Emil Eitel.

Kollwitz in connection with an article in the Soviet periodical *Izvestia* in which she had been mentioned. They gave her the choice of supplying information and retracting what she had said or of being sent to a concentration camp. The next day, when another Gestapo officer called, she decided to provide the retraction, but refused to supply the names of other unidentified German artists who were also quoted in the *Izvestia* article; she knew that such betrayal would not only violate her principles but doom her colleagues. Although her work continued to be severely criticized and reviled, Kollwitz was never again threatened. After the interrogation, however, both Käthe and Karl carried vials of poison in the event they should be incarcerated by the Nazis at a future time.

Now in her seventies, Kollwitz continued to work on various sculptures and design gravestone reliefs, but her work was labeled "degenerate" by the Nazis and could not be displayed. When the Nazis finally banned Karl's medical practice altogether, the two became quite poor. An American offered her refuge in the United States, but she declined, unwilling to be separated from her family.

In 1940, the year after the outbreak of World War II, Karl became completely bedridden. Käthe was his constant nurse and companion; on July 19, 1940, he died. From that day on, Käthe used a cane when she walked (Kearns, 1976, p. 216). Her loneliness intensified when her grandson Peter (her son Peter's namesake) joined the army. At age seventy-four she executed her last graphic—*Seed For The Planting Must Not Be Ground.* This time the seeds for planting—sixteen-year-old boys—surround the mother, anxious to break loose. But the mother will not allow her sons to go, indicating that they must be ready for life and not for war. On October 14, 1942, Hans brought Käthe word that Peter had been killed in action. It was a terrible wrenching irony that he should have had the same fate as his namesake.

In 1943, Käthe created the last of her eighty-four self-portraits. In this work, she is passive, reflective, accepting of

414   CHILDHOOD BEREAVEMENT AND ITS AFTERMATH

the forces about her; one has the impression she is truly
waiting for death. As the bombing of Berlin grew dangerous,
she was evacuated to the country by some friends. Six
months after leaving Berlin, her tenement building was hit by
bombs and burned to the ground. A sizable portion of her
work was destroyed—and this in the wake of the earlier
deliberate destruction of her art by the Nazis. Even in the
country, life became difficult, with no heat, very reduced
food rations, and the constant danger of air raids. She was
evacuated a second time and accompanied by her granddaughter. On April 22, 1945, four months before the end of
World War II, she died without worldly possessions and away
from her home of fifty years. She was a symbol to those who
knew her or merely knew of her, an ideal and an inspiration to
those who were oppressed and threatened. She was a creator
of art, of children, and of a household in which she and her
husband lived harmoniously throughout their lives.

IV

The life and artistic career of Käthe Kollwitz are extremely
relevant to a topic that I have explored in several previous
publications (Pollock, 1975b, 1978a,b): the complex inter-
relationship between mourning and creativity. I have attempted to demonstrate both the regularity with which a
successfully completed mourning process issues in creative
activity and the significant degree to which the artistic
products that result from this activity are shaped by issues
that have figured in the mourning work. The case of Käthe
Kollwitz dramatically highlights the import of a lifetime of
mourning on the thematic preoccupation of a significant
twentieth-century artist.

I have elsewhere (1978a, pp. 453–454) called attention
to the instrumental role of Käthe's childhood sibling loss—
the death of her younger brother Benjamin when she was

eleven years old—in accounting for the despairing subject matter of her later art. Here, having reviewed Kollwitz's life in greater detail, we can see that her mourning actually irradiates in both directions from this important childhood loss. We have noted that two older brothers had already died at the time of her birth, and that Käthe's childhood was significantly shaped by the prolonged pathological mourning of her mother. It was Katherina Schmidt's continuing grief for her lost children that rendered her remote and physically unexpressive with their surviving siblings. In the case of Käthe, Katherina's failure to provide adequately warm and loving care engendered a panoply of physical and emotional symptoms including stomach pains, anxiety at losing the mother, and temper tantrums. With the benefit of psychoanalytic hindsight, we can see beneath these symptoms not only Käthe's resentment at her mother's inability to provide "empathic" maternal care, but an intractable survivor guilt that paralleled the mother's equally intractable grief over the loss of Käthe's two older brothers. We find a vivid expression of this survivor guilt in the eleven-year-old Käthe's terror-stricken reaction to the news of her brother Benjamin's death: the child, we recall, believed Benjamin's death was punishment for her playful offerings to Venus before the "pagan" temple she had built of blocks.

In adult life, Käthe's inability to work through the losses of her childhood would be significantly highlighted by her virtually incapacitating reaction to the serious illness of her older son Hans and, in subsequent years, by her serious difficulty in tolerating her sons' extended departures from home. The gripping culmination of Käthe Kollwitz's life of losses, of course, was the death of her younger son Peter at the beginning of World War I; by way of tragic postscript, it would be followed twenty-eight years later by the death of her eldest grandchild and only grandson, Peter, in World War II.

Like Edvard Munch and other artists, Kollwitz presented us with self-portraits from her youth to her old age. I believe the progression of her self-image as contrasted with actual photographs of her self at the corresponding ages of her self-depiction gives us a window into her conception of herself. I have undertaken this comparison when I could locate the actual photos (see Kollwitz, 1981). The discrepancies and similarities seemingly confirm my hypothesis. The artist is the subject of her drawing and she is also the instrument for depicting what she sees. The distortions, the special emphases, the expressions give us glimpses of the self of the artist that photographs do not and portraits by artists other than the self-artist cannot bring out. This parallels the difference between autobiography and biography. Self-portraits are visual autobiographies. When we have some idea about the life circumstances, past and present, of the self-artist, we may be able to understand her message. In Käthe Kollwitz's productions we follow her aging through the course of her life and see how these relate to her repetitive themes of death, mourning, and concern. Kinneir (1980) has noted that "Self-portraiture is unique. It gives us access to an intimate situation in which we see the artist at close quarters from a privileged position in the place of the artist himself and through his own eyes" (p. 15). I do not agree with Kinneir's suggestion that the artist in the self-depiction "intends to communicate only with himself" (1980, p. 15). The artist wishes to express what she feels, sees, and can put on her canvas. This is part of the mourning process. With the expressions comes liberation—internally. Thus the artist can use the repeated self-depictions to continue her mourning process and, it is hoped, to achieve more and more freedom. For mothers who have lost children, the mourning process is never fully completed; they feel they have not been able to adequately preserve their child's life. The protective aspects of Kollwitz's later Pietàs seemingly illustrate this. Kollwitz lived in a private world of pain, hardship, great sadness, fear, and loss. She found these in the external world; in her art work she brought inside together with outside and forged an enduring creative product: her art.

That Kollwitz's life was punctuated by a series of tragic losses is a matter of historical record. What remains of psychoanalytic interest is the way in which she was able to make the lifelong mourning process that accompanied these losses subserve her artistic creativity. There is no evidence that Kollwitz was able, during any interval of her life, to resolve fully her mourning–liberation process. But there is abundant evidence that she was consistently able to mobilize her ongoing attempts at resolution on behalf of her art. Throughout her adult life, that is, she was able to mourn through her creative products. To this extent, she exemplifies a thesis I have propounded elsewhere, namely, that in certain individuals "great creativity may not be the outcome of the successfully completed mourning process but may be indicative of attempts at completing the mourning work. These creative attempts may be conceptualized as restitution, reparation, discharge or sublimation. Though they may not always be successful in terms of mourning work solutions, the intrinsic aesthetic or scientific merit of the work still may be great despite the failure of mourning completion" (Pollock, 1978b, p. 267).

H. F. Deutsch (1959) has suggested that loss of one's own body integrity or of a love object may be related to the use of creativity in the service of restitution. In the three examples he cites, interestingly all had losses through death: Auguste Rodin, G. Ambrosi, and Käthe Kollwitz. Deutsch suggests that Kollwitz's art work was in the service of atonement for her death wishes. I believe Deutsch's well-reasoned position can be explained by Kollwitz's identification with and reaction to a pathologically mourning mother who deprived her of maternal care, communication, and comfort. The destructive and reconstructive impulses undoubtedly were present, but the evidence here is inferential. The loss of siblings threatened Käthe Kollwitz but perhaps not only through reawakened guilt over infantile hostile wishes against the lost object. The "loss" and "abandonment" by the chronic grieving mother who was unavailable could well have been a more significant source of guilt and depression than the loss of two brothers one of whom she never knew. Nonetheless, the urge to create can be a means of undoing the effects of the unconscious fantasy of destruction. One gives life—not death.

We have seen how Kollwitz's childhood identification with a mourning mother and the fated assumption of this very status in her own adulthood provided a central, recurrent theme in her art work. More specifically, her creative efforts from 1914 were integral to the mourning process that followed the tragic death of her son in that year, whereas the artistic products that resulted from these efforts were concrete representations of her mourning. These works, and especially the memorial sculptures for the Roggevelde cemetery, were not only created to memorialize Peter; they were simultaneously undertaken *on behalf* of Peter, whose untimely death denied him the opportunity of realizing his own artistic promise. Kollwitz's creative activity, in this regard, derived from energy that was liberated through identification with the slain child who had seemed destined to be creative.

But Kollwitz's art embodies a meaning that ranges beyond the personal losses of the artist. To the extent that her artistic creations are successful, they constitute not only a poignant statement of her personal grief and suffering, but a successful attempt to canalize her mourning into the advocacy of certain humanitarian ideals. I have previously posited that "an outcome of the mourning process following the loss of a significant object may be the reinvestment in an ideal" (Pollock, 1975a, p. 347), and I have discussed such ideals at the level of visions of utopia espoused by political revolutionaries, among others. Käthe Kollwitz, whose bleak view of the human condition is poles apart from the utopian mentality, nonetheless illustrates this development. In her lithographs and woodcuts of the 1920s and 1930s, the various depictions of human suffering and economic hardship all subserved a renunciation of war that, for Kollwitz, was the political legacy of losing her son. Thus, if Kollwitz's creative activity derived from energy liberated by identification with her lost son, it was an energy destined to be reabsorbed continually in the aesthetic representation of a pacifist ideal that was the political lesson of Peter's death. She did not respond to object loss by elaborating a full-blown utopian fantasy (Pollock, 1975a), but she did use the energy liberated by her mourning process to produce art work that was conducive to political and social reform. In the wake of Peter's death, her earlier revolutionary zeal was supplanted by an independent socialism of embracing humanitarian import. Käthe Kollwitz became a champion of social justice and peace even as she mourned her victimization by war.

Summary and Conclusions

Sol Altschul, M.D.

This volume is the culmination of combined studies, conducted at the Chicago Institute for Psychoanalysis, of children and adults who suffered the loss of a parent by death in childhood. The intent of the volume is to enlarge upon and contribute to the knowledge, understanding, and clarification, first, of the possible mechanisms of adaptation and/or mechanisms of pathology, and second to consider preventive measures and interventions when necessary to facilitate and maximize healthy growth and development in bereaved children.

Questions have been raised as to how children adapt to loss and whether children can or cannot adapt through engaging in the mourning process. Some investigators have felt that even very young children can mourn, while others have been concerned with how much and what kind of psychic structure must be developed before a mourning process can be traversed. Mourning is the psychological process by which an individual adapts to the loss of a loved object. In Freud's terms, that loss may vary in degree and extent from the loss of a loved person by death, to the loss of a relationship, or the loss of an ideal or country. It is a process that entails stages and phases with alternating expression and emphasis on affects of sadness and/or anger, recathecting memories, disbelief of the reality, and finally acceptance of the loss. Mourning has also been described as a process of disorganization and reorganization (Bowlby 1961, 1963). There is despair, anger, and protest in the disorganization with a subsequent reworking of affects, memories, and reality, leading ultimately to a reorganization of psychic structure and renewed interest in life. With these stages and expression of the intense affects there is a piecemeal processing of memories with working through of the loss sufficient to reinvest in new relationships and life activities. This is the ideal adaptation and endpoint that we hope can and will take place in all bereaved individuals. However, such an outcome is not universally reached even in adults, and under ordinary circumstances, one would expect children to have more difficulty in attaining this endpoint.

The mechanisms which characterize the mourning process are, in fact, constant elements in human psychological functioning that can be observed in all life situations that require adaptation. Any challenge to the individual's status quo, whether it be reaching a new developmental stage, a significant life choice, or even psychoanalytic treatment, can be dealt with in this piecemeal fashion whereby conflicts, developmental tasks, and accompanying affects are met with and faced bit by bit until a new equilibrium is achieved. This process is especially true of traumatic situations and defenses against trauma, as described in chapter 1.

Children faced with the death of a parent and the traumatic aspects of such an event are therefore faced with one of life's formidable challenges. Certainly children must adapt or adjust in some fashion. How a child adapts varies; some adaptations are in the service of the individual child's growth, development, and future well-being, while other adaptations, as observed in the adult patients described in this volume, fit the needs of the individual at the time of the loss but lead to deviations and arrested development.

There is no question that the children observed by the staff of the Barr-Harris Center experienced profound reactions to parental loss. Almost all the children, during the first year of bereavement, were symptomatic, as outlined in chapter 2. They most certainly began the process of mourning exemplified by the grief reactions and depressive aura that could be observed even in very young children. The experience of grief, while an integral part of the mourning process, is, however, not equivalent or comparable to the working through of the loss necessary to reinvest in life's activities. Children's adaptations to bereavement depending on their previous growth and development, tend in general always to be more complicated than the adaptations seen in the adult. Bereavement for children depends primarily on two aspects: their internal makeup, organization, and struggles, and the environment in which they exist and function. In the best sense, children adapt to parental death in ways which are compatible with their stage of development and allow for continuing psychological growth. The fact that the working through is incomplete does not by itself imply pathology, since the child is still in a dynamic developmental process and the unfinished issues can be revived when either a new stage of development is reached or a more opportune time ensues, and then the mourning process can be reactivated and proceed to a new, more comprehensive working through. In fact, this sequence may be the hoped-for ideal in the immature child. It should be noted that mourning in the sense of decathexis of the lost object is never complete, even in the adult, nor would such a state be desirable. Memories of the lost object are available and can be a source of comfort to the bereaved individual (adult or child) long after a loss. There is evidence in our experience that some children do have the capacity to go through a significant mourning experience (see chapters 8, 9, and 11). Johnny, one of these individuals, demonstrates the capacity to grieve and mourn, but his experience also demonstrates complications met in the process. Children invariably need support from the surviving parent to negotiate the painful, difficult process of mourning. Parents bring their children in for evaluation because they are concerned about their welfare, even if the parents' primary motivation is to seek help for themselves because they feel overwhelmed by their own grief and loss. This fact often gives one the opportunity to begin counseling with the parent, which in turn allows the benefits to extend to the child and facilitates the child's mourning process as well. In the course of the ordinary experience of mastering conflict, the child relies (more or less depending on the degree of stress) on the parent as an auxiliary ego. When you add the extraordinary burden of mourning, both child and surviving parent are taxed in their adaptive capacities. In the Barr-Harris experience, approximately 25 percent of the surviving parents are capable of tolerating their own and their children's painful affects so that they can support and facilitate the child's mourning process. The remaining parental survivors will usually require some assistance, at least in the initial stages of mourning. The necessary assistance may be achieved through brief counseling and guidance or it may, in other instances, require strenuous efforts, including psychotherapy for either or both child and surviving parent, as described in chapters 5 and 6. E. Furman has noted that parents generally want to be good parents, and it is possible to appeal to their self-esteem as parents to assist them in supporting their children's efforts to engage in the mourning process.

Adult cases of childhood loss are important from several points of view. On the one hand, they demonstrate the effects where there is inadequate response and support for the child's grieving/mourning process. The case described by Dr. Seidenberg (chapter 13) demonstrates the devastating effect parental death can have on a very young child when the surviving parent reacts to her own loss with depression and withdrawal. The immature child could not begin to deal with or appreciate the father's death when her more immediate care and security were severely jeopardized. The case of the adolescent girl, who was sent away by her parents in order to insure her survival, in more subtle ways demonstrates the effects of both the uncertainty and confusion about the actual fate of the parents and the absence of parental support, and pressure to deal with her loss, as well as the adolescent task of separation. The other adults with childhood loss by death described by Brockman and Forman (chapters 14 and 15) reflect in their subsequent adult difficulties the combined issues of struggles in dealing with parental death, inherent in their structural development at the time, and the relative unavailability of the surviving parent manifested by their inability to appreciate the child's needs and dilemma, and provide an appropriate, facilitating atmosphere in which to grieve. In these adult patients, when the regression and reactivation of conflicts was facilitated by the psychoanalytic process, the loss could be brought into focus and mourning resumed and worked through toward the ideal endpoint of more appropriate investment in new objects, activities, and interests; much like the process of disorganization and reorganization of a developmental stage or critical periods in development.

When individuals suffer arrests in development (such as the adult cases described in section V) one can also observe with greater clarity the developmental tasks and conflicts, so that our knowledge and understanding of the various phases is enhanced. One can contribute to determining the kind of mechanisms utilized in the defensive reactions that foster arrests in development as well as how growth and development can proceed when the pathways of normal development are reopened through the psychoanalytic treatment. Study of these patients also shows how the needs and internal struggles of the child contribute to the mechanisms of adaptation utilized by the child who become the adult patient, independent of the question of parental availability.

In addition, one is able to observe the developmental structures due to ego arrests and then to observe the unfolding of developmental difficulties and/or progression as the psychoanalytic therapy proceeds with greater or lesser success.

Treatment issues of when and how to intervene become very important when dealing with bereaved children at the time of loss. The diagnostic period is utilized to make a decision as to which individual in the family is the potential patient and whether the best approach to the situation would be through the child or surviving parent. The diagnostic evaluation can be used as a form of intervention in that it may allow for the opening up and expression of the affects of grief including sorrow, anger, frustration, hopelessness, and so on. It also serves to alert the surviving parent to the affects present in the child and necessary for him to undergo the mourning process, and thus may serve to facilitate the parent's capacities to tolerate and assist in the child's mourning process. In chapter 2 we see described a situation where, through parental guidance, the parent was able to be patient and be available to the child when the opportunity arose more appropriately at a later date.

One elusive aspect in the study of bereaved children is the fate of the internalized object. Of course the developmental level of the child at loss will determine how stable the image of the parent is or can be. What is remembered about the deceased parent? Does or can the image or internal representation change over time or with development? Does the impression of the parent remain static according to the internal representation at the time of loss or does the image change with the mourning process and distance from the unfortunate event? One source of evidence of arrested development or disturbance in the developmental process is when a child's memories are stereotypic in that the descriptions of the parent remain static or are consistently avoided, and the fantasies and play of the child remain the same. Garber, in his treatment of a child who was essentially preverbal at the time of loss, demonstrates that assisting the child to gain a more comprehensive and stable image of the lost mother facilitated the treatment process and helped fill in the void of a very limited image of the mother. This leads one to believe that as the child enters new phases of development a more comprehensive image of the dead parent can also be developed.

Finally, the essay by Pollock demonstrates the creative and liberating process that adaptation to loss can set in motion. In another context, he has demonstrated how James Barrie, in an effort to help his bereaved mother, began to write stories for her amusement. This coincided with his own reactions to the loss of his sibling and contributed to the development of his illustrious career (Pollock, 1978a).

On a somewhat lesser scale, some of our Barr-Harris children have adapted to the loss by efforts to memorialize their parents through useful productive projects and through positive identifications with the parental goals and ideals.

It is clear that parent loss by death in childhood is a profound experience but that children can adapt successfully, even creatively at times. However, almost all children will need the support and assistance of the surviving parent or an important consistent adult. If such support is not available, the child may follow adaptations that are useful at the time but set the stage for future psychopathology. Guidance is usually useful for parent and/or child, but treatment itself may not be appropriate for the child as he may be more amenable to the mourning process at a later phase of development. At any rate, it is important that adults and professionals engaged in the care of children be aware of the possibly deleterious outcomes to childhood bereavement and be alert to the special needs and possible interventions for such children.

We do not answer all the questions originally asked by our group, but we believe we have expanded the knowledge of the subject. In process, to be reported on in future communications, are the correlation of death and divorce with school difficulties, specific reactions to variables such as age and sex, or the kind of loss, whether due to illness or violence. For instance, our population at the Barr-Harris Center has a greater number of latency boys in the study who lost fathers than one would anticipate, and they appear to have the most difficulty adapting to the losses. Such issues, however, will need to be addressed in future communications from the Barr-Harris Center of the Insitute for Psychoanalysis.

References

Abraham, K. (1924), A short study of the development of the libido. In: *Selected Papers on Psychoanalysis.* London: Hogarth Press.

Adam, K., Bouckoms, A., & Steiner, D. (1982), Parental loss and family stability in attempted suicide. *AMA Arch. Gen. Psychiat.,* 39:1080–1085.

Adler, G. (1985), *Borderline Psychopathology and Its Treatment.* New York, London: Jason Aronson.

Agee, J. (1957), *A Death in the Family.* New York: McDowell Obolensky.

Altschul, S. (1966), Object loss by death of a parent in childhood. In: Panel on depression and object loss. Reporter, S. Levin. *J. Amer. Psychoanal. Assn.,* 14:142–153.

———— (1968), Denial and ego arrest. *J. Amer. Psychoanal. Assn.,* 16:301–317.

———— (1973), Discussion of a paper by Gilbert Kliman presented April 5, 1973. In: Lecture series *Children Under Stress.* Institute for Psychoanalysis of Chicago and Northwestern University.

———— Beiser, H. (1984), The effect of early parent loss on future parenthood. In: *Parenthood,* ed. R. Cohen, B. Cohler, & S. Weissman. New York: Guilford Press.

Barenboim, C. (1977), Developmental changes in the interpersonal cognitive system from middle childhood to adolescence. *Child Develop.,* 48:1467–1474.

Basch, M. F. (1977), Developmental psychology and explanatory theory in psychoanalysis. *The Annual of Psychoanalysis,* 5:229–263. New York: International Universities Press.

Beiser, H. R. (1980), Ages eleven to fourteen. In: *The Course of Life,* Vol. 2, *Latency, Adolescence and Youth,* ed. S. I. Greenspan & G. H. Pollock. Washington, DC: U.S. Department of Health & Human Services, pp. 293–308.

Bell, A. (1961), Some observations on the role of the scrotal sac and testicles. *J. Amer. Psychoanal. Assn.,* 9:261–286.

_____ (1965), The significance of scrotal sac and testicles for the prepubertal male. *Psychoanal. Quart.*, 34:182–206.

_____ (1968), Additional aspects of passivity and feminine identification in the male. *Internat. J. Psycho-Anal.*, 49:640–647.

_____ (1970), Some observations concerning the development of sexual identity in young males between four and a half to seven and a half years of age. In: Panel on the development of the child's sense of sexual identity. Reporter, V. L. Clower. *J. Amer. Psychoanal. Assn.*, 18:165–176.

Benedek, E. (1985), Children and disaster: Emerging issues. *Psychiat. Ann.*, 15:168–172.

Benedek, T. (1938), Adaptation to reality in early infancy. *Psychoanal. Quart.*, 7:200–215.

_____ (1956), Toward a biology of the depressive constellation. *J. Amer. Psychoanal. Assn.*, 4:389–427.

_____ (1959), Parenthood as a developmental phase. *J. Amer. Psychoanal. Assn.*, 7:389–417.

_____ (1970), Parenthood during the life cycle. In: *Parenthood: Its Psychology and Psychopathology*, ed. E. J. Anthony & T. Benedek. Boston: Little Brown, pp. 185–206.

Beres, D. (1974), Trauma. In: *Monograph V, The Kris Study Group. Trauma and Symbolism.*, ed. H. F. Waldhorn & B. Fine. New York: International Universities Press.

Blanck, G., & Blanck, R. (1979), *Ego Psychology II: Psychoanalytic Developmental Psychology.* New York: Columbia University Press.

Blos, P. (1958), Preadolescent drive organization. *J. Amer. Psychoanal. Assn.*, 6:47–56.

_____ (1962), *On Adolescence.* New York: Free Press of Glencoe.

_____ (1970), *The Young Adolescent.* New York: Free Press.

_____ (1974), The genealogy of the ego ideal. *The Psychoanalytic Study of the Child*, 29:43–88. New Haven, CT: Yale University Press.

_____ (1976), The child analyst looks at the young adolescent. In: *Twelve to Sixteen*, ed. J. Kagan & R. Coles. New York: W. W. Norton.

_____ (1980), Modifications in the classical model of adolescence. *Psychoanal. Quart.*, 49:351–352.

Blotcky, M. J., & Looney, J. B. (1980), Normal female and male adolescent psychological development: An overview of theory and research. In: *Adolescent Psychiatry*, Vol. 8., ed. S. C. Feinstein & P. L. Giovacchini. Chicago: University of Chicago Press.

Blum, H. P. (1977), The prototype of preoedipal reconstruction. *J. Amer. Psychoanal. Assn.*, 25:757–785.

_____ (1980), The value of reconstruction in adult psychoanalysis.

Internat. J. Psycho-Anal., 61:39–52.

Bowlby, J. (1960a), Separation anxiety. *Internat. J. Psycho-Anal.,* 41:89–113.

—— (1960b), Grief and mourning in infancy and early childhood. *The Psychoanalytic Study of the Child,* 15:9–52. New York: International Universities Press.

—— (1960c), Separation anxiety: A critical review of the literature. *J. Child Psychol. Psychiat.,* 1:251–269.

—— (1961), Process of mourning. *Internat. J. Psycho-Anal.,* 42:317–340.

—— (1963), Pathological mourning and childhood mourning. *J. Amer. Psychoanal. Assn.,* 11:500–541.

—— (1973), *Attachment and Loss,* Vol. 2, *Separation.* New York: Basic Books.

—— (1980), *Attachment and Loss,* Vol. 3, *Loss.* New York: Basic Books.

Brody, S. (1961), Some aspects of transference resistance in prepuberty. *The Psychoanalytic Study of the Child,* 16:251–274. New York: International Universities Press.

Brownell, G. J. (1977), Dealing with pubertal developmental tasks in the classroom. In: *The Sexual and Gender Development of Young Children,* ed. T. Oremland & E. K. Oremland. Cambridge, MA: Ballinger Publishing Co.

Burgner, M., & Edgecumbe, R. (1972), Some problems in the conceptualization of early object relationships: Part II. The concept of object constancy. *The Psychoanalytic Study of the Child,* 27:315–333. New York: Quadrangle Books.

Call, J. (1976), Effects on adults of object loss in the first five years of life. In: Panel. Reporter, M. Wolfenstein. *J. Amer. Psychoanal. Assn.,* 24:659–668.

Carroll, L. (1946), *Alice in Wonderland and Through the Looking Glass.* Illustrated Junior Library. Kingsport, TN: Grosset & Dunlap.

Chess, S., & Thomas, A. (1977), Temperamental individuality from childhood to adolescence. *J. Amer. Acad. Child Psychiat.,* 16:218–226.

Chethik, M. (1976), Work with parents: Treatment of the parent–child relationship. *J. Amer. Acad. Child Psychiat.* 15:453–463.

Clayton, P. J., Desmarais, L., & Winokur, G. (1968), A study of normal bereavement. *Amer. J. Psychiat.,* 125:168–178.

—— Halikas, J. A., Maurice, W. L., & Robins, E. (1973), Anticipatory grief and widowhood. *Brit. J. Psychiat.,* 122:45–51.

Curtis, H. (1982), Construction and reconstruction: Clinical aspects. In: Panel. Reporter, A. Malin. *J. Amer. Psychoanal. Assn.,* 30:213–233.

DeLeon-Jones, F. A. (1979), The role of transference in mourning. *The*

Annual of Psychoanalysis, 7:133–157. New York: International Universities Press.

Deutsch, F. (1959), Creative passion of the artist and its synesthetic aspects. *Internat. J. Psycho-Anal.,* 40:38–51.

Deutsch, H. (1937), Absence of grief. *Psychoanal. Quart.,* 6:12–22.

———— (1944), *The Psychology of Women,* Vol. 1. New York: Grune & Stratton.

Dewald, P., & Kramer, S., reporters (1976), Dialogue on the role of family life in child development. *Internat. J. Psycho-Anal.,* 57:403–409.

Dulit, E. (1972), Adolescent thinking à la Piaget: The formal stage. *J. Youth & Adol.,* 1:281–301.

Erikson, E. (1959), The Problem of Ego Identity. *Psychological Issues,* 1:1. New York: International Universities Press.

Esman, A. H. (1982), Fathers and adolescent sons. In: *Father and Child,* ed. S. H. Cath, A. R. Gurwitt, & J. N. Ross. Boston: Little, Brown.

Feigelson, C. I. (1976), Reconstruction of adolescence (and early latency) in the analysis of an adult woman. *The Psychoanalytic Study of the Child,* 31:225–236. New Haven, CT: Yale University Press.

Fenichel, O. (1945), *The Psychoanalytic Theory of Neurosis.* New York: W. W. Norton.

Fleming, J. (1963), The evolution of a research project in psychoanalysis. In: *Counterpoint: Libidinal Object and Subject,* ed. H. S. Gaskill. New York: International Universities Press, pp. 75–105.

———— (1969), Sequellae of parent loss in childhood. Discussion of papers by M. Mahler and C. Pinderhughes. Presented at American Psychoanalytic Association meeting, May 1969.

———— (1972a), Early object deprivation and transference phenomena. *Bull. Assn. Psychoanal. Med.,* 11:39–42.

———— (1972b), Early object deprivation and transference phenomena: The working alliance. *Psychoanal. Quart.,* 41:23–29.

———— (1975), Some observations on object constancy in the psychoanalysis of adults. *J. Amer. Psychoanal. Assn.,* 23:743–759.

———— Altschul, S. (1963), Activation of mourning and growth. *Internat. J. Psycho-Anal.,* 44:419–431.

———— ———— Zielinski, V., & Forman, M. (1958), The influence of parent loss in childhood on personality development. Paper presented at American Psychoanalytic Association meeting, May 1958.

Forman, M. (1966), Resistances and defenses against the work of mourning. Paper presented at American Psychoanalytic Association meeting, May 1966.

_____ (1983), Four types of resistance to mourning in adults with parent loss in childhood. Paper presented at Parent Loss Conference, Chicago, September 24, 1983.

Fraiberg, S. (1955), Introduction to therapy in puberty. *The Psychoanalytic Study of the Child,* 10:264–286. New York: International Universities Press.

_____ (1969), Libidinal object constancy and mental representation. *The Psychoanalytic Study of the Child,* 24:9–47. New York: International Universities Press.

Frank, R. A., & Cohen, D. J. (1979), Psychosocial concomitants of biological maturation in preadolescence. *Amer. J. Psychiat.,* 136:1518–1524.

Freud, A. (1936), *The Ego and the Mechanisms of Defense.* New York: International Universities Press.

_____ (1958), Adolescence. *The Psychoanalytic Study of the Child,* 13:255–278. New York: International Universities Press.

_____ (1960), Discussion of Dr. John Bowlby's paper. *The Psychoanalytic Study of the Child,* 15:53–62. New York: International Universities Press.

_____ (1962), Assessment of childhood disturbances. *The Psychoanalytic Study of the Child,* 17:149–158. New York: International Universities Press.

_____ (1965), *Normality and Pathology in Childhood: Assessments of Development.* New York: International Universities Press.

_____ (1967), Comments on trauma. In: *Psychic Trauma,* ed. S. Furst. New York: Basic Books, pp. 235–245.

_____ Burlingham, D. (1944), *Infants Without Families.* New York: International Universities Press.

Freud, S. (1893), On the psychical mechanism of hysterical phenomena: Preliminary communication. *Standard Edition,* 2:3–17. London: Hogarth Press, 1955.

_____ (1905a), Fragment of an Analysis of a Case of Hysteria. *Standard Edition,* 7:3–112. London: Hogarth Press, 1953.

_____ (1905b), Three essays on the theory of sexuality. *Standard Edition,* 7:125–244. London: Hogarth Press, 1953.

_____ (1917a), Mourning and melancholia. *Standard Edition,* 14:243–258. London: Hogarth Press, 1957.

_____ (1917b), Part III. General theory of the neurosis. *Standard Edition,* 16:273–285. London: Hogarth Press, 1963.

_____ (1923), The ego and the id. *Standard Edition,* 19:12–66. London: Hogarth Press, 1961.

_____ (1924), The loss of reality in neurosis and psychosis. *Standard Edition,* 19:183–187. London: Hogarth Press, 1961.

_____ (1926), Inhibitions, symptoms and anxiety. *Standard Edition,* 20:87–175. London: Hogarth Press, 1959.

———— (1937), Analysis terminable and interminable. *Standard Edition*, 23:216–253. London: Hogarth Press, 1964.

———— (1939), Moses and Monotheism. *Standard Edition*, 23:3–137. London: Hogarth Press, 1964.

Furman, E. (1974), *A Child's Parent Dies: Studies in Childhood Bereavement*. New Haven, CT: Yale University Press.

———— (1981), Treatment-via-the parent: A case of bereavement. *J. Child Psychother.*, 7:89–101.

———— (1984), Childrens' pattern in mourning the death of a loved one. In: *Childhood and Death*, ed. H. Wass & C. Carr. New York: Hemisphere Publishing Corp., pp. 185–203.

Furman, R. A. (1964), Death and the young child: Some preliminary considerations. *The Psychoanalytic Study of the Child*, 19:321–393. New York: International Universities Press.

———— (1978), Some developmental aspects of the verbalization of affects. *The Psychoanalytic Study of the Child*, 33:187–211. New Haven, CT: Yale University Press.

Furst, S. S. (1967), *Psychic Trauma*. New York: Basic Books.

Gadpaille, W. J. (1978), Psychosexual developmental tasks imposed by pathologically delayed childhood: A cultural dilemma. In: *Adolescent Psychiatry.*, Vol. 6, ed. S. C. Feinstein & P. Giovacchini. Chicago: University of Chicago Press.

Galenson, E. (1982), The effects of parent loss on the development of psychic structure. Summarized report on the Vulnerable Child Discussion Group. American Psychoanalytic Association, Boston, May 1982. Chairman, T. B. Cohen. *J. Prevent. Psychiat.*, 1:33–44.

Garber, B. (1981), Mourning in children: Toward a theoretical synthesis. *The Annual of Psychoanalysis*, 9:9–19. New York: International Universities Press.

Gaskill, H. S. (1963), Ed., *Counterpoint: Libidinal Object and Subject*. New York: International Universities Press.

Gedo, J., & Goldberg, A. (1973), *Models of the Mind*. Chicago: University of Chicago Press.

Gill, M. M. (1979), The analysis of the transference. *J. Amer. Psychoanal. Assn.*, 27:263–288.

Glenn, J. (1976), Panel, Reconstruction in child and adult analysis. *Psychoanal. Assn. of New York Bull.*, 13:11–13.

Greenacre, P. (1956), Experiences of awe in childhood. *The Psychoanalytic Study of the Child*, 11:9–30. New York: International Universities Press.

———— (1960), Woman as artist. *Psychoanal. Quart.*, 29:208–227.

———— (1975), Differences between male and female adolescent sexual development as seen from longitudinal studies. In:

Adolescent Psychiatry, Vol. 4, ed. S. C. Feinstein & P. Giovacchini. New York: Jason Aronson.

———— (1976), On reconstruction. *J. Amer. Psychoanal. Assn.*, 23:693–712.

Hamburg, B. A. (1974), Early adolescence: A specific and stressful stage of the life cycle. In: *Coping and Adaptation*, ed. G. V. Coelho. New York: Basic Books.

Harley, M. (1971), Some reflections on identity problems in prepuberty. In: *Separation-Individuation*, ed. J. B. McDevitt & C. F. Settlage. New York: International Universities Press.

Harris, M. (1976), Infantile elements and adult striving in adolescent sexuality. *J. Child Psychother.*, 4:29–44.

Hetherington, E. M. (1980), Divorce, a child's perspective. In: *Annual Progress in Child Psychiatry and Child Development*, ed. S. Chess & A. Thomas. New York: Brunner/Mazel, 1980 pp. 277–291.

Hilgard, J. R., & Newman, M. F. (1959), Anniversaries in mental illness. *Psychiatry*, 22:113–121.

———— ———— Fisk, F. (1960), Strength of adult ego following childhood bereavement. *Amer. J. Orthopsychiat.*, 30:788–798.

———— ———— (1963), Early parental deprivation as a functional factor in the etiology of schizophrenia and alcoholism. *Amer. J. Orthopsychiat.*, 33:409–420.

Hoffman, M. (1984), The parent's experience with the child's therapist. In: *Parenthood: A Psychodynamic Perspective*, ed. R. Cohen, B. Cohler, & S. Weissman. New York: Guilford Press, pp. 164–172.

Isay, R. A. (1975), The influence of the primal scene on the sexual behavior of an early adolescent. *J. Amer. Psychoanal. Assn.*, 23:535–553.

James, H. (1908), *The Awkward Age. Novels and Tales of Henry James*, Vol. 9. New York: Kelley Publications.

James, M. (1964), Interpretation and management in the treatment of preadolescents. *Internat. J. Psycho-Anal.*, 45:499–511.

Joffe, W. G., & Sandler, J. (1965), Pain, depression, and individuation. *The Psychoanalytic Study of the Child*, 20:394–424. New York: International Universities Press.

Kagan, J. (1980), Family experience and the child's development. In *Annual Progress in Child Psychiatry and Child Development*. New York: Brunner/Mazel, pp. 21–30.

Kaplan, G. C. (1977), The early pubertal student. In: *The Sexual and Gender Development of Young Children: The Role of the Educator*, ed. T. Oremland & E. K. Oremland. Cambridge, MA: Ballinger, pp. 65–72.

Kearns, M. (1976), *Käthe Kollwitz: Woman and Artist.* Old Westbury, NY: Feminist Press.

Keiser, S. (1967), Freud's concept of trauma and a specific ego function. *J. Amer. Psychoanal. Assn.,* 15:781–794.

Kennedy, H. (1971), Problems in reconstruction in child analysis. *The Psychoanalytic Study of the Child,* 26:386–402. New York/Chicago: Quadrangle Books.

Kernberg, O. (1975), *Borderline Conditions and Pathological Narcissism.* New York: Jason Aronson.

Kestenberg, J. S. (1980), Eleven, twelve, thirteen: Years of transition from the barrenness of childhood to the fertility of adolescence. In: *The Course of Life,* Vol. 2, *Latency, Adolescence and Youth,* ed. S. I. Greenspan & G. H. Pollock. Washington, DC: U.S. Department of Health & Human Services, pp. 229–263.

———— (1981), Notes on parenthood as a developmental phase, with special consideration of the roots of fatherhood. In: *Clinical Psychoanalysis,* Vol. 3, ed. S. Orgel & B. D. Fine. New York: Jason Aronson, pp. 199–234.

———— Marcus, H., Sossin, K. M., & Stevenson, R. Jr. (1982), The development of parental attitudes. In: *Father and Child,* ed. S. H. Cath, A. R. Gurwitt, & J. M. Ross. Boston: Little, Brown, pp. 205–218.

Khan, M. M. R. (1963), The concept of cumulative trauma. *The Psychoanalytic Study of the Child,* 18:286–306. New York: International Universities Press.

Kinneir, J., Ed. (1980), *The Artist by Himself: Self-portrait Drawings from Youth to Old Age.* New York: St. Martin's Press.

Klein, M. C., & Klein, H. A. (1975), *Käthe Kollwitz: Life in Art.* New York: Schocken Books.

Kliman, G. (1973), The impact of parent loss. Paper presented at series on Children Under Stress, sponsored by Institute for Psychoanalysis of Chicago and Northwestern University.

———— Feinberg, D., Buchsbaum, B., Kliman, A., Lubin, H., Ronald, D., & Stein, M. (1969), Facilitation of mourning during childhood. *Amer. J. Orthopsychiat.,* 39:247–248.

Kohrman, R., Fineberg, H., Gelman, R., & Weiss, S. (1968), Technique in child analysis. *J. Amer. Acad. Child Psychiat.,* 7:639–662.

———— ———— ———— (1971), Technique of child analysis: Problems of countertransference. *Internat. J. Psycho-Anal.,* 52:487–497.

Kohut, H. (1971), *The Analysis of the Self.* New York: International Universities Press.

Kollwitz, H., Ed. (1955), *The Diary and Letters of Kaethe Kollwitz.* Chicago: Henry Regenery.

Kollwitz, K. (1981), *Käthe Kollwitz: Graphics Posters, Drawings,* ed. R. Hinz. New York: Pantheon Books.

Kris, E. (1956), The recovery of childhood memories in psychoanalysis. *The Psychoanalytic Study of the Child,* 11:54–88. New York: International Universities Press.

Lazarus, R. S., Averill, J. R., & Opton, E. M. Jr. (1974), The psychology of coping: Issues of research and assessment. In: *Coping and Adaptation,* ed. G. V. Coelho, D. A. Hamburg, & J. E. Adams. New York: Basic Books, pp. 249–315.

Lifton, R. J. (1982), The psychology of the survivor and the death imprint. *Psychiat. Annals,* 12:1011–1020.

Lindemann, E. (1944), Symptomatology and management of acute grief. In: *Death and Intensity,* ed. R. Fulton. New York: John Wiley, 1965 pp. 186–201.

Loewald, H. (1960), On the therapeutic action of psychoanalysis. *Internat. J. Psycho-Anal.,* 41:16–33.

Lopez, T., & Kliman, G. (1979), Mourning in the analysis of a four year old. *The Psychoanalytic Study of the Child,* 34:235–271. New Haven, CT: Yale University Press.

Madison, D., & Walker, A. (1968), The health of widows in the year following bereavement. *J. Psychosom. Med.,* 12:297–301.

Mahler, M. S., Pine, F., & Bergman, A. (1975), *The Psychological Birth of the Human Infant.* New York: Basic Books.

Marris, P. (1974), *Loss and Change.* London: Routledge & Kegan Paul Ltd.

Meiss, M. (1952), The oedipal problems of a fatherless child. *The Psychoanalytic Study of the Child,* 7:216–229. New York: International Universities Press.

Miller, D. (1978), Early adolescence: Its psychology, psychopathology and implications for therapy. In: *Adolescent Psychiatry,* Vol. 6, ed. S. Feinstein & P. Giovacchini. Chicago: University of Chicago Press.

Mishne, J. M. (1983), *Clinical Work with Children.* New York: Free Press.

Murphy, L. B., & Moriarty, A. E. (1976), *Vulnerability, Coping and Growth from Infancy to Adolescence.* New Haven, CT: Yale University Press.

Nagera, R. (1970), Children's reactions to the death of important objects: A developmental approach. *The Psychoanalytic Study of the Child,* 25:360–400. New York: International Universities Press.

_____ (1981), *Developmental Approach to Childhood Psychopathology.* New York: Jason Aronson.

Nochlin, L. (1971), Why are there no great women artists? In: *Women in Sexist Society: Studies in Power and Powerlessness,* ed. V. Gornick & B. K. Moran. New York: New American Library, pp. 480–510.

Offer, D., & Peterson, A. (1982), Adolescent psychiatry: A brief research note. *J. Amer. Acad. Child Psychiat.*, 21:86–88.

Ottenstein, D., Wiley, K., & Rosenblum, G. (1962), Some observations on major loss in families. *Amer. J. Orthopsychiat.*, 32:299–300.

Palombo, J. (1981), Parent loss and childhood bereavement: Some theoretical considerations. *Clin. Soc. Work J.*, 9:3–33.

Parkes, C. M. (1965), Bereavement and mental illness. *Brit. J. of Med. Psychol.*, 38:1–26.

———— (1970), Nature of grief. *Internat. J. Psychiat.*, 5:435–438.

———— (1972), *Bereavement: Studies of Grief in Adult Life.* New York: International Universities Press.

———— Brown, R. J. (1972), Health after bereavement: A controlled study of young Boston widows and widowers. *Psychosom. Med.*, 34:449–461.

———— Weiss, R. S. (1983), *Recovery from Bereavement.* New York: Basic Books.

Piaget, J. (1952), *The Language and Thought of the Child.* New York: Humanities Press.

Pollock, G. H. (1961), Mourning and adaptation. *Internat. J. Psycho-Anal.*, 42:341–361.

———— (1975a), On mourning, immortality, and utopia. *J. Amer. Psychoanal. Assn.*, 23:334–362.

———— (1975b), Mourning and memorialization through music. *The Annual of Psychoanalysis,* 3:423–436. New York: International Universities Press.

———— (1978a), On siblings, childhood sibling loss, and creativity. *The Annual of Psychoanalysis,* 6:443–481. New York: International Universities Press.

———— (1978b), Process and affect: Mourning and grief. *Internat. J. Psycho-Anal.*, 59:255–276.

———— (1981), Aging or aged: Development or pathology. In: *The Course of Life: Psychoanalytic Contributions Toward Understanding Personality Development,* Vol. 3, ed. S. I. Greenspan & G. H. Pollock, Washington, DC: U.S. Government Printing Office, pp. 549–585.

Pruett, K. D. (1979), Home treatment for two infants who witnessed their mother's murder. *J. Amer. Acad. Child Psychiat.*, 18:647–657.

———— (1984), A chronology of defensive adaptations to severe psychological trauma. *The Psychoanalytic Study of the Child,* 39:591–612. New Haven, CT: Yale University Press.

Raphael, B. (1983), *The Anatomy of Bereavement.* New York: Basic Books.

Rochlin, G. (1953), Loss and restitution. *The Psychoanalytic Study of the Child,* 8:288–309. New York: International Universities Press.

Ryan de Brun, S. (1981), The psychological dimensions of preadolescence. *Adolescence,* 16:913–918.

Sandler, J. (1960), On the concept of superego. *The Psychoanalytic Study of the Child,* 15:128–162. New York: International Universities Press.

–––––– (1967), Trauma, strain and development. In: *Psychic Trauma,* ed. S. Furst. New York: Basic Books, pp. 154–174.

–––––– Kawenoka, M., Neurath, L., Rosenblatt, B., Schnurmann, A., & Sigal, J. (1962), The classification of superego material in the Hampstead Index. *The Psychoanalytic Study of the Child,* 17:107–127. New York: International Universities Press.

–––––– Rosenblatt, B. (1962), The concept of the representational world. *The Psychoanalytic Study of the Child,* 17:128–145. New York: International Universities Press.

Sarnoff, C. (1976), *Latency.* New York: Jason Aronson.

Scharfman, M. A. (1977), Preadolescence, puberty, and early adolescence. In: *Understanding Human Behavior in Health and Illness,* ed. R. Simons & H. Pardes. Baltimore, MD: William & Wilkins, pp. 156–163.

Scharl, A. E. (1961), Regression and restitution in object loss: Clinical observations. *The Psychoanalytic Study of the Child,* 16:471–480. New York: International Universities Press.

Schur, M. (1960), Discussion of Dr. John Bowlby's paper. *The Psychoanalytic Study of the Child,* 15:63–84. New York: International Universities Press.

Seidenberg, H. (1966), Resistances in the initial phase of analysis. Paper presented at the American Psychoanalytic Association meeting, May 1966.

Settlage, C. F. (1977), The psychoanalytic understanding of narcissistic and borderline personality disorders: Advances in developmental theory. *J. Amer. Psychoanal. Assn.,* 25:805–834.

Shakespeare, William (Macbeth), *Complete Works of William Shakespeare.* Cambridge Edition Text, ed. W. A. Wright. Garden City, NY: Garden City Publishing, 1936.

Silverstein, S. (1976), *The Missing Piece.* New York: Harper & Row.

Sklansky, M. A. (1980), The pubescent years: Eleven to fourteen. In: *The Course of Life,* Vol. 2, ed. S. I. Greenspan & G. H. Pollock. Washington, DC: U.S. Department of Health & Human Services, pp. 265–292.

Smith, S. (1982–83), Interrupted treatment and forced terminations. *Internat. J. Psycho-Anal.,* 9:337–352.

Sours, J. (1978), An analytically oriented approach to the diagnostic evaluation. In: *Child Analysis and Therapy,* ed. J. Glenn. New York: Jason Aronson, pp. 598–613.

Spanier, G. B., & Glick, P. C. (1980), Path to remarriage. *J. Divorce,* 3/3:283–298.

Spitz, R. (1957), *No and Yes.* New York: International Universities Press.

——— (1960), Discussion of Dr. John Bowlby's paper. *The Psychoanalytic Study of the Child,* 15:85–94. New York: International Universities Press.

Statistical Abstract of the United States (1980). U.S. Dept. of Commerce, Bureau of the Census, Social Security Administration. Unpublished data. Washington, DC.

Stein, M., Keller, S. E., & Schliefer, S. J. (1985), Stress and immunomodulation. The role of depression and neuroendocrine function. *J. Immunol.,* 135:827s–833s.

Sullivan, H. S. (1953), *The Interpersonal Theory of Psychiatry.* New York: W. W. Norton.

Tanner, J. M. (1959), Physical maturing and behavior at adolescence. *National Children's Home Convocation Lecture, 1958.* Harpenden, Herts: Printing Technical School.

——— (1972), Sequence, tempo and individual variation in growth and development of boys and girls aged twelve to sixteen. In: *Twelve to Sixteen: Early Adolescence,* ed. J. Kagan & R. Coles. New York: W. W. Norton.

Terr, L. (1979), Children of Chowchilla, a study of psychic trauma. *The Psychoanalytic Study of the Child,* 34:547–623. New Haven, CT: Yale University Press.

——— (1983), Chowchilla revisited: The effects of psychic trauma four years after a school-bus kidnapping. *Amer. J. Psychiat.,* 140:1543–1550.

Tolpin, M. (1971), On the beginnings of a cohesive self. *The Psychoanalytic Study of the Child,* 26:316–352. New York: Quadrangle Books.

——— (1978), Self-objects and oedipal objects: A crucial developmental distinction. *The Psychoanalytic Study of the Child,* 33:167–184. New Haven, CT: Yale University Press.

Waelder, R. (1967), Trauma and the variety of extraordinary challenges. In: *Psychic Trauma,* ed. S. Furst. New York: Basic Books, pp. 221–234.

Wallerstein, J. S. (1984), Children of divorce: Preliminary report of a ten-year follow-up of young children. *Amer. J. Orthopsychiat.,* 54:444–458.

——— Kelly, J. B. (1980), *Surviving the Breakup: How Children and Parents Cope with Divorce.* New York: Basic Books.

Weiss, S. (1979), Conceptualizing the nature of the therapeutic action of child analysis. Paper presented to the Chicago Psychoanalytic Society, February 27, 1979.

Wieder, H. (1978), The psychoanalytic treatment of preadolescents. In: *Child Analysis and Therapy,* ed. J. Glenn. New York: Jason Aronson.

Winnicott, D. W. (1960), Parent–infant relationship, maternal processes and the facilitating environment. In: *Maturational Processes and the Facilitating Environment.* New York: International Universities Press, 1979 pp. 37–55.

_____ (1965), A child psychiatry case illustrating delayed reaction to loss. In: *Drives, Affects, and Behavior,* Vol. 2, ed. M. Schur. New York: International Universities Press.

Wolfenstein, M. (1966), How is mourning possible? *The Psychoanalytic Study of the Child.,* 21:93–123. New York: International Universities Press.

Zilbach, J. J. (1979), Family development and familial factors in etiology. In: *Basic Handbook of Child Psychiatry,* Vol. 2., *Disturbances of Development,* ed. J. D. Noshpitz. New York: Basic Books, pp. 62–87.

Name Index

443

Steiner, D., 28, 429
Stevenson, R., Jr., 374, 436
Sullivan, H.S., 351, 440

Tanner, J.M., 353, 354, 440
Terr, L., 5, 13, 102, 440
Thomas, A., 431, 434
Thornburg, 358
Tolpin, M., 33, 440

Waelder, R., 6, 9, 440
Waldhorn, H.F., 430
Walker, A., 38, 437
Wallerstein, J.S., 21, 440
Wass, H., 434

Webber, C., xii, 77
Weiss, R.S., 107, 438
Weiss, S., 78, 190, 228, 272, 436, 441
Weissman, S., 429, 434
Wieder, H., 357, 358, 441
Wiley, K., 108, 438
Winnicott, D.W., 81, 188, 441
Winokur, G., 38, 431
Wolfenstein, M., xxi, 34, 240, 372, 431, 441
Wright, W.A., 439

Zielinski, V., xiii, xix, 278, 309, 377, 432
Zilbach, J.J., 38, 441

Subject Index

Action memories, 25
Active mastery, 31
Adaptation, xx
  assessment of, 104
  of child, role of parent in, 108
  developmental progression and, 94
  negative, risk for, 95, 96–101
  trauma and, 3–15
  verbalization and, 122, 127–128
Adaptive movement, 178
Adolescence
  parental death and, 300
  reconstruction of, in adult case study,
    351–376
Adolescent personality structure in
    adult, 282
Adultomorphic model of mourning,
    147, 161–162
Affect
  depressive, xx, 312
  of mourning process, 153–154
  parental interference in expression
    of, 153
Affect states, parental functioning and,
    31
Affective expression, 42
Affective grief components in
    mourning, 167
Aggression, 302
  inadequate mastery of, 252
Aggressive drive impulse, 362
Alcohol use, 329, 330
  bereavement and, 40
  parental, 375

Alice in Wonderland, 354, 355
Ambivalence, 302, 332
Anal fixation, 352, 360
Anal stimulation, 368
Analysis, initial phase of, 313–321
Analyst-patient relationship, 318, 320
Anger, 42, 55
  toward deceased parent, 154, 155
  toward deceased spouse, 124
  mourning process and, 40, 153
  pathological mourning and, 59
  recognition of, 155
Anniversary phenomena:
  mourning process and, 133
  pathological mourning and, 57
Anorexia, 312
  mourning and, 40
Anticipatory mourning, 30
Anxiety, 197, 214, 217, 312, 338
  motoric activity and, 120
  mourning process and, 40, 153
  separation, *see* Separation anxiety
Approach-avoidance behavior, 210
  parental, 217
Arrested development, xxii–xxiii, 3, 8,
    13, 15, 36, 95, 220, 239, 279, 300,
    310, 340, 342, 348, 352, 378,
    425–426
Artistic production, mourning-
    liberation and, 393
Authority, attitude toward, 314
Autonomic dysfunction, 5
Auxiliary ego, therapist as, 116
Awareness of self, 197

447